READ HARD

EDITED BY
ED PARK AND
HEIDI JULAVITS

BELIEVER BOOKS

a division of
MCSWEENEY'S

BELIEVER BOOKS
a division of
McSWEENEY'S

These pieces appeared between March 2003
and June 2009 in *The Believer* magazine.

All illustrations by Tony Millionaire, except for "Gidget on the Couch," courtesy of
the Frederick Kohner Estate, "Like Cormac McCarthy, but Funny," by Paul Davis,
"'And Suppress the Unpleasant Things'" and "The Bad Mormon," by Jaime Hernandez,
"How Far Can You Press a Poet?" by Stevie Smith, "Waiting for the Bad Thing,"
by Sylvie Christophe, "Whirl," courtesy of the *Evening Whirl*, "The American
Vicarious," courtesy of New Directions, and "Transit Byzantium," by Tim Rossiter.

www.believermag.com

Cover design by Brian McMullen

Printed in Canada by Westcan Printing Group

ISBN: 978-1-934781-39-5

CONTENTS

READ
HARD

INTRODUCTION

Hello!

If you're reading this introduction, there's a good chance you've already purchased this book, possibly because you're a fan of *The Believer*, or maybe you have no idea what *The Believer* is, but you patronize an independent bookstore with a very pushy and opinionated (and armed) sales staff.

There's also the chance that you're reading this introduction *in* a bookstore, meaning the attractive cover caught your eye, and the title speaks to you (you've always found reading to be a bit arduous, truth be told), and now you've opened to the introduction to discover what, exactly, is this *Believer*.

Possibly you've half-baked a few forgivably incorrect preconceptions.

Despite what our name might lead you to think, *The Believer* is not the official trade publication of the Utah Branch Davidians or the National Association for Terminally Ill Theologians or the Society of Gay Muslim American Republicans or the group that goes by the acronym WODWAGTATPLCOSB—Women of the Dakotas Who Ask God To Award Them the Posthumous Love Child of Samuel Beckett.

The *Believer* is a monthly magazine, not, as many people mistake us to be, a literary journal. As a monthly we do not publish on a quarterly schedule, thus we are not a quarterly. We do not have (though we would love to have) a benefactress who wears rhinestone-studded cat's-eye glasses, or an illustrious board of directors, or an office (we do, however, have a very nice desk). We do not publish fiction.

Though we do not publish fiction, and though (if you've turned to the table of contents) many of the essays collected here do not overtly concern fiction, fiction, is, in a way, our rallying concern.

When we started the *Believer*—our first issue was published in March 2003—fiction was in the state it's been in since possibly forever—that of a ritually bemoaned tailspin—and though we, the founding editors, were naturally concerned about this purported tailspin, we decided that the best way to make fiction matter again was not to publish more fiction ourselves, but to attempt to rejuvenate the way fiction, and books generally, are written about. We started by making a rule: we wouldn't publish any essays that were less than four thousand words. Then we vowed that we would pay writers comparatively little money in exchange for writing four thousand words for us, which is to say we pay an impressive 12.5 cents per word. Despite the fact that we pay 12.5 cents per word, we've been lucky enough to publish essays from writers of a caliber represented by this collection's table of contents—Rick Moody, William T. Vollman, Tayari Jones, Jonathan Lethem, Richard Powers. We also proudly publish writers you've never heard of before, really fantastic young writers who, in order to avoid homelessness, inevitably graduate to better-paid gigs.

But our thinking about the four-thousand-word limit was this: once you write (or read) four thousand words about a book, you discover that the book about which you're writing (or reading), and books generally, which have come to be treated as a solitary and somewhat hermetically self-referencing—even *irrelevant*—pastime, are in fact natural introductions to all corners of the culture—political corners, film corners, self-help corners, evangelical-rock corners, young-adolescent-boy fantasy-gaming corners, depraved-French-novelists-on-California-road-trips corners, transgendered-music-festivals-in-backwoods-Michigan corners. And so our magazine—called, originally, for reasons none of us can remember, the *Balloonist*—started to evolve from a long-format book review into a magazine that considered any topic books considered as their province—which is to say, everything.

Our essays attempt to extend literature into culture (or culture into literature)—so while we publish essays about individual writers such as Cormac McCarthy, W. G. Sebald, and Michel Houellbecq, a more prototypical piece might be the one included in this collection called "Gidget on the Couch," which examines the rise of Malibu surfing culture via the works of Sigmund Freud and Robert Musil, among other notable Austro-Hungarians, and which begins with an epigraph from *Life* magazine, a quote from a surfer that says, "If I had a couple bucks to buy a book, I wouldn't. I'd buy some beer."

For obvious reasons, this is not the epigraph of this collection. We're hoping that if you have a couple of bucks, you'll buy this book, because—unless it's very pricey and imported—a beer won't introduce you to the wonders of a female poet/novelist named Stevie, it won't help you see the connections between *Little House on the Prairie* and the gentrification of a "bad" Chicago neighborhood, and its fleeting high won't pleasantly inebriate you over the course of (because reading is really hard, but in a good way), weeks, months, years.

—*Heidi Julavits*

NO MAN'S LAND

DISCUSSED: *Laura Ingalls Wilder, Kansas, Bonnets, "A Great Many Colored People," Copper Gutters, Martin Luther King Jr., People Who Know Nothing about Gangs, Scalping, South Africa, Unprovoked Stabbing Sprees, Alarming Mass Pathologies, Chicago, Haunted Hot-Dog Factories, Gangrene, Creatures from the Black Lagoon, Tree Saws, Headless Torsos, Quilts, Cheerleaders, Pet-Grooming Stores, God*

ON THE PRAIRIE

"What is it about water that always affects a person?" Laura Ingalls Wilder wrote in her 1894 diary. "I never see a great river or lake but I think how I would like to see a world made and watch it through all its changes."

Forty years later, she would reflect that she had "seen the whole frontier, the woods, the Indian country of the great plains, the frontier towns, the building of the railroads in wild unsettled country, homesteading and farmers coming in to take possession." She realized, she said, that she "had seen and lived it all...."

It was a world made and unmade. And it was not without

some ambivalence, not without some sense of loss, that the writer watched the Indians, as many as she could see in either direction, ride out of the Kansas of her imagination. Her fictional self, the Laura of *Little House on the Prairie,* sobbed as they left.

Like my sister, like my cousin, like so many other girls, I was captivated, in my childhood, by that Laura. I was given a bonnet, and I wore it earnestly for quite some time. But when I return to *Little House on the Prairie* now as an adult, I find that it is not the book I thought it was. It is not the gauzy frontier fantasy I made of it as a child. It is not a naïve celebration of the American pioneer. It is the document of a woman interrogating her legacy. It is, as the scholar Ann Romines has called it, "one of our most disturbing and ambitious narratives about failures and experiments of acculturation in the American West."

In that place and time where one world was ending and another was beginning, in that borderland between conflicting claims, the fictional Laura, the child of the frontier, struggles through her story. She hides, she cowers, she rages, she cries. She asks, "Will the government make these Indians go west?" and she asks, "Won't it make the Indians mad to have to—" but then she is cut off and told to go to sleep. She falls ill and wakes from a fever to find a black doctor attending her. She picks up beads at an abandoned Indian camp and strings them for her sister. The real Laura grows up riding back and forth in covered wagons across the Middle West, passing through immigrant towns and towns where she notes in her diary seeing "a great many colored people." She marries a farmer named Almanzo and settles, finally, in the Ozarks.

Laura Ingalls Wilder loved the land enough to know exactly what had been stolen to make her world. "If I had been the Indians," she wrote in her 1894 diary, as she looked out over a river and some bluffs in South Dakota, "I would have scalped more white folks before I ever would have left it."

ON THE BORDER

Shortly after we married, my husband and I moved to a part of Chicago that was once known as "No-Man's-Land." At the turn of the century, when Chicago had already burned and been rebuilt again, this was still a sandy forest of birch and oak trees. It was the barely populated place between the city of Chicago and the city of Evanston, the place just north of the boundary that once designated Indian Territory, a place where the streets were unpaved and unlit.

Now this neighborhood is called Rogers Park, and the city blocks of Chicago, all paved and lit, run directly into the city blocks of Evanston, with only a cemetery to mark the boundary between the two municipalities. The Chicago trains end here, and the tracks turn back in a giant loop around the gravel yard where idle trains are docked. Seven blocks to the east of the train station is the shore of Lake Michigan, which rolls and crashes past the horizon, reminding us, with its winds and spray, that we are on the edge of something vast.

There are a dozen empty storefronts on Howard Street between the lake and the train station—a closed Chinese restaurant, a closed dry cleaner, a closed thrift shop, a closed hot-dog place. There is an open Jamaican restaurant, a Caribbean American bakery, a liquor store, a shoe store, and several little grocery markets. Women push baby carriages here, little boys eat bags of chips in front of the markets, and men smoke outside the train station while the trains rattle the air.

We moved to Chicago because I was hired to teach at the university in Evanston, which is within walking distance of Rogers Park. Walking to campus along the lakeshore for the first time, I passed the cemetery, and then a block of brick apartment buildings much like the ones on my block, and then I began to pass houses with gables and turrets and stone walls and copper gutters and huge bay windows and manicured lawns and circular drives. I passed beaches where sailboats were pulled up on the sand, where canoes and kayaks were stacked; I passed fountains, I passed parks with willow trees, I passed through one block that was gated at both ends. I passed signs that read PRIVATE ROAD, NO ACCESS, POLICE ENFORCED.

Evanston was still an officially segregated city in 1958 when Martin Luther King Jr. spoke there about the Greek concept of agape, love for all humanity. On my first visit to Evanston, after my job interview, I experienced a moment of panic during which I stood with the big cool stone buildings of the university and its lawns and trees behind me while I called my sister to tell her that I was afraid this might not be the life for me. I was afraid, I told her, that if I became a professor I would be forever cloistered here, forever insulated from the rest of the world. My sister, who is herself training to be a professor, was not moved. There are, she reminded me, worse fates.

Of the seventy-seven official "community areas" of Chicago, twenty-four are populated by more than 90 percent of one race, and only twelve have no racial majority. Rogers Park is one of those few. It is celebrated as the most diverse neighborhood in a hyper-segregated city. By the time I moved to Rogers Park, quite a few people had already warned me about the place. Two of them were my colleagues at the university, who both made mention of gangs. Others were near strangers, like my sister's roommate's mother, who asked her daughter to call me on the day I was packing my moving truck to share her suspicion that I might be moving somewhere dangerous. And then there was my mother, who grew up in a western suburb of Chicago but has, for almost twenty years now, lived in an old farmhouse in rural New York. She told me that she had heard from someone that the neighborhood I was moving to might not be safe, that there were gangs there. "Ma," I said to her, "what do you know about gangs?" And she said, "I know enough—I know that they're out there." Which is about as much as I know, and about as much as most white folks who talk about gangs seem to know, which is to say, nothing.

IN THE IMAGINATION

Gangs are real, but they are also conceptual. The word *gang* is frequently used to avoid using the word *black* in a way that might be offensive. For instance, by pairing it with a suggestion of fear.

My cousin recently traveled to South Africa, where someone with her background would typically be considered neither white nor black, but colored, a distinct racial group in South Africa. Her skin is light enough so that she was most often taken to be white, which was something she was prepared for, having traveled in other parts of Africa. But she was not prepared for what it meant to be white in South Africa, which was to be reminded, at every possible opportunity, that she was not safe, and that she must be afraid. And she was not prepared for how seductive that fear would become, how omnipresent it would be, so that she spent most of her time there in taxis, and in hotels, and in "safe" places where she was surrounded by white people. When she returned home she told me, "I realized this is what white people do to each other—they cultivate each other's fear. It's very violent."

We are afraid, my husband suggests, because we have guilty consciences. We secretly suspect that we might have more than we deserve. We know that white folks have reaped some ill-gotten gains in this country. And so, privately, quietly, as a result of our own complicated guilt, we believe that we deserve to be hated, to be hurt, and to be killed.

But, for the most part, we are not. Most victims of violent crimes are not white. This is particularly true for "hate" crimes. We are far more likely to be hurt by the food we eat, the cars we drive, or the bicycles we ride than by the people we live among. This may be lost on us in part because we are surrounded by a lot of noise that suggests otherwise. Within the past month, for example, the *Chicago Tribune* reported an "unprovoked stabbing spree," a "one-man crime wave," a boy who was beaten in a park, and a bartender who was beaten behind her bar, the story being, again and again, that none of us are safe in this city.

IN THE CITY

In the spring of 2006, the *New York Times* published an analysis of all the murders that had been committed in New York City during the previous three years—a total of 1, 662 murders. The article revealed one trend: people who were murdered tended to be murdered by other people like them. Most of the killers were men and boys (a disturbing 93 percent—a number that, if we weren't so accustomed to thinking of men as "naturally" violent, might strike us as the symptom of an alarming mass pathology), and most killed other men and boys. The majority of children were killed by a parent, and in more than half of all the cases, the victim and the killer knew each other. In over three fourths of the killings, the killer and the victim were of the same race, and less than 13 percent of the victims were white or Asian.

Even as it made this point, the article undid its own message by detailing a series of stranger murders. There was the serial murderer who shot shopkeepers, the KFC customer who stabbed a cashier, the man who offered a ride to a group of strangers and was then murdered for his car. These are the murders we find most compelling, of course, because these are the murders that allow us to be afraid of the people we want to be afraid of.

In a similar layering of popular fantasy with true information, the article went on to mention specific precincts in Brooklyn, the Bronx, and Harlem where murders were concentrated, and then quoted Andrew Karmen, an expert in victimology, who explained, "The problem of crime and violence is rooted in neighborhood conditions—high rates of poverty, family disruption, failing schools, lack of recreational opportunities, active recruitment by street gangs, drug markets. People forced to reside under those conditions are at a greater risk of getting caught up in violence, as victims or as perpetrators." In other words, particular neighborhoods are not as dangerous as the conditions within those neighborhoods. It's a fine line, but an important one, because if you don't live in those conditions, you aren't very likely to get killed. Not driving through, not walking through, not even renting an apartment.

I worked, during my first year in New York, in some of the city's most notorious neighborhoods: in Bed-Stuy, in East New York, in East Harlem, in Washington Heights. That was before I knew the language of the city, and the codes, so I had no sense that these places were considered dangerous. I was hired by the Parks Department to inspect community gardens, and I traveled all over the city, on train and on bus and on foot, wearing khaki shorts and hiking boots, carrying a clipboard and a Polaroid camera.

I did not understand then that those city blocks on which most of the lots were empty or full of the rubble of collapsed buildings would be read, by many New Yorkers, as an indication of danger. I understood that these places were poverty stricken, and ripe with ambient desperation, but I did not suspect that they were any more dangerous than anywhere else in the city. I was accustomed to the semirural poverty and postindustrial decay of upstate New York. There, by the highways, yards were piled with broken plastic and rusting metal, tarps were tacked on in place of walls, roof beams were slowly rotting through. And in the small cities, in Troy and Watervliet, in Schenectady and Niskayuna, in Amsterdam and in parts of Albany, old brick buildings crumbled, brownstones stood vacant, and factories with huge windows waited to be gutted and razed.

Beyond the rumor that the old hot-dog factory was haunted, I don't remember any mythology of danger clinging to the urban landscape of upstate New York. And the only true horror story I had ever heard about New York City before I moved there was the story of my grandmother's brother, a farm boy who had gone to the city and died of gangrene after cutting his bare foot on some dirty glass. "Please," my grandmother begged me with tears in her eyes before I moved to New York, "always wear your shoes."

And I did. But by the time I learned what I was really supposed to be afraid of in New York, I knew better—which isn't to say that there was nothing to be afraid of, because, as all of us know, there are always dangers, everywhere.

But even now, at a much more wary and guarded age, what I feel when I am told that my neighborhood is dangerous is not fear but anger at the extent to which so many of us have agreed to live within a delusion—namely that we will be spared the dangers that others suffer only if we move within certain very restricted spheres, and that insularity is a fair price to pay for safety.

Fear is isolating for those who fear. And I have come to believe that fear is a cruelty to those who are feared. I once met a man of pro-football-size proportions who saw something in my body language when I shook his hand that inspired him to tell me he was pained by the way small women looked at him when he passed them on the street—pained by the fear in their eyes, pained by the way they drew away—and as he told me this he actually began to cry.

One evening not long after we moved to Rogers Park, my husband and I met a group of black boys riding their bikes on the sidewalk across the street from our apartment building. The boys were weaving down the sidewalk, yelling for the sake of hearing their own voices, and drinking from forty-ounce bottles of beer. As we stepped off the sidewalk and began crossing the street toward our apartment, one boy yelled, "Don't be afraid of us!" I looked back over my shoulder as I stepped into the street and the boy passed on his bike so that I saw him looking back at me also, and then he yelled again, directly at me, "Don't be afraid of us!"

I wanted to yell back, "Don't worry, we aren't!" but I was, in fact, afraid to engage the boys, afraid to draw attention to my husband and myself, afraid of how my claim not to be afraid might be misunderstood as bravado begging a challenge, so I simply let my eyes meet the boy's eyes before I turned, disturbed, toward the tall iron gate in front of my apartment building, a gate that gives the appearance of being locked but is in fact always open.

IN THE WATER

My love of swimming in open water, in lakes and oceans, is tempered only by my fear of what I cannot see beneath those waters. My mind imagines into the depths a nightmare landscape of grabbing hands and spinning metal blades and dark sucking voids into which I will be pulled and not return. As a charm against my terror of the unseen I have, for many years now, always entered the water silently repeating to myself this command: *Trust the water.* And for some time after an incident in which one of my feet brushed the other and I swam for shore frantically in a gasping panic, breathing water in the process and choking painfully, I added: *Don't be afraid of your own feet.*

I am accustomed to being warned away from the water, to being told that it is too cold, too deep, too rocky, that the current is too strong and the waves are too powerful. Until recently, what I learned from these warnings was only that I could safely defy them all. But then I was humbled by a rough beach in Northern California where I was slammed to the bottom by the surf and dragged to shore so forcefully that sand was embedded in the skin of my palms and my knees. That beach happened to have had a sign that read HOW TO SURVIVE THIS BEACH, which made me laugh when I first arrived, the first item in the numbered list being DO NOT GO WITHIN 500 FEET OF THE WATER.

It is only since I have discovered that some warnings are legitimate that my fears of open water have become powerful enough to fight my confidence in my own strength. I tend to stay closer to shore now, and I am always vigilant, although for what, exactly, I do not know. It is difficult to know what to be afraid of and how cautious to be when there are so many imagined dangers in the world, so many killer sharks, and so many creatures from the Black Lagoon.

Now that we share a bookshelf, I am in possession of my husband's dog-eared, underlined copy of Barry Glassner's *The Culture of Fear.* Every society is threatened by a nearly infinite number of dangers, Glassner writes, but societies differ in what they choose to fear. Americans, interestingly, tend to be most preoccupied with those dangers that are among the least likely to cause us harm, while we ignore the problems that are hurting the greatest number of people. We suffer from a national confusion between true threats and imagined threats.

And our imagined threats, Glassner argues, very often serve to mask true threats. Quite a bit of noise, for example, is made about the minuscule risk that our children might be molested by strange pedophiles, while in reality most children who are sexually molested are molested by close relatives in their own homes. The greatest risk factor for these children is not the proximity of a pedophile or a pervert but the poverty in which they tend to live. And the sensationalism around our "war" on illegal drugs has obscured the fact that legal drugs, the kind of drugs that are advertised on television, are more widely abused and cause more deaths than illegal drugs. Worse than this, we allow our misplaced, illogical fears to stigmatize our own people. "Fear Mongers," Glassner writes, "project onto black men precisely what slavery, poverty, educational deprivation, and discrimination have ensured that they do not have—great power and influence."

Although I do not pretend to understand the full complexity of local economies, I suspect that fear is one of the reasons that I can afford to live where I live, in an apartment across the street from a beach, with a view of the lake and space enough for both my husband and me to have rooms in which to write. "Our lake home," we sometimes call it, with a wink to the fact that this apartment is far better than we ever believed two writers with student-loan debt and one income could hope for. As one Chicago real estate magazine puts it: "For decades, a low rate of owner occupancy, a lack of commercial development... and problems with crime have kept prices lower in East Rogers Park than in many North Side neighborhoods." And so my feelings about fear are somewhat ambivalent, because fear is why I can afford to swim every day now.

One of the paradoxes of our time is that the War on Terror

has served mainly to reinforce a collective belief that maintaining the right amount of fear and suspicion will earn one safety. Fear is promoted by the government as a kind of policy. Fear is accepted, even among the best-educated people in this country, even among the professors with whom I work, as a kind of intelligence. And inspiring fear in others is often seen as neighborly and kindly, instead of being regarded as what my cousin recognized it for—a violence.

On my first day in Rogers Park, my downstairs neighbors, a family of European immigrants whom I met on my way out to swim, warned me that a boy had drowned by the breakwater not too long ago. I was in my bathing suit when they told me this, holding a towel. And, they told me, another neighbor walking his dog on the beach had recently found a human arm. It was part of the body of a boy who had been killed in gang warfare, and then cut up with a tree saw. The torso was found later, they told me, farther up the shore, but the head was never found.

I went for my swim, avoiding the breakwater and pressing back a new terror of heads with open mouths at the bottom of the lake. When I retold the neighbors' story to my husband later, he laughed. "A tree saw?" he asked, still laughing.

ON THE FRONTIER

When the Irish immigrant Phillip Rogers built a log cabin nine miles north of the Chicago courthouse in 1834, there were still some small Indian villages there. He built his home on the wooded ridges along the north shore after noticing that this is where the Native Americans wintered.

Rogers built just south of the Northern Indian Boundary Line, which was the result of an 1816 treaty designating safe passage for whites within a twenty-mile-wide tract of land that ran from Lake Michigan to the Mississippi River, a treaty that was rendered meaningless by the Indian Removal Act of 1830, which dictated that all of the land east of the Mississippi would be open to white

settlement. The Northern Indian Boundary Line, which was originally an Indian trail, would eventually become Rogers Avenue.
And my apartment building would be built on the north corner
of Rogers Avenue, just within the former Indian Territory.

During my first weeks in Rogers Park, I was surprised by
how often I heard the word *pioneer*. I heard it first from the
white owner of an antiques shop with signs in the windows that
read WARNING, YOU ARE BEING WATCHED AND RECORDED. When
I stopped off in his shop, he welcomed me to the neighborhood
warmly and delivered an introductory speech dense with code.
This was a "pioneering neighborhood," he told me, and it needed
"more people like you." He and other "people like us" were
gradually "lifting it up."

And then there was the neighbor across the street, a white man
whom my husband met while I was swimming. He told my husband that he had lived here for twenty years, and asked how we
liked it. "Oh, we love it," my husband said. "We've been enjoying
Clark Street." The tone of the conversation shifted with the mention of Clark Street, our closest shopping street, which is lined with
taquerias and Mexican groceries. "Well," the man said, in obvious
disapproval, "we're pioneers here."

The word *pioneer* betrays a disturbing willingness to repeat the
worst mistake of the pioneers of the American West—the mistake
of considering an inhabited place uninhabited. To imagine oneself
as a pioneer in a place as densely populated as Chicago is either
to deny the existence of your neighbors or to cast them as natives
who must be displaced. Either way, it is a hostile fantasy.

My landlord, who grew up in this apartment building, the
building his grandfather built, is a tattooed Harley-riding man who
fought in Vietnam and has a string of plastic skulls decorating the
entrance to his apartment. When I ask him about the history of this
neighborhood he speaks so evasively that I don't learn anything
except that he once felt much safer here than he does now. "We
never used to have any of this," he says, gesturing toward the back
gate and the newly bricked wall that now protects the courtyard

of this building from the alley. "We never even used to lock our doors—I used to come home from school and let myself in without a key."

For some time, the front door of the little house that Laura's Pa built on the prairie was covered with only a quilt, but when Pa built a door, he designed it so that the latchstring could be pulled in at night and no one could enter the house from outside. Pa padlocked the stable as soon as it was built, and then, after some Indians stopped by and asked Ma to give them her cornmeal, Pa padlocked the cupboards in the kitchen. These padlocks now strike me as quite remarkable, considering that Pa did not even have nails with which to construct the little house, but used wooden pegs instead.

In one scene of *Little House,* the house is ringed by howling wolves; in another, a roaring prairie fire sweeps around the house; in another a panther screams an eerie scream and the girls are kept inside. And then there are the Indians. The Indians who ride by silently, the Indians who occasionally come to the door of the house and demand food or tobacco, the Indians who are rumored—falsely, as Pa reveals—to have started the prairie fire to drive out the settlers. Toward the end of the book, the Indians hold a "jamboree," singing and chanting all night so that the family cannot sleep. Pa stays up late making bullets, and Laura wakes to see Pa sitting on a chair by the door with his gun across his knees.

This is our inheritance, those of us who imagine ourselves as pioneers. We don't seem to have retained the frugality of the original pioneers, or their resourcefulness, but we have inherited a ring of wolves around a door covered only by a quilt. And we have inherited padlocks on our pantries. That we carry with us a residue of the pioneer experience is my best explanation for the fact that my white neighbors seem to feel besieged in this neighborhood. Because that feeling cannot be explained by anything else that I know to be true about our lives here.

The adult characters in *Little House,* all of them except for Pa, are fond of saying, "The only good Indian is a dead Indian." And for this reason some people don't want their children reading the book. It may be true that *Little House* is not, after all, a children's book, but it is a book that does not fail to interrogate racism. And although Laura is guilty of fearing the Indians, she is among the chief interrogators:

> "Why don't you like Indians, Ma?" Laura asked, and she caught a drip of molasses with her tongue.
>
> "I just don't like them; and don't lick your fingers, Laura," said Ma.
>
> "This is Indian country, isn't it?" Laura said. "What did we come to their country for, if you don't like them?"

With the benefit of sixty years of hindsight, Laura Ingalls Wilder knew, by the time she wrote *Little House,* that the pioneers who had so feared Native Americans had been afraid of a people whom they were in the process of nearly exterminating. And so as a writer she took care, for instance, to point out that the ribs of the Indians were showing, a reminder that they came, frighteningly, into the house for food not because they were thieves but because they were starving. They were starving because the pioneers were killing all their game. If anyone had a claim on fear, on terror, in the American frontier, it was obviously the Indians, who could not legally own or buy the land they lived on, and so were gradually being driven out of their lives.

Near the very end of *Little House,* after the nights of whooping and chanting that had been terrifying the Ingalls family, and after many repetitions of the phrase "the only good Indian is a dead Indian," Pa meets an Indian in the woods, the first Indian he has met who speaks English, and he learns from him that the tall Indian who recently came into the house and ate some food and smoked silently with Pa has saved their lives. Several tribes came together for a conference and decided to kill the settlers, but this tall Indian refused, thus destroying a federation of tribes and saving the settlers. On reporting the news to his family, Pa declares, "That's one good Indian."

This turn of events has the advantage of offering a lesson and also of being a fairly accurate account of what took place in Kansas in 1869. Because Laura Ingalls Wilder was actually only a toddler during the time her family lived in Kansas, she did quite a bit of research for *Little House,* traveling back to Kansas with her daughter and writing to historians, in the process discovering the story of the tall Indian, Soldat du Chene.

And so Wilder, the writer and the researcher, knows that the land the Ingallses have made their home on in *Little House* is part of the Osage Diminished Reserve. It is unclear whether Pa knows this, but it is clear that he knows he is in Indian Territory. He goes into Indian Territory on speculation, because he has heard that the government is about to open it up to settlers. At the end of the book, he gets word from his neighbors that the government has decided to uphold its treaty with the Indians, and soldiers will be coming to move the settlers off the land.

"If some blasted politicians in Washington hadn't sent out word it would be all right to settle here, I'd never have been three miles over the line into Indian Territory," Pa admits, in a rare moment of anger and frustration. "But I'll not wait for the soldiers to take us out. We're going now!"

The Ingalls family did indeed leave their home in Kansas under these circumstances. But the possibility the book suggests, by ending where it does, is that the settlers left Indian Territory to the Indians. "It's a great country, Caroline," Pa says, as they ride off in their covered wagon. "But there will be wild Indians and wolves here for many a long day."

This is how it could have been, Laura Ingalls Wilder seems to be proposing. The government could have enforced a fair policy. The settlers could have left and stayed away. But, as it happened, the government revoked its treaty with the Plains tribes within what one historian estimates was a few weeks after the Ingalls family abandoned their house in Kansas.

Laura Ingalls Wilder does not tell us this. She tells us, instead, that Pa digs up the potatoes he just planted and they eat them for dinner. The next day they get back into their covered wagon, leaving the plow in the field and leaving their new glass windows, leaving their house and their stable, and leaving the crop they have just planted. This is the end of the book, and this, I believe, is the moral of the story.

ON THE LAKE

Leaving my apartment one morning, I found a piece of paper on the sidewalk that read, "Help! We have no hot water." This message was printed in pink ink above an address that I recognized as nearby, but farther inland from the lake. The paper was carried by the wind to the water's edge, I imagined, as a reminder of the everyday inconveniences, the absent landlords and the delayed buses and the check-cashing fees, of the world beyond.

"Everyone who lives in a neighborhood belongs to it, is part of it," Geoff Dyer writes in *Out of Sheer Rage*. "The only way to opt out of a neighborhood is to move out...." But this does not seem to hold true of the thin sliver of Rogers Park bordering the lake, which many of our white neighbors drive in and out of without ever touching the rest of the neighborhood. They do not walk down Howard to the train station, do not visit the corner store for milk or beer, do not buy vegetables in the little markets, do not, as one neighbor admitted to me, even park farther inland than one block from the lake, no matter how long it takes to find a spot.

Between my apartment building and the lake there is a small park with a stony beach and some cracked tennis courts where people like to let their dogs run loose. In the winter, the only people in the park are people with dogs, people who stand in the tennis courts holding bags of shit while their dogs run around in circles and sniff each other. In the summer, the park fills with people. Spanish-speaking families make picnics on the grass and Indian families have games of cricket and fathers dip their babies in the lake and groups of black teenagers sit on the benches and young men play volleyball in great clouds of dust until dusk.

"The warm weather," my landlord observed to me not long after
I moved in, "brings out the riffraff."

When my landlord said this, I was standing on the sidewalk
in front of our building in my bathing suit, still dripping from
the lake, and a boy leaving the park asked if I had a quarter.
I laughed and told the boy that I don't typically carry change in
my bathing suit, but he remained blank-faced, as uninterested as a
toll collector. His request, I suspect, had very little to do with any
money I may have had, or any money he may have needed. The
exchange was intended to be, like so many of my exchanges with
my neighbors, a ritual offering. When I walk from my apartment
to the train I am asked for money by all variety of people—old
men and young boys and women with babies. Their manner of
request is always different, but they are always black and I am
always white. Sometimes I give money and sometimes I do not,
but I do not feel good about it either way, and the transaction
never fails to be complicated. I do not know whether my neighbors believe, like I do, that I am paying paltry reparations, but
I understand that the quarters and dollars I am asked for are a
kind of tax on my presence here. A tax that, although I resent it,
is more than fair.

One day in the late summer after we moved to Rogers Park,
my husband came home from the fruit market with a bag of tomatoes and a large watermelon he had carried the half mile from
the market to our house, stopping once to let some children feel
how heavy it was. He was flushed from the sun and as he split the
melon, still warm, my husband mused, "I hope more white people
don't move here." My husband isn't prone to sentimentality of any
kind, or to worrying about white people, so I asked him why and
he said, "Because kids were playing basketball by the school, and
they had cheerleaders cheering them on, and black men say hello
to me on the street, and I love our little fruit market, and I don't
want this place to change."

But this place probably will change, if only because this is not
a city where integrated neighborhoods last very long. And we are

the people for whom the new coffee shop has opened. And the pet-grooming store. "You know your neighborhood is gentrifying," my sister observes, "when the pet-grooming store arrives." *Gentrification* is a word that agitates my husband. It bothers him because he thinks that the people who tend to use the word negatively, white artists and academics, people like me, are exactly the people who benefit from the process of gentrification. "I think you should define the word *gentrification*," my husband tells me now. I ask him what he would say it means and he pauses for a long moment. "It means that an area is generally improved," he says finally, "but in such a way that everything worthwhile about it is destroyed."

My dictionary defines *gentrification* as meaning "to renovate or improve (esp. a house or district) so that it conforms to middle-class taste." There is definitely the sense among the middle-class people in this neighborhood that they are improving the place. New condos fly banners that read LUXURY! The coffee shop and pet-grooming store have been billed as a "revitalization." And if some people lose their neighborhood in the process, there is bound to be someone like Mrs. Scott of *Little House* who will say, "Land knows, they'd never do anything with this country themselves. All they do is roam around over it like wild animals. Treaties or no treaties, the land belongs to folk that'll farm it. That's only common sense and justice."

Meanwhile, when I walk home from the train station at night, I watch unmarked cars pull up in front of black teenagers who are patted down quickly and wordlessly. Some of the teenagers, my husband observes, carry their IDs in clear cases hanging from their belts for easy access. One evening, I watch the police interrogate two boys who have set a large bottle of Tide down on the sidewalk next to them, and I cannot forget this detail, the bottle of Tide, and the mundane tasks of living that it evokes. I consider going to one of the monthly beat meetings the police hold for each neighborhood and making some kind of complaint, but month after month I do not go.

Walking down Clark Street, I pass a poster on an empty store-front inviting entrepreneurs to start businesses in Rogers Park, "Chicago's most diverse neighborhood."

It takes me some time, standing in front of this poster, to under-stand why the word *diverse* strikes me as so false in this context, so disingenuous. It is not because this neighborhood is not full of many different kinds of people, but because that word implies some easy version of this difficult reality, some version that is not full of sparks and averted eyes and police cars. But still, I'd like to believe in the promise of that word. Not the sunshininess of it, or the quota-making politics of it, but the real complexity of it.

ON THE COAST

There are three of us here on the beach, with Lake Michigan stretching out in front of us. We are strangers, but we have the kind of intimacy that can exist between people who are lying on the same deserted beach. Aisha, a young black woman, sits on one side of me, and Andre, a middle-aged Polish immigrant, sits on the other.

We bury our feet in the sand and talk of the places we have lived. Aisha is from Chicago, and she has never, in her twenty-one years, lived anywhere else. Andre left Poland when he was seventeen, looking for more opportunities. Now, he says, he isn't entirely sure that he didn't make a mistake. We all fall silent after this confession.

This beach is a kind of no-man's-land. To the south are the last city blocks of Chicago, where the beaches are free but rocky and plagued with chunks of concrete. To the north are the first city blocks of Evanston, where the beaches are expansive and sandy but require a fee of seven dollars. To the west, beyond the wall of rocks directly behind us, is the cemetery that separates Chicago from Evanston, and a sign that forbids entry to this stretch of beach. To the east is an endless prairie of water.

When I mention that yesterday a lifeguard from Evanston came down in a boat while I was swimming and informed me that it was illegal to be here and that I had to leave because this land belongs to Evanston, Aisha rolls her eyes and says, gesturing back toward the cemetery, "This land belongs to the dead people." Andre, the immigrant, the pioneer, looks out across the water and says, "This land belongs to God." ✶

PETER LUNENFELD

GIDGET ON
THE COUCH

DISCUSSED: *Surfing's Premier Nihilist, Yet Another Papa-Centric Tale, Double-Secret-Crypto Jews, Something You Buy v. Something You Do, Weimar on the Pacific, A Man Named Tubesteak, Hitchcockian Voyeurs, Sexual-Coming-of-Age Novels, Teaching Sally Field to Surf*

If I had a couple bucks to buy a book, I wouldn't. I'd buy some beer.
—Malibu surfer in *Life* magazine, right after *Gidget* was published

AN ANALYSIS OF A CASE OF
A LITTLE GIRL WITH BIG IDEAS

hile sports, life, and style have been around for a while, the "sports lifestyle" as a distinct market is a mere half century old. Like much else of cultural import in the years since World War II, this niche is the product of the human laboratory we call California, and specifically of its coastline. Surfing is enjoying (or despising, depending on your perspective) one of its periodic peaks in the general consciousness,

which makes it appropriate to look back the five decades to the moment when the sport broke free of its cult status and became the urtext of athletic sports retailing. The publication of *Gidget* in 1957 did not just introduce us to the barely fictionalized account of a girl's summer in Malibu; it started a chain reaction that introduced surfing to the rest of the country and spread it to the world at large. The novel was licensed for three hit movies, and later made into numerous television shows. Within a few years, the Beach Boys, woodies, hangin' ten, and board shorts were as popular in Kansas City as in Santa Cruz.

The thing to remember is that, since 1957, surfing as something you buy has overshadowed surfing as something you do. I would hazard that no other activity has ever generated as many products among people who neither know how to do it nor follow those who do.[1] The archetypal surfer might be a sun-bleached, vacant-eyed, deracinated beach boy, but there are deeper stories beneath surfing's glossy surface. Like Los Angeles, surfing often seems to be outside the realm of history, trapped in a permanent present. In this story, though, noir eclipses sunshine; high culture paves the way for low commerce; utopia inspires and disappoints in equal measure; and the surf shops of Huntington Beach owe an unacknowledged debt to the sweet scents of Viennese coffee houses.

Before Gidget, however, there was a real girl named Kathy Kohner who learned to surf Malibu in the summer of 1956. From her house in Brentwood, it was a trip of fewer than fifteen miles, but one that took her out of American suburbia and into an emergent youth subculture, though nobody called it a subculture back then. California was full of rebels against conformity—bikers in Bakersfield, Beats in San Francisco, low-riders from East L.A., and guys riding what looked like planks spread out from Oceanside near San Diego to Santa Cruz up north. Malibu fell somewhere in the middle, seventeen miles of unincorporated land, just north of

---

[1] This distinguishes surfing from NASCAR, which generates a rabid fan-following at the same time as it moves literally tons of merchandise.

Los Angeles, and over the hill from the rapidly filling suburbs of the San Fernando Valley. Kathy's mother, an exceedingly minor player in this papa-centric tale, was of the opinion that her movie-crazy fifteen-year-old should get out into the sunshine, so she forced her to go to the beach every weekend with two older male cousins. Bored and curious, Kathy wandered from one side of the Malibu pier to the other. What she saw was a collection of great-looking young men riding the waves. She walked up to one and asked, "Am I bothering you?" to which he responded, "You're breathing, aren't you?" Unlike the beach bunnies who were already hopping along the shore, Kathy decided that she wanted to join the men in the water and brought sandwiches with her to trade for time on their boards. The "boys" all had nicknames like the Big Kahuna, Tubesteak, and Da Cat (more on him later). Kathy—five feet tall, and ninety-five pounds when wet—was evidently a girl and, in the estimation of the surfers, quite small: hence, Girl-Midget, or Gidget, a name that reeks of both schoolyard taunts and Freudian condensation (the trick of the dreamwork that yields the equation GIRL + MIDGET = GIDGET). Eventually, Kathy/Gidget bought a board for thirty dollars and taught herself to surf.

It was at the point that Kathy decided to commit her experiences to paper that things become more complicated. She was planning to write a book about that summer, but her father convinced her that he should write it. This made some sense, as Frederick Kohner was a professional writer, and an accomplished one at that. Born in Teplitz-Schönau, the Czech spa town that inspired Ibsen to write *An Enemy of the People,* Frederick got his PhD in Vienna, and then moved to Berlin to work in film. His brother had moved to Los Angeles in 1921, and so when the Nazis made Berlin increasingly inhospitable for Jews in all fields, Frederick followed in 1933. The newcomer gained steady work and even received an Oscar nomination for coauthoring *Mad About Music* (1938). Frederick would be all but forgotten, had it not been for the book he wrote about the new friends his daughter Kathy made the summer of her sophomore year in high school.

27

That famous son of Vienna, Sigmund Freud, never made it out west, and the closest he ever came to New World beach culture was a day trip to Coney Island in 1909, but we might well turn to him now, because the full title of the novel, *Gidget: The Little Girl with the Big Ideas,* sounds alarmingly like one of the great doctor's case studies.

1. Frederick began to listen in on his daughter's phone calls—with Kathy's permission, but not her friends'—in order to "get the language right." Consider a photo from a *Life* magazine shoot after the success of the novel. Kathy's on the phone, while her father, pipe in mouth, lurks in the shadowy doorway, looking for all the world like a Hitchcockian voyeur. But Frederick was hardly the passive type. Having appropriated his daughter's life, he proceeded to sell it as a transmedia property to publishing, film, and television.

2. Frederick is both prurient and ambivalent about his fictional daughter's sexual awakening. On the one hand there is much '50s-era talk of breasts like "fangled chassis that would put Jayne Mansfield to shame." On the other, the poor girl doesn't know the meaning of the word *orgy.* She looks it up in her "old man's" *Funk & Wagnall's,* traces its etymology back to Pythagoras, but never figures out its sexual meaning.[2]

3. *Gidget* is very much the outsider's book, a girl watching boys being watched by her émigré father. In the novel, Gidget's dad is a professor of German literature at USC and a *Mitteleuropean* gloss pervades the description of Gidget's life. There are sabbaticals in Berlin, side trips to Venice, and "that bitchen Mondsee in Austria." Gidget reads Françoise Sagan's French sexual-coming-of-age novel *A Certain Smile* three times, listening to Fats Domino. Gidget's brother-in-law is a psychoanalyst, a "disciple of Freud and

---

[2] *Gidget* was released within weeks of the first American version of *Lolita.* It must have been something in the air.

Rorschach" with a Beverly Hills practice specializing in children. Freudian language pervades the novel. "I guess you would call this fetishism or something," as Gidget says. Relocate *Jules et Jim* from Paris to SoCal, and they're Moondoggie and the Great Kahuna, with Sandra Dee subbing in for Jeanne Moreau.

4. Like fellow icons Mr. Spock and the Thing from the Fantastic Four, Gidget is Jewish, but nobody knows. To complicate matters even further, Gidget is the obvious inspiration for Malibu Barbie. Ruth Handler, the cofounder of Mattel, named Barbie after her own Jewish daughter, Barbara. This lineage means that Malibu Barbie, the ultimate California blonde, is a double-secret-crypto-Jew.

As Gidget moved from the page to the screen—from the "real" Kathy Kohner to Sandra Dee (herself "really" Alexandra Zuck) to Sally Field to the many other actresses who have played her—she followed the great American trajectory of willful forgetting of ethnic and regional roots. The cinematic and televisual Gidgets came from bland American families and generic, WASP moms and dads. Within half a decade, her deracinated status as a commodity was complete. Also erased was Gidget's status as a feminist heroine. The book concludes with Gidget riding a wave by herself for the first time. "I was so jazzed up that I didn't care whether I would break my neck or ever see Jeff again—or the Great Kahuna. I stood, high like on a mountain peak, and dove down, but I stood it." Standing on the board ("getting up") and angling down the face of the wave is the first lurching movement out of kookdom and into the ranks of real surfers. The literary Gidget gives voice to the physicality of surfing, the hard work and terrifying joys peculiar to all gravity-driven thrills.

By the time the novel was adapted for films and television, seeing "Jeff again" regained its supremacy and Gidget the inspiration became Gidget as played by a succession of Hollywood actresses, using Malibu as a backdrop for the Hollywood dyad of girl meeting boy. But before she moved on, Kathy/Gidget left an indelible mark on the place where she was named. As surf journalist Paul Gross has written, "Malibu is the exact spot on earth where ancient surfing became modern surfing," and Gidget announced this to the world. This transformation has always been seen as a move east from Hawaii to California, but it was, as we have seen from the Kohner family saga, touched by the flow west of refugees from Europe's near suicide in the first half of the twentieth century.

DA CAT ON HIS BOARD

Of the surfers that Gidget hung with that fabled summer, none was more ambivalent about the transformation of Malibu than the mysterious and gifted Miki Dora, who was likewise a child of that move from Europe to California. Dora was the master of the Malibu waves, an innovative iconoclast, a true rebel in a sea of poseurs, "a Kerouac in shorts," as the *London Times* put it. Born Miklos Sandor Dora III in Budapest, he had more aliases than a master thief, which later in life he became. He was Miki Dora, but sometimes Mickey Dora, occasionally Dickie Mora, and for a while he took his stepfather's last name and became Mickey Chapin. Then there were the nicknames—the Black Knight or the Gypsy Darling for his dark Magyar good looks; Malibu Mickey, King'Bu, the Fiasco Kid; and most famous of all, Da Cat, for his feline grace on a board.

Before we get any deeper into the stories about Dora—and they are legion, often unverified and unverifiable—we should make clear the one thing that all who saw and knew Dora agreed upon. Dora was an artist. He lived only for the moment of being and being seen on the wave. The master of small to medium-wave surfing, he was a graceful longboarder in complete sync with the elements, famed for his light stance on the board and ultranimble footwork—hence *Da Cat*. On and off the water, he was omnipotent and inscrutable, wearing trench coats or top hats down to the beach, shooting rockets off the pier, painting swastikas on his board (less fascist impulse than a last-ditch effort to *épater le bourgeois*). He drove the fastest cars, dated Hollywood starlets, and never, *never*, held down a real job.

Others of his generation might have been surfing bigger waves or winning more contests, but Dora was about style above all else. He was the Muhammad Ali of his sport, the original haole soul surfer.

Miki's father was a Royal Calvary officer who met a beauty from Los Angeles and moved with her to Hollywood. He opened a restaurant on Sunset Boulevard called the Little Hungary, and there young Miklos met regulars Billy Wilder, Michael Korda, and Greta Garbo. These were film colonials who hungered for the culture that had disappeared along with the rest of the Austro-Hungarian Empire, and access to them meant that Hollywood and its parties were as open to Miki as were the waters on the coast.

After his mother divorced his father, she married a very different sort of man, surf pioneer Gard Chapin, a roughneck rebel who never fit into polite society. If Miki's biological father connected him to Hollywood, stepfather Chapin's obsession with the development of surfboards brought the young Miki into the high-tech world of California's industrial design, including visits to Charles and Ray Eames's studio. The legacy of Miki's two patriarchs, the Hungarian hussar and the surfing redneck, determined the course of his life. Miki might have been born to ride waves, but he never shared the sunny obliviousness of postwar California teens. Instead, along with his boards and wax, he brought European nihilism to the beach.

Miki started surfing when virtually no one did. He and a few others had the waves to themselves. The late '40s and early '50s were to Dora an unrecapturable Eden, a mythic space of freedom that a ninety-five-pound girl-midget destroyed. Yet Miki was also willing to cash in, as an extra in the awful beach-party films shot in Malibu, happily grabbing a free trip to Hawaii to stunt-double for *Ride the Wild Surf,* teaching actress Sally Field how to handle herself on a board when she was television's first Gidget. Dora was the prototype for the new sports-lifestyle icon of independence, the extreme outlaw who decries selling out at the very moment he cashes in. When he finally agreed to do a signature board in 1966, it was the biggest seller in history, not only when it first hit the market, but

again a quarter of a century later when it was re-released. Even the
ads for Da Cat boards were famous; they featured quixotic shots of
a melancholy Dora, ruing his lost utopia. It was an odd marketing
strategy—including an infamous shot of Miki crucified on a cross
constructed from two surf boards—but successful beyond anyone's
wildest dreams. This ambivalence is quintessentially American: as old
as the cowboys who decried the legend at the same time they sold
their stories to the dime novels, and as contemporary as pierced and
tattooed X Games athletes talking about keeping it real at the same
time as they license their bad-boy images for the highest dollar.

Dora was the first literary superstar of the surfing world. He
crafted a snarling, witty persona in interviews, and wrote short essays for *Surfer* magazine about the end of his personal Eden. "Bad
omens," he wrote, "are in the air." Whereas *The Day of the Locust*
famously concludes with a fire ravaging the assorted cretins and
hucksters of Nathanael West's Los Angeles, Dora's twist on the
apocalyptic imagination presages our own fears of global warming
and rising waters. Dora was forever waiting for that moment when
"the sea gods come and reclaim their domain."

Before those gods arose from their depths, Miki was determined to have the best and most interesting time he could.[3] There's
a contact sheet of head shots Miki did in 1962 with two-day stubble
and a cigarette dangling from his lips, where he looks like nothing
so much as a Magyar Marlon Brando (whom Miki had met and

---

[3] That kind of image, linked to his otherworldly skills, meant that he ruled the beach, and
he knew all the famed surfers and shapers of his era, from Dale Velzy to Greg Noll, but Miki
was also a player inland. He hung out with the Beats and dropped acid with Tim Leary. He
raced antique cars with Steve McQueen and hung out at the Ferus Gallery with Billy Al
Bengston (the "real" Moondoggie and the most famous artist who ever surfed well) and
Bengston's gallery mates like conceptualist/painter Ed Ruscha and actor/photographer/
legend Dennis Hopper. Miki claimed to have met Barbara Handler, the "real Barbie," while
she was living out of a van, complaining that her parents stole her life and image. He surfed
with Hollywood Ratpacker and Camelot princeling Peter Lawford, and is rumored to have
accidentally run his board over JFK while the president was bodysurfing at Lawford's place
in the Malibu Colony. Miki was even at the Ambassador Hotel the night that RFK was
assassinated by Sirhan Sirhan, one of the few parts of the Dora story that can be checked
against police records (he is on the interview list for that fateful night).

liked). The photographs of this period show Miki and his compatriots perfecting beach cool. Look at Miki leaning against a wall, wearing faded khakis, a T-shirt, and a crooked smile and you see the American image of youth, power, and inchoate rebellion that every active sports-retail brand the world over sells for billions.[4]

Miki supported his intriguing life with an endless series of scams and subterfuges. When he got free tickets to an event, he would immediately sell them and then sneak in. He and three friends took an infamous "surf ambassador tour" of South America, including a scam that got him into the Governor's Ball in Rio, topped off with kiting a check for fifty-thousand dollars' worth of jewels. Miki hustled at golf, tennis, racing, anything to keep moving forward. Eventually, Da Cat just took off. In his last competition, the 1967 Malibu Invitational Surf Classic, he caught a great wave, turned his back on the judges, spectators, photographers, hangers-on, and assorted kooks, and dropped his trunks, mooning the whole lot of them—a postadolescent version of Garbo's wanting to be alone. He spent the next four decades roaming the globe, surfing waves, charming some, stealing from others. He served federal time for fraud and grand larceny. In 2002, at the age of sixty-seven, he died of cancer, in his father's house in Montecito. To this day, worldwide, but especially in the Pit at Malibu, you can still see the graffiti that the surfers he inspired to their own acts of rebellion and renunciation put up in honor of their mysterioso missing Magyar mentor: "Dora Lives!"

SCHINDLER IN HIS HOUSE

The word *Kakania* sounds like it could come from a luau in *Gidget Goes Hawaiian*. Likely Miki Dora would have brought it back from

---

[4] When Abercrombie & Fitch decided to create a sub-brand appealing to adolescents, it created the fictional "surf brand" Hollister: "Surfing is one of those sports that, whether you do it or not, you are inspired by the lifestyle. It represents freedom, it's exciting, it's dangerous, it's difficult to do. It's very aspirational."

the islands to Malibu's Pit, just because it sounded scatological.[5] Kakania is, in fact, the nonsensical name that novelist Robert Musil coined to refer to the Austro-Hungarian Empire, "that misunderstood State that has since vanished." Musil's pitiless masterpiece, *The Man Without Qualities,* offers a postmortem of the last days of *der österreichisch-ungarischen Monarchie,* and to comprehend Musil's in-joke requires both knowledge of German and some historical understanding of the political forces pulling at either side of the country's hyphen. Austria-Hungary was seen as both *kaiserlich-königlich* (*k.k.,* Imperial-Royal) as well as *kaiserlich und königlich* (*k und k,* Imperial and Royal). The nitpicking about what was *k.k.*—specifically Austrian—or *k und k,* which included the Central European peoples like the Hungarians, caused the subjects of the Dual Monarchy much angst. In spite of all these cascading *K*s, or perhaps even because of them, Kakania gave birth to much genius. Freud, Kafka, Erdos, von Neumann, Wittgenstein, Klimt, Schrödinger, Schoenburg, Schumpeter, Loos, and others too numerous to mention were born into the Empire.[6] Whatever the field, from music to mathematics, physics to architecture, Kakanians were inventing modernisms across their vast realm. But then Kakania vanished and more than a quarter century of misery, depression, pestilence, and war ensued.[7]

So many of the best left, and some of the more talented ended up on the shores of the New Eden. Los Angeles in the 1930s and '40s has been called Weimar on the Pacific, but I like to think of it as Kakania on the Koast. There were enough of them to create a

---

[5] Amazingly enough, in 1846 *The Knickerbocker: Or, New-York Monthly Magazine* used the word *kakania* as pidgin Hawaiian in an ersatz letter to the magazine from the king of that then-independent island paradise. (God, do I love Google Book Search.)

[6] The author of *Mein Kampf,* Kakania's most infamous son, is intentionally omitted from this list.

[7] The Austro-Hungarian Jewish writer Joseph Roth referred to the conflict of 1914–18 as a world war, "not because the entire world had conducted it but because, owing to it, we all lost a world, our world."

community, but it was a small enough group to ensure remarkable crossovers. If Bertolt Brecht could make the film *Hangmen Also Die!* with Fritz Lang, just before Thomas Mann, advised by Theodor Adorno, wrote *Dr. Faustus* featuring a character based on Arnold Schoenberg, all these giants living within a few miles of each other, then we can posit the following fiction about a late-summer evening in the middle of the twentieth century:

> The Kohner family drives east on Sunset from Brentwood to the Little Hungary, where Miki Dora's father greets them at the door. Miki's not there. He's sleeping in the Pit at Malibu, waiting for the dawn break. The Kohners are seated next to a table where the Budapest-born actress Hedy Lamarr sits alone, puzzling over the frequency-hopping torpedo protection technology that earned her a patent and the grateful thanks of the War Department.[8] As the Kohners leave, they pass an older man coming in. He is an architect who has walked up to the Sunset Strip from his house on King's Road. Did they all have goulash, or was there a special on schnitzel? Given that this is sheer invention, I choose goulash.

The latecomer to this fictional dinner was Rudolph M. Schindler, who, though close to forgotten at mid-century, is now acknowledged to be one of the two finest modern architects to have worked in Los Angeles, and among the most influential worldwide. The modest residence from which he walked to the Little Hungary is now universally acclaimed as the first great modern private house. The Schindler House is the last stop on our connectionist journey around Southern California, because it both prefigures and outlives the cultural and economic transformations to which Gidget and Da Cat contributed.[9]

---

[8] See U.S. Patent 2,292,387.

[9] Another point of connection here is that Miki Dora, at the time of this fictional dinner, lived almost exactly midway between the Schindler House and the Little Hungary. After his parents' divorce, Miki moved in with his father's mother, Madame Nadina DeSanctis. The

Schindler wasn't running away from persecution in 1914, when he left Vienna and headed for America. Instead, he was seeking space, light, and opportunity, the classic California triad. Along the way, he stopped in Chicago for a few years to work for Frank Lloyd Wright, and it was Wright who convinced him to head even farther west. The plan was to have Schindler supervise the construction on Wright's Barnsdall House in Hollywood. After breaking away from Wright, Schindler and his wife, Pauline, decided he should stay in Los Angeles, and establish a combination residence and studio, on the model of Wright's own Taliesin. The Schindlers forged a relationship with Clyde and Marian Chace. Pauline and Marian had been friends in college, and Clyde was a builder interested in new materials and construction. All were utopian modernists, interested in remaking the world through form and action. They decided to pool their resources and create a new way of living in which each of the residents would function as an artist, a communal space in which cooking was transformed from womanly drudgery into shared pleasure, in which the boundary between family and community, between the personal and the political, and between work, life, and play, would dissolve.

Erected in then only partially developed West Hollywood, Schindler's 1922 house was radical from the plan forward. Nothing about the way they lived was as radical as the space in which they were living, though. Two couples were intended to share the main house, which was arranged in a symmetrical pattern. There was an additional studio attached for the use of a single individual. The materials were simple: concrete, unadorned timber, glass. The construction was unconventional, with lean-up walls and slits for windows, and numerous sliding panels, designed to facilitate movement across boundaries, from interior to exterior and among the

---

Madame, a concert pianist, had arrived from Vienna in 1937, and supported herself in exile as a vocal coach. While Gard and Miki's mother were living in the Valley in a reconverted garage amid GI housing and sprouting TV aerials, Miki's father and paternal grandmother were the young surfer's link to Kakanian elite culture.

couples' shared spaces. There were Japanese theatrical performances in the garden, the residents would occasionally wear toga-like garments free of buttons and zippers, the politics were left of center, rumors of polygamous pairings were bandied about. All in all, the neighbors were scandalized. Reyner Banham famously described Schindler as coming close to designing "as if there had never been houses before."

The radical break with earlier architecture is the melding of interior and exterior. The landscape flows into the home; the home, via its outdoor patios, fireplaces, and sleeping porches, intermingles with the outdoors. While his erstwhile friend, colleague, and even Schindler House–mate Richard Neutra became more famous, Schindler was there first. The style that Schindler and Neutra developed on the fringes of architectural civilization became central two decades later to the program of *Arts & Architecture,* the seminal magazine of West Coast modernism. The magazine sponsored the case-study house program from 1945–1966, and its pictures (often by renowned photographer Julius Schulman) of the new style of architecture influenced the entire postwar building boom. The ranch home with pool, sliding glass doors, and a stripped-down aesthetic, the seamlessness of experience and the purchase of experience, whether kitsched up for the suburbs or not, owes its mass appeal to these case-study homes, but even more to the photographs of them.

Just as surfing is a sport that most people experience through photography, so too is high-modern architecture something generally encountered through images. It can even be said that surfing and modern architecture are designed for the perfect moment of photography: the instant in the tube before the wave closes in, that brief interval between completion of construction and the arrival of the clients. There's another odd symmetry between soul surfing and the West Coast's high-modern architecture. Each claimed the desire for a personal connection to and communion with nature, achieved through the spare use of the most contemporary materials and techniques. Yet this communion, often discussed in the loftiest of terms, was also quite exclusive, and those who achieved its satori often fought to keep others away. Miki Dora was famous for his vicious localism after the Gidget crowds roared in; what are we to make of Pauline Schindler's decade-long attempt to restrict King's Road to zoning for single-family homes? No renters, or even condos, in her workers' paradise, I suppose.

Like Miki, Pauline wanted to keep her cool exclusive, but they were both fundamentally out of step with the second half of the twentieth century. Cool was no longer the province of the avant-gardes, the rebels, the margin dwellers. Cool had become a brand. Gidget, and even more so the opportunistic Frederick, were among the first to surf this wave. The X-treme sports industry, which sells board shorts, skate shoes, watches, hoodies, and wraparound shades in lieu of experience, owes its fortunes to the pint-size daughter of an émigré father on the run from the ruins of the Austro-Hungarian Empire. It's gnarly on the *Ringstrasse,* dude![10] ✶

---

[10] If you are in need of shorts or wax, I would recommend Surfinsel, Vienna's full-service surf shop, at 126 Margaretengürtel.

LIKE CORMAC McCARTHY, BUT FUNNY

DISCUSSED: *Dr. Slaughter, Gringos, The Dog of the South, Turnip Greens, a Japanese Napkin-Folding Club, Ink-Stained Wretchdom, Gore, True Grit, the Old Testament, Glen Campbell, the Covered Path, Occult Mischief, Ambidextrous Romanians, Pure Nitro*

I. AMONG THE JOURNALIST ANTS

In 1964, in the midst of so-called Swinging London, Charles McColl Portis had Karl Marx's old job. Portis (who turns seventy this year) was thirty at the time, not yet a novelist, just a newspaperman seemingly blessed by that guild's gods. His situational Marxism would have been hard to predict. Delivered into this world by the "ominous Dr. Slaughter" in El Dorado, Arkansas, in 1933, Charles Portis— sometimes "Charlie" or "Buddy"—had grown up in towns along the Arkla border, enlisted in the Marines after high school, and fought in the Korean War. Upon his discharge in 1955, he majored in journalism at the University of Arkansas (imagining it might be "fun and not very hard, something like barber college"), and after graduation worked at the appealingly named *Memphis Commercial Appeal*. He soon returned to his native state, writing for the *Arkansas Gazette* in Little Rock.

He left for New York in 1960, and became a general-assignment reporter at the now-defunct *New York Herald-Tribune*, working out of what has to be one of the more formidable newsroom incubators in history—his comrades included Tom Wolfe (who would later dub him the "original laconic cutup") and future *Harper's* editor Lewis Lapham. *Norwood's* titular ex-Marine, after a fruitless few days in Gotham, saw it as "the hateful town," and Portis himself had once suggested (in response to an aspersion against Arkansas in the pages of *Time*) that Manhattan be buried in turnip greens; still, he stayed for three years. He apparently thrived, for he was tapped as the *Trib's* London bureau chief and reporter—the latter post held in the 1850s by the author of *The Communist Manifesto* (1848). (More specifically, his predecessor had been a London correspondent for the pre-merger *New York Herald*.) Recently, in a rare interview for the *Arkansas Gazette* Project at the University of Arkansas, Portis recalls telling his boss that the paper "might have saved us all a lot of grief if it had only paid Marx a little better."[1]

Indeed, as Portis notes in his second novel, the best-selling *True Grit* (1968), "You will sometimes let money interfere with your notions of what is right." If Marx had decided to loosen up, Portis wouldn't have gone to Korea, to serve in that first war waged over communism, and (in the relentless logic of these things) wouldn't have put together his first protagonist, taciturn Korea vet Norwood Pratt, in quite the same way. Perhaps the well would have run dry—fast. Instead of writing five remarkable, deeply entertaining novels (three of them surely masterpieces, though which three is up for debate), Portis could be in England still, grinding out copy by the column inch, saying "cheers" when replacing the phone.

---

[1] Many of the biographical details about Portis in this piece have been gleaned from this leisurely interview, conducted by Roy Reed on May 31, 2001.

* * *

In any event, Portis left not only England but ink-stained wretch-dom itself—"quit cold," as Wolfe writes in "The Birth of the New Journalism: An Eyewitness Report" (1972), later the introduction to the 1973 anthology *The New Journalism*. After sailing back to the States on "one of the *Mauretania*'s last runs," he reportedly holed up in his version of Proust's cork-lined study—a fishing shack back in Arkansas—to try his hand at fiction.

These journalists work pretty fast, and the slim picaresque *Norwood* appeared in 1966, to favorable notice. Portis's signature drollery and itinerant protagonist (Norwood Pratt, auto mechanic and aspiring country singer, ranges from Ralph, Texas, to New York City and back, initially to recover seventy dollars loaned to a service buddy) are already in place. The supporting cast includes a midget, a loaf-groping bread deliveryman, and a sapient chicken, and a looser hand might have plunged the tale into mere chaos or grotesquerie. But Portis's sense of proportion is flawless, and the resulting panorama, clocking in at under two hundred pages, stays snapshot-sharp throughout—a road novel as indispensible as *On the Road* itself.[2]

With reportorial precision, and without condescension, *Norwood* captures all manner of reflex babble, the extravagant grammar of commercial appeal—stray words bathed in the exhaust of a Trailways bus. This omnivorous little book has a high metabolism, digesting everything from homemade store signs (I DO NOT LOAN TOOLS) and military-base graffiti to actuarial come-ons and mail-order ads for discount diamonds. Appropriately enough, the characters are constantly chowing down. On one leg of the journey, Edmund B. Ratner (formerly the "world's smallest perfect

---

[2] Whereas Kerouac was said to have been more passenger than driver, Portis knows his cars inside out, and his oeuvre overflows with automotive asides. Even the *Gazette* interview is graced with these vehicular discursions: speaking of his stint at the *Northwest Arkansas Times*, Portis conjures up the vehicle he drove to work in, a 1950 Chevrolet convertible, "with the vertical radio in the dash and the leaking top," and notes the species-wide "gearshift linkage that was always locking up, especially in second gear."

man," before he porked out) and Norwood's new sweetheart, Rita Lee Chipman, are described as having eaten their way through the Great Smoky Mountains. *Norwood's* decidedly humble (call it American) menu nails the country's midcentury gastronomy with a precision that today takes on near-archaeological value: canned peaches, marshmallows, Vienna sausages, cottage cheese with salt and pepper, a barbecue sandwich washed down with NuGrape, a potted-meat sandwich with mustard, butter on ham sandwiches, biscuit and Brer Rabbit syrup sandwiches, an Automat hot dog on a dish of baked beans, Cokes and corn chips and Nabs crackers, a Clark bar, peanuts fizzing in Pepsi, a frozen Milky Way.

No bloat for Portis, and no sophomore slump, either: in 1968 the *Saturday Evening Post* serialized *True Grit*, a western that both satisfies and subverts the genre. (The only title of his to have remained almost continuously in print, *True Grit* has just been republished by Overlook, joining that press's recent paperback reissues of the author's four other books.) The novel, published later that year by Simon & Schuster, could hardly seem more out of step with the countercultural spirit of '68.[3] Writing in 1928 (i.e., on the eve of the Great Depression), a spinster banker named Mattie Ross revisits the central chapter in her life: the winter of 1873, when, as a fourteen-year-old from Yell County, Arkansas, she hunted down her father's killer, Tom Chaney, with the help of a tough U.S. marshal that she hired (the "old one-eyed jasper" Rooster Cogurn) and a young Texas Ranger (the cowlicked LaBoeuf).

"Thank God for the Harrison Narcotics Law," Mattie declares, in what might have read as a sort of antediluvian rebuke to the era of one-pill-makes-you-listen-to-Jefferson-Airplane. "Also the Volstead Act." Mattie never minces words or judgments—she's not from Yell County for nothing—and the poles of wrong and right

[3] The new *Portable Sixties Reader*, ed. Ann Charters (Penguin, 2003), does not mention Portis at all.

are firmly fixed. Unlike Huck Finn, to whose narrative hers is sometimes compared, Mattie knows the Bible back to front, handily settling spiritual debates by citing chapter and verse. To those men of the cloth, for example, who might conceivably take issue with her belief that there's something sinister about swine, she says: "Preacher, go to your Bible and read Luke 8: 26–33."[4] (Portis's father was a Scripture-studying schoolteacher, and his mother—whose name he gives to the steamer *Alice Waddell*—was the daughter of a Methodist minister.) Her steadfast, unsentimental voice—Portis's sublime ventriloquism—maintains such purity of purpose that the prose seems engraved rather than merely writ.

When Roy Blount Jr. says that Portis "could be Cormac McCarthy if he wanted to, but he'd rather be funny," he may be both remembering and forgetting *True Grit*, which for all its high spirits is organized along a blood meridian, fraught with ominous slaughter. Blood literally stains the book's first and last sentences, and Rooster, though admirable in his tenacity and his paternal protectiveness of Mattie, has a half-hidden history of trigger-happy law enforcement and less defensible acts of carnage. Indeed, the Overlook reprint provides a necessary corrective for latter-day Portis enthusiasts, a prism for the acts of violence in his other books: the cathartic fistfight punctuating Norwood's homecoming and *Gringos's* startlingly gory if swift climax. (The latter novel's narrator, Jimmy Burns, is also a Korean War vet, and Norwood reveals to Rita Lee that he killed two men "that I know of" in that conflict.) Portis's current reputation as a keen comedian of human quirks, though well deserved, is limiting. Put another way: after cars, Portis is most familiar with the classification and care of guns. (Even Ray Midge, the ever-observant milquetoast who tells his story in *The Dog of the South*, knows his firearms.)

---

[4] Mattie also has strong opinions on particular political matters, but the issues could not be at a more distant remove for the general reader in 1968 (or today), lending an air of comedy and verisimilitude. On Grover Cleveland: "He brought a good deal of misery to the land in the Panic of '93 but I am not ashamed to own that my family supported him and has stayed with the Democrats right on through, up to and including Governor Alfred Smith, and not only because of Joe Robinson."

Not that *True Grit* stints on comedy—in one of the funniest set pieces to be found in all of Portisland, Rooster, LaBoeuf, and a Choctaw policeman suddenly break into an escalating marksmanship contest, pitching corn dodgers two at a time and trying to hit both, eventually depleting a third of their rations. Mattie's precocious capacity for hard-bargain-driving (selling back ponies to the beleaguered livestock trader Stonehill) is revealed in expertly structured repartee, and her rock-ribbed responses to distasteful situations amuse with their catechism cadences. (When Rooster, in his cups, offers sick Mattie a spoonful of booze, she intones, "I would not put a thief in my mouth to steal my brains.") But Mattie also re-creates, poignantly and despite herself, her stark discovery of a world gone suddenly wrong, and what had to be done to set it right. Old Testament resonances are always close at hand: her father's killer bears a powder mark on his face, a Cain figure to say the least, and not to be pitied, and her own taste for frontier justice will lead her into a pit of terror, biblically populated by snakes. The price that Mattie pays may be greater than she knows.

True Grit's fame, of course, extends well beyond the book itself. The phrase has lodged in the culture, somewhere below *Catch-22* and above *nymphet*. And Henry Hathaway's enjoyable if foreshortened film version (1969) firmly yokes the story to John Wayne, who at sixty-two won his only Oscar for his portrayal of Rooster. Alas, the movie (which also stars Kim Darby as Mattie and Glen Campbell as LaBoeuf) doesn't capture the retrospective quality of Mattie's voice, as she fixes on the events over the widening gulf of years ("Time just gets away from us," she writes, in the book's penultimate and heartbreaking line). Wayne, in a full-bodied performance, draws the focus away from his employer/charge, so that the title refers far more to Rooster than to Mattie.[5]

---

[5] If the film of *True Grit* somewhat revises the book, the less-known screen adaptation of *Norwood* (Jack Haley Jr., 1970), also scripted by Marguerite Roberts, scrambles both *Norwood* and *True Grit*. Glen Campbell (*Grit*'s LaBoeuf) here plays Norwood, and Kim Darby (Mattie) is Rita Lee Chipman; Mattie's unacknowledged teenage longing for LaBoeuf ("If he is still alive and should happen to read these pages, I will be happy to hear from him," Mattie

Some see the book as Portis's albatross. Ron Rosenbaum, whose enthusiasm for the novelist's lesser-known works was instrumental in their republication, found it necessary (in a 1998 *Esquire* piece) to distance Portis from his most famous creation ("too popular for its own good"), in order to make his case for the *true* gems of the Portis canon. But the novel occupies a position similar to that of *Lolita* in relation to Nabokov's works: though it might not be your personal favorite, it cannot be subtracted from the oeuvre; nor can his other writings fall outside its shadow.[6] If Portis's subsequent novels—*The Dog of the South, Masters of Atlantis, Gringos*—have as a shared theme the seriocomic echo of lost, irretrievable greatness,[7] it's possible that *True Grit* is the genuine article—a book so strong that it reads as myth. As Wolfe notes of Portis's enviable success: "He made a fortune.... A fishing shack! In Arkansas! It was too goddamned perfect to be true, and yet there it was." And here it is—here it is, again.

---

writes at the novel's close) becomes consummated in *Norwood*, or just about. Roberts's *Grit* script shunted Mattie in favor of the bigger-than-life Rooster; for this film the screenwriter dilutes some of Norwood's cool by revealing that Rita Lee has been made pregnant by another man before they met—a significant, possibly feminist tweak of the original plot. (Incidentally, the contra-hippie theme that runs through Portis, made more explicit in *Gringos*, is elaborated in this film, most notably when Campbell-as-Norwood takes the stage after a numbing sitar exhibition. He sings a good-timey country number presciently called "Repo Man" to the uncomprehending, wigged-out crowd, until a more lysergically inclined combo unseats him.)

As it's unlikely I'll ever have the chance to write about this film again, let it be noted that the date of *Norwood*'s theatrical release, a year after *Midnight Cowboy* won the Academy Award for Best Picture, lends Campbell-as-Norwood a certain Voightian frisson during the scenes in New York, where he sticks out like a Stetsoned sore thumb. Which makes the bit in *Cowboy* where Voight regards himself in the mirror and says approvingly, "John Wayne," a sort of anticipatory gloss on Wayne costar Campbell's future appearance in Gotham. (The celluloid *True Grit* also spawned a 1975 sequel, *Rooster Cogburn*, starring Wayne and Katharine Hepburn.)

[6] Toward the end of *Norwood*, a conversational non sequitur seems to anticipate *True Grit*'s heroine. Someone mentions a Welsh doctor to the British-born midget Ratner: "Cousin Mattie corresponded with him for quite a long time. Lord, he may be dead now. That was about 1912."

[7] In books and in blood, as in this analysis from *Masters*: "One's father was invariably a better man than oneself, and one's grandfather better still."

*   *   *

In *The New Journalism*, Wolfe invokes the original laconic cutup, who happened to sit one desk behind him at the *Trib* office south of Times Square, as stubborn proof that the dream of the Novel—with its fortune-changing, culture-denting potential—never really died, even at a time when journalists were discovering new narrative ranges, fiction-trumping special effects. There was only one trophy worth typing for, one white whale worth the by-line and fishing wire, the Great, or even just the Pretty Good, American Novel, and Charlie Portis was going to try and snag it.

Or maybe the scoopmonger's life just bugged him. In "Your Action Line," a two-page lark published in the *New Yorker* at the end of 1977 (still in the eleven-year no-novel zone between *True Grit* and *The Dog of the South*), Portis addressed such pressing queries as "Can you put me in touch with a Japanese napkin-folding club?" (If a similar peep had emerged from Camp Salinger, it would scan as Zen koan.) The exchange ends with encyclopedia-caliber dope on a heretofore obscure insect:

> Q—My science teacher told me to write a paper on the "detective ants" of Ceylon, and I can't find anything about these ants. Don't tell me to go to the library, because I've already been there.
>
> A—There are no ants in Ceylon. Your teacher may be thinking of the "journalist ants" of central Burma. These bright-red insects grow to a maximum length of one-quarter inch, and they are tireless workers, scurrying about on the forest floor and gathering tiny facts, which they store in their abdominal sacs. When the sacs are filled, they coat these facts with a kind of nacreous glaze and exchange them for bits of yellow wax manufactured by the smaller and slower "wax ants." The journalist ants burrow extensive tunnels and galleries beneath Burmese villages, and the villagers, reclining at night on their straw mats, can often hear a steady hum from the earth. This hum is believed to be the ants sifting fine particles of information with their feelers in the dark. Diminutive grunts can sometimes be heard, too,

but these are thought to come not from the journalist ants but from their albino slaves, the "butting dwarf ants," who spend their entire lives tamping wax into tiny storage chambers with their heads.

If Portis had long since escaped the formicary, his books nevertheless continued to draw on his previous work environment. Here and there, fixed in amber, his former fellow ants appear.

Heading the London bureau, Portis kept getting entangled in "management comedies," expending too much precious time trying to stamp out unscrupulous freeloaders; he describes (for the *Gazette* Project) setting up a small sting operation to nab a writer who was using a tenuous *Trib* association—a single review, written years prior—to score theater tickets gratis. But Portis's fictional portraits of the less-upstanding members of the trade are not without a certain affection. The rogues are legion: Norwood breaks bread in Manhattan with Heineman, a freelance travel writer (supposedly on deadline for a *Trib* piece) who writes articles on Peru from his Eleventh Street digs and frankly aspires to the freeloading condition. (Laziness, he confesses, holds him back.) In *Masters of Atlantis*, hack extraordinaire Dub Polton, commissioned to compose the biography of Gnomon Society head Lamar Jimmerson, has a formidable reputation ("He wrote *So This Is Omaha!* in a single afternoon," says one awed Gnomon), and is so confident in his vision for *Hoosier Wizard* that he doesn't take down a single note. The master of this subspecies of charlatan might be overweening travel writer Chick Jardine. In Portis's jaunty 1992 story for the *Atlantic*, "Nights Can Turn Cold in Viborra," the consummate insider confesses to his readers, "I seldom reveal my identity to ordinary people," while taking pains to mention his "trademark turquoise jacket"—perhaps a gentle dig at the dapper Wolfe. Chick has also devised a product called the Adjective Wheel, which he sells to his fellow (well, lesser) travel writers at $24.95 a pop.[8]

---

[8] Travel writers, not to say *Homo britannicus*, get ribbed by Portis again in "Motel Life, Lower Reaches," part of the *Oxford American's* relaunch issue (January–February 2003). Describing

More abusive than even writers, of course, are editors. In the *Gazette* Project interview, Portis mentions a job in college for a regional paper, where he edited the country correspondence:

> ...from these lady stringers in Goshen and Elkins, those places. I had to type it up. They wrote with hard-lead pencils on tablet paper or notebook paper, but their handwriting was good and clear. Much better than mine. Their writing, too, for that matter. From those who weren't self-conscious about it. Those who hadn't taken some writing course. My job was to edit out all the life and charm from these homely reports. Some fine old country expression, or a nice turn of phrase—out they went.

Perhaps as penance for these early deletions, he created Mattie Ross, whose idiosyncratic style is most immediately identifiable by her liberal, seemingly arbitrary use of "quotation marks"—as if to let a phrase "stand alone" was to risk having it "fall by the wayside" at the whim of some "blue pencil." (A brief list of Mattie's punctuated preferences would include "Lone Star State," "scrap," "that good part," "moonshiners," "dopeheads," "Wild West," "land of Nod," "pickle," and "night hoss.") The punctuation not only highlights the phrases in question—some of them perhaps "old country expressions" of the time—but also comes to reflect her thriftiness. If *True Grit* is Mattie's true account, meant for publication, then the quote marks act as preservatives—insurance that her hard work will not be weeded out by some editorial know-it-all. Quotation marks mean the thing is true—to the degree that someone said it, or that it had some currency then.[9]

---

a cheap motel in New Mexico, he notes a small population of "British journalists named Clive, Colin, or Fiona, scribbling notes and getting things wrong for their journey books about the real America, that old and elusive theme."

[9] Portis is well aware of the seemingly disproportionate effects of punctuational caprice. In *Masters of Atlantis*, Whit and Adele Gluters' suitcase bears their surname in caps and quotes, leading to this flight of fancy: "Babcock wondered about the quotation marks. Decorative strokes? Mere flourishes? Perhaps theirs was a stage name. Wasn't Whit an actor? The bag did have a kind of backstage look to it. Or a pen name. Or perhaps this was just a handy way of

For Mattie has, apparently, tried her hand at the freelance game. An earlier experience with the magazine world came to grief. She had written a "good historical article," based mostly on her first-hand observation of a Fort Smith trial, prior to meeting Rooster Cogburn. Though the piece had a rather vivid (or as she would say, "graphic") title—"*You will now listen to the sentence of the law, Odus Wharton, which is that you be hanged by the neck until you are dead, dead dead! May God, whose laws you have broken and before whose dread tribunal you must appear, have mercy upon your soul. Being a personal recollection of Isaac C. Parker, the famous Border Judge*"—the magazine world "would rather print trash."

As for newspapers, the cheapskate editors "are great ones for reaping where they do not sow"—always hoping to shortchange contributors, or else sending reporters around to get an interview gratis. Ever the banker, Mattie means for her story to make money—which *True Grit* went ahead and did.

Totting up his fee sheets, a struggling Rooster opines that un-schooled men like himself have a raw deal. "No matter if he has got sand in his craw, others will push him aside, little thin fellows that have won spelling bees back home." A century hence, this ortho-graphical ace might be Raymond E. Midge, the twenty-six-year-old ex-copy-editor and perpetual college student who narrates *The Dog of the South*. That Portis effortlessly makes Midge, a nitpicking,

---

setting themselves apart from ordinary Gluters, a way of saying that in all of Gluterdom they were the Gluters, or perhaps the enclosure was to emphasize the team aspect, to indicate that 'THE GLUTERS' were not quite the same thing as the Gluters, that together they were an entity different from, and greater than the raw sum of Whit and Adele, or it might be that the name was a professional tag expressive of their work, a new word they had coined, a new infinitive, to gluter, or to glute, descriptive of some new social malady they had defined or some new clinical technique they had pioneered, as in their mass Glutering sessions or their breakthrough treatment of Glutered wives or their controversial Glute therapy. The Gluters were only too ready to discuss their personal affairs and no doubt would have been happy to explain the significance off the quotation marks, had they been asked, but Babcock said nothing. He was not one to pry."

book-burrowing cuckold, as indelible and appealing as the battle-scarred man of action (or strong-willed girl revenger) is ample proof of his scope and skill.

Thanks to a few wizards of international fiction, the proof-reader has had some pivotal roles—Hugh Person in Nabokov's *Transparent Things* (1972), Raimundo Silva in Jose Saramago's *The History of the Siege of Lisbon* (1996). Denizens of the copy desk have not enjoyed a similar literary profile. Though the professions bear some resemblance, the latter's task is more Sisyphean and perhaps more conducive to despair—sweating the details on something as disposable as a newspaper, in most cases gone inside a week, if not a day. No novel captures the occupation's particular brand of virtues and neuroses as well as *The Dog of the South*; it's the perfect job (or former job) for a character so constitutionally driven to remark on deviations from the norm. (At twenty-six, he's lived as many years as there are letters in the alphabet.) Ray Midge sets out for British Honduras to recover his car and perhaps Norma, his wife[10]—both stolen by his former coworker, the misanthropic Guy Dupree. Dupree's errant behavior—he's finally investigated for writing hostile letters to the president—and burgeoning anarcho-communist tendencies reflect a harsh if hysterical worldview possibly aggravated by his days in the newspaper office: "He hardly spoke at all except to mutter 'Crap' or 'What crap' as he processed news matter, affecting a contempt for all events on earth and for the written accounts of those events."[11]

Midge, conversely, pays enormous attention to all events on Earth, and *The Dog of the South*, his written account of them, allows the reader to share his pleasure. "In South Texas I saw three interesting things," he writes, and then lists them. Indeed, he's inordinately

---

[10] Midge himself, with his rules against record playing after nine p.m. and aversion to dancing, is a deviation from the norm, or from Norma—at least in the eyes of his mother-in-law, who calls him a "pill."

[11] At a small museum in Mexico, Midge finds Dupree's comments in the guestbook: "A big gyp. Most boring exhibition in North America."

proud of his better-than-average vision, noting that he can "see stars down to the seventh magnitude." Perhaps it is something to boast about, but in compensation for his assorted failings, he seems to have attributed to his eyesight super-hypnotic powers:

> I watched the windows for Norma, for flitting shadows. I was always good at catching roach movement or mouse movement from the corner of my eye. Small or large, any object in my presence had only to change its position slightly, by no more than a centimeter, and my head would snap about and the thing would be instantly trapped by my gaze.

A military-history buff with "sixty-six lineal feet" of books on the topic (he would know the exact dimensions), Midge sees himself on a mission, and in his hilarious, unconscious self-inflation, he makes vermin sound like panzer units trying some new formation.

Freed from copyediting, then, Midge proceeds to read the world at large, the way any good Portis protagonist would—but his job training means his observations are that much more acute. He contemplates spelling errors (a strange man hands him a card that reads, inscrutably, "adios AMIGO and watch out for the FLORR!"), the abysmal Spanish-language skills of his traveling companion, Dr. Reo Symes, and the bizarrely mangled locutions of the chummy Father Jackie (e.g., *wanter* instead of *water*). Encountering an emergency flood-relief effort, Midge fervently pitches in, but is nevertheless distracted when a British officer reprimands someone "to stay away from his vehicles 'in future'—rather than 'in *the* future.'" It's funny enough the first time; when a similar omission occurs twelve pages later, after Midge discovers Norma in the hospital ("I would have to take that up with doctor—not 'with *the* doctor'"), the repetition alleviates, if just for an instant, the unspoken sadness that's dawning on him.

In British Honduras, Midge meets Melba, the friend of Dr. Symes's mother's. At Symes's insistence, he reads two of her stories, and like an amateur Don Foster, he notes certain compositional tendencies:

Melba had broken the transition problem wide open by starting every paragraph with "Moreover." She freely used "the former" and "the latter" and every time I ran into one of them I had to backtrack to see whom she was talking about. She was also fond of "inasmuch" and "crestfallen."

Like all good copy editors, Midge is something of a pedant; nevertheless he seems more to relish than disdain such human details. He may debate, at length, some nicety of Civil War lore, but he rarely passes judgment on the people he meets, even when they forget his name: Dr. Symes calls him Speed; an addled Dupree mistakes him for Burke (yet another copy editor); for some reason, Father Jackie thinks his name is Brad. But names are important, as a character asserts in *Masters of Atlantis*. Midge notes the nominal errors with exclamation points, but no real outrage, until the end of his quest, when a dazed Norma calls him by Dupree's first name—not just once, but repeatedly. It's the only slip that really hurts.

"I was interested in everything," Midge confesses early on, and in the book's final paragraph, right before his quietly devastating revelation which colors all that has come before, Midge notes that upon his return to Little Rock he finally received his BA, and is contemplating graduate work in plate tectonics. He wants to literally read the world, to study its layers and its lives.

II. THE BALLOONIST

At age nine, a daydreaming Portis conducted underwater-breathing experiments at Smackover Creek—a lifesaving measure, rehearsed in the eventuality of pursuit by Axis nasties. The toponym, he explains in "Combinations of Jacksons" (published in the May 1999 *Atlantic*), is "an Arkansas rendering of 'chemin couvert,' covered path, or road."

Few could have predicted that after the brisk gestation of *Norwood* and *True Grit*, eleven years would pass before *The Dog of the*

South emerged, a period that constitutes a *chemin couvert* of sorts. Silence, with side orders of cunning and exile, can lend luster to a writer's work. Deep processes are afoot, some calculus of genius or madness, penury or plenty. Given the Central American trail of *Dog* and *Gringos*, and the occult mischief of *Masters*, one imagines Portis hitting the road, unearthing pre-Columbian glazeware, eavesdropping in hotel bars—and reading, reading, reading: Ignatius Donnelly's *Atlantis* and Colonel James Churchward's *The Lost Continent of Mu*, special-interest magazines like the ufological *Gamma Bulletin*, dense books "with footnotes longer than the text proper," to say nothing of the whole of Romanian fiction, which contains "not a single novel with a coherent plot."

That earlier Portisian lag, alas, is now officially smaller than the one between 1991's *Gringos* and whatever he's currently working on. In Portis's last book to date, Jimmy Burns observes of a fellow expat:

> Frank didn't write anything, or at least he didn't publish anything.... The Olmecs didn't like to show their art around either. They buried it twenty-five feet deep in the earth and came back with spades to check up on it every ten years or so, to make sure it was still there, unviolated. Then they covered it up again.

Is a new cycle of Portisian activity on the horizon, at the end of a decade-and-change? The recent magazine appearances of "Combinations of Jacksons" (1999) and "Motel Life, Lower Reaches" (2003), memoiristic pieces that bookend the Overlook reprint project, are enough to make one wonder whether (or if you're me, pray that) Portis is writing at length about his life.

Maybe he'll fill in the blanks, reveal what he's been up to all these years, though if anyone understands the character of silence, the value of secrets, it's Charles Portis. *The Dog of the South* contains its own Portis doppelgänger—its own commentary on authorial mystique—in the figure of John Selmer Dix, MA, the elusive writer of *With Wings as Eagles*, which he penned entirely on a bus, a board across his lap, traveling from Dallas to L.A. and back again for a year. His whereabouts remain a mystery; assorted reported sightings, like those of Bigfoot or Nessie, cannot be taken at face value. Dr. Reo Symes, the most vigorous, wildly comic jabberjaw in all of Portisland, is *Wings*'s unlikely champion ("pure nitro," he calls it)—a huckster on the skids who maintains an unlikely reverence for what appears to be nothing more than a salesman's primer and its reticent creator.

Symes's limitless patter circles the indissoluble truths contained in this criminally overlooked document, and his earnest-rabid claims for *With Wings as Eagles* sound not unlike those of Portis fanatics to the uninitiated: "Read it, then read it again.... The Three T's. The Five Don'ts. The Seven Elements. Stoking the fires of the U.S.S. Reality. Making the Pep Squad and staying on it." All else in the world of letters is "foul grunting." When Midge modestly counters that Shakespeare is considered the greatest writer who ever lived, the doctor responds without hesitation, "Dix puts William Shakespeare in the shithouse." Midge, "still on the alert for chance messages," reads a few pages of Symes's copy of *Wings*, but finds its dialectical materialism a touch opaque:

> He said you must save your money but you must not be afraid to spend it either, and at the same time you must give no thought to money. A lot of his stuff was formulated in this way. You must do this and that, two contrary things, and you must also be careful to do neither.

As important to Symes as the visible text is what happened after its publication, the story behind the story, during the time when Dix "repudiated all his early stuff, said *Wings* was nothing but trash, and didn't write another line, they say, for twelve years." Symes has an alternate theory: he believes Dix continued writing, at greater length and with even more intense insight, but "for some reason that we can't understand yet he wanted to hold it all back from the reading public, let them squeal how they may." Thousands of pages repose in Dix's large tin trunk—which, of course, is nowhere to be found.

*   *   *

Portis's trunk resurfaces, after a fashion, in his next book, *Masters of Atlantis* (1985), which sustains its seemingly one-joke premise through tireless comic invention and an ever-shifting narrative focus. At once the oddest ball among his works and a full-vent treatment of themes common to *Dog* and *Gringos*, a clearinghouse of obscurantist scribblings and a satire that skewers without malice, Portis's sprawling third novel loosely follows the life of Lamar Jimmerson, whose eventual sedentary existence is in perverse contrast to the typical Portis rambler. Jimmerson's destiny crystallizes after the First World War, when a grateful derelict gives him a booklet crammed with Greek and triangles—an *n*th-generation copy of the Codex Pappus, containing the wisdom of lost Atlantis. Portis's inspired tweaking of subterranean belief systems touches on alchemy, lost-continent lore, and reams of secret-society mumbo-jumbo. The original codex, written untold millennia ago, survived its civilization's destruction in an ivory casket, which eventually washed ashore in Egypt, to be decoded after much effort by none other than Hermes Trismegistus (the mythical figure deified by the Egyptians as Thoth, the Greeks as Hermes, and the Romans as Mercury). Hermes became the first modern master of the Gnomon Society, which counts among its elite ranks Pythagoras, Cagliostro, and, as it happens, Lamar Jimmerson of Gary, Indiana.

That the document is bunk is the obvious joke, but Portis wraps it in antic bolts of faith and failure. Indeed, *Masters of Atlantis* works as a thoughtful, whimsical companion to Frances A. Yates's *Giordano Bruno and the Hermetic Tradition* (1964), a study of the magical and occult reaches of Renaissance thought. Yates lays her cards on the table, explaining that the "returning movement of the Renaissance with which this book will be concerned, the return to a pure golden age of magic [i.e., the supposed era of ancient Egyptian wisdom], was based on a radical error of dating.... This huge historical error was to have amazing results."

The amazing result in *Masters* is an alternately deadpan and

high-flying pageant of secret sharers, unreadable tracts,[12] and highly
dubious theories, determining the rise and fall—and rise?—of an
institution insulated from the American century unfolding outside
by nothing more than the unshakable belief of its adherents. The
adept cultivate their secrecy and self-regard by maintaining rules
against dissemination to outsiders, or "Perfect Strangers," a code as
strict as it is arbitrary. For instance, the Romanian-born alchemist
Golescu, a caretaker at the Naval Observatory, would seem a shoo-in
for Gnomonic acceptance. His achievements read like a variation on
Symes's catalog of Dixian wisdom:

> Through Golescuvian analysis he had been able to make positive
> identification of the Third Murderer in *Macbeth* and of the Fourth
> Man in Nebuchadnezzer's fiery furnace. He had found the Lost
> Word of Freemasonry and uttered it more than once, into the air,
> the Incommunicable Word of the Cabalists, the Verbum Ineffabile.
> The enigmatic quatrains of Nostradamus were an open book to
> him. He had a pretty good idea of what the Oracle of Ammon had
> told Alexander.

But Golescu doesn't make the cut. He knows too much—or
at least says too much. His strident claims betray an insufficiently
covered path. The point of the Verbum Ineffabile—the unspeak-
able word— is that you don't say it.

Most mortals, it seems, are doomed to remain Perfect Strangers,
but at least there's the possibility of writing something oneself, a
validating work of comprehensive greatness. In *Gringos*, freelance
bounty hunter and former antiquities dealer Jimmy Burns journeys to the Inaccessible City of Dawn, bringing along his friend
Doc Flandin, an ailing Mexico hand. Doc is ever on the lookout
for the Mayan equivalent of Dix's tin trunk or the hermetically

---

[12] Many years after the publication of *Gnomonism Today*, a sharp-eyed disciple discovers that
the printers have omitted every other page.

unsealed casket—a fabled cache of lost *libros* that would provide
further pieces to the puzzle of that vast and vanished civilization.
Burns doubts any such books even exist. In any case, Doc claims
to be nearly finished with his own "grand synthesis" of Mexican
history, a scholarly tour de force explaining the truth behind myths
and answering ancient riddles; among other things, Doc's book
would "tell us who the Olmecs really were, appearing suddenly
out of the darkness, and why they carved those colossal heads that
looked like Fernando Valenzuela of the Los Angeles Dodgers."

Somewhere in limbo, apart from or behind the printed
ephemera—confession magazines and pre-1960 detective novels
and something called *Fun with Magnets*—that crop up in Portis's
novels more frequently than any work of high literature, is a dream
library stocked entirely with vanished books and unwritten ones,
impossible genius texts that tantalize from across the void. Chances
are that Doc's unfinished manuscript will join the rest of those
ghostly titles. But time doesn't always run out, and at least once
the dream becomes manifest. Mattie Ross waits half a century to
write *True Grit*, and during those years the factual grit of her life
story at last forms a pearl. Though Portis's compositional time-
frame isn't quite as long as Mattie's, his periodic absences from the
thrum of publication help give each one of his books what those
Burmese journalist ants call a "nacreous glaze," a shimmering coat
of perfect strangeness.

Portis has published a single work of fiction since *Gringos*—"I Don't
Talk Service No More," a spare, haunting short story that appeared
in the May 1996 *Atlantic*. The unnamed narrator, an institutionalized
Korean War veteran, sneaks into the hospital library every night to
make long-distance calls to his fellow squad members, participants
in something called the Fox Company Raid. He remembers their
names, though some other details have grown hazy. At the end of
this call, his fellow raider "asked me how it was here. He wanted to
know how it was in this place and I told him it wasn't so bad. It's

not so bad here if you have the keys. For a long time I didn't have the keys."

Instead of closure, the last sentence casts a pall over the story, and the mention of keys conjures the great locked enigmas drifting through Portis's last three books. In *Dog*, Symes disputes an alleged Dix sighting, musing, "*Where were all his keys?*" (According to Dixian lore, the great author, wise with answers, never went anywhere without a jumbo key ring on his belt.)

The "Service" narrator's resounding isolation connects with the loneliness found in so many Portis characters. Norwood Pratt and Jimmy Burns, wry loners capable of brute force, wind up married and in more or less optimistic situations. But happiness eludes the other protagonists. Lamar Jimmerson and most of the Gnomons in *Masters of Atlantis* can't form mature emotional attachments; Jimmerson barely notices as his wife leaves him and his son avoids him. And how is it that *The Dog of the South*, Portis's finest comic achievement, subtly shades into melancholy? When Midge finds Norma, by chance, in the hospital, he calls it a "concentrated place of misery"; his earlier angst-free, even chipper take on his cuckoldry suddenly shifts, in her presence, to a terrible feeling of rejection. The mere fact of his being strikes her as wearisome:

> "I don't feel like talking right now."
> "We don't have to talk. I'll get a chair and just sit here."
> "Yes, but I'll know you're there."

Dog's last two lines erase miles of cheer that have come before. *True Grit*'s matter-of-fact final sentence ("This ends my true account of how I avenged Frank Ross's blood over in the Choctaw Nation when snow was on the ground") harbors a more cosmic sadness; as pathetic fallacy, it feels like an American cousin to the faintly falling snow that closes Joyce's "The Dead." Portis carries over this precipitous finish to his own life in "Combinations of Jacksons." A "peevish old coot" himself now, he peers back over the years to when his Uncle Sat showed him scale maps of tiny Japan and the immense U.S., to dispel his boyhood fears of a protracted war. The last lines run: "I can see the winter stubble in his fields, too, on that dreary January day in 1942. Broken stalks and a few dirty white shreds of bumblebee cotton. Everyone who was there is dead and buried now except me."

Portis is careful to keep the tears at bay with laughter; to borrow the impromptu skeet targets from Rooster and company, he's a literary corn dodger. In *Dog*, Dr. Symes's mother, a missionary, periodically grills Midge on his knowledge of the Bible, a knowledge he repeatedly professes not to have. "Think about this," she says, pointedly fixing his thoughts to the matter of last things. "All the little animals of your youth are long dead." Her companion Melba promptly emends the truism: "Except for turtles."

The statement, at once hilariously random but completely realistic, neutralizes the threat of gloom; it's the sort of bull's-eye silliness that pitches Portis's reality a few feet above that of his fellow page-blackeners. Significantly, he gives Lamar Jimmerson some experience with skyey matters: *Masters of Atlantis* opens with the young man in France during the First World War, "serving first with the Balloon Section, stumbling about in open fields holding one end of a long rope."

The truth is up there—well, maybe. (*Gringos*, among its other virtues, navigates UFO culture with more than cursory knowledge and without easy condescension.) Of all the moments when Portis's prose turns lighter than air, my personal favorite involves the aforementioned Golescu, whose chaotic turn in *Masters of Atlantis* gives the book an early-inning jolt. In addition to claiming membership in various sub rosa brotherhoods, some of them seemingly contradictory, Golescu possesses the talents of a "multiple mental marvel," to borrow magician Ricky Jay's term. Asking for "two shits of pepper," he takes pencils in hands and demonstrates for a bemused Lamar Jimmerson his ambidexterity and capacity for cerebral acrobatics, in a rapid-fire paragraph of undiluted laughing gas. It's what Dr. Symes would have called pure nitro.

"See, not only is Golescu writing with both hands but he is also looking at you and conversing with you at the same time in a most natural way. Hello, good morning, how are you? Good morning, Captain, how are you today, very fine, thank you. And here is Golescu still writing and at the same time having his joke on the telephone. Hello, yes, good morning, this is the Naval Observatory but no, I am very sorry, I do not know the time. Nine-thirty, ten, who knows? Good morning, that is a beautiful dog, sir, can I know his name, please? Good morning to you, madam, the capital of Delaware is Dover. In America the seat of government is not always the first city. I give you Washington for another. And now if you would like to speak to me a sequence of random numbers, numbers of two digits, I will not only continue to look at you and converse with you in this easy way but I will write the numbers as given with one hand and reversed with the other hand while I am at the same time adding the numbers and giving you running totals of both columns, how do you like that? Faster, please, more numbers, for Golescu this is nothing...."

Read it, then read it again—at a spittle-flecked rush, with a mild Lugosi accent—and observe how everything turns into nothing, how all that is solid melts into air. ✳

HOW TO BE A
CHRISTIAN ARTIST

DISCUSSED: *Franny and Zooey, Vince Guaraldi, Record Clubs,
Caterwauling, Spiritual Frailty, Aretha Franklin, The Reverend
Al Green, Improvised Testifying, Medical Garb, Kramer, Churchgoing
Intellectuals, Psychedelia, I-IV Progression, Cock-Rock Posturing, Dante,
Early B-52s, Overdubbed Exhalations, Doubt*

I like music that makes other people uncomfortable. I like
Pere Ubu a lot, for example, and my favorite Pere Ubu
album is *New Picnic Time,* an album that has sent many
listeners screaming from the room. Captain Beefheart is
another favorite, in which case I like *Lick My Decals Off,
Baby,* an album of great rhythmic complexity and impressionistic lyrics. Rhys Chatham's out-of-tune guitar pieces. Tony Conrad's violin
pieces for just intonation, LaMonte Young's minimalisms, free jazz
from the mid-sixties, the Sun City Girls, the Slits, Daniel Johnston,
the Shaggs, Wesley Willis, Syd Barrett's most ominous solo work,
the most experimental David Grubbs, etc. It's not that I think this
music is interesting simply because it's *unusual.* This music brings
me genuine pleasure. I like pop songs, too, of course, in reasonable
doses. But often the work that makes an indelible impression on

me comes from a place of singularity. This work doesn't give up its
secrets easily. It makes demands. In the process of reckoning with it,
you feel as though you've helped make it what it is.

An example: a few years ago I was invited to a record club in
Lower Manhattan by a painter friend. The record club worked this
way: each of the twelve attendants brought two songs that they
were *in love with* at the moment, and, according to a sequence generated by randomly dealt playing cards, we circled the room in two
rounds with everyone playing his or her songs in turn. Though
I've never really been a book-club sort of guy, I was taken with
the spirit of this gathering right away.

On the Friday night in question, the record club was march-
ing along, doing what it does, glancing off of jazz, electronica,
Britpop, early rock and roll, Old Time, when suddenly there
emerged from the speakers the most strangled, desperate racket
I had heard in ages.

The first problem was the singer's voice. The singer sang in a
tortured falsetto, or most of the time he did. Sometimes he hovered just above and below the line that separated his chest voice
from his falsetto. In the tenor range, he had a boyish drawl, sort
of like Kurt Cobain, if Kurt had been raised in the Ozarks. But
then there was his boy soprano, into which he lurched for various
pitches, where he was silly and ghostly and a little bit shrill all at
the same time.

Having noted the singer, I shifted my focus to the accompanying ensemble: acoustic guitar, organ, celeste, two rather primitive
drummers. The band would probably have sounded *adorable,* like
the sound track to the tugboat in *Mister Rogers' Neighborhood*, were
it not for the structure of the song itself, which I later learned
was entitled "Holy Kisser's Block Party." It began with an alarm
clock, followed by a section A, some kind of whispery chant in
which Daniel, the lead vocalist, and some girl backup singers
intoned their rhetorical intention, "I do vow, / here and now, /
I will kiss again / It starts right now." This was followed by section
B, in which the celeste, or chimes, dominated, and a very different

melody was explored, followed by a section C, in which varieties of love were described and suggested by the narrator, "Begin your loving to the one who bothers most," this in turn followed by a section D, an actual chorus, in which piano propelled the rhythms, major triads, while above hovered some really strange counterpoint between Daniel and the backup singers, his *sisters.* Did I not say that the band in question, the Danielson Famile, really are a family? Daniel on acoustic guitar and vocals; Rachel on vocals and flute and sometimes organ; Megan on bells and vocals; David and Andrew on drums and percussion, respectively. "Get your rear in gear, lend an ear, have no fear, draw near, my dear, bring the cheer, take time to hear." And then a section E, which was really section B in a minor key, consisting only of a repetition of the line "As coals of fire rest on their heads," with minimal accompaniment. Back to section A.

I thought it was some of the worst caterwauling I had ever heard. And I *like* caterwauling.

The record club always produces a little anthology—the minutes of the proceedings, if you will—and so I had the opportunity to hear "Holy Kisser's Block Party" again, in my car, because that's often where I first listen to compact discs, and I confess I was a little shocked by the song. I resisted its complex demands. And yet when I stumbled on it, periodically, when playing the anthology of the record-club event, I realized that I was beginning to think the song was indisputably great.

After a couple of years, I was invited again to the record club (visit its website: *recordclub.org*), this time along with my wife, Amy. By coincidence, Julia Jacquette, the painter who'd first issued the invitation to me, had *again* selected a Danielson Famile song, as though she'd been thinking of nothing else in the intervening years. On this occasion, the song was the hit, sort of, from the brand-new Danielson album, *Fetch the Compass Kids,* viz., "We Don't Say Shut Up," again composed of a bunch of rather diverse sections that in this case featured really great counterpoint writing between the piano and the acoustic guitar, and great vocal arrangements, etc. At first, I had no idea what the song was about, really, except that it extolled the notion of "quiet time," and the author of this "quiet time" seemed to be the "holiest of ghosts." However, with proximity and familiarity I was beginning to understand something quite elemental about the Danielson Famile that had escaped my notice—they were evangelical Christians.

Julia Jacquette, my painter friend, had made a pilgrimage to see them perform live, and she said it was sort of an amazing thing. For example, the singer and acoustic-guitar player, Daniel, performed the entire show from inside of a large textile tree, which must have made it rather difficult to play all the chords properly. The rest of the family wore medical garb. The motives for the costumes and props were not explained to the audience, but upon reflection it now appears likely that they had something to do with the laboriously worked-out theology of songwriter Daniel Smith.

My first reaction to the evangelical dimension of the work was, naturally, to resist. What I liked best was the *sound* of this album, which, frankly, was and is unlike anything else that is being produced today. Half-innocent and half-cultivated. *Compass Kids,* which was released in early 2001, was produced by Steve Albini, the man behind some of Nirvana, some of P. J. Harvey, some of Will Oldham, and the most recent album by Godspeed! You Black Emperor. You can tell a lot more thought went into the recording this time, since Daniel's voice is mixed back a bit as the vocal choir of Megan, Rachel, and others is brought forward. Also, for a band that has no bass player, the album feels nicely bass-heavy, with strange keyboard sounds and bits of distorted guitar filling in the low end. Also, some of the music writing on *Compass Kids* is divided between Daniel and the keyboardist Chris Palladino, with the result that the piano and acoustic guitar interact almost uncannily in spots, in a way that calls to mind the sublime Vince Guaraldi, and his music for the *Peanuts* cartoons.

My wife became obsessed, too, and we bought *Fetch the Compass Kids* and played it for a long stretch. Not as in my youth, when I pored over the lyrics of albums (back then, I remember reading with intense disappointment an interview with Mick Jagger, wherein he remarked that lyrics were "just something to sing"), these days I tend to play things because I like how they sound, with an indifference to the "message." I never knew what Michael Stipe was singing, and I never cared; I never cared what Bob Mould was singing; I never cared what Paul Westerberg was singing; I certainly didn't care what Kurt Cobain was singing. Around our house, we played *Compass Kids* because the music rewarded attention, because the piano and acoustic guitar traded the downbeats in different verses, and because the time signatures were unusual, because the instrumentation was bizarre, and because there was something charming about the ominous innocence of the entirety.

Later, however, I did start to wonder about the lyrics. It was perhaps when my wife bought one of the earlier albums. On the first track from *Tell Another Joke at the Old Choppin' Block,* released in 1997, Daniel chants "I love my Lord, I love my Lord, I love my Lord." Pretty straightforward, huh? And, later, on "Flesh Thang," I noticed the following: "It's a house of the Lord. It's a house of the Holy Ghost but the house be speakin' at times. Haunted house is bein' tricky. You better only be hearin' the holiest of ghosts." Similarly, on "Smooth Death," the title of which acts as a leit-motif on *Choppin' Block,* there is an allusion to the wine of the Eucharist: "Take a bath in the blood, it's gonna be a smooth death, take it slow." Maybe it's possible that I didn't notice the Christian dimension of the Danielson lyrics at first because I didn't *want* to have to think about Christian imagery in what is, for all its eccentricity, an example of so-called indie rock. And yet the specific musical characteristics of *Choppin' Block* made avoidance of the lyrics almost impossible. *Choppin' Block* was produced by the one-named Kramer, who also brought you Galaxie 500 and Low and Bongwater, et al. It follows that the album rings with echo and reverb, with the repetition of open chords. The litanical reiteration of phrases like "I love my Lord," or "It's time to rest, my son," from the song entitled "Jersey Loverboy," falls naturally into this reboant space, with the incantatory quality that we associate, perhaps, with a certain kind of psychedelia. Daniel could just as easily be singing: "Mother? Yes, son. I want to kill you."

Or: what is psychedelia but entry-level spiritual investigation? I first understood that the Danielsons were singing about God when I understood that the music on *Choppin' Block* sounded as if they were singing about God. There's a misuse of the litanical in some rock and roll. There's a perversion of the litanical, and you hear it, for example, in Lou Reed, the reliance on the I-IV progression, while he sings, in this case, about heroin. In such a context, that is, the secular *is* spiritual. "Heroin," that is, is spiritual, or it wants to borrow from a spiritual tradition in its repetitions and its life-or-death concerns. He does, after all, feel like Jesus' son.

Choppin' Block reaches a similar zenith of repetitions in "Quest for Thrills," a song composed largely of one chord, which advances a relentless and slightly humorous passion play over its drone: "Hungry humans, rootless man, just a number, avoid the question of the truth. Get the injection, the good infection, take a drink of spirited tunes, spirited pop, spirited tunes, pop tunes, poppy tunes. Fifth dimension, belt of truth, Bible belt. Thirty minutes after death, something called *E. coli* is detected in your nose. You'll be decomposing in the dirt, and you're cryin' yourself to sleep... dead man's wishes is bein' sacred." Soon after, the song proceeds into a second droning passage where Daniel chants "Amen, brother," for a good couple of minutes.

Choppin' Block concludes with a longish instrumental, actually recorded in a funeral home, consisting of an orchestra of tuba, flute, sax, and clarinet, all playing the big, ominous drone that one imagines has everything to do with the idea of the *smooth death,* as enunciated earlier on the album, here perhaps embodying the passage *through* the smooth death of evangelical experience, into the afterlife. When the vocals finally break out at the end of the unnamed instrumental, they consist merely of the words *I believe* repeated ad infinitum.

In the African American tradition of musical evangelism, there exists a profound and seductive ambiguity that clouds the differences between spiritual and earthly love. God's *caritas* and *agape* are adjacent to the *eros* of the first world, so that when Al Green says, "Let's Stick Together," he could either mean, *Let's you and I work this thing out,* or he could mean that he is spiritually frail and in desperate pursuit of some kind of certainty of *divine* love, a certainty that is often framed in the context of doubt, because doubt is the human thing. You find this same evangelical origin in a lot of black popular music, of course: in Aretha Franklin, whose Gospel roots are well known, but even in Motown, where songs like "Ain't No Mountain High Enough" trade on the conflation of the earthly and the spiritual. The other salient feature of this African American musical evangelism is its lack of punitive imagery. There's little in these songs about the theology of Hell.

The theology of (white) rock and roll is often much less forgiving. From "Great Balls of Fire," by Jerry Lee Lewis, which makes love and brimstone bedfellows, right up to the heavy-metal theology of AC/DC (in "Highway to Hell," and "Hell's Bells"), you feel that the spiritual in the rock-and-roll tradition is mainly obsessed with sin and penitence (or the lack thereof), with the downright *fallen* qualities of mankind, with doubt, with all that is harrowing about Christian experience, not a moment given over to forgiveness, except perhaps in that awful song by Don Henley "The Heart of the Matter," or in the bland affirmations of the contemporary "country" radio format.

The Danielsons sidestep all prior solutions to the problem of how to be evangelical recording artists. On the one hand, the Danielson Famile are so far from the Gospel idea of a musical ministry that it's hard to consider what they do as being in the same league at all. There's none of the improvised *testifying* of an Al Green or a Solomon Burke here, none of the reliance on scriptural citation and preordained Old Testament imagery that turns up again and again in the Gospel music tradition. And at the other extreme, notwithstanding their love of the occasional bar chord, the Danielsons avoid the bombastic cock-rock posturing of Creed and their brethren, wherein the evangelical involves the inevitable removal of the lead singer's shirt.

The Danielsons, I think, sketch out a sonic diagram of the difficulty of contemporary faith, because they make music that is incredibly ungainly and awkward, as faith itself is ungainly and awkward, though no less fervent for its homeliness. Well, perhaps there *is* some consistency between the way Rev. Al Green uses his music and the way that Daniel Smith uses his in the aforementioned repetition of phrases. This has everything to do, believe it or not, with *Franny and Zooey.* You remember, of course, that Franny goes out to a luncheon on the day of the big game, and despite the loving and affable affection of her suitor, she *passes out* at lunch. The reason for this fainting spell is often given in literature classes as a *spiritual crisis* of some kind. In particular, it is said, Franny Glass faints because of her attempts to repeat the Jesus prayer: "Lord Jesus Christ, have mercy on me, a poor sinner." In fact, in *The Way of the Pilgrim,* where this prayer technique was first given mass-market evocation, the idea was to repeat the prayer so constantly and so perfectly that your heart is able to say it with each muscular pulsation. When you get to that point, amazing things begin to happen, your life improves, your relationships improve, doors open that once were closed, etc., and, I suppose, you experience loss of consciousness. This is the way the Danielsons use a phrase like "I believe." They use it like the phrase has magical properties, and they use it like they definitely believe, and like they know that if they repeat a phrase often enough, life improves, the door opens that once was closed, etc.

Fetch the Compass Kids, the 2001 masterpiece of the Danielsons, comes immediately after a two-album package called *Tri-Danielson Alpha* and *Tri-Danielson Omega,* in which Daniel Smith tries to play in three separate group contexts: (1) in a primarily acoustic guise, (2) with the Danielson Famile as described above, and (3) with a sort of a conventional rock group, replete with electric guitar. The Trinitarian model is obviously premeditated on *Tri-Danielson,* but it's also a bit facetious, since the same Smith siblings and the same cast of side characters play in all three groups. The results also vary more widely than on any other Danielson album. A hilarious song like "Rubbernecker," a dead ringer for the early B-52s, can be followed by something that really relies on Daniel's obsession with downwardly moving chromatic melodies, wherein there is no chorus and no hook. *Tri-Danielson* is hilarious and moving in spots, but it's also big and sloppy.

Not so with *Compass Kids*. You emerge from the diffuse ambitions of *Tri-Danielson* into a record that is thoroughly composed, where the band is better organized than ever before, where the young drumming Smiths suddenly seem to be first-rate drummers, and where the evangelical context of the album seems entirely organized around a single idea, which is the pursuit of a moral compass in a dangerous and modern secular world. "It's an incredibly confusing time / been told I must be in my prime," Smith observes on "Rallying the Dominoes," "It's too much of a confusing time, / 'you forgot to eat again,' but I don't mind." Or elsewhere, on "Singers Go First": "Poppa pushed me out the boat again, my morning face says I cannot swim, did not eat again." Or, on "The Wheel Made Man": "Fear comes where loves was then love comes where fear was, the wheel within wheel in the sky, who am I?" Of course there are the usual protestations of faith on *Compass Kids*: "Happy and sad gonna sing the wide and long and high and deep, oh Lord," or "In Him do we move and live and do become." And yet in general, *Compass Kids* attempts a more subtle evocation of the frailties of the spiritual life. It attempts to evoke these frailties gently and compassionately, while it continues to demonstrate the evangelical properties of music and religious imagination, all of this in the context of a musical idiom that I suspect most people would find too strange for their listening delectation. The result is that the contradictions implicit in such an undertaking emerge as massive, overpowering, and, for me, incredibly interesting.

Which is to say that I find I have come somehow to *identify* with the Danielson Famile. I identify with them, in that rock-and-roll way, and I am reassured by them. Here's why. Because in the literary community, at present, one of the worst career moves you can make is to admit that you are a person who *believes,* a person who goes to church and who finds value in it. To say both that you go to church and that you consider yourself an intellectual is to court skepticism and even disdain in your peers. I have been asked by at least one editor not to talk about churchgoing because "people don't want to think about you as a churchgoer." And the reason for this is that *churchgoing* has come to mean *literalist fundamentalism.*

I should qualify my experience for the purposes of these remarks. I don't have particular adherence to Episcopalianism, the religion in which I was raised, to the extent of including or ruling out adherence to any other sect. I don't believe in Christianity as the one true faith; I don't believe in the Christian God as the one true God, excluding all others. I don't believe that the ancient Abrahamic faiths are more correct than some Druidic sun-worshipping commune in eastern Oregon. At various moments, I have been just as taken by the Quaker faith, or Tibetan Buddhism, as by Episcopalianism, and I am a fan of the Qur'an and Talmudic scholarship. A friend of mine sends me daily prayers from the Lubavitchers, and I think they're fabulous. While I find Madonna's obsession with the kaballah kind of self-congratulatory, I don't rule it out. I love the church of my birth because I love the ritual of the church of my birth, the bells, the censer, the sung liturgy, the emphasis on textual interpretation. Moreover, I like the repetition of certain kinds of rituals, simply because things repeated are pleasing. And I love that Episcopalianism is the locus of debates, now, about what scripture means on the subject of homosexuality. I love that my church has been brave enough to lead in the matter of ordaining gay bishops.

Do I believe every day? I believe every day, and I doubt every day. I cannot conceive of faith without doubt. I can't conceive of a relationship to the God of my faith without conceiving of terrifying overpowering silences that make me wonder what the hell it is that I think that I'm doing when I am praying and when

I am addressing myself to the divine. I have never found that my faith has completely eliminated the fleshly appetites, and I don't even know if it's *meant to be* that faith eliminates these fleshly appetites—because we wouldn't have these bodies if were weren't meant to wrestle with the significance of having them.

Did I also say that I love the music of the church? As Dylan remarked, I understand the spirit, whatever it is, through music. Music somehow actualizes belief in the face of doubt, in the face of the considerable secular pressures in my life and professional community, so that I feel myself made stronger by music and literature. And this seems to be the sort of thinking at the very center of *Compass Kids,* as when Daniel Smith says, "I will empty all my accounts to become a waiter on hand and foot and tend to invisible hammers, guitars, and pens; everything returns with purpose again."

What does music sound like when it is rendering these sorts of complexities, the paradoxes of belief in a modern age? It doesn't sound *easy.* Daniel Smith came up through the music department at Rutgers, and he learned composition, and his thesis was the first Danielson Famile album, *A Prayer for Every Hour,* and even in that far more primitive recording, you can already feel him aspiring toward punk rock, prog, children's music, and the high-art tradition of contemporary classical music. Likewise, lyrically, he is already longing for an architecture of Christian symbolism that is not tainted by overuse, sentimentality, and tradition. In a way, Smith is like Dante, wanting to conceive of an imagination so rich that in understanding his words and his protagonists, you will have automatically worked through some of the mystery of Christianity: "Making a point of being disappointed, that rule of thumb will take you far in this life, 'cause I know I'm always being disappointed by my plans, by my boys and girls and by my plans. I now know I need, I now know I'm needy, I need to me [*sic*] a King. King of the jungle. There's a good fire and a bad fire, my flame's burnin' at both ends. The one's gotta go, the other's gone wild. My wild fire is my feeling tank, my tank or heart is not mine. There's no me involved, it's the Great Comfort moving man, amen, brother." Already, the experience of listening to the music and coming to parse the lyrics is the experience of being faithful, which is an experience of much confusion, and much disappointment, and much that is *not* reassuring, and not simple, and not easy. Or, as a friend once preached at my parish in New York City, people would quit asking for angels to visit if they bothered to read up on when exactly angels turned up. Angels are terrifying. The appearance of angels always brings with it cataclysmic changes in life and circumstance. They aren't hovering outside to make sure that your tax return arrives promptly. They appear to tell *you* that *you* are about to be impregnated by the power that created all space and time. Or they appear to tell you that the world as you know it is going to end, and that you may perish among the billions.

Consider the allusive quality of the most beautiful song on *Compass Kids,* "Can We Camp at Your Feet": "I get down from my sky high chair to camp at your feet / with what can I get away? Your love will have your way with us / anything that we can do? Water all the gifts in my shipshape children, bless this mess. Water all the gifts in my compass children / feet of good news." There's nothing screechy about the music on this one, just a morose stillness to Daniel's harmony with one of his sisters. The pulse of a backbeat begins with the line "with what can I get away?" which, as anyone who has ever tried to be religious will tell you, is the line that your brain utters with greatest regularity: *Why should I bother to do this, I get very little respect for trying to do this here on earth, where the options are between some mindless adherence, which seems to involve wearing blinders and condemning everyone I love to a fiery eternity, why bother with the coffee hour with the Republicans after a church service in which they have ignored everything they have just heard, why should I bother, couldn't this possibly just pay off a little bit, couldn't the thing that I'm supposedly praying to, the thing that supposedly created all this stuff around me, just respond once to my pleas, couldn't it just one time, this thing, make life a little bit easier instead of making it more complicated? Isn't there a reward for people who go through with all this stuff and give away a lot of money because that's what you're supposed to do, isn't there one meager reward for doing this in terms of actual gifts given, or results conveyed, because if there's no reward, when everyone else is outside doing all the stuff they get to do, buying what they get to buy, sleeping in on Sunday, why should I bother to do this, because it really would be a lot more fun not to have to do it?* "Can We Camp at Your Feet" brings this difficulty into relief, suggesting what is frankly heretical in most sects of Christianity, that the believer should take his or her faith directly to the unnamed omnipotence (Christ is almost never mentioned in the entirety of the Danielson oeuvre, for example), *around* the intervening authorities, the bishops, ministers, etc., *around* the commentators who say it should be done this way and no other way. In doing so, the song proceeds toward a truly magnificent instrumental coda in which, after the line "your love will have your way," there is a beautiful overdubbed *exhalation,* by the vocal chorus, and this exhalation, the breath of God, I guess, recurs through the chord progression, while the backup singers sing the word *good,* from the *good news* of the last line, and the drummers stop and start in some kind of martial style, with myriad snare rolls, and the song threatens to end three times, always with these exhalations, the breath of God, the thing worshipped brought near, away from the history of a religion, away from the religious controversies of the moment, away from the sectarianism, away from the battles between Christianity and Islam, away from the anti-Semitism of fundamentalism, and in a musical style that any smart kid on any college campus in this country would recognize and respond to, a musical idiom that is full of instruments actually being *played,* instead of machines being played, mistakes and awkwardnesses preserved, barely an amplifier turned on, all because this is the way things really are, they are insurmountable, they are irreconcilable; it's hard to get through any twenty-four-hour period, that's what it means to be a Christian artist, it means that you understand what it's like to be here, and you don't presume to know more, you presume to care about what other people think and feel, which is emphatically what most Christians do *not* do, that's how it is. ✱

WILLIAM T. VOLLMANN

"AND SUPPRESS THE UNPLEASANT THINGS"

DISCUSSED: *Shostakovich, Dresden, Propaganda, Tolstoy, Vonnegut, Victor Klemperer, Céline, Complicity, Aida, The Anguish of Jean Améry, Raskolnikov*

ccording to my *Jane's Fighting Aircraft of World War II,* RAF Bomber Command dropped 45,517 British tons (2,240 pounds) of bombs on Berlin, 36,420 tons on Essen, 34,711 tons on Cologne,[1] and (as Kurt Vonnegut kept saying in *Slaughter-house-Five*) so it goes.

Like Vonnegut, I remain especially haunted by the incineration of Dresden on February 13 and 14, 1945. Fifty thousand people were killed. I have been told by older Germans, rightly or wrongly I don't know, that the second wave of planes, the American B-17 bombers, machine-gunned more civilians as they

---

[1] *Jane's Fighting Aircraft of World War II* (New York: Military Press, 1989 repr. of 1946–47 ed.), p. 34 ("Tonnage of Bombs Dropped by Bomber Command by Cities").

went through. At any rate, this raid eventually discomfited even Winston Churchill. Dresden hangs over me almost as balefully as Auschwitz and Leningrad as I finish writing my collection of short stories set largely in Germany and Russia during World War II. (If the book has a protagonist, it would be Shostakovich, whose Eighth String Quartet [1960] was composed in the course of a visit to the ruins of Dresden. That piece of music is one of the saddest and angriest ever written.)

"Horror" is an inadequate description of what occurred in Dresden, because the horror is almost over now. The broken churches, the roasted children, the black skeletons in their sometimes strangely unburned Nazi uniforms exist in the memories of those who survived, but in a few more decades at most those rememberers and their trauma will all be dead. But when the horror is buried, the loss will remain. Page through any picture book of Dresden as it used to be, and you'll see how beautiful the city once was. I happen to own a very thick volume of such photographs, and it never ceases to shock me how many images are captured with such helpful indicators as *"1945 zerstört,"* or sometimes, more pedantically, *"1945 zerstört, später abgebrochen"*— "1945 destroyed, later demolished."[2]

Thus Dresden, and Dresden was but one inferno of many. Multiply Dresden by Nuremberg, Berlin, and their kindred German cities sacrificed to the war, and the magnitude of this atrocity begins to emerge—or was it an atrocity? Did the laws of war somehow legitimize it?

In a posthumous collection of essays, entitled *On the Natural History of Destruction,* W. G. Sebald reminds us that "the majority of Germans today know, or so at least it is to be hoped, that we actually provoked the annihilation of the cities in which we once lived" (p. 103). And obviously World War II was to a great extent

---

[2] Fritz Löffler, *Das Alte Dresden: Geschichte Seiner Bauten* (Leipzig: E.A. Seemann Verlag, 1999 repr. of 1995 ed.).

Hitler's war,[3] fought with Hitler's methods. To what extent World War II was, however, a *German* war remains less clear. On 31 August 1939, a prominent American journalist in Berlin wrote in his diary: "Everybody against the war. People talking openly. How can a country go into a major war with a population so dead against it?" The journalist then comments: "Despite all my experience in the Third Reich I asked such a naive question! Hitler knew the answer very well." That answer was *propaganda.*[4]

To what extent the German people were complicit from the start in the war and the Holocaust, and to what extent they were manipulated into complicity, will never be decided according to any consensus. And in a way the question is irrelevant. It wasn't Hitler personally who killed the millions of Poles, Russians, Jews, et cetera. Nonetheless, the catastrophe which Germany, considered as a national unit, brought upon itself, would seem more "fair," partaking of retributive justice to a greater degree, if most Germans could be known to have wholeheartedly supported Hitler's hideous program—less so if they didn't. In my thinking about this matter over the past several years, I have not been able to come to any firm conclusions as to the responsibility of "the average German." In my short stories I fall, perhaps too conveniently, into an empathetic approach. I put myself into the shoes of a person born in Germany (or Russia), and necessarily exposed year after year to nothing but the local totalitarian propaganda, and I'm inclined to say: "They were led." Then I read the memoirs of a Jew who found himself threatened and tormented daily by his fellow Germans, and my heart hardens again.

Most parties concerned developed pretty hard hearts. To call

---

[3] While the appeasers such as Neville Chamberlain come in for their share of blame, appeasement might possibly have been effective with someone other than Hitler, who pretended to be temperate and even peaceful but was really, as hindsight can easily see, determined have his conquests no matter what.

[4] William L. Shirer, *The Rise and Fall of the Third Reich* (New York: Simon and Schuster, 1960), p. 593.

the Blitzkrieg in Poland "bestial" gives beasts a bad name. The Germans were the first to take up aerial bombing of cities. What we did to Dresden, they did to Warsaw. The conquered Poles couldn't retaliate; the unconquered British could, and after Pearl Harbor the Americans joined them. The *Oxford Companion to World War II* notes that the air war against Germany killed a hundred thousand Anglo-Americans and up to a million Germans[5] (the figure employed by Sebald is six hundred thousand). Even had those Germans all been civilians, they got off easily in comparison to the defenseless victims of their Final Solution. Sebald is right. What Germany got is what Germany provoked.

By all means let's begin with that judgment. The aerial bombing of Germany was, unfortunately, justified. But we need not end there. Sebald's book, which is frequently brilliant and almost always stylistically felicitous, deals with "the way in which memory... deals with experiences exceeding what is tolerable" (p. 79). (I see a family in an air-raid shelter, everybody roasted golden brown. I hear Shostakovich's Eighth String Quartet.) Given the carnage of the air war, why haven't more Germans written about it? What does their silence say?

We are advised by the former Panzer commander Hans von Luck that the only way to bear the kill-or-be-killed strain of soldiering is: "Learn to endure all things with equanimity." This accomplishment requires that the soldier "builds up an immune system of his own against the feelings of fear and sympathy and probably, to a certain degree, even against matters of ethics, morals and conscience... He learns through a long process of habituation to suppress images of horror, to distance himself from his neighbor in order to remain capable of rational action."[6]

In his "Notes for Officers," Tolstoy warns of "that time—and

---

[5] I.C.B. Dear and M.R.D. Foot, ed., *The Oxford Companion to World War II* (New York: Oxford University Press, 1995), p. 1072 (entry on strategic air offensives).

[6] Panzer Commander: *The Memoirs of Colonel Hans von Luck* (New York: Random House/ Dell, 1989 repr. of undated Praeger ed.), p. 57.

this will soon appear for each one of you—when you will stand face to face with an unarmed crowd of peasants or factory workers, and be ordered to shoot at them. And then, if anything human remains in you, you will have to refuse to obey, and, as a result, to leave the service."[7] Perhaps soldiers cannot possess the luxury of continuing to be human in Tolstoy's sense. As I write these words, my foolish, wicked president seems intent on ordering American soldiers to begin raining destruction on Iraqis who in comparison might as well be unarmed, although I am sure they will retaliate in any way they can. What can our soldiers do (unless, of course, they leave the service), except take von Luck's course of immunizations?

In the fall of 1942, our Panzer leader gets invalided home from Africa. "I was determined to make the most of my enforced leisure and suppress the unpleasant things, as all frontline soldiers do whenever they have the chance."[8]

In 1956 he visits a former Resistance fighter in Paris. "Two officers, who had once confronted each other as enemies, had becomes friends in the best sense of the word. Everything divisive was forgotten and forgiven."[9]

What if that were true? I want it to be true. In his introduction to von Luck's memoirs, the military historian Stephen Ambrose praises the kindness and gentle compassion of this old man, who had a very rough stint as a POW in the Soviet Union but expresses no bitterness. The only veteran whom Ambrose likes better than von Luck is Eisenhower. "I urge those American readers who still believe, as I once did, that all the good Germans are either dead or long ago emigrated to the United States, to give Hans a fair

---

[7] Leo Tolstoy, *Writings on Civil Disobedience and Nonviolence* (Santa Cruz: New Society Publishers, 1987), p. 37 ("Notes for Officers"). I have discussed this passage at more length in my longish essay on violence, *Rising Up and Rising Down.*

[8] Ibid, p. 104.

[9] Ibid, p. 341.

reading. He deserves your attention and respect."[10] I do give him that. Moreover, I have, or want to have, an image of a convivial lounge where the former tools of Nazi imperialism clink glasses with the former incinerators of German civilians, each respecting the other's stories, and remembering without hating to the extent that that's possible. To the extent that it isn't, "everything divisive was forgotten and forgiven." And why shouldn't it be?

Sebald's answer to that question is as follows: "Such a preoccupation with retrospective improvement of the self-image they wished to hand down was one of the main reasons for the inability of a whole generation of German authors to describe what they had seen"—Sebald is referring to the air war—"and to convey it to our minds."[11]

In other words, someone who claims that everything divisive has been forgotten and forgiven might well be lying to us and to himself.

One reads that theatrical performances continued to be held in Berlin's famous Schauspielhaus right through the air war, that the playhouse caught fire in the course of one raid, that in the final days of the Battle of Berlin, the Berlin Philharmonic performed *Aida*. I for my part consider this fact to be evidence of nobility and courage; I admire it. Moreover, as a descendant of the victors it behooves me to be kind in my judgments. Sebald seems a trifle less kind: "Who could deny that the audiences of the time, eyes shining as they listened once more to the sound of music rising in the air all over the country, were moved by a sense of gratitude that they had been saved? Yet we may also wonder whether their breasts did not swell with perverse pride to think that no one in human history had ever placed such overwhelming tunes or endured such suffering as the Germans" (p. 44).

What does he want? Does he want them to have stayed home

---

[10] Ibid, p. 2.

[11] Sebald, pp. ix–x.

and boycotted any sort of public life? Given that their public life was so thoroughly corrupted by the Third Reich, I could certainly respect any Tolstoyan soul who made that choice. On the other hand, I can hardly condemn people whose brothers and fathers might have already fallen on the Eastern Front, and who themselves might be killed by an American bomb that very night, from trying to "endure all things with equanimity." Or if they did feel sorry for themselves, why shouldn't they?

Over and over, Sebald finds himself appalled by the inappropriate cheerfulness, busyness, et cetera, of the people he studies. "You do not expect an insect colony to be transfixed with grief at the destruction of a neighboring anthill" (p. 42), but it does seem inhuman to him that in not-yet-destroyed slices of German cities people could be sitting on their balconies drinking coffee, while a few steps away everyone is dead and rat-eaten. How inhuman is this, actually? I'd say, not at all. "You get numb to it after a while," I was told by people in besieged Sarajevo who lost a friend every week or two. "I was determined to suppress the unpleasant things." I've met stoical children of murdered fathers—it doesn't matter to my sympathy for the child whether the father was guilty of anything—pathologists who joke and drink coffee during autopsies, journalists whose black humor about the suffering they see might appear cynical if you didn't know it was a defense mechanism. How else can they get by?

Sebald does allow that carrying on in the face of disaster "is a tried and trusted method of preserving what is thought of as healthy human reason" (p. 42), and it is one of the most maddening features of this book, as well as evidence of its author's anguished sincerity, that he leaves such contradictions hanging in the air without artificially resolving them. By no means do I want to dismiss this book, which I cannot shake from my mind. I disagree with much of what Sebald says, and with the harsh way that he says it. Nonetheless, he has begun something very important. To the extent that World War II remains relevant to our time, it can no longer be relevant through primary perception—the battles are over—but through *memory*. The war is now a story. How will it get told? What will be repressed, and what will be emphasized? Hitler had his story of World War I: the German military was never defeated on the battlefield, but betrayed by a "stab in the back" from certain government circles, which in due time he associated with "international Jewry." This dangerous lie was widely believed. And Sebald very urgently and legitimately asks: if Germans tell themselves the story of World War II in a certain consistent way, always omitting what happened during the air war, then could some similarly dangerous purpose be served by that omission?

Accordingly, what he seems to want most of all in his "natural history" is to characterize, analyze, define—above all, to distinter what has been repressed. "We Germans today are a nation strikingly blind to tradition and lacking in history" (p. viii). I myself, a foreigner, can't say whether or not this is true; but if it is, why might that be? Our author's answer: because history shows that Germans were complicit in the Third Reich's crimes.

In the course of exploring his eminently reasonable thesis, Sebald frequently commits the sort of error which used to prevail under Nazism, or for that matter socialist realism: If I write a fiction, it is acceptable, and frequently appropriate, for me to make my protagonist as meaning-laden as I can, right down to his name and the color of his eyes. But if I categorized real human beings on this basis, I wouldn't be far removed from the Nazi who imparted all sorts of meanings to the personality, phenotype, politics, et cetera of his Jewish neighbor: every aspect of each Jew must somehow prove his *badness*. (This particular interpretation of the other finds its equally debased equivalent in Soviet novels where the landlord's daughter will always prove treacherous and selfish in the end, and the stern, grizzled old machinist can be relied upon.) It would comfort self-interested categorizers if life were this way; and Sebald, whose intentions are far nobler than theirs, and who remains tortured by "the harmless, conversational tone that is so strikingly disproportionate to the reality of the time" (pp. 84–85), seeks comfort, too; specifically, he seeks the comfort of insight. His mistake is to totalize what insight he finds.

An example: when he savages the author Alfred Andersch, whom he accuses, with some plausibility, of having been morally compromised during the Nazi epoch, he makes great capital out of the man's egotism, for instance quoting repeatedly from his letters to his mother; he writes he that is "in the middle of working on a great new radio play" (p. 108), et cetera. I can't help my own reaction; a man's self-praise to his mother, however extreme, seems harmless to me. But Sebald wishes to present Andersch as a person who is righteously sure of himself, an "extraordinary man," let's say, a Raskolnikov. And for Raskolnikov the end justifies the means. Hence Sebald characterizes his quarry as "quick to compromise again at the first opportunity" (p. 112) when he seeks to ingratiate himself with the previously hostile critic Reich-Ranicki.

So far, Andsersch doesn't sound very different from most writers I know, including myself. I'm guilty of having a high regard for my own work, and while I might not have brown-nosed any critics, I've certainly compromised; I survive financially by permitting magazines to butcher my stories for money. I guess that's just the kind of writer I am. And what kind of writer is Andersch? In *Kirschen der Frieheit*, "memory acts very selectively; decisive tracts of experience are entirely omitted" (p. 114). (This of course is the central thesis of Sebald's book; this is what makes Andersch relevant.) Among the events which Andersch's memory has selected out is his temporary union with Angelika Albert, who happened to be of Jewish extraction. He married her in 1935—and divorced her in 1943, an act which of course exposed her (and their child) to imminent risk of being sent to the gas chamber.

In his diaries, which have recently been translated into English[12] and which I highly recommend, Victor Klemperer describes how humiliating and perilous it was to be even the most "privileged"

---

[12] Victor Klemperer, *I Will Bear Witness: A Diary of the Nazi Years 1942–1945,* trans. Martin Chalmers (New York: Random House, 1999).

Jew married to an Aryan; in the end, Klemperer was scheduled to be sent off for slaughter just the same, and only one thing saved him—the Allied bombing of Dresden, which destroyed records and kept SS personnel busy burning German bodies.

For Andersch to un-privilege his wife in the midst of the Final Solution therefore seems callous, to say the least, and it scarcely improves our opinion of the man to learn that in 1944 we find him complaining to his Allied captors about the creative shackles he'd endured, "my wife being a mongrel of Jewish descent" (p. 119).

(On the other hand, why did he marry her two years after Hitler took power? Every German must have known by then that it would scarcely help one's prospects in the Third Reich to espouse a Jew. That is why to me Andersch's acts seem confused, rather than steadily, expediently malignant. I wish that Sebald had made more of that wedding date.)

After citing from Andersch's *Sansibar* a descriptive passage that is to me in part accomplished, in part a trifle overblown, Sebald waves his sword some more, insisting that "it is one thing for the words really to take off, another for them to be tastelessly overloaded… with recherché adjectives, nuances of literary color, a tinselly glitter, and other cheap ornaments." So far, this is just literary criticism. But distaste (or snobbishness) abruptly becomes polemic in the next sentence: "When a morally compromised author claims the field of aesthetics as a value-free area it should make his readers stop and think" (pp. 130–31). I simply cannot agree. Thomas Jefferson was a slave owner, but that fact cannot invalidate the good that Jefferson did. Céline was a fascist, and so was Ezra Pound; while it might have been proper to punish those two authors for whatever material support, if any, they lent to the fascist cause, I see no reason on earth to disavow their aesthetics on any nonaesthetic account. Céline, whose egotism reminds me a bit of Andersch's, is a great novelist who continues to deserve reading today. Kurt Vonnegut asserts that "every writer is in his debt." (Vonnegut also argues, as I'm not sure I would, that "since the Nazi nightmare is so long ago now, it may at last be possible to perceive a twisted sort of honor in his declining to speak of remorse or to offer excuses of any kind."[13]) In any event, Céline's books are good or bad because they are good or bad, period.

Sebald sums up Andersch, very possibly rightfully, as "plagued by ambition, egotism, resentment, and rancor. His literary work is the cloak in which those qualities wrap themselves, but its lining, which is less attractive, keeps showing through" (p. 142). So what? "When a morally compromised author claims the field of aesthetics as a value-free area it should make his readers stop and think." I'd revise that sentence thus: When a morally compromised author, a saintly author, or any author at all claims the field of aesthetics as a value-free area, it should make his readers say to themselves: On that much, at least, we're all in agreement. What is aesthetics if not value-free? What do Andersch's recherché adjectives have to do with the way he treated his wife, or his reaction to national socialism? Exactly nothing.

Sebald's chapter on the anguish of Jean Améry is much better. This writer's essays "contain insights, based on the most direct experience, into the irreparable condition" of Hitler's victims—for Améry himself had been tortured until his arms were dislocated. "It is from such insights alone that the true nature of the terror visited upon them can be extrapolated with some precision. It is part of the psychic and social condition of the victim that he cannot receive compensation for what was done to him" (p. 147)—a sentiment obviously at odds with von Luck's comforting notion that "everything divisive was forgotten and forgiven." What if Améry rather than von Luck had said this? Would Sebald accept it then? If anyone has the right to forgive and forget, it must be the victim, but it seems to me that even he can invoke that right only on his own behalf. At any rate, Améry doesn't say this at all; he suffers from his personal form of memory's pain, "as if every fragment of memory touched a sore point," writes Sebald, "as

---

[13] Louis-Ferdinand Céline, *Rigadoon*, trans. Ralph Manheim (New York: Penguin Books, 1975; orig. French ed. 1969), pp. xiv, xvi.

if he were compelled to ward off everything immediately and translate it into effective form to make it at all measurable by any standard" (p. 149).

Sebald himself is obviously suffering from this pain. His book is an attempt, both fine and flawed, to translate and measure the agonizing memories of his countrymen. He informs us that he was personally exempt from much of the misery, in part on account of his extreme youth during the war. Nevertheless, he obviously partakes of it; he, too, is a victim, and my heart goes out to him.

Given the times in which we unfortunately live, I would be remiss if I failed to draw some correspondences between the German case and our own.

Obviously, the events of September 11, 2001, traumatized us Americans severely, and our nation will feel the resulting grief, anger, and fear for the indefinite future. I continue to hope that the people who bear direct responsibility for those attacks will be captured or killed.

Unlike the Germans of 1943, the Americans of 2003 are not particularly stoical. There seems to be little danger of our quietly, proudly rebuilding the World Trade Center into something bigger or better than it was before, then moving on. The main reason for that is simple: at the moment we are the most powerful nation on earth, and we are on the warpath. The Germans were losing their unjust war. We are preparing to launch the next phase of a war that many of us believe to be just.

Earlier in this essay, I criticized our president, and I stand by that criticism. This does not mean that I am against attacking nests of terrorists. It simply means that their guilt, and our danger, must first be proved. I do not intend my remarks to be inflammatory. Whether our war against Afghanistan, Iraq, North Korea, the Philippines, and wherever else we go is just or unjust need not be debated here. And no matter how unjust it might be, I certainly don't think it will stand comparison with what the Nazis did (the Yemenis, Afghans, Pakistanis, Iraqis I've interviewed frequently beg, rather stridently, to differ). America is not the Third Reich. The point is this: what happened on September 11, 2001, was a tremendous shock to us. None of my fellow citizens expected it. No one saw it coming. Afterward, my phone began to ring. People wanted me to explain "why they hate us."

The nation in which I live has consistently horrified me with its ability to forget. I remember visiting Iraq in 1998. Although they certainly know it now, the vast majority of my friends and neighbors had no idea then that we were still at war with that country; and one of the most painful things I had to do in Baghdad was listen to Iraqis' desperately intense questions about what the Americans were thinking about them, and then to honestly answer: "The Americans are not thinking about you at all. They've forgotten Iraq, and they don't care."

I remember when we invaded Panama and carried off its head of state into an eternal American prison. (He used to "work for us," I'm told.) Who else remembers?

I remember when we began to bomb Yugoslavia in the interests of the Albanian majority in Kosovo, and I, who felt conflicting emotions, tried to tell a neighbor as accurately as I could how the Serbian Kosovars had also suffered. I have always felt that our intervention in Kosovo would have been arguable either way, and it was not argued. I watched my neighbor going blank. I told her about a certain atrocity committed by Muslims against Serbs, and she cried, "Oh, you're so right! That's just what the television says! Oh, those vicious, evil Serbs!"

I remember that all through the eighties I kept trying to publish articles about the plight of the Afghans under Soviet oppression, and every editor said, "But no one's interested in the Afghans anymore."

Sebald believes that Améry's stance, which is founded on "implacable resentment" (p. 156), "makes no concession to history but exemplifies the necessity of continuing to protest, a dimension so strikingly lacking from postwar German literature" (*loc. cit*). What would making a concession to history entail? "Learn to endure all things with equanimity." After all, I didn't invade Panama myself, and as I write, the invasion of Iraq will probably happen no matter what I do. Dresden was destroyed; what good would it do to remember the screams? By all means, let's suppress the unpleasant things. ✭

BEN EHRENREICH

THE BAD MORMON

DISCUSSED: *Dark Property, Gordon Lish, Provo, Death-by-Bees-in-Sewn-up-Mouth, Sadism, Klaus Barbie, Ivar the Boneless, Altmann's Tongue, Contagion, Murderous Rural Cretins, Bad Literary Images = Bad Man, The Din of Celestial Birds, Scugs*

Around me all was dark with the darkness of the world in the night of language, words eating at my skin.
    —From "The Polygamy of Language," by Brian Evenson

hen Brian Evenson's first book, *Altmann's Tongue*, came out in 1994, it made barely a ripple in the centers of established literary might. It swiftly created a small and cultish buzz, but critics didn't seem to know what to do with this bizarre collection of twenty-eight taut, almost relentlessly brutal short stories—here a boy finds his stepfather dead, his mouth stuffed with bees and sewn shut with carpet thread, there a cheerful skeleton named Bone Job rattles down the road in search of God—and a cerebral novella that seemed to borrow

as much from the *nouveau roman* as the stories did from Hierony-
mus Bosch. When not ignored completely, Evenson was judged
a slightly distasteful curiosity. In a capsule review, the *Los Angeles
Times* nervously conceded that "there is a talent here," albeit, "an
eldritch one."

In faraway Utah, though, *Altmann's Tongue* was taken quite seriously. For Brian Evenson is something of an odd bird, an eldritch
one even. Not only the author of fictions whose emotionless violence mocks human flesh, Evenson was also a Mormon of no little
piety. Raised in quiet, conservative, churchgoing Provo, he was at
one point even a member of the high priesthood of the Church of
Jesus Christ of Latter-Day Saints. To thicken the brew, Evenson is
also a scholar with a Ph.D. in critical theory. He was one of the main
players in the brief flap over Gordon Lish's influence on Raymond
Carver a few years back, and has just published a monograph on
Robert Coover's fiction. Quotes from Kristeva and Artaud introduce stories in *Altmann's Tongue,* and an accolade from Gilles De-
leuze adorns the back cover of *Dark Property,* Evenson's latest book.

It was in Provo, where the then-twenty-seven-year-old Evenson had just begun teaching in Brigham Young University's English department, that Evenson would receive his harshest reviews.
In the fall of 1994, a few months after its publication, a Brigham
Young student wrote a letter to Mormon authorities labeling
Altmann's Tongue "a showcase of graphic, disgusting, pointless violence." She only made it to page eighty-four—the conclusion of
the aforementioned death-by-bees-in-the-sewn-up-mouth story,
called "Stung," which ends with more than a suggestion of in-
cest—before she had to quit, feeling "like someone who has eaten
something poisonous and is desperate to get rid of it." She was, she
wrote, "terrified to think that a man who is capable of creating and
perpetrating this kind of mental imagery on others was able to be
hired as a professor at BYU."

By spring, shortly after Evenson won an NEA grant on the
merits of one of the stories in *Altmann's Tongue* ("The Munich Window," a wry tale narrated by a man who, having murdered his wife

years ago, is grudgingly called back to murder his daughter as well),
a university spokesman had told the *Deseret News*, "We don't want
this kind of stuff coming out of this institution. We are not talking about literature in general. We're talking about extreme, brutal,
sadistic, and violent depictions of violence." University and church
officials alike made it clear to Evenson that if he kept writing similar works he would not only lose his job, but might face excommu-
nication from the church, a cataclysm for a devout believer.[1]

Evenson chose to leave Brigham Young. He has since published two novels and two more short-story collections, each as
uncompromisingly sanguineous as the first, with *Contagion*, the
most recent collection, surpassing it by far in sophistication and
complexity. "I don't want to have to make a choice between the
Mormon Church and my work," he told the *London Times* in 1997,
"but if I do I will be on the side of art, even though I still have my
faith." Even on a second or third read, *Altmann's Tongue*, which was
reissued by the University of Nebraska Press last year with a new
introduction by the philosopher Alfonso Lingis, is still a profoundly
unsettling book, shocking as much for the rawness and vitality of
its prose and for the mythic strangeness of the world it depicts as
for any of the variety of corporeal indignities perpetrated therein.
It is a world not only of violence but of profound affectlessness, in
which death and mutilation appear with all the banality of a dirty
shoe. It is at times a world recognizably our own (Altmann, after
all, is the name taken by Klaus Barbie, the onetime "Butcher of
Lyons," while in hiding in Bolivia), at times a nightmarescape of
desert fortresses and walking dead, peopled with characters bearing
names like Ivar the Boneless, Hébé, Bosephus.

Some of the stories are bare and simply bleak. In "The Father,
Unblinking," a man finds his daughter dead of fever and secretly
buries her in a corner of the barn. "You seen your little lullaby?"

---

[1] For a detailed account of the controversy at Brigham Young, see Bryan Waterman and
Brian Kagel's *The Lord's University: Freedom and Authority at BYU* (Signature Books, 1998),
pp. 326–341.

his wife asks. "I haen't seen her," he lies, and runs off searching for a shovel. Some are cruelly comic, like "Killing Cats," about a chirpy couple who enlist the sublimely passive narrator's help in disposing of their pets: when the husband "saw the cats climb up there to lick the plates, he wanted to 'blow their furry bodies right off the table.' He had wanted to 'blast the cats away' for quite some time, he said, Checkers most of all, he said, but Oreo and Champ were no exception." Or "The Boly Stories"—three tales of murderous rural cretins, relayed in an almost slapstick vernacular ("Boly looked up and got a spatter of blood eyewise. He woped the eye clean and seed other blood red-spatter down on the leaves around him and on him too"), like Cormac McCarthy's Appala-chian novels perversely bred with a Donald Barthelme yarn and fed raw to Gordon Lish.

Some of the stories are simply creepy. "Having sewn Jarry's eye-lids shut, Hébé found himself at a loss as to how to proceed," begins one, which doesn't go much further than that. Others are creepily religious, like the title story, which begins, "After I had killed Alt-mann, I stood near Altmann's corpse watching the steam of the mud rising around it, obscuring what had once been Altmann. Horst was whispering to me. 'You must eat his tongue. If you eat his tongue, it will make you wise,'" and, its final sentence reveals, is narrated by a vulture, or an angel, or perhaps a winged demon. The starkly minimalist "After Omaha" depicts a scene from a war between men and angels (or maybe vultures, or winged demons): the protagonists hang bacon from the trees, cut the lights, and crouch in wait "for the dull flapping of heavy holy wings." Three interconnected sto-ries portray, in gore-stained Borgesian allegory, the inhabitants of a lone fortress who declare themselves under siege, and commence to devour one another. Another lightheartedly depicts the travails of Bone Job, a skeletal sort—"He ate rot and tree mold, shat grubs and maggots. He swabbed the insides of his ribs clean with handfuls of grass. Masticated mint leaves worked miracles for his breath"—as he wanders in search of God and a coveted Redline axe.

In response to his accusers at Brigham Young, Evenson declared his work to be in fact "uncompromisingly moral." *Altmann's Tongue*, he wrote at the time in a thirteen-page apologia, was an attempt "to paint violence in its true colors and to let it reveal for itself how terrible it is." The stories offer, he wrote, "a violence that cannot be enjoyed—in response to the kind of glamorization of violence that television and movies provide." It's no surprise, really, that his attack-ers were unconvinced. If their analysis (bad literary images = bad man) lacked sophistication, Evenson's seemed disingenuous. Certainly he does portray violence shorn of all context—ideological, religious, or even narrative—that might render it meaningful, and in doing so bares its full horror. And while perhaps only a deeply moral individual could be capable of creating—or even recogniz-ing—a world so fully stripped of moral content, there is far too much humor in these stories, too much aesthetic delight in the syn-tax of even the most gruesome episodes, for Evenson to pass himself off as a simple pedant.

A few years later, in an interview with *Story Quarterly*, Evenson gave a more interesting account of his work. "My stories have little explicit reference to my belief system or to any belief system that might save the characters from the immediacy of their existence," he said. "Religion and morality, if present at all, are present in the reader's recognition of their absence." This of course still leaves plenty of room for didacticism, but it wasn't Sunday-school homi-letics that Evenson was after. "The religion my fiction offers, which is a religion of the collapse of the ethical will, is hopeless from the start: it will convert nobody." That, however, is the point, or a good part of it. "Good writing unsettles," Evenson said. "It causes rifts and gaps in belief which make belief more complex and more textured, more real."

It is hard not to see Evenson's work in part as rebellion, as an attempt to cleave some rifts in the unrelenting cheeriness of con-temporary Mormonism, a culture of firm handshakes and toothy smiles stretched hopefully over a bloody and painful history. That history, of course, is no more or less violent (or beset by excesses of kitsch-induced optimism) than that of the American West, which provides the setting for much of Evenson's fiction. The unending barrenness of the Western deserts—in which blood evaporates as quickly as water and corpses surrender themselves swiftly to sun, buzzards, and sand, in which the forces of nature are neither kind nor gentle, and God, if deemed present at all, can be discovered only through the manifest evidence of his cruelty—provides a convenient metaphoric backdrop, the vicious sun chasing all comfort of shade from even the dark night of the soul.

Evenson's interest in violence has other sources as well. He is a writer, not a mystic, and an extraordinarily precise and skilled linguistic craftsman. So he is interested in words, and intensely conscious of the violence language does to the world by abstracting it, flattening out its infinite particularities into the finitude of what can be said. Thus Evenson not infrequently uses grammatical terms to describe mutilations, as in "There was no simple way to parse the torso." And, a good student of late-twentieth-century literary criticism, he is ever-conscious of the violence language inevitably does itself, dissolving the very meanings it hopes to disseminate. "Words, when they brush up against people," he writes in his second collection, "swell and split and branch. They become unmanageable." Thus, says a character in *Dark Property*, in what might easily stand as a motto for Evenson's literary approach, "Truth cannot be imparted, it must be inflicted."

In 1997, Evenson published a volume of earlier stories, *The Din of Celestial Birds* (the title is borrowed from an Alfonso Lingis essay), which date before those collected in *Altmann's Tongue* to a period in which he had apparently not yet learned that lesson, and was still trying to impart truth in the conventional fashion. It's a disappointing book, adrift in a murky magical realism, largely set in or near a fictional Latin American village, with an overlapping cast of characters, all of whom are reeling in one way or another from violence and its aftereffects. It is perhaps because the violence is here given context— a mythologized but still-familiar setting of revolutionary conflict and bloodthirsty indigenous spirits—that these stories lack the painful impact he would later achieve. They are almost moralizing: people kill and are haunted by their deeds; violence begets violence. Only one story, appropriately titled "Altmann in Bolivia," hints at that later territory of uncategorizable absurdity, tearing violence from the level of historic comprehensibility and rendering it inexplicable, uncanny, removing all the banality from evil, and returning it to the realm of the monstrous. The title refers to Klaus Barbie, responsible for the slaughter of thousands of French Jews, but the story depicts a night-marish figure dressed in rags, his chest "crossed through by bando-leers, strung with holstered scissors and shears," who wanders from town to town cutting hair and lopping off heads, slaughtering chil-dren and stray dogs, hanging them from his belt "in a skirt of bone."

If church authorities had hoped to silence Evenson, the 1998 release of *Father of Lies*, his first published novel, made it clear that they would not. With a dedication to "the stiff men in dark suits, well pressed and ready for burial," it tells the story of a psychiatrist named Feshtig (the name means, more or less, "strong"—Evenson loves his German), who learns that one of his patients, a respected provost with "the largely conservative religious sect the Corpora-tion of the Blood of the Lamb," also called "Bloodites," has been raping and murdering local children, and that the church hierar-chy is doing all it can to cover for his crimes. Feshtig, a Bloodite himself, is ordered by church authorities to hand over his notes and tacitly participate in the cover-up. Unwilling to hide the bru-tal truth, he is persecuted in a manner that will be very familiar to anyone who followed the controversy over *Altmann's Tongue* at Brigham Young. "I was made to understand that my worthiness to be a member of the Bloodite faith was being called into question," Feshtig writes. "I was told that someone had reported that in my psychiatric practice I was 'preaching a vision of the world and the soul contradictory to the true vision offered by the restored gospel of Jesus Christ'... and that I was 'openly preaching a nihilistic re-jection of the soul that contradicted the Church's recent Statement in Support of Family Values.'"

As a novel, *Father of Lies* has its shortcomings. Fochs, the murderous provost, is too simply and purely monstrous, the church lackeys too stereotypically craven, Feshtig too, well, strong. And Evenson seems ill at ease on the drab plains of realism. His prose is unremarkable, even flat, and his dialogue, usually sharp and subtle, is clumsy here. ("We want to convict someone quickly to put the community at ease," a police officer declaims.) Evenson perhaps should have waited a few years before writing it—his anger may have been too raw to be transformed with any grace into literature, and *Father of Lies* functions more effectively as rebuke, a bitter insistence that "Hell is crammed full of godly men."

The same point is made to far subtler effect in *Contagion*, Evenson's most accomplished collection to date, released in 2000. Published by the same small publisher that released *The Din of Celestial Birds,* Wordcraft of Oregon, *Contagion* went almost entirely unnoticed in the press, but it remains one of the most strange and powerful books of the new millennium. The book contains just eight stories, none of them dispensable. It is perhaps Evenson's most explicitly Mormon work, largely set in the desert, deeply concerned with language, with writing and testimony (Mormons are encouraged to keep journals, and the religion was founded through an act of writing—Joseph Smith's legendary transcription of the Book of Mormon from golden plates revealed to him by the angel Moroni), crowded with polygamists, heretics, visionaries, self-proclaimed prophets, and killers of all stripes.

It goes without saying that these stories, most of them anyway, are violent, but the violence is more incidental here. *Contagion*'s characters are engaged in absurd, quasi-metaphysical quests, and metaphysics is for Evenson, like everything else, wound up with violence. In "The Polygamy of Language" the narrator murders two polygamists to take over the shelter they had prepared in anticipation of the apocalypse. "Here I hoped to finally force into words the thoughts which would, when properly formulated, unravel the problem of all possible language... by solving this problem all other problems would be resolved." It doesn't quite work. There are the corpses to deal with, and all manner of distractions, including plenty of opportunities for grim Evensonian slapstick: "The polygamists were still dead, though they had slipped from where I had heaped them, falling so it seemed as if the first was eating the other's ear, though I knew this was not the way of the dead."

In the title story, two men, hired to maintain the length of a barbed-wire fence, encounter a frightful plague, which causes blood to seep through its victims' pores like sweat. They are ordered not to turn back, but to follow the fence-line to the source of the disease. They encounter bandits, cultists, and many dead. Plague and fence alike soon take on huge metaphoric weight, and their task becomes a quest. "What is the connection between wire and contagion, if any?" one scrawls in his journal. "When will I die?" Some of the stories spiral into the queasy vortexes of what Hegel called "bad infinity"—the endless repetition of finite phenomena, as opposed to the good kind of infinity, the capital-*I* Infinity, from which Evenson's characters are decidedly excluded. Psychiatric interns are ordered to live in unfurnished apartments and observe other psychiatric interns living in other unfurnished apartments (they all get a little crazy); a frontier lynch mob fiendishly perpetuates itself.

Some of *Contagion*'s stories are family dramas, though with properly perverse Evensonian twists. Two brothers fall apart after one murders their parents. (He asks the other whom he loves now that their parents are dead. "God," the other answers. "In *this* world,' [says] Theron, kicking Aurel in the face. 'God isn't in this world. Think, goddamn it.'") Two half brothers, sons of a polygamous father, survive their mothers' suicides and, a window between them, plot their own. ("We are all flesh, in constant decay," one whispers. "If we are not dead yet it is because we are too busy dying to know we are dead. Every moment we do not kill ourselves is an unpardonable sin committed against ourselves.") A boy lives alone with his father and comatose mother in an endless labyrinth of dusty hallways and locked doors, gathering keys and trying all the locks. "Let's speak frankly," the father says. "Do you think collecting keys is the best choice for you?"

*   *   *

This last fall saw the publication of *Dark Property*, a short novel that dates back to roughly the same period in which Evenson wrote the stories that *Altmann's Tongue* comprises. It's a strange little book, an extended crawl through a terrain of utter damnation. Despite the title (which refers obliquely to the soul), *dark* is not quite the word for this world, in which light is no more blessed. The sun—and it is indeed, we learn early on, "God's sun"—only reveals corpses unseen in the night. It beats down with unrelieved cruelty, its heat spurring its victims to further evils, and to madness. The distinction between light and dark is immediately collapsed, and with it falls any hope of transcendence. Evenson's epigram from the Gospel of Matthew ("If therefore the light that is in thee be darkness, how great is that darkness!") is twisted out of context to occlude the very possibility of salvation. The word *freedom* appears but once in this book, in this sentence about a boy being chased through the desert: "The boy stumbled, effected a brief freedom, fell to earth." His pursuers stomp him to death, then butcher and eat him.

All creatures devour one another in *Dark Property*. Crows pick apart the dead, and fall upon each other in their hunger. Even the landscape is dying ("Uprooted brush stumbled vagrant down the faint decline that slid into the flat. The trees sparsed out. The sage contorted, contracted into brittle fistocks. The road shivered though its last curves, threw itself straight"), and the heavens themselves are endangered ("Star-sprewn clouds shone feebly down... In the dark the crests of the mountains unwove, mingled their warp and woof with the dark tangle of night. Vast eddies of cloud swallowed and disgorged stars").

Preluding each chapter with further epigrams—untranslated and unattributed, wrenched slyly out of context—from Heidegger, Hegel, and Nietzsche, Evenson follows two figures through this waste. An unnamed woman, in a solitary incidence of nurture and care, carries her dying infant in a rucksack on her back. At the same time a huge, brutal man, ironically named Kline, drags a grown woman in a sack of his own, stopping occasionally to kick it until blood seeps through the burlap. (In a rare comic moment, the pair meet and, just before Kline attacks the grieving mother, she deadpans, "Somebody always has to have a sack, don't they.") They both encounter cannibals, a shack in which dwells a throat-cut corpse, and a seaside fortress peopled by the "righteous," a cult of identically clad believers (in dark suits, natch) dedicated to reawakening the dead by replacing their organs with balloons, fruit, and string, sewing, taping, or stapling them back together, and breathing life in through metal tubes screwed into the throat. The two wanderers proceed, their fates inexplicably joined, a living, stumbling dialectic of striving and despair.

The language of *Dark Property* is everywhere as alien—and alienating—as its landscape, its syntax as tortured, its vocabulary as odd. Evenson digs up obscure and obsolete terms, employs them rather naughtily (using verbs as adjectives, nouns as verbs), and sprinkles them throughout. Thus despite the boy's *frement*, he is *strampled*, his body *flitched* and *flenched*. Unforgettably, the book's one love scene goes like this: "She neither regarded his face nor chose to squirm under him. Their swollen scugs tottered the walls, gave utterance in dark tongues that mocked all flesh." (Scugs, by the by, are shadows, and also squirrels.) There are echoes of Cormac McCarthy everywhere—both are strangely enamored with the word *sprent*—but here McCarthy's sprawling Western lyricism has been replaced by a tight, almost Beckettian absurdism, like *Blood Meridian* boiled down to an oozy ichorous syrup. Evenson's world is far stranger; if McCarthy tilts occasionally into the surreal, Evenson is really only at home there.

The first of *Dark Property*'s rather show-offy German epigrams is taken from Heidegger's essay "Language." Evenson ransacks Heidegger's original statement, shifting its subject and ditching most of it in ellipses, leaving only a fragment which translates as "The sentence... leaves us to hover over an abyss..." Here and elsewhere Evenson, perhaps heroically, perhaps perversely, does his best to drag it—and us—down and in. ✶

WHY LOOK AT FISH?

What is it about aquariums? Walk into the cool, humming darkness of the zoo's aquatic counterpart and something magical happens. Burbling blue light, darkened corridors, a silvery flash of fin, a ripple of aquatic wings: aquariums quiver with the promise of unearthly visions. In *The Lady from Shanghai*, Orson Welles's passionate clinch with Rita Hayworth unfolds before an aquarial tank: the aquarium's allure, after all, is not unlike the appeal of illicit sex. Aquariums, like adultery, draw us into a shadowy underworld of unspoken sensual pleasures, an engrossing, exotic environment harboring dangers of mythic proportion.

It's partly the mystery of it all. The ocean has long been our repository for ideas of the monstrous and the unknowable. "Canst thou draw out leviathan with a hook?" God demands of Job. We can't control the sea's creatures—we can barely comprehend them. They challenge our most basic ideas of creatureliness. Creatures have recognizable parts—but in the sea they can be diaphanous clouds of membrane, without eyes, face, stomach, spine, or brain. Creatures move, but oysters drift, and corals are rooted like plants. Creatures have physical integrity, but a starfish chopped in half will grow into two separate beings. Or consider the Portuguese man-of-war, a creature that acts like an individual but is actually a huge colony of beings moving as one. There are fish that can freeze without dying, and other sea creatures living at temperatures above boiling. Recent research around volcanic vents has found tiny organisms that breathe iron. As for reproduction, even the most ordinary fish can be deliriously perverse. They're hermaphrodites. They switch genders. Males give birth. Some corals and bivalves reproduce by "broadcast spawning," in which males cast off huge nets of sperm that drift capriciously to any available egg, while snails and leeches mate through what scientists call "traumatic insemination," where the male fires a detachable sperm-filled harpoon at the unsuspecting body of a female—Jesse James meets Johnny Wad.

As naturalist Loren Eiseley once wrote, "If there is magic on this planet, it is contained in water."

A visit to an aquarium does little to diminish this sublime terror. Even as it strives to inform, with wall copy and touch screens and neat placards of exhibit-speak, the aquarium mesmerizes visitors, overflowing and short-circuiting its own pedantic intent. No touch screen on earth can match the allure of a live reef shark, rippling your way with a sinister, toothy smile.

We must love this. Aquariums are currently all the rage. Of the forty-one American aquariums accredited by the American Zoo and Aquarium Association in 2003, more than half opened since 1980, sixteen since 1990 alone. These are not traditional halls of fish tanks but huge, immersive environments with increasingly exotic fish in ever more realistic habitats: live coral reefs, artificial currents, indoor jungles, and living kelp forests. Massive public/private endeavors, the new breed of aquarium has flourished in an era of ambitious urban renewal aimed at reviving derelict inner-city waterfronts. Their prominent role in such schemes has caused the *Wall Street Journal* to dub the last two decades "the age of aquariums." We are in love with looking at fish. But why?

POSEIDON AND ATHENA

There's a standard story about the history of animal display. It begins with the menagerie, a beast-collection used since ancient times as a sign of princely power and dominance. According to zoo historians, Roman praetors introduced the idea in the West, sending tigers, elephants, snakes, and other exotic fauna back to the capital as symbols of conquest. Other heads of state followed suit. Louis XIV established a menagerie at Versailles. In England, the tradition of keeping a menagerie at the Tower of London seems to have begun with Henry I, who started his collection of exotic critters at Woodstock. It was common practice for royals to present allies with gift animals.

Sometime in the mid-nineteenth century, the story goes, animal collections evolved a new purpose. As the Industrial Revolution fostered the rise of an urban working class, animal displays transcended the crass display of dominance, shifting their focus to education. Menageries became "zoological gardens," sites of learning that forwarded human enlightenment and progress not only through scientific knowledge but through edifying contemplation of the Creator's work. Where menageries had been private, aristocratic, and designed to intimidate, zoological gardens were public, democratic, and designed to educate. At the same time, technological advances solved some of the problems of maintaining aquatic environments. The first aquarial exhibit in London opened in 1853 and was quickly followed by others in Europe and America.

Nigel Rothfels, in *Savages and Beasts: The Birth of the Modern Zoo* (2002), outlines how scholars have attacked as a sham this idea of a "transformation" from intimidation to education. In reality, debunkers say, regardless of format, the display of animals is always underwritten by social, political, and economic imperatives. Modern zoos operate as signs of dominance, but they bear witness to civic pride rather than princely power. The formation of aquariums supports this view. In Paris, for instance, the first public aquarium was built in 1931 for the Colonial Exposition. It brought together a stunning array of sea creatures—the plundered riches of France's far-flung conquests. (The surrealists, grasping the imperialist implications, demonstrated against it.)

America's first public aquarium launched a different struggle. According to Jerry Ryan's *The Forgotten Aquariums of Boston* (Finley Aquatic Books, 2001), the first "pure" aquarium in America was the Boston Aquarial Gardens, begun by James Cutting in 1859. There were already aquarial exhibits in the U.S., most notably at P. T. Barnum's American Museum, but these were, according to Ryan, "a collection of curiosities and freaks and 'pure humbug.'" The Aquarial Gardens, on the other hand, were not crassly commercial, but "dedicated to the appreciation of marine life and the education of the public." No Feejee Mermaids for Cutting.

But not for long. In 1862 Barnum bought the struggling attraction from Cutting, renaming it the Barnum Aquarial Gardens and repurposing it to the kind of hokum and spectacle purveyed by his American Museum. The reopening, Ryan relates with scorn, involved a "Great National Dog Show." Thereafter, the fish shared the limelight not only with dogs, but babies, midgets, albinos, and "dramatic performances." "The marine life exhibits," Ryan sighs, "were mere background." Thus opens the history of American aquariums: with an agon between study and spectacle, teaching and unabashed trade.

LOAVES AND FISHES

The current U.S. aquarium boom can be dated from the opening of the New England Aquarium in 1969. Located on an unpromising stretch of Boston's derelict waterfront, the New England Aquarium was the first designed by Peter Chermayeff and his groundbreaking exhibit design firm, Cambridge Seven. The Central Wharf, where the aquarium was built, was purchased from the city of Boston for one dollar, and the rest of the project was financed with $6 million in corporate and individual donations.

Estimates were that somewhere around six hundred thousand visitors a year would pass through the aquarium's doors. Shortly after the opening, a million had attended. Within walking distance of Faneuil Hall's new complex of shops and eateries, the aquarium provided the missing waterfront piece of Boston's urban renaissance. Downtown Boston took off. The site the aquarium occupies is now valued at more than $50 million.

Chermayeff and his associates went on to re-create this magic formula—aquarium + shopping malls = urban renewal—in Baltimore, designing and building the National Aquarium on the dilapidated Inner Harbor. After a 1990 study by the Maryland Department of Economic and Employment Development concluded that the National Aquarium had generated $128.3 million in income for the local economy, blighted city centers began lining up for their fish. New Orleans already had its project in place; it opened in 1990. In the decade following, Corpus Christi, Columbus, Dallas, Tampa, Charlotte, Pittsburgh, and Charleston all became proud owners of new aquariums. Soon, even smaller struggling cities began to see aquariums as economic development catalysts: one of the first was Camden, New Jersey, already federally designated an "Empowerment zone." Others followed: Long Beach, California; Chattanooga, Tennessee; even Newport, Kentucky, a riverfront adult-entertainment strip known to its Cincinnati neighbors as "sin city."

"A lot of cities have looked at aquariums as an economic panacea," Debra Kerr Fassnacht, executive vice president of Chicago's Shedd Aquarium, told the *Christian Science Monitor.* So many cities added aquariums to their development wish list that recent articles in the *Monitor* and the *Wall Street Journal* raise the specter of a market oversaturated with fish. Even so, a number of new aquariums are in the works: Atlanta, Georgia; New Bedford, Massachusetts; Los Angeles, California. One project currently in proposal stage is the Great Waters Aquarium for Cleveland, Ohio. It's planned for the riverfront of the Cuyahoga—a body of water so polluted that it holds the dubious distinction of being the only moving river ever to have caught fire.

BIOPHILIA

What is the link between aquariums and urban renewal? True, an aquarium is more likely to generate popular interest than, say, an art museum. But there are deeper connections, too. Since the nineteenth century, animal displays have been argued to provide moral uplift for the working classes. In an attempt to secure funds for Hamburg's zoological gardens in 1911, Dr. J. Vosseler summarized the view:

> Intimacy with the living world makes people indigenous, and awakens and sustains the sense of home and the love of Nature and her creatures as the best counterbalance to the social disadvantages of modern life.

The "social disadvantages of modern life" assuaged by the zoo are represented more explicitly for us by a 1904 visitor to the New York Zoological Park:

> It matters little whether Michael Flynn knows the difference between the caribou and the red deer. It does matter a lot, however, that he has not sat around the flat disconsolate, or in the back room of the saloon, but has taken the little Flynns and Madam Flynn out into the fresh air and sunshine for one mighty good day in which they have forgotten themselves and their perhaps stuffy city rooms.

In this way, zoological gardens and parks were more critical to the "lower orders" than they were to the upper classes, providing not only relief from "stuffy city rooms," but an alternative to the inevitably degraded amusements they would seek otherwise. In

1869, as concerned citizens raised money to establish a zoological garden in Central Park, the *New York Times* published an editorial titled "The Necessity of Amusements for the Poor." The editors argued that "the class of amusements supplied now to the poor is nasty and odious... If there be no amusements of even a pretence of decency, the young man and young girl seek their enjoyment in such places as the Water-street dance-cellars, or the innumerable liquor saloons" (July 4, 1869).

But zoos were more than just distractions; they were sites of instruction, offering "moral improvement" for the working classes not only by diverting their natural tendencies toward drinking, gambling, and fighting, but by illustrating the higher principles on which society depended. Zoos provided training in middle-class behavior standards, banning alcohol, polka music, the shooting of songbirds, and even, in some cases, restaurants, for fear of creating a "low" atmosphere. Furthermore, the zoological garden's focus on taxonomies upholds a view of the world—including the human part of it—as hierarchical. The *New York Times* editorialized:

> The true destination of Zoological Gardens would be to serve as a stage for facts and experiments in natural history. An investigation into the laws, by virtue of which animals pass from the savage into the domestic state, attempts at acclimatization, the improvement of the conquered races and re-education of those that remain to conquer—such, in our view, is the field of practical studies in which Zoological Gardens ought to limit their instructions (July 18, 1868).

Assimilation is in the best interest, then, of cows as well as people. In a nation doubling in population, as the U.S. did between 1860 and 1900 in part due to immigration, that message could hardly fall on deaf ears.

Today's "Michael Flynn"s continue to be offered moral betterment through education in the normative—defined now as conservation. But it's a particularly personal form of conservation that aquariums propound. Visitors are urged to take individual action: stop littering, use public transportation, avoid banned products like corals, snakeskin, and sea horses. And they are exhorted to *care*. The local, urban population, particularly urban youth, is the primary focus of this message. As the Monterey Bay Aquarium says on its website:

> Children today need to grow up to be better stewards of nature because of all of the threats to this world. But if they don't know about the sea and its creatures, how can they care about them?

The implication is that individual action is what counts—and that city kids, with less exposure to nature, are a bigger threat to conservation than, say, the executive board at Exxon Mobil, or the sycophants at George Bush's new, pollution-friendly EPA.

In a more general sense, aquariums are argued to support moral improvement by inspiring a broad appreciation for life itself. Again, Chermayeff has led the charge, moving away from the educational, information-heavy designs of earlier aquariums like Boston's, and toward a more spectacular, emotion-based approach meant to create a sense of wonder in the viewer. An aquarium should be "an emotional thing, not a science lesson," he told *Harvard Magazine*. Chermayeff frequently borrows biologist E. O. Wilson's term *biophilia* to describe the response he is aiming for: the innate human attraction to other forms of life. According to Wilson, biophilia is one of the things that defines our humanity. We are human in part because we long to look.

RICH AND STRANGE

Looking at fish is not like looking at zoo animals. Most zoo creatures are at least partly familiar. Even the creepy denizens of the reptile house or the bat exhibit are critters we might come across in our daily lives. But fish don't come from our habitat. The aquarium is a terrestrial embassy from a nonterrestrial world. If fish went about on land, making themselves visible out the kitchen window or from the car as we sped past them on the highway, they wouldn't be half as fascinating. We'd look—we're lookers after all—but we wouldn't look with the same feeling of excitement, that thrill of transgression we get from gazing through that foot or so of acrylic that makes the formerly unseeable seen.

John Berger's classic essay "Why Look at Animals?", printed in the collection *About Looking* (Pantheon, 1980), asks why we are so doomed to disappointment at animal parks. The inevitable feeling at a zoo, he claims, is baffled unfulfillment: "Why are these animals less than I believed?"

Berger proposes an answer: while we long to see animals as connected to us, in fact the very conditions of their visibility highlight how separate they are. Placed in faked habitats, lit by artificial means, and footnoted with informational copy, they become merely "objects of our ever-extending knowledge." We see them, but the gaze is one-way. They don't see us. The technologies that make them visible and interpretable only serve to differentiate and distance them further: "What we know about them is an index of our power, and thus an index of what separates us from them."

Berger blames this on modernity: the very historical conditions that gave rise to zoos also ensured the disappearance of animals from everyday life. With urbanization and the Industrial Revolution, machines replaced animal labor, while factories took over breeding them. Along with cuddly animal toys, anthropomorphized animal imagery, and urban pets, zoos became monuments to the disappearance of true beasts from our lives, "an epitaph to a relationship which was as old as man."

Following Berger's construct, one might read the aquarium boom of the eighties and nineties as a monument to the disappearance of sea creatures not only from our lives, but from the planet. In *The Empty Ocean* (Shearwater Books, 2003) biologist Richard Ellis outlines the various ecological disasters now making the oceans what he calls "the next environmental battleground." Among them is the disappearance of fish. A seemingly inexhaustible resource has been depleted, in many cases beyond recovery. Among the missing: miles-long swarms of cod off the Grand Banks, gray whales that once roamed the Atlantic, the giant Patagonian toothfish of South

America, nearly extinguished in the two short decades since its 1982 L.A. debut under the stage name Chilean sea bass. The world's leading sardine canneries, on Cannery Row in Monterey, closed in the seventies when sardine stocks became too skimpy to support an industry. As if to illustrate Berger's point, the old cannery has become the site of the highly acclaimed Monterey Bay Aquarium, built by Lucile and David Packard of Hewlett-Packard.

But Berger's formula falters when we consider aquarium technology. For Berger, the zoo's technology distances the animals from us. But fish are invisible without those technologies. Hence, in aquariums, technology is not disguised. Habitats may aim for realism, but the pumps and plate glass aren't embarrassing necessities, like the camouflaged fence limning the captive tiger's fake jungle. In aquariums, the technology that makes the creatures available to us is part of what we come to admire, what creates our sensation of awe and wonder. Aquariums know this and are immensely fond of citing their stats: the number of tank gallons, the thickness of the acrylic walls, the sophisticated filtration and aeration systems that make it all possible. In flaunting this technological prowess, aquariums reach for the sublime.

The ocean has always been sublime, which is to say it has always been capable of instilling wonder and awe, appreciation tinged with terror. The age of reason borrowed the notion of the sublime from the ancients as a counterpoint to mere beauty. In the late eighteenth and early nineteenth centuries, poets and painters valorized the sublime, and turned to nature to evoke it. Then, only the natural world had the scale and complexity to be sublime. Today, that's no longer true: sublimity resides best in the man-made world. David Nye, in *American Technological Sublime* (MIT Press, 1994), argues that this is an American phenomenon: where once we looked at nature and gleaned a sense of the divine, now we look at technology and glean a feeling of national pride. Leviathan is superseded by levees.

We have come a long way from the question of why aquariums might be good devices for slum clearance. Or have we?

AN ART THAT NATURE MAKES

Writing in *Communique,* the magazine of the American Zoo and Aquarium Association, John Bierlein, exhibit manager at Seattle's Woodland Park Zoo, states a truism in contemporary exhibit design: animal displays must create awareness and appreciation not only of animals, but of the habitats that sustain them. "One of our goals," he writes, "is to accentuate the inseparable connection between the survival of animal species and the survival of their wild habitats" (March 2003).

But the zoo or aquarium's very existence suggests the opposite. Increasingly, endangered animal populations are kept alive only by conservation parks—the best husbandry might be done not by nature but by man. Without zoo and aquarium captive-breeding programs, many recovering animal species, including the California condor and the Arabian oryx, might still be languishing on the endangered list, or, worse, might be entirely extinct. No longer viewed as unfortunate captives or pale imitations of their wild counterparts, zoo and aquarium animals are now considered a fortunate, treasured few.

The aquarium not only improves on nature; in substituting the technological sublime for the natural sublime, it improves on our relationship to it. Ecologically adept and technologically brilliant, the aquarium is a twenty-first-century utopia, a place where culture and nature unite to induce wonder. Publicity photos offered by aquariums make this clear. They have evolved a standard vocabulary of awe and absorption to indicate the new heights of sensation achieved in this artificial world.

Publicity photos are mostly of two types. First is the animal close-up. These tend to feature either anthropomorphized creatures—otters, toads, turtles—or wildly strange or scary ones— sharks, jellies, lionfish, sea horses. Regardless of subject, they follow an unwritten set of rules. Framed according to the conventions of traditional portraiture and engaging the camera eye directly, the fish—or otter or shark or turtle—is a direct refutation of Berger's claim that the animal has no gaze with which to return ours. (There are exceptions: the leafy sea dragon, a creature straight out of a cartoon, is almost always shown in profile: to grant it a gaze would undermine its adaptive resemblance to its kelp habitat.) They look right at us, and their expressions mirror the intelligence and thoughtful interest that these encounters promise to inspire in us. Sometimes they appear in pairs or groups, and their relationships are always idyllic—devoted couples, attentive parents, cooperative social units. Signs of strife, dominance, or struggle are absent—as they largely are in the aquarium itself, where the copper sulfate used to treat water for algae and parasites also reduces the natural aggressiveness of fish and sharks.

The second kind of photo shows humans interacting with the aquarium environment. Here, too, a standard vocabulary prevails, its predominant gestures connoting both the aquarium's magnitude and the human response to it. Pointing or reaching hands are common. Faces are shown angled upward, lips parted in wonder. The sensation of sublimity is often indicated by composition as well. One of the most popular shots, for instance, is a panorama of a large, backlit tank with one or more people silhouetted in front of it. The aquarium environment, the shot tells you, is completely absorbing: you lose yourself in it.

The Tennessee Aquarium media library includes one particularly interesting photo. It shows a young African American boy in a pop-up tank—a large tank with a bubble-shaped window on its floor, giving viewers a vantage point from inside the tank habitat. The boy is looking at a sea horse, and the angle of the shot makes it look as if the sea horse is gazing back at him. His expression—eyes wide, mouth a circle of delighted astonishment—is striking. Next to him, you can just make out the pink coat and hair braids of a slightly taller girl—his classmate? His sister? It doesn't matter. The boy's expression of joy is the shot's focal point. He is Tennessee's twenty-first-century answer to "Michael Flynn," a (presumably) urban youth having his eyes—literally—opened, his perspective changed through contact with another living thing. The highly mediated nature of that contact is elided—the tank walls separating sea horse and boy vanish—and yet that very mediation is in some sense the subject of the photo. The photo is not depicting the boy, nor the aquarium's nifty acrylic sphere, but the experience made possible by their encounter. That experience is coded as an exchange of sympathies between two beings—our Michael Flynn and a sea horse—and, by extension, between gritty urban reality and the magical world of nature.

THOSE ARE THE PEARLS

The new aquariums propose a reconciliation of nature and technology. In doing so, they offer to reconcile environmentalism and corporate culture. Sometimes this can be quite explicit: in Baltimore, for example, each exhibit has a corporate sponsor. Placards over each tank inform you that, for instance, the electric eels are brought to you by Tristate Electricity Suppliers. That connection may inspire a chuckle, but for the most part, the signs are subtle. It takes some looking to realize that every inch of the so-called National Aquarium is underwritten by American business. The picture is clearer on the website. The section on corporate sponsors lists 216 corporations and businesses that have supported the aquarium to the tune of anywhere from $850 to more than $25,000. It includes General Motors, IBM, Procter & Gamble, Castrol HDL, Lockheed Martin Naval Electronics, Aegon, and, alone in the "Corporate Circle," defense contractor Northrop Grumman.

Baltimore isn't alone. Clearly, corporate PR departments have seen the relatively worry-free advantage of associating themselves with something as crowd-pleasing and uncontroversial as an aquarium—no *Piss Christ*s or Mapplethorpes here. Coca-Cola and SunTrust Banks are presenting sponsors of the Tennessee Aquarium. Coca-Cola reappears as an institutional sponsor of the New England Aquarium, along with Comcast and Sovereign Bank. PepsiCo underwrites the Oregon Coast Aquarium in Newport, Oregon, and the South Carolina Aquarium in Charleston,

South Carolina, where it is joined by Philip Morris, Alcoa, BMW, and Chevron.

Somehow, it seems appropriate for the new breed of mega-aquariums to thrive on corporate sponsorship. With their expensive, advanced technology, they seem like they must be brought to us by the companies that build printers or cars. But it's more than that. We expect public museums to be like the outdated National Aquarium in Washington, D.C.—rows of medium-size fish tanks in the basement of the Department of Commerce. It's interesting—they're still fish—but bland, staid, educational. Instead, the highly planned, affective environments of the splashy new aquariums have a corporate feel: the glitzy crowd appeal, the slick presentation of easy-to-digest facts; the obsession with their own stats. It's the real thing.

Furthermore, aquariums are telling a pro-corporate story. They posit a world in which the chief danger to nature is individual apathy. Baltimore's National Aquarium, for instance, offers cautious tips for how individuals can promote conservation: Recycle! Install water-saving showerheads! Conserve electricity! As for cars, it suggests Americans drive fuel-efficient vehicles—which it defines as thirty-two miles to the gallon, knocking about ten miles off what environmentalists typically advocate. When it comes to driving less, they are more guarded. "Sharing a ride just once or twice a month," they point out, "can have a tremendous impact."

Corporate behavior, on the other hand, is never questioned. In fact, it is nature's friend. Example: the star exhibit at the Audubon Aquarium of the Americas in New Orleans, a four-hundred-thousand-gallon Gulf of Mexico tank boasting a replica of an abandoned oil rig. Behind thirteen inches of acrylic, sharks, rays, groupers, gars, and turtles meander around shellfish-encrusted pilings. Abandoned oil rigs, the wall copy explains, should be considered valuable ecosystems, improvements on nature, not eyesores.

Another placard, likely to be passed over by schoolchildren, displays the logos of companies that sponsor the Gulf of Mexico tank: Amoco. Shell. Exxon Mobil. Chevron. Kerr-McGee. Auto-parts maker Tenneco. Oil-field-couplings manufacturer Wheeling Machine Products.

The one aquarium that has tried to avoid leaping into the sponsorship fray is the pioneering New England Aquarium, in Boston. Its freedom from corporate donors is evident when you read its display copy: global warming, overfishing, overuse of fossil fuels—no punches are pulled in its conservation message. Sadly, this freedom can't last. The New England Aquarium's dire financial situation caused the AZA to revoke its accreditation in March of 2003. According to President and CEO Edmund Toomey, "the Aquarium is engaged in an ambitious strategic planning process and has launched several initiatives to strengthen its financial position." Undoubtedly these initiatives will include increasing the number of corporate underwriters—and whatever content adjustments are required to keep them happy.

ROLL ON, THOU DEEP
AND DARK BLUE OCEAN

Built as part of a plan to redevelop Chattanooga's riverfront, the Tennessee Aquarium focuses on the Tennessee River ecosystem. But the Tennessee River can really no longer be considered a river at all. Rather, it's a system of reservoirs, linked by some thirty-five dams. In re-creating the "original" Tennessee River environment, the aquarium is creating a monument to a body of water that no longer exists. This is not odd: more and more, it's part of what aquariums do. In fact, it wouldn't be unreasonable, every time you saw a fancy new aquarium, to ask *What body of water has been destroyed here?* You might then want to look at the corporate donors and ask a further question: *How might they be implicated?*

Witness the Florida Aquarium, in Tampa. One of the nation's top-ten busiest ports, Tampa Bay is Florida's largest open-water estuary. Its naturally shallow harbor requires continual dredging and channel-digging to support the port's heavy traffic in phosphates, petroleum, and seafood. By the late 1970s, this constant dredging and filling, combined with nitrogen-polluted water, had led to algae-bloom, fish kills, and the death of more than half the sea grasses that provided natural nurseries for the area's fish.

The Florida Aquarium opened on Tampa Bay in 1995. One of its corporate sponsors is Cargill, developers of the phosphate industries that necessitate the harbor's regular dredging, and one of the world's largest producers of the nitrogen fertilizers that choke the bay. Today, these fertilizers pour down the Mississippi from the Corn Belt and into the Gulf of Mexico, where, according to a National Oceanic and Atmospheric Administration report, they are the primary drivers of a seasonal "Dead Zone": an area the size of New Jersey—and growing—in which nothing can live from May to September.

Or consider the Great Lakes Aquarium, a freshwater aquarium located in Duluth, Minnesota. Duluth Harbor was created in 1871, when mayor J. B. Culver and fifty men with picks and shovels, racing against a federal injunction, dug a channel in the sandbar that separated the St. Louis River from Lake Superior. By the time the cease-and-desist order arrived, it was all, as they say, water under the bridge. Since then, Duluth Harbor has become one of the busiest Great Lakes ports, and the St. Louis River has become one of Lake Superior's most polluted tributaries. Local industries, most notably U.S. Steel, released PCBs, mercury, cyanide, and other volatile organic compounds into it for over fifty years. In the eighties, the area was designated a Superfund site and the closed U.S. Steel plant put on the National Priorities List. U.S. Steel is a business partner at the Great Lakes Aquarium.

There are many more examples. Paper-and-packaging giant Sonoco, having dumped thousands of pounds of PCBs into Lake Michigan via the Fox River, sponsors the South Carolina Aquarium. Cinergy, the coal-heavy utility singularly responsible for 1 percent of the earth's greenhouse gas emissions, bought naming rights to the Cinergy Theater at Kentucky's Newport Aquarium. Aquariums have become a sort of consolation prize for communities whose drinking water has been despoiled, whose fish have been poisoned, whose runoff has turned toxic, and whose water-fronts have been left to die.

"In a world full of simulations and clever illusions, zoos and aquariums increasingly become the authenticators of what is real and still alive," John Bierlein writes. But it isn't just fish we want to imagine alive; it's the sea itself. Baltimore's Inner Harbor. Charleston Harbor. Monterey Bay, the Tennessee River, Lake Superior, even the noxious Cuyahoga. Few big aquarium projects are land-locked, because the aquarium feeds nostalgia not only for vanishing sea creatures, but for a lost connection to the waterfront itself. Inland water travel is a distant memory; sea travel is a hobby for retirees; even our fishing and canning industries are dying as our fisheries, one by one, are depleted. The vibrant maritime metropolis celebrated in Alfred Stieglitz's early-twentieth-century photos of docks, ships, disembarking crowds, and commercial water traffic has vanished.

In his brilliant photo essay *Fish Story* (Richter Verlag, 1995), Allan Sekula recounts how the rise of container shipping in the 1960s led to the removal of commercial ports to the urban margins. New York's port, for instance, is now in Elizabeth, New Jersey. As the increasingly automated working harbor moved out of sight, city dwellers lost track of the huge amount of labor—grubby, backbreaking, and poorly remunerated—that underwrites a global economy predicated on the transfer of goods and workers. The container, according to Sekula, is "the very coffin of remote labor-power," a banknote-shaped sarcophagus enabling "the transnational bourgeoisie's fantasy of a world of wealth without workers, a world of uninhibited flows."

Thus bereft of purpose and meaning, urban waterfronts be-came derelict and dangerous, ripe for commercial redevelopment. They're reborn as retail-driven fantasy ports like Baltimore's Inner Harbor, now trumpeted as "one of America's oldest seaports—and one of the world's newest travel destinations." Tampa Bay's Chan-nelside is similar, as is Chattanooga's riverfront, rechristened Ross's Landing, where the Tennessee Aquarium paved the way for one hundred new stores and restaurants, property-value increases of 124 percent, and an economic impact estimated to be around a billion dollars. All these waterfront complexes, in addition to aquariums, feature Disney-like re-creations of waterfront life: scenic boat tours, shopping malls with seaside themes, maritime museums and plenty of chain-operated seafood restaurants to serve up the last of the vanishing cod, once so thick off the Grand Banks that fishermen drew them up by the basketful.

We want to see the ocean as rich and teeming with life when all over the world it is dying, fisheries collapsed, tidal basins clogged by development, coral reefs bleached to lifelessness. We want to see the waterfront as a vital source for economic growth, but magically free of the ugly trappings of hazardous cargos, grimy industry, and unions. Even as it becomes more obviously the barometer of our ability to kill, we cling to the notion of the sea as the cradle of life. And we are nostalgically reconstructing the seaside—an improved, sanitized version—before we have even finished eradicating it.

The zoo, as Berger contends, may be an epitaph for our lost connection to animals, but the aquarium is a headstone—a great big, titanium-clad one—for our lost connection to water.

A SHADOW OF MAN'S RAVAGE

On Good Friday, 1989, the *Exxon Valdez*, a 987-foot, single-hulled tanker, ran aground on Bligh Reef in Alaska's Prince William Sound. At least eleven million gallons of heavy crude oil—125 Olympic-pools-full—gushed into the sound's pristine waters and began to spread, eventually oiling 1,300 miles of coastline. The immediate, countable damage was dramatic: at least a quarter-million dead seabirds, 2,800 dead sea otters, 300 dead harbor seals, 250 dead bald eagles. The uncountable effects on the ecosystem were even more disastrous, including what scientists estimate to be billions of destroyed salmon and herring eggs and juveniles, along with genetic malformations affecting generations to come.

The *Exxon Valdez* disaster put Prince William Sound on the

map. News footage and photos of seabirds, otters, and eagles slicked with oil were a PR disaster for one of the world's wealthiest corporations. Exxon went to work immediately to repair its image. More than a decade after the spill, it seemed to have succeeded. Exxon stock had tripled, and it merged with Mobil to become the world's largest oil corporation, with more than $12 billion in profits annually. The *Economist* recently declared it "the world's best-run energy company." But even before the merger, as it appealed the 1994 U.S. District Court decision slapping it with $5 billion in punitive damages, Exxon had repaired its public image enough to turn its massive resources to the job of helping to sink U.S. participation in the Kyoto Protocol on global warming, a goal met in March 2001 with President Bush's scrapping of the accord.

The environmental cleanup has been less successful than the publicity one. While Exxon describes the sound's environment as "healthy, robust and thriving," the Oil Spill Trustee Council, an organization created by the government to disburse the millions of dollars in reparations Exxon paid in settlements, disagrees. Of the thirty "injured resources" being tracked, the OSTC lists only seven as recovered fifteen years later. Among the species posted as "not recovering" are the common loon, three species of cormorants, harbor seals, the harlequin duck, the pigeon guillemot, and one of the sound's foundation species, the Pacific herring.

Around thirty-nine million dollars of the Exxon Valdez Oil Spill Settlement Fund went toward building an aquarium. The Alaska SeaLife Center in Seward opened in May 1998, with the declared purpose of "understanding and maintaining the integrity of the marine ecosystem of Alaska through research, rehabilitation and public education." Designed by the Cambridge Seven, the Center was designed to combine a marine research and rehabilitation center with a tourist attraction.

Many of the species still suffering from the effects of the spill— and facing further threats from climate change and overfishing—can now be seen in the Center. Harbor seals, the pigeon guillemot, and the Pacific herring are thriving at the Center, even as they falter in the wild. One can find Steller's sea lions there, a marine mammal whose 93 percent decline in population over the last thirty years has landed it on the endangered list. "We probably have the best habitat in the world for these animals," then–executive director Kim Sundberg told the *Seattle Post-Intelligencer* in 1998. "Everything's been designed to accommodate full-sized adult Steller sea lions." It's a far cry from their natural habitat, particularly Prince William Sound, where the continued post-spill lack of nutrient-rich herring has driven sea lions to eat pollack, a fish that marine biologists call "the junk food of the sea." At the SeaLife Center, the sea lions enjoy their herring iced: it's Canyon Ranch for marine mammals.

The SeaLife Center is officially owned by the city of Seward, population 2,500, and operated by the Seward Association for the Advancement of Marine Science, a nonprofit affiliated with the University of Alaska. Exxon, however, has done little to disguise its role. Most of the press around the opening of the Center mentioned Exxon's restitution settlement as its main funding source. But Exxon's fingerprints remain on more than the money. The corporation's very language has structured discussion of the disaster from the beginning, and now shapes debate on the status of the cleanup.

According to Exxon's press release on the state of Prince William Sound, the Oil Spill Trustee Council's declarations of incomplete recovery can't be trusted. This is because some populations might have been in decline before the *Valdez* spill. Addressing the issue of the common murre, a seabird failing to thrive, Exxon's release states that "there was little information about the size of the murre population prior to the spill. Yet for the trustees, murre population recovery is dependent on a return to pre-spill conditions—when it is obvious that no one knows what those conditions were, or what the population would have been had no oil been spilled."

The SeaLife Center's executive director, Tylan Schrock, uses very similar language to describe the Center's function. "When the

Exxon Valdez went aground and had that terrible natural disaster," he told KNLS, a World Christian Broadcasting radio station, "one of the things that came out of that was a recognition that we didn't even know what the baseline information from that ecosystem' was. That was one of the real strong messages that came out of the oil spill. We can construct a world-class research institution that will provide that baseline data. And we never want to see that type of a natural disaster up here again, but we're not gonna kick ourselves for not having the information the second time around if it does happen to us."

Schrock, intentionally or not, is telling an authorized story—as does the SeaLife Center itself. The Cambridge Seven design, borrowing features from other successful projects, is calculated to tell an uplifting story of cooperation between corporate culture and the public trust. Like the firm's other designs, the Center leads visitors through a predetermined tour route, starting with an escalator trip to the second level. When the Center opened, after an initial exhibit introducing Alaska's marine life, visitors were led into a room entirely devoted to the *Valdez* disaster. Text, photos, maps, and day-by-day accounts described the damage and the clean-up effort.

Emerging from this area, visitors would see the Center's research facility, overlooking the research deck and wet lab as they moved toward the realistic Resurrection Bay habitat in which many of the area's struggling species—sea lions, seals, puffins, and murres—could be seen enjoying themselves. They then descended to the first level, where they got an underwater view of the habitat.

The progression of the tour could best be described as triumphal. The viewer began, after some preliminary facts, with disaster. The negative feelings spurred by this display were immediately qualified by the Center's scientific capabilities. The final impression was one of a better-than-real-life habitat in which endangered species were hearty, thriving, and accessible. As the *Atlanta Journal-Constitution* reported in a 1998 article on the Center, "Here, children could spend hours communing with the noses and faces of chocolate-brown seals and sea lions." Through its rehabilitation programs and its ability to make animals visible, the Center posed itself as an example of how technology can improve on nature.

Today the Center is arranged on a slightly different plan. The *Valdez* disaster display has been relocated from the beginning of the tour to the end. After viewing the underwater tanks, visitors can listen to an audio exhibit called "*Exxon Valdez* Oil Spill: The Continuing Legacy." The text gives an update on species affected by the disaster. The final display, however, is a video of Stellar's sea lions. The visitor ends, again, with the image of thriving, magnificent animals.

The SeaLife Center suggests a story that is in keeping with the one Exxon tells through its press releases—the story of a tragic accident that, through corporate accountability and the use of advanced technology, was prevented from causing serious, long-term harm. It's tempting to see this narrative as a brazen and prejudicial imposition on an unwilling public. But what's happening is more complicated. If Exxon's story appeals, it isn't just because Exxon wants it to. Exxon is telling the story people long to believe, the story at the heart of our use of aquariums as agents of urban renewal. People want to believe that technology and nature can be united, that corporate culture tends to forward the public good. That's the story aquariums tell, all by themselves. In yoking technology and nature as if there were no conflicts between them, aquariums sit astride what Leo Marx called "the contradiction at the heart of culture that would deify the Nature it is engaged in plundering."

REFINING THE FUTURE

Senegalese conservationist Baba Dioum once said, "In the end, we will conserve only what we love." The quote is often cited as a rationale for spending large sums on animal display. Aquariums, their promoters claim, help us to love fish. They help us love the wonders of the sea, in all their richness and all their strangeness, too. Only by looking a harbor seal or a leafy sea dragon in the eye will we really see that there is something there to be valued.

Do aquariums achieve this end? And if they do, does it matter? A recent book of photographs is the best current document of the worldwide aquarium boom. *Aquarium* by Diane Cook and Len Jenshel (Aperture, 2003) juxtaposes the work of two photographers whose pictures pose very different answers to such questions. Cook's black-and-white photos are texturally rich and often abstract, focusing mostly on what mesmerizes aquarium visitors themselves: the delicate tendrils of a jellyfish, the comic cartwheel of a crab, the rippling rows of suckers on an octopus's underside. When there are human subjects in them, they commune with the animals. In one, a walrus turns its head as it swims past a child's hand pressed to the tank window. The window seems to disappear, so the walrus appears to be pressing its muzzle against the child's stubby fingers. It's a false sense of intimacy—exactly what aquariums, at their best, create.

Len Jenshel's color pictures, in contrast, draw out the separation between human and animal, between observers and observed. His people are blurred and indistinct; his viewing subjects always seem to be missing the view. A single woman in a red skirt stands in an underwater tunnel at the Bahamas' Atlantis resort, a large gold handbag under her arm. A school of silvery fish arc over the tunnel above her, their luminescent curves echoing her shiny bag. She gazes, not up at them, but at something unseen off to the left, so the school's spectacular swoop goes unnoticed, except to us. In another tunnel shot in the same aquarium, a woman in shorts and a bikini top is seen leaving as a mournful looking fish floats in the foreground, disconsolate. A joke on a break-up scene, the photo dramatizes the separation that, as John Berger would have it, is the only relationship possible between displayed animals and their observers.

Looking at Cook's photos, one is struck with the awe and wonder that sea creatures have the ability to inspire. Looking at Jenshel's, one takes a step back from that awe and asks *Is it enough?* Will our oceans be saved by a sea turtle's wise face, or the luminous, ethereal beauty of a tank full of jellies? A more fundamental question underlies that one: What does education have to do with love? Is instilling a sense of wonder truly a higher educational goal, the root of real understanding? Or is it simply the easiest effect to induce in the overstimulated MTV generation? David Powell, former director of live-exhibit development at the esteemed Monterey Bay Aquarium, would argue for wonder. "My original goal," he writes in his memoir, *A Fascination for Fish* (2001), "was to bring as much factual understanding as possible to the visitor... Now I see things quite differently. I've come to realize that perhaps our true goal in the aquarium world is to inspire awe, to create a sense of wonder and appreciation that will grow into caring. Communicating facts is all well and good, but without awakening a sense of caring we have accomplished little."

It's a convincing argument, but it fails to account for the ways in which aquariums are making an argument, even as they seem to offer simply the visual spectacle of nature in all its glory. *Here is where you can find this*, they say, presenting their acres of sparkling acrylic. *Here is what we have done for nature.*

When you visit an aquarium, there are usually boxes or cute parking meters where you can drop in a quarter for wetlands preservation, or a "save the Amazon rainforest" charity. But you're more likely to be overwhelmed by the technological sophistication of a facility that could clearly be funded only by corporate America. Exxon Mobil, and its cronies, continue to support the aquarium boom. And they continue to bankroll the ever-dwindling number of scientists who will question the reality of global warming and the still-plentiful politicians who will ignore it.

Meanwhile, the ocean's fisheries dwindle, the waterfront retreats from view, and historical memory founders on the reefs of complacency. After the *Valdez* disaster, Congress legislated that all oil tankers in Prince William Sound must be double-hulled by the year 2015. Most tanker-owners are beginning to comply. The only major oil company that has not yet built a double-hulled tanker is

Exxon Mobil. As for the *Valdez*, Exxon refloated it, towed it to San Diego (after Portland refused to harbor it), and repaired it. It changed the ship's name to the *Mediterranean*, and its subsidiary's name from Exxon Shipping to Sea River Maritime. Exxon then petitioned to have a 1990 law barring the ship from Alaskan waters declared unconstitutional. When that failed, it filed a "takings" claim against the federal government, demanding $125 million in reparations. Currently, the *Sea River Mediterranean* carries oil between Europe, Africa, and the South Pacific. At last sight, it was continuing Exxon Mobil's commitment to education: as part of a project called "Refining the Future," the children of Hallett Cove South Primary school in Adelaide, Australia, are in regular email contact with the ship and its crew. ✷

TOM BISSELL

"SIR, PERMISSION TO GO AWOL FROM THE INTERESTING, SIR!"

DISCUSSED: *How to Play Five-String Banjo, Grendel, How to Write a Damn Good Novel, The Hunt for Red October, The Notebook, The Firm, Aspects of the Novel, Mystery and Manners, Ancient Evenings, The Making of the Atomic Bomb, The Tommyknockers*

The first idea was not our own.
—Wallace Stevens, "Notes Toward Supreme Fiction"

ASPIRANTS

To linger around the bookstore alcove dedicated to how-to-write books is to grow quickly acquainted with the many species of human expectation. One after another the aspirants come—the good-sport retiree who has decided to tell her life story, the young specter of manhood with scores to settle and truths to tell, the Cussler-and-Patterson-overdosed executive aiming to blockbust his way to lakefront property and setting his alarm for ten—and shyly pull books off the packed shelves, level upon level of volumes promising to atomize the frustratingly numerous barriers between them and their dreams. Yet most of the people who frequent the how-to-write section will never become writers. It gives me no pleasure to make that observation, just as it gives me no pleasure to admit that I will never play swingman for the Indiana Pacers.

The question is whether these people will never become writers because they are not talented or because the books that congest the shelves of the how-to-write section are mostly useless. This sounds much sharper than I intend. Look around the how-to section. To your left: books on how to garden. To your right: computer programming. Down the way a bit more: *How to Play Five-String Banjo*. Most of the people who buy *these* books will not become professional gardeners or computer programmers or banjoists either. Would a successful computer programmer sneer at a person seeking to explore the pleasures of writing a few lines of code? Somehow one doubts it. Dreams, after all, are many, often mundane, and their private pursuit is the luxury of every dreamer.

But an even dustier (and probably unanswerable) question must first be posed: can writing be taught? Both congratulation and flagellation tend to accrue upon the answers this question receives. Those who maintain that writing cannot be taught are in effect promoting the Priesthood Theory of writing. In short, a few are called, most are not, and nothing anyone does can alter this fated process. Those who maintain that writing can be taught are, on the other hand, in grave danger of overestimating their ultimate value as teachers, though most of the writing teachers I know are squarely agnostic on the issue. My own view, if it matters: Of course writing can be taught. Every writer on the planet was taught, via some means, to write. Even those lacking the guildlike background of an MFA program or the master apprentice experience of studying beneath an attentive teacher taught themselves to write—most likely by reading a lot of literature. To think about this question for more than a few moments quickly reduces it to the absurd.

All human activity is taught. The only thing any human being is born to do is survive, and even in this we all need several years of initial guidance.

Harder to judge is the possibility of teaching a beginning writer how to be receptive to the very real emotional demands of creating literature. To write serious work is to reflexively grasp abstruse matters such as moral gravity, spiritual generosity, and the ability to know when one is boring the reader senseless, all of which are founded upon a distinct type of aptitude that has little apparent relation to more measurable forms of intelligence. Plenty of incredibly smart people cannot write to save their lives. Obviously, writerly intelligence is closely moored to the mature notion of *intellect* (unlike math or music, the adolescent prodigy is virtually unknown to literature) because writing is based on a gradual development of psychological perception, which takes time and experience. Writing can be taught, then, yes—but only to those who are teachable. Strong writers, especially, can be made, with sensitive guidance, even stronger. This is, in part, the service professional book editors provide. The problem is, truly fine writers have emerged from every cultural, sociological, and educational milieu imaginable. An even bigger problem, at least for those who teach beginning writers, is that no one can predict who *is* teachable. Perhaps it is best, then, to teach them all.

ON BECOMING
A NOVELIST

If any of this sounds familiar, it is because I am cribbing from John Gardner's *On Becoming a Novelist,* the book that did, in fact, teach me how to write. It is probably the most important book I have ever read—or rather the most important book ever read by the aspiring writer who became the person writing this sentence. Gardner, an erratically brilliant novelist, solid short-story writer, underappreciated critic, legendary creative-writing teacher, habitual animadvert, massive hypocrite, and awe-inspiring pain-in-the-ass, died in a motorcycle accident at the age of forty-nine in 1982, having written more than thirty books; *Novelist* is one of the last he completed. With the exception of *Grendel,* his genre-shattering masterpiece, most of his books are, today, out of print. (I should disclose here that, as a young editor at W. W. Norton, I was behind *Novelist's* restoration to print. I tried the same daring rescue op with some of his fiction. That mission failed.) Why is *Novelist* so good? "Either the reader [of this book] is a beginning novelist who wants to know whether the book is likely to be helpful," Gardner writes in his preface, "or else the reader is a writing teacher hoping to figure out without too much wasted effort what kind of rip-off is being aimed this time at that favorite target of self-help fleecers." Instantly we see the many virtues of Gardner's approach: honesty, an up-front acknowledgment of the typical how-to-write book's worth, and a forgiving awareness of human limitation: "More people fail at becoming businessmen than fail at becoming artists." It was Gardner's unfakeable gift to write advice that feels laser-beamed into the cortex of each individual reader. *Me,* one thinks with amazement while reading. *He is talking to me.* Or so I felt, reading *Novelist* for the first time at a writer's workshop in Bennington, Vermont.

I was eighteen, had never been to a workshop before (and have, with a couple of exceptions, stayed away from them since), had never even been *east* before (I was then a community-college student in Michigan), and was surrounded, for the first time, by people crazy about writers and books. It was overwhelming, and after two days I wanted to go home. I did not have talent, was galactically outclassed by the Harvard students on their résumé-building summer vacations, and suddenly had no idea why I'd ever believed my deeply rural imagination would ever be capable of producing literary art. My teacher, sensing my distress, handed me *On Becoming a Novelist,* and by the end of the day I had nearly conked out my highlighter. One paragraph in particular saved my literary life, as I was then struggling with the demands of telling "the truth" about the asses and idiots every young man imagines living all around him. I remember the passage so vividly I scarcely need to consult the source:

> One of the great temptations of young writers is to believe that all the people in the subdivision in which he grew up were fools and hypocrites in need of blasting or instruction. As he matures, the writer will come to realize, with luck, that the people he scorned had important virtues, that they had better heads and hearts than he knew. The desire to show people proper beliefs and attitudes is inimical to the noblest impulses of fiction.

Thunder! Lightning! Read that again, please. These are the words of a fundamentally good man attempting to show the young writer one honest way in which to think, to *see*. (When I found out that the aesthetically conservative Gardner was actively loathed by many of his fellow writers—Joseph Heller called him "a pretentious young man"!—I loved him even more.) If I belabor the point with autobiography—and there will not be any more, or at least not very much—I do so to make a point. Most writers have thoughts about writing as an act, as a way of understanding oneself, or as a way of being, and these thoughts are often interesting. I have any number of thoughts about writing, all of which I find incomparably fascinating. How fascinating to others, though, might they be? A how-to-write book saved my life, then, but it did so existentially, not instructively. Many of the best books about writing are only incidentally about writing. Instead, they are about how to live.

USER'S MANUAL

There are several types of how-to-write books. The first is the rigorous handbook-style guide that does not concern itself with creating interesting characters or crafting exciting scenes. Rather, it concentrates on how to write a decent sentence that means what one intends it to mean: a User's Manual to the English language. The most famous is William Strunk Jr. and E. B. White's

The Elements of Style. If one wishes to write *New Yorker*–style prose, this is the book to read. Of course, the *New Yorker* style is a fine style with which it is eminently worth getting acquainted, but it is not the only style. Nor is it, in every case, even the most preferable style. One truly interesting thing about the *New Yorker* style is that it can serve both as a hiding place for mediocrity and as the lacquered display table for masters rightfully confident in their powers. Used well, the *New Yorker* style is what one imagines the style of God might be, if there were any indication that God spoke English. Used poorly, the *New Yorker* style is all gutless understatement, decorous to a Fabergé extreme.

Composed of five parts ("Elementary Rules of Usage," "Elementary Principles of Composition," "A Few Matters of Form," "Words and Expressions Commonly Misused," and "An Approach to Style"), *Elements* is a hand-holding book, in the best sense. The first four parts are, as one might guess, almost ridiculously elementary, with brief and noticeably impatient advice as to how to punctuate ("A common error is to write *it's* for *its*," "Do not use periods for commas") and employ basic literary logic ("As a rule, begin each paragraph either with a sentence that suggests the topic or with a sentence that helps the transition"). The last part, "An Approach to Style," opens with Strunk and White admitting, "Here we leave solid ground," and that "no key unlocks the door." It must surely rank among the most winning and incisive twenty pages on writing that have ever been published. "With some writers," *Elements* tells us, "style not only reveals the spirit of the man but reveals his identity.... The beginner should approach style warily, realizing it is an expression of self, and should turn resolutely away from all devices that are popularly believed to indicate style." In other words, when it comes to the most important stuff, kid, you are on your own.

Nevertheless, there is much within *Elements* to debate. Many have quibbled with Strunk and White's imperative to "write with nouns and verbs, not with adjectives and adverbs." In fact, the passage in which this advice appears is actually an apologia for the much-maligned adverb. "Use adverbs *well*" seems to be the actual, hidden point of this initially restrictive diktat. "Avoid fancy words," Strunk and White tell us, and, if the wearisome battles I have had with copy editors and family members is any indication, the entire planet now agrees. "Anglo-Saxon," we are informed, "is a livelier tongue than Latin, so use Anglo-Saxon words." Well, according to whom? Charlemagne? The "fancy words" Strunk and White unveil as examples—*beauteous*, *curvaceous*, and *discombobulate*—are less fancy words than incredibly dumb words. One thing a "fancy words" embargo does is squelch and stifle a certain kind of young writer—the kind of young writer who happens to love and cherish unusual words, and who can, more significantly, divine the appropriateness of a dumb word and a word of high contextual potential. "Do not inject opinion," *Elements* goes on. Dear Lord in heaven, why not? "We all have opinions about almost everything, and the temptation to toss them in is great.... To air one's views at an improper time may be in bad taste." But good writing, like a good joke, is very rarely in good taste. It could be said—in fact, I will say it—that *all a writer has, in the end, is his or her opinions*. Hemingway believed that personal courage was the defining component of one's life; that is of course an opinion, and his entire body of work is shot to the core with it. "Do not inject opinion" is itself an opinion! This is not advice for a young writer seeking a stately style. This is advice one receives in a Toastmasters public speaking class.

I do not really believe that Strunk and White thought opinion had no place in writing, or believed "fancy words" were inherently ill-advised. *The Elements of Style* is not proscriptive, despite its many proscriptions. It is suggestive, and wisely so. It has made and will continue to make many people write better, and more clearly. So shouts out. But it seems unlikely to help anyone already on his or her way toward becoming an artist. If even this most ideal of books is read at the wrong time, it may actually damage (or at least discombobulate) the young artist.

GOLDEN PARACHUTE

What of the how-to-write books with more financially liberating titles? I speak, of course, of Daniel H. Jones's *How to Write a Best-Seller While Keeping Your Day Job!,* Judith Appelbaum's *How to Get Happily Published,* James N. Frey's *How to Write a Damn Good Novel,* James N. Frey's *How to Write a Damn Good Novel II,* and so on. Quite a few of these Golden Parachutes are penned by people who have rarely written anything *but* how-to-write books. They are usually hack books for hacks. Most are fairly, and forgivably, straightforward about this. The self-aware hack is, after all, one of our more pardonable literary coevals, largely because hacks pose no threat to an actual artist.

Artist. That is a grand word, and you might think that most of the Golden Parachute how-tos care little about the artier aspects of writing: integrity, truth, vision, and the like. You would be wrong. Many care deeply about art, as they care about advances and careers and publicity. Such books nanny every facet of writing equally, giving us a portrait of the artist as a fragile Hummel figurine.

Donald Maass's *Writing the Breakout Novel* is both a case in point and not. Maass, an established literary agent who, according to his biography, "is the author of fourteen pseudonymous novels," does not at first blush appear to be the most sensitive minister to the literary soul. Take, for instance, some of his clients, such as the historical-romance novelist Anne Perry, one of the two girls whose real-life matricidal crimes were the subject of Peter Jackson's film *Heavenly Creatures.* Indeed, Perry provides the book's foreword: "Put yourself on the page and all that you think and feel about life, but do it with discipline; do it with skill. Then the good agents and the good publishers will get your work into the hands of the good readers." And then the good fairies and elves will approach your front door carrying bags of gold, and the leprechauns will come, and the gnomes, and the friendly talking monkeys will sing, oh sing! outside your window! Although Perry's is some of the most insincere advice I have ever read, it is not even her preface's silliest moment. That would be: "Good luck. There's room for us all. They'll just build bigger bookshops!"

Maass is much shrewder than all that. *Writing the Breakout Novel* is about just what it claims: breaking out. Intended mainly for the already-published novelist marooned upon the Isles of Midlist, *Breakout* is largely a fiduciary affair, as breaking out has little to do with art and much to do with sweaty calculation. Maass acknowledges this, more or less. He also acknowledges that people in the publishing industry, most often, "do not have the foggiest idea" why some authors break out and some do not. Authors who have broken out, Maass writes, "toss around wholesale numbers like baseball stats, and generally display the ease and confidence of someone who has made it big through long and dedicated effort." Such writers are often called assholes. However, these assholes have learned something. That is, "the methods [of] developing a feel for the breakout-level story." The breakout-level story is one "in which lightning seems to strike on every page," written by authors who "run free of the pack." To write a breakout novel "is to delve deeper, think harder, revise more, and commit to creating characters and plot that surpass one's previous accomplishments." But! "I am not interested in punching out cookie-cutter best-sellers, so-called 'blockbuster novels.'" Rest assured, "a true breakout is not an imitation but a breakthrough to a more profound individual expression."

Cynics would not be blamed for suspecting that Maass is sleeping in both bunks, as it were. But the fact is, agents are not the brainless dollar-zombies routinely imagined by lit-biz chatterboxes. Virtually all of them know the difference between a work of art and a work of commerce, Maass included. Here is a man who can, in the space of one page, excerpt from and discuss the work of both Nicholas Sparks ("You have probably noticed from these excerpts that the prose and dialogue in *The Notebook* is rudimentary") and Colson Whitehead ("His fully developed premise meets all of my breakout criteria"). In his extremely good discussion of "Tension on Every Page" Maass holds up not, say, Robert Stone or Neal Stephenson, but John Grisham. Maass admits that "it is fashionable to put down [Grisham's] writing: *His prose is plain… his characters are cardboard cutouts.* There is some truth to those charges, but one cannot deny that Grisham compels his readers to turn the pages." I have read two Grisham novels, *The Firm* and *A Time to Kill,* and though my eyes rolled skyward several dozen times, I did, indeed, finish them both. In the case of *The Firm,* I could scarcely turn the pages fast enough. There *is* that to learn from Grisham, as Maass notes, "even in the absence of artistic prose."

But can one *learn* how to keep readers turning pages? Can one *learn* some magical method of "Building a Cast" of support-ing characters, as one of Maass's subchapters is headed? "Needless to say," Maass writes, "the more complex you make your second-ary characters, the more lifelike and involving your story will be." One can almost hear the scribbly note-taking accompanying that insight. Maass is not wrong; it *is* needless to say. But seeking to provide writers with some surefire method of injecting complex-ity into secondary characters seems a sloggy concern more along the lines of a De Palma than a Dos Passos. How would one do this, if not intuitively—if not *naturally*? Well, let us try. Say I have just created a secondary character named Jake. Jake works at a zoo. He is overweight, conscious of his body, and has no girlfriend. OK. Complexity now. He was once kicked in the face. By a zebra. That Jake, he hates zebras. This is pointless, of course. Characters, along with their hang-ups and complexities, appear in the mind of a writer and are honed or dispatched accordingly. It is as simple and dreadfully complicated as that. Writers who are able to summon up a lot of interesting secondary characters have one of two things go-ing for them: they have had a lot of life experience and met many interesting people, or they are imaginative swamis.

Maass's book is at its best while destroying certain tightly held notions of why writers do not succeed. Writers whose books have not broken through, Maass notes, "would rather put their faith in formulas, gossip, connections, contract language—*any-thing* but their own novels." This is certainly true, but who can blame them? The powerful counterargument is that dozens and dozens of writers (Joanna Scott, Brian Hall, Donald Harington, Gary Sernovitz, Wilton Barnhardt) have written brilliant, exciting, innovative *breakthrough*-style books and not yet bathed in the fountain of universal acclaim. I once asked a writer friend, whose first book had won an important literary prize, what that was like. He answered, "Like running around on a football field with a hundred other people and being the only one struck by lightning." *Getting Struck by Lightning* is an ungainly title, and its premise is rather cracked. Ultimately, though, its premise is no more cracked than that of *Writing the Breakout Novel*.

Writing the Breakout Novel is published by Cincinnati's own Writer's Digest Books, possibly the most sinister malefactor of Panglossian expectations in the literary world today. Some of its books, like Maass's, are useful. Most are pandects of stupidity. From *The Insider's Guide to Getting an Agent* to *The Writer's Guide to Character Traits* to *Fiction Writer's Brainstormer*, Writer's Digest Books preys on hopefuls' dreams. *How to Write and Sell Your First Novel*, by the literary agent Oscar Collier and the freelance writer Frances Spatz Leighton, is no doubt something of a landmark book for these dreamers, as it sells them a vision not of publishing but publi$hing: "Publishing has become a $32 billion industry in the United States, and authors are beginning to appear on annual lists of America's biggest earners." So quit your job and buy a boat, why don't you? "Writers," we are told, "are continuing to move away from the typewriter toward computers." And Model Ts are beginning to roll down the cobbled streets of old Manhattantown. "A less promising development," Oscar and Frances tell us, "has been the appearance of novels devoted almost entirely to extreme violence." But first novels without such nasty bits still get published all the time. And what a feeling for the agent! "If I," Oscar confides, suddenly ditching poor Frances, "can get such a charge from merely *discovering* a new novelist, think how much more you can benefit from *becoming* one." Holy shit!

What does it take to write a salable novel? Let us see: "a feeling for characterization," "a passable plot," and an "interesting and well-detailed setting." What are the writer's chances at publishing his or her first novel? Oscar does some casual arithmetic and comes up with the following: "[Y]ou have a once in ten chance of getting published, unless you do it yourself." I would say that this is off the mark by a factor of, oh, two million or so. Oscar/Frances then give us the success stories, all set forth in one helluva Larry Kingian prose: "You couldn't get more obscure than John Wessel who worked in a bookstore." But Wessel sold his book to Simon & Schuster for $900,000. And since then Wessel has written… uh, let us move on. Tom Clancy! The admittedly interesting publishing history of *The Hunt for Red October* is addressed at length, and then: "Novels continued to explode out of Clancy." Alack, yes. But what *is* a novel, Oscar? "A novel is a story. It's just a story. It has a beginning, a middle and an end. That's all there is and you can handle it." This seems about as convincing and heartfelt as a Sigma Chi preparing a drunken coed for her first anal goosing. "Writing about what you know is fine, and writing what you only dream about in your mind is fine, too." Everything is fine, in fact. How do you make characters sympathetic? "In many ways." How do you make people sound natural in a novel? "How do real people talk? They talk like you. They talk like me." But what about finding the time to write a novel? "Steven Linakis worked full time as a book-keeper, commuted long hours on the Long Island Rail Road and still managed to write a first novel that earned him more than $200,000." You know, Steven Linakis. He wrote… that book. That book that sold for $200,000.

NUTS & BOLTS,
TEA & ANGELS

Probably the most well-known (and well-bought) species of how-to-write book is authored by someone who has published a few successful works of fiction or nonfiction and decided to share with the world his or her incunabulum of literary secrets. Such books are often aridly titled, highly theoretical, exercise-driven, and contain generous tissue samples of other writers' prose to be peeled and vivisected until the student-reader knows, as the plumber knows gallons-per-flush, why the passage "works." Madison Smartt Bell's *Narrative Design* and Josip Novakovich's *Fiction Writer's Workshop* are both fine and helpful examples, as is John Gardner's *The Art of Fiction,* an oak-solid Nuts & Bolts that is an interesting companion to his more philosophical *On Becoming a Novelist.* All of these books should be read, and not only by beginners. But this category breaks down into more Linnaean classification. Alongside the various Nuts & Bolts how-tos of solidly accomplished writers, one finds what I will call the Tea & Angels how-to. These are often deeply mystical affairs.

There is a place for mysticism when discussing writing, as much of the process is bloodcurdlingly strange. So many things happen in any given piece of writing that cannot be explained: hauntingly unintentional thematic echoes, unplanned characters who arrive as though by séance, moments all but impossible to describe to the nonwriter, when one does not feel as though one is writing but *transcribing.* Amazing, all of it. But the majority of writing is not like this, and should not be discussed as though it is, or can be.

Natalie Goldberg's *Writing Down the Bones: Freeing the Writer Within* is more mystical than ten Sufis trapped in a macrobiotic eatery. Get the right pen, Goldberg advises, and the right notebook ("Garfield, the Muppets, Mickey Mouse, Star Wars. I use notebooks with funny covers") and just *go.* Keep your hand moving, she coaches. There is another activity that requires you keep your hand moving. The important things are not to cross out, think, or get logical. And keep a big wad of Kleenex nearby. "Lose control," she commands. Goldberg is Saint Paul on the topic of the First Thought: "First thoughts have tremendous energy.... You must be a great warrior when you contact first thoughts and write from them."

Goldberg tells us, "I teach the same methods over and over again." Unfortunately, she also makes the same points over and over again. "What is said here about writing can be applied to running, painting, anything you love." Indeed, writing is like cooking, she says at one point. Writing is like singing, she says at another. Writing is like running, she says (again). Actually, writing is like writing. Where did Goldberg pick up this breathtakingly inclusive view of writing? "In 1974 I began to do sitting meditation." Uh oh.

Goldberg is also a very cunning egomaniac, as when she describes with dewy wonder how a friend of hers once spent the afternoon reading over her (Goldberg's) old notebooks. "If you could write the junk you did then and write the stuff you do now," this friend tells Goldberg, "I realize I can do anything." Later on, she shares that she always brings a "date" to her readings: "I told the friend that as soon as I was finished reading, 'Come right up to me, hug me, tell me how beautiful I looked and how wonderful I am.'" Of course, nearly all writers are needy monsters, but that is no reason for Goldberg to unwisely encourage this lamentable condition.

And yet some of what Goldberg says is beautiful:

> We are important and our lives are important, magnificent really, and their details are worthy to be recorded. This is how writers must think, this is how we must sit down with pen in hand. We were here; we are human beings; this is how we lived.

That is a lovely few lines of sentiment, and Goldberg is to be honored for sharing them. Equally salutary is her realistic appraisal of money and writing, so unlike Golden Parachutes and the troughs of lucre they promise: "I feel very rich when I have time to write and very poor when I get a regular paycheck and no time to work at my real work." One begins to like Goldberg—with qualifications, absolutely—but, all the same, one really begins to admire her spirit and goofiness, and then she says something like "If you read good books, when you write, good books will come out of you" and you bow your head. In *Bones*'s epilogue, she describes the day she finished writing the selfsame book and going to a local café: "I looked at everyone, spoke to no one, and kept smiling: 'I've finished a book. Soon maybe I can be a human being again.' I walked home relieved and happy. The next morning I cried. By the afternoon I felt wonderful." Reading this book feels a little like being in a long, doomed relationship with a manic-depressive. One also feels ruthlessly certain that, despite the fact that it has sold well over 150,000 copies, no one who ever read *Writing Down the Bones* became a writer by anything but sheer accident.

Of well-known how-to-write books by established authors, Anne Lamott's *Bird by Bird: Some Instructions on Writing and Life* is, despite her healingly mild approach, the most fun to read. The title comes from a story out of Lamott's childhood. Her brother, overwhelmed by a grade-school writing project on birds, despaired of his ability to finish it. Lamott's father put his arm around the boy and said, "Bird by bird, buddy. Just take it bird by bird." Perhaps one feels a small temptation to snigger at this advice—how easily it is imagined upon a crocheted pillow—but this temptation should be fought, for a simple reason: like much of what is found on crocheted pillows, it is memorable and quietly true. *Bird by Bird*'s introduction offers a portrait of Lamott's father, himself a writer, who died early, of a stroke, at fifty-five. Lamott's first novel, published when she was twenty-six, concerned a family coming to terms with its patriarch slowly dying. Intended as a gift to the man, it was written as he succumbed. Not having read the book, I have no idea if it is any good. Having read Lamott's introduction, with its description of a dying father weakly raising his fist to his daughter as new pages are delivered, I can say I never want to: it could not be as good as that image, or as beautiful.

Like Natalie Goldberg, Lamott has a marked fondness for magical mystery tours ("December is traditionally a bad month for writing") but she is tougher, funnier, and more honest. Her admission of why she writes ("I am completely unemployable") may not be helpful, exactly, but it moved at least one reader to put down the book and laugh with warm recognition. Evidently, Lamott teaches quite a lot, and I was on guard for the moistly encouraging tone that I would imagine many career creative-writing teachers are, for their humanity's sake, forced to adopt. But getting published, Lamott writes, "will not open the doors that most of [her students] hope for. It will not make them well." (To indulge, briefly, in further autobiography, my first published book has just appeared in stores. The last year of my life—the year of finishing it, editing it, and seeing it through its various page-proof passes—ranks among the most unnerving of my young life. It has not felt good, or freeing. It has felt nerve-shreddingly disquieting. Publication simply allows one that much more to worry about. This cannot be said to aspiring writers often or sternly enough. Whatever they carry within themselves that they believe publication cures will not, I can all but guarantee, be cured. You just wind up living with new diseases.)

One learns many things about Anne Lamott in *Bird by Bird*. Quite likely, one learns far too much. We meet her friends Carpenter and the gay Jesuit priest Tom and Ethan Canin and a friend who died—far too young—of breast cancer. Lamott's son, Sam, keeps popping up, too, often to say something enchantingly cute, such as when he decides that night air "smells like moon." One or two instances of this would have been tolerable, but being held at parental gunpoint by Lamott so many times grows irritating.

However, a good deal of what Lamott says is terrific; she rewards you for hanging in there. Much of the beauty of writing is, she writes, "the beauty of sheer effort." A whole chapter titled "Shitty First Drafts" argues, hilariously so, for the necessity of such drafts. Another chapter, about her multiple failures to "fix" a novel that seemed obdurately resistant to fixing (meanwhile her money was running out) is not only useful and heartening but undeniably wrenching. "To be a good writer," she says, "you not only have to write a great deal but you have to care." Elsewhere she notes that writing "is about hypnotizing yourself into believing in yourself, getting some work done, then unhypnotizing yourself and going over the material coldly." In recounting a workshop that saw a good writer suddenly, viciously assault a bad writer after the class had offered the bad writer some patronizing praise, Lamott refuses any pat conclusions. Admirably refusing to criticize the good writer for her attack, she judges only that "you don't always have to chop with the sword of truth. You can point with it, too." She brilliantly and, I believe, accurately diagnoses the sort of student writer who routinely rips the spinal column from his classmates as a heathen seeking "pleasure that is almost sexual in nature."

Less terrific is some of her advice:

> Write down all the stuff you swore you'd never tell another soul. What can you recall about your birthday parties?... Scratch around for details.... Write about the women's curlers with the bristles inside, the garters your father and uncles used to hold up their dress socks, your grandfathers' hats, your cousins' perfect Brownie uniforms.

There is such a thing as too specific guidance, and I fear it will take some time for anyone who has read *Bird by Bird* to write about a birthday party *without* mentioning all the hair curlers and garter socks and Brownie uniforms. Lamott simply beats one to the writing. Also, for a writer of such shrewdness, Lamott allows herself to get lost among some awfully simple terrain. A longish section intended to inspire beginners who do not know what to write about sees Lamott throwing out suggestions as unpromising as school lunches and carrot sticks. Yes, an ode to the carrot stick will get one writing, but *Bird by Bird* is not, I don't think, intended for children but reasonably intelligent adults interested in writing. The whole question is beneath Lamott, and her suggestion is beneath her readers. Norman Mailer once said that if a writer does not know how to get a character across the room, he is dead. I would append that: If a writer does not know what to write about, has no idea where even to *begin*, he was never alive to begin with.

OLYMPUS

"I do not think novelists—good novelists, that is—are altogether like other people." This insight comes fifteen lines into Norman Mailer's *The Spooky Art,* which was published on Mailer's eightieth birthday, in January of 2003. This sentence places us high upon the mountainside of a different sort of how-to-write book, the Olympus, which only rarely deigns to address the actual processes of solid fiction-making. Instead, it focuses on the philosophy of writing—again, how to live—enjoying frequent, rather stark expeditions into the joys and terrors of literature. Reading such books is not always easy: the mountain analogy is apt. One's pack is too heavy, the snow is thick, the guide is unforgiving, self-involved, but far too knowledgeable to ignore. One constantly feels as though one has to prove oneself worthy of his or her company.

The Olympus is always the work of a highly esteemed writer who has elected—perhaps for money, perhaps because the writer believes he or she has something interesting to say—to set aside the scepter for a short while and share with fans and hopefuls how and why he or she writes, and what a beginning writer can do to improve him or herself. With their mandarin tones and necessary overstatements, such books routinely annoy and worry beginners. Beginners are probably right to be worried and annoyed, and it is no coincidence that the typical Olympus is not usually read by aspiring writers but rather by its author's fans and foes. The particles of their allure have an altogether different electricity: the insights are less global and more personal, more spiritual and less emotional. Not surprisingly, the Olympus also tends to have a much longer shelf life than other how-to books, from E. M. Forster's *Aspects of the Novel* to Flannery O'Connor's *Mystery and Manners* to Margaret Atwood's *Negotiating with the Dead*. Joyce Carol Oates's recent (and excellent) *The Faith of a Writer* will, I suspect, outlast a good deal of her other work.

Mailer's *The Spooky Art* was greeted by notably hostile reviews. Many critics charged that it was simply one big microwaved potluck of Maileriana that contained only the stray spice of anything new. This charge was indisputably true, but some of us card-carrying Mailer fanatics are willing to read the man on topics as bleak as poodles or Madonna. (Indeed, some of us *have* read the man on poodles or Madonna.) Yes, Mailer devotees will be familiar with most of what appears in *The Spooky Art*. I will go perilously far out on a limb here to say that, if only for its arrangement and augmentations, it is still very much worth perusal. Here is something:

A man lays his character on the line when he writes a novel. Anything in him which is lazy, or meretricious, or unthought-out, complacent, fearful, overambitious, or terrified… will be revealed in his book…. No novelist can escape his or her own character altogether. That is, perhaps, the worst news any young writer can hear.

This is a reversal of the mysticism one encounters in a book such as *Writing Down the Bones,* which promises that unlocking the inner writer will release only lemon-scented elation. Mailer suggests that the inner life of a writer is a vast, terrible ocean of doubt and despair. The former view will make for happier workshops and pleasanter emotional weather, certainly, but it is not likely to encourage a writer to "settle for nothing less than making a revolution in the consciousness of our time," as Mailer summarized his own goals in 1958. ("And I certainly failed," Mailer adds now, "didn't I?") There is much in *The Spooky Art* that few writers would be willing to say. "You can write a very bad book," Mailer tells us (and as anyone who has read *Marilyn* or *Ancient Evenings* or *Of Women and Their Elegance* or *An American Dream* can tell you, he would know), "but if the style is first-rate, then you've got something that will live—not forever, but for a decent time…. Style is half of a novel." Of writing in the first person, Mailer says, with his characteristic admixture of wisdom and buffoonery, "It is not easy to write in the first person about a man who's stronger or braver than yourself. It's too close to self-serving. All the same, you have to be able to do it." As for novel writing (I will hopefully assume he really means writing, as Mailer's chief accomplishment lies in nonfiction, which is no small thing, whatever he may believe or wish to believe), "It may be that [writing] is not an experience. It may be more like a continuing relationship between a man and his wife. You can't necessarily speak of that as an experience, since it may consist of several experiences braided together; or of many experiences braided together; or indeed it may consist of two kinds of experiences that are antagonistic to one another." If this sounds confused, one suspects it is supposed to, and it is inversely stirring to see a writer of Mailer's stature recklessly unable to come to terms with what, exactly, writing *is*.

In his bravely titled *How to Write: Advice and Reflections*, Richard Rhodes takes an opposite tack than that of his Olympian colleagues: "If you want to write, you can. Fear stops most people from writing, not lack of talent, whatever that is.... You're a human being, with a unique story to tell.... We need stories to live, all of us." Rhodes, the Pulitzer Prize–winning author of, among other books, *The Making of the Atomic Bomb* (a great work of nonfiction everyone should read) and *Making Love* (a queasy memoir of all the sex Rhodes has had, which I do not advise reading), has written a decent, old-fashioned Olympus that honors writing and the writer equally. That does not mean he will brook any of the delaying measures to which writers routinely subject themselves:

> If you're afraid of what other people will think of your efforts, don't show them until you write your way beyond fear. If writing a book is impossible, write a chapter. If writing a chapter is impossible, write a page. If writing a page is impossible, write a paragraph. If writing a paragraph is impossible, write a sentence.

One is not likely to encounter any advice in a how-to book as commendably intolerant of writerly self-delusion as that. One will find in Rhodes, though, goodly helpings of advice that sound awfully close to the advice of Natalie Goldberg and Anne Lamott and any number of other Tea & Angels writers. To the stalled writer, Rhodes offers this encouragement: "Everyone knows how to do something: describe a process. How do you tie your shoe? How do you brush your teeth? How do you plant a bulb, drive a car, read a map?" Perhaps this K–8 tone can be traced to Rhodes's early career as a Hallmark card writer (about which he is unapologetic; he considers all types of writing, no matter how cheap, to be tools in the writer's box), but I do not believe it should be. Rather, many of these books sound so alike—from the atom-splitting concentration they bring to bear upon the minutiae of their authors' lives to their nakedly desperate exhortations simply to write *anything*—because the questions the beginning writer needs answered are so depressingly similar: How do you start? What do you write about? How do you know if you are any good? Often you feel that these accomplished and famous writers are merely talking to themselves, since, in many ways, they still *are* that tremblingly uncertain scribbler. The how-to-write genre begins to feel less like an effort to instruct and more like a rearguard action to reinforce the garrisons of their authors' own slaughtered confidences. Just about all how-to-write books have at least a little worth, and some, like Rhodes's, have great worth. For instance, Rhodes's discussion of the cardinal importance of "voice" in writing ("'Natural' is a hopeless word; it has always meant and continues to mean whatever the speaker wants to exclude from discussion") is as good as anything one can hope to find on the topic. But what begins to rise up from these pages are the iodine and lotions of self-healing. You start to wonder if you are responding not to the how-to writer who is least crazy, but the how-to writer who is crazy in the same way you are crazy. You want to be healed, too.

On its face, Stephen King's *On Writing: A Memoir of the Craft* is *primarily* about self-healing—written, as it was, in the wake of the nearly fatal accident King suffered while walking along a country road in the summer of 1999. (The man who ran King down, one Bryan Smith, was later found, in a very King-like twist, dead of undetermined causes in his trailer home.) Most of the decisions about which how-to-write books to discuss in this essay have been due to my familiarity with their authors' less subsidiary work. In King's case, I confess to having read everything from *Carrie* to *The Tommyknockers*. (The latter's demonically murderous flying soda machine made me realize, with what I can only call the shock of unexpected maturity, that perhaps I had outgrown this sort of thing. But it comes as no shock in *On Writing* when we learn that King wrote *The Tommyknockers* with "cotton swabs stuck up my nose to stem the coke-induced bleeding.") In other words, I have read, by quick estimate, about fifteen thousand pages' worth of Stephen King's prose—and I do not regret one folio of it. Whether because of his success ("I've made a great deal of dough from my fiction"), his profligacy ("There's one novel, *Cujo,* that I barely remember writing at all"), or the simple likability of his voice ("Creative people probably *do* run a greater risk of alcoholism and addiction than those in some other jobs, but so what? We all look pretty much the same when we're puking in the gutter"), there are not many living writers whose views on writing will be as enthusiastically received by hacks, would-be hacks, artists, would-be artists, and civilians alike. On King's Olympus, God walks alongside man.

"This is a short book," King explains in the second of his three forewords, "because most books about writing are filled with bullshit." This is fairly representative of *On Writing*'s tone, though its anti-intellectualism is more akin to that of Abbie Hoffman than Rush Limbaugh. The approach results in some passages of wonderful bullshitlessness. For example, King's strident belief that a work of prose is about brutally controlled paragraphs rather than artful, free-flowing sentences ("If your master's thesis is no more organized than a high school essay titled 'Why Shania Twain Turns Me On,' you're in big trouble") seems that delightful thing: an insight that is both unexpected and true. His insistence that carefully placed fragments in a scene of action (King's example: "Big Tony sat down, lit a cigarette, ran a hand through his hair") nail down the writing, giving it a kind of vivid breather, is advice good enough to pay for. But King's dirt-plain line of attack also results in some massively wrong-headed counsel. "Remember," he writes, "that the basic rule of vocabulary is *use the first word that comes to your mind, if it is appropriate and colorful.* If you hesitate and cogitate, you will come up with another word... but it probably won't be as good as your first one, or as close to what you really mean." It seems to me that only willfully obtuse people don't realize that the mind very rarely says what it means to say in the heat of any given moment, writing included. One's first word or thought is usually imprecise, muddy, and wrong. Writing is seeing, but revision is reflecting on what one has seen. And the first word that comes to one's mind when one is writing about anything even remotely technical is all but *guaranteed* to be the wrong word. The same goes for characters whose professions or interests are unfamiliar to us: one *has* to go back and vivify those "dogs" and "trees" and "wiry-type things" that, in every first draft, exist lifelessly on the page. The many nuances of King's advice will be teased out by more advanced beginners, but to the less skilled, one fears it will seem that King is giving prose permission to go AWOL from the interesting. "No one can be as intellectually slothful as a really smart person," King writes. No one, perhaps, but an incredibly defensive dumb person. King is the furthest imaginable thing from dumb, and it is unappetizing to watch him pretend that he is.

But one quickly comes back to the good King, Saint King:

> I am approaching the heart of this book with two theses, both simple. The first is that good writing consists of mastering the fundamentals... and then filling the third level of your toolbox with the right instruments. The second is that while it is impossible to make a competent writer out of a bad writer, and while it is equally impossible to make a great writer out of a good one, it is possible, with lots of hard work, dedication, and timely help, to make a good writer out of a merely competent one.

"Life," King writes elsewhere, "isn't a support-system for art. It's the other way around." Of course, the world is filled with those who will sniff at the notion of making good writers out of competent writers, who will despair at the prospect of these empowered good writers writing their good novels and stories and filling the world with competent, merely interesting writing. That is, in part, what I believe angers so many writers about the how-to-write genre—and I would be fibbing greatly if I did not admit to regarding it with a certain amount of skepticism myself. Every writer's road is hard, and lonely, and forever covered by night, and even the best how-to books splash the path with an artificial spotlight and claim it is the sun.

Nevertheless, one wonders. Just when was it that "competent" became such a terrible fate? Like "cute," it is a word that has somehow culturally capsized and spilled its initial, positive meaning. And since when have merely good writers been deserving of barbed wire and gruel? I, for one, am glad of the world's good novels. I am reading a good novel right now. I hope to write a good novel someday. (I have already written several bad ones. That does not really seem such terrible providence either, in the end.) Writers who fail are not pathetic; they are people who have attempted to do something incredibly difficult and found they cannot. Human longing exists in every person, along every frequency of accomplishment. It is the delusions endemic to bad writers and bad writing that need to be destroyed. Here are a few: *Writing well will get you girls, or boys, or both. Writing well will make you happy. Fame and wealth are good writing's expected rewards. Writing for a living is somehow nobler than what most people do.* What needs to be reinforced is the idea that good writing—solid, honest, entertaining, beautiful good writing—is simultaneously the reward, the challenge, and the goal. Some of us will be great, but, as King says, that will be an accident, and its determination is beyond our power, no matter how many books we read or write. Perhaps especially if those books are about writing.

A BEAGLE'S LAMENT

There is a final book about writing that I need to talk about. God help us, it is published by Writer's Digest Books, so allow me to encourage anyone interested to steal it forthwith, preferably from the warehouses of Writer's Digest Books. It is called *Snoopy's Guide to the Writing Life,* and forms a handsome collection of *Peanuts* Snoopycentrism. Snoopy, of course, is a long-suffering writer, and some of Charles Schulz's funniest strips have been devoted to his worthy beagle's literary frustrations; they are gathered here, in their glorious entirety. My second-favorite strip gives us Snoopy in full profile, bent over his typewriter, diligently typing. "Gentlemen," he writes. "Enclosed is the manuscript of my new novel. I know you are going to like it." And in the final panel: "In the meantime, please send me some money so I can live it up." In my favorite strip, Snoopy gives Lucy van Pelt a draft titled "A Sad Story." "This isn't a sad story," Lucy complains. "This is a dumb story!" Snoopy takes back the draft and holds it close to his protuberant face. He thinks, "That's what makes it so sad."

That *is* what makes it so sad. That is also why we laugh. But it is a good laughter, a pure laughter, and not at all at Snoopy's expense. It is the laughter of necessity, laughter rich with the hope that, eventually, all of our stories will be happier. ✷

TRANSMISSIONS FROM CAMP TRANS

DISCUSSED: *Porto-Janes, Sex-to-Order Surgery, Post-Dyke Queer Scene, Spring Break for Trannyboys, Floridian Retiree Role-Play, Dirty Dancing, Susan Powter, J. J. Bitch, The Fat-Tastics, Fat Caucus, ADD Caucus, Heat Death in France, The Bearded Transrevolution, Beefalo, Youth Travel Culture, "King Shit of Fuck Mountain," A Safe Space to Fuck Up, A New Civil Rights Movement*

Unless you've spent some time as a lesbian, or perhaps are the sort of straight lady who enjoys the music, politics, and occasional abandoning of the menfolk that a particularly earthy strain of "women's culture" offers, you've probably never heard of the Michigan Womyn's Music Festival. It's been happening for the past twenty-eight years, taking place each August on a lush chunk of woodland in northern Michigan, planned to coincide with summer's final full moon. While womyn's music is the festival's alleged purpose—the guitar stylings of folksters like Holly Near and Cris Williamson as well as post-riot-grrrl acts like Bitch and Animal, the Butchies, and Le Tigre, to draw in the younger generation—the real purpose is to hunker down in a forest with a few thousand other females, bond, have sex in a fern grove, and go to countless workshops on everything from sexual esoterica to parading around on stilts, processing various oppressions, and sharing how much you miss your cat. The festival aims to be a utopia, and in most ways it hits its mark. Performers are paid well, and all performers are paid the same amount, regardless of if they're famous, like the Indigo Girls, or some virtually unknown girl band. You can come for free as a worker, taking on jobs like child care, kitchen work, or driving shuttles on and off the land, and even women who pay the hundreds of dollars to come in are required to pull their weight by picking up a couple of work shifts. The only dudes allowed in the space are the ones who rumble in late at night, in giant trucks, to vacuum the sludge from the hundreds of Porta-Potties, called Porta-Janes. They are preceded by a woman who hollers, "Man on the land! Man on the land!"—a warning to skittish nymphs to hop into a tent or a bush. I've been to the festival four or five times, and can attest to the deeply stunning feeling of safety and peace there. The absence of guys does make for an absence of threat; everyone's guard is down, finally, and a relaxation level is hit that is probably impossible to access in the real world. Pretty much everyone who attends bursts into tears at some point, saddened at all the psychic garbage that females are forced to lug around and grateful for a week of respite. It's no wonder the women who come to the festival are zealots about it, live for August, and get totally obsessed with and protective of the culture that springs up within its security-patrolled boundaries.

In 1991 a transsexual woman named Nancy Jean Burkholder was evicted from MWMF. Transsexual women, for those not up to date with the growing transgender revolution, are women who were born in male bodies and have been fighting against that ever since. They may or may not be on hormones, which can be costly or unavailable. Same goes for sex-reassignment surgery, which is often prohibitively expensive and not covered by insurance. Nancy Jean's eviction is famous in Michigan lore, for it sparked a fierce debate about the inclusion of transsexual women, which has been raging for over a decade. A lot of women inside the festival want to keep trans women out. Some staunchly insist that these individuals are not women but men in dresses trying to ruin the feminist event. Others concede that trans women are women, but because they were born boys and may still have penises, the festival is not the place for them. Trans women and their growing number of allies say these feminist justifications are straight-up discrimination, no different from that of the rest of the world, which routinely denies that trans women are "real" women and bars their access to everything from jobs to housing, domestic-violence counseling to health care. Off and on for the past decade, a small group of transpeople and their supporters have set up a protest camp, Camp Trans, across the road, in the hope of changing the policy that left Nancy Jean stranded in the Midwest twelve years ago.

NANCY JEAN BURKHOLDER

"I appreciate women's space, and after checking with festival literature I couldn't see that I wasn't welcome. I had talked to people, and their opinion was, if you think of yourself as a woman, you're welcome. I'd gone with a friend of mine, Laura. We drove out together, and we were number thirty-three in line. We got there early; we were really excited about going. We set up camp up in Bread and Roses. It's kind of the quiet area. Then we each did a work shift, shuttle duty. Hauling people from the front all the way back. That evening Laura was having a friend come in on the shuttle bus from Grand Rapids, so we walked down to the gate about nine p.m. to meet the bus. Turned out the bus was late and didn't get there till about eleven. We were hanging out at the fire pit, just kind of joined the group of people that were hanging out and talking. When the bus came in at eleven, Laura went up to the gate to meet her friend, and I waited by the fire pit. At that point a couple of women approached me and asked if I knew that this was a festival for women. It kind of surprised me. I said, 'Yeah, uh-huh.' About that time Laura was coming back, so I asked her to come over; something didn't seem right about what these women were asking. I think one of them asked me if I was transsexual. I said, 'My history is none of your business.' I asked, 'Why are you asking?' and she said that transsexuals weren't welcome. I think I remember saying, 'Are you sure? How do you know?' And so she went at that point and talked to the festival producers. She came back in about an hour; it took a while. She said that transsexuals were not welcome at the festival, and was I transsexual? At one point I offered to show them my driver's license, which said female, and also to drop my drawers, and she said, 'I wouldn't be comfortable with that.' Which I thought was kind of off, given the amount of nudity at the festival. She asked again, 'Are you transsexual?' and I said, 'It's none of your business.' At that point she said, 'Well, I'm empowered to expel any woman, at any time, for any reason. You have to leave.' I knew there was no arguing with them.

"They wouldn't let me leave the area around the main gate. Instead, Laura went with a couple of festival security guards back out to my campsite, scooped up all my equipment, and brought it back to the main gate. It must have been about one o'clock in the morning by then. They arranged for us to stay at a motel in Hart, [Michigan]; I think we got there around two o'clock. And it was a dump. It was cold; there was mildew in the carpet; wet; trucks running by on Route 10. I couldn't believe it. I was devastated. The next day Laura took me down to Grand Rapids, and I paid for a plane ticket and flew home to New England. I flew to Worcester, Massachusetts, and Laura's partner arranged for a taxi to take me back to their house, where my car was. Laura went back to the festival for two reasons: she was doing a workshop, and also she went back to tell my friends what happened to me. Otherwise I would have disappeared without a trace. One of the friends she told was Janis Walworth. Janis and Laura spent the rest of the festival talking to people and telling them what happened. I was back in New Hampshire, and I called *Gay Community News,* a newspaper in Boston, to tell them what happened. I think they were a little taken aback and weren't quite sure what to do with this. They did say, 'If you want to write an editorial, we'll publish it.' So, Laura wrote a letter to the editor, and they published it with my editorial, and we took up a whole page in the newspaper. That kind of started the whole controversy.

"The important piece that doesn't always get reported is that Janis organized a bunch of people to go back in 1992. She brought her sister, a male-to-female postoperative transsexual, and also an intersex person and a butch female. They distributed buttons and leaflets and did a survey. The survey indicated that 72 percent approved of transsexuals being at the festival. 23 percent did not, for a variety of reasons. Out of that Janis categorized the reasons why people didn't want transsexuals, and she compiled gender myths, twenty-four of them."

TWENTY-FOUR GENDER MYTHS

1. Although male-to-female transsexuals have surgery to change their anatomy and take female hormones, they still act like men.

2. Male-to-female transsexuals are not women-born-women (or womyn-born-womyn).

3. Male-to-female transsexuals have been socialized as men, and this socialization cannot be changed.

4. Male-to-female transsexuals are trying to "pass" as women. They try to make themselves as much like nontranssexual women as possible.

5. Male-to-female transsexuals take jobs away from women because they had access to better training when they were men.

6. To lessen the power of patriarchy in our lives, we must purge

our community of everything male, including women who once had male anatomy.

7. Most women can easily prove they are not male-to-female transsexuals, if they are challenged to do so.

8. Male-to-female transsexuals have been raised as boys, have never been oppressed as women, and cannot understand women's oppression.

9. Women's space is not "safe" space if male-to-female transsexuals are allowed in it.

10. Transsexuals have surgery so they can have sex the way they want to.

11. Male-to-female transsexuals are trying to take over the lesbian community.

12. The sex assigned to a person at birth is that person's "real" sex.

13. The lesbian and women's communities have nothing to gain by including transsexuals.

14. Nontranssexual women have the right to decide whether transsexuals should be included in the women's community.

15. Transsexuals are guilty of deception when they don't reveal right away that they are transsexuals.

16. Male-to-female transsexuals are considered men until they have sex-change surgery.

17. People can be categorized as transsexual or nontranssexual—there's no in-between.

18. Women who want to become men have bought into societal hatred of women or are hoping to take advantage of male privilege.

19. A person's "true" sex can be determined by chromosome testing.

20. Transsexualism is unnatural—it is a new problem brought about by sophisticated technology.

21. "Real" women, certainly those who belong to the lesbian community, rejoice in their womanhood and have no desire to be men.

22. Since Festival policy was made clear, there have been no transsexuals at Michigan.

23. Transsexuals have caused trouble at Michigan, resulting in their expulsion.

24. Nontranssexual women at Michigan don't want male-to-female transsexuals to be present.

AIRPLANE OVER SOUTHWEST, AUGUST 15, 2003

I'm reading *Jane* magazine because my plane could, of course, crash; this could be my last moment alive, and I will not deny myself the small delight. *Jane* is the most innocent of the guilty pleasure that is women's magazines, as it at least aspires toward a sensibility affirming that women shouldn't look starved for cheeseburgers and that gay people are cool. Printed beneath a small column in which the actor who plays the exchange student on *That '70s Show* gives advice to lovelorn teenage girls is this bit of information:

Wesleyan University now offers the nation's first "gender-blind" dorm for students who don't label themselves as male or female.

I am zooming through the air toward a patch of national forest presently populated by a horde of people who don't label themselves as male or female, as well as bunches of folks whose identities settle somewhere beneath the transgender banner. Now, before we land in Grand Rapids, an emergency glossary.

EMERGENCY GLOSSARY OF GENDER-IDENTITY TERMINOLOGY

(Partially plagiarized from the website Antny's Place [antnysplace.org])

Genderqueer: Individuals who may identify as both male and female, or sometimes as male and sometimes as female, or decline to identify with any gender whatsoever. They are not necessarily on hormones or pursuing surgery.

Transsexual: (1) A person who feels a consistent and overwhelming desire to transition and fulfill their lives as a member of the opposite gender. Generally taking hormones and pursuing surgery. (2) A person who believes that his or her actual biological (or "born") gender is the opposite of the one it should have been.

Trans man: A female-to-male transsexual (FTM). Also known as a *trannyboy,* if younger.

Trans woman: A male-to-female transsexual (MTF).

Pre-op: Has not yet had sex-reassignment surgery.

Post-op: Has had sex-reassignment surgery.

Non-op: Has no intention of having sex-reassignment surgery.

*   *   *

I am headed to Camp Trans, now in the tenth year of its on again/
off again standoff with the Michigan Womyn's Music Festival
across the road. Started by Nancy Jean and friends in the years after
her eviction, the protest camp faded away in the mid-nineties. A
new generation of young transgender activists picked up the torch
in 1999 and resumed the confrontational face-off. In the scant four
years since, there has been an unprecedented boom in people
identifying as trans, mostly female-assigned people transitioning to
men or staking out a third-sex genderqueer territory. Flocking to
Camp Trans for both the political struggle and the party, they have
changed the outpost in significant ways. The focus of the trans
struggle in recent years has drifted away from its original intention
of getting trans women into women-only and lesbian spaces. Trans
men have generally been welcome—if not totally fetishized—by
contemporary dyke communities, particularly in young, urban
enclaves. The same is not true for trans women, even lesbian trans
women. This influx of trannyboys and their lesbian admirers has
not only alienated many of the trans women at Camp Trans, it's
also blown up attendance so high they can no longer set up right
across the street from the festival gates. The encampment is now
located up the road a bit, in a forest-lined field between the music
festival and a nudist camp.

I've never been to Camp Trans, though I stopped attending
MWMF a few years back, too conflicted about this exclusion of
trans women. Today I'm picked up at the airport by a girl named
Ana Jae who volunteered to get me so she can get the hell out of
the woods. Ana hates camping; she says the bugs are attacking like
mad and it's really bad when you drop your shorts to piss in the
woods and they start fluttering around your bare ass. Ana can't use
the Porta-Potties because she's been traumatized by the 1980s
B–horror flick *Sleepaway Camp II,* in which terrible things happen
within one plastic, fetid chamber; so she is forced to piddle among
the bugs. I'm antsy to hear of the mood at Camp Trans, and Ana

confirms that the trans men far outnumber the trans women, complains about a general devaluing of femininity in the young, post-dyke queer scene, and tells me about a sex party that somehow went awry the night before and is this morning's main drama. Our immediate drama is that we get outrageously, wildly lost on the way back to the woods, careening through quaint Michigan townships for hours, hopelessly passing farm stands selling fresh vegetables, rows of exploding sunflowers and cornstalks, trees and trees and more trees, gigantic willows with long whipping branches that drape and swag, and large single-family homes with porches and pools and tractors in their front yards. We know that we've unscrambled our cryptic directions when we pass a gas station that has a flapping sign that says WELCOME WOMYN in its parking lot, and loads of sporty females loading cases of beer into their cars. We follow a camper with a bumper sticker that reads SEE YOU NEXT AUGUST down a road so heavily traveled that the foliage that lines it is coated with a thick dusting of brown dirt like an apocalyptic snowfall. We pass the front gates of the festival and see its huge parking lot crammed with vehicles, women in neon orange vests directing the flow of females through the gates, and we keep going. It's a disappointment not to see Camp Trans boldly arranged there at the mouth of the festival, and I wonder how its political point can be clearly made if it's tucked out of sight, around the curving road. The former vigil has turned into a sort of alternative to the festival, one that's free of charge, one that a lot of MWMF attendees mistake as a happy, friendly, seperate-but-equal campsite. A place for dykes who think trannyboys are hot to spend a night cruising and partying with, and who then return to their gated community up the road. For the trans women relying on Camp Trans as a site of protest, this new incarnation—as a sort of spring break for trannyboys and the dykes who date them—has been infuriating. Which is why Sadie Crab-tree, a trans woman and an activist from D.C., has emerged as the sort of head leader this year. It is her intention, backed up by the other organizers, to bring the focus of Camp Trans back around to the trans women it originally meant to serve.

CAMP TRANS WELCOME STATION

Everyone who comes to Camp Trans, either to camp or to visit on a day pass from the festival, has to pause at the welcome tent and check in, and MWMF attendees who arrive tonight for entertainment are charged three dollars. Behind a table made from boards and sawhorses sits a couple of Camp Trans welcomers, women doing their work shifts and acclimating visitors to their new environment. Like the festival across the way, everyone here is expected to lend a hand. The camp isn't nearly as large as the music festival—MWMF's parking lot is bigger than Camp Trans's entire area—but it still takes a lot of work to make it run. I spy a kitchen tent with a mess of pots and pans and water jugs strewn before it. Another tent is garlanded with Christmas lights that are beginning to shine as the hot summer sun sinks. This is the performance area, bulked with DJ and other sound equipment. There's a medic tent and a roped-off area for "advocates," armbanded individuals whose job is to answer touchy questions, listen to complaints, and defuse conflicts.

At the welcome tent I sign in on a form that doubles as a petition calling for the dropping of the festival's womyn-born-womyn policy. I'm handed a slip of paper welcoming me to Camp Trans.

From "WELCOME TO CAMP TRANS 2003":

> Camp Trans is an annual protest against the Michigan Womyn's Music Festival's policy that bars transsexual women from attending. MWMF's so-called "womyn-born-womyn" policy sets a transphobic standard for women-only spaces across the country, and contributes to an environment in women's and lesbian communities where discrimination against trans women is considered acceptable. For trans women who are consistently refused help from domestic violence shelters and rape crisis centers, this is a matter of life and death.

Some posterboards are stuck with Post-it notes that outline each day's workshops and meetings; another posterboard is cluttered with bright notes soliciting amour in the woods. One bemoans a throat atrophied with lack of use, another is looking for couples to participate in a Floridian-retiree role-play. Interested parties can respond by slipping scrawled replies into corresponding envelopes. There are zines for sale, silkscreened patches that say CAMP TRANS SUPPORTER in heavy-metal letters, buttons that squeak I ♥ CAMP TRANS, and T-shirts that say NOT GAY AS IN HAPPY BUT QUEER AS IN FUCK YOU. There is also a notebook labeled LETTERS TO LISA VOGEL.

Lisa Vogel is the sole captain of the SS Michigan Womyn's Music Festival. There is no one but her behind the wheel; she wrote the policy, and she is the only one who can lift it. Of the many rumors I hear this weekend, most involve her. One rumor says that she offered Camp Trans a sum of money somewhere between $7,500 and $75,000 to start its own damn festival. This is totally unlikely, as her own festival is suffering financially. Another rumor says that transsexual women will be allowed into her festival over her dead body, an extreme pledge that makes me think of Lauryn Hill's "I'd rather my babies starve than white kids buy my records" quote. Who knows what's true. Vogel is famously tight-lipped about the whole controversy, and has never made an attempt to negotiate with Camp Trans. In the face of past protests she has simply reiterated the policy, which, I also hear, has suddenly been removed from all MWMF web pages. There is much speculation on what this means, but no one is naive enough to believe that it means the policy has been dropped and trans women are now welcome. More likely the immense controversy, which now involves not just a boycott of the festival but also of the performers, is wearing on festival producers, and targets for attack are being shuffled out of the line of fire.

Excerpts from LETTERS TO LISA VOGEL:

> I love the festival and it has to become a safe space for everyone. It can happen, everyone would benefit. As feminists we cannot become our oppressors.

> A transpositive environment will only improve the festival experience for all. There are plenty of information sources on how to do this.

I've been to many trans-inclusive events in my hometown, including a woman's bathhouse. I feel totally safe around trans women, and I know lots of other women my age who feel the same way.

Behind the treeline is where people are camping, and the arc of green has been segmented into three campsites: loud substance, which means campers are getting bombed and fucking right outside your tent; loud no substance, meaning sober people lashed to trees and moaning loudly; and quiet no substance, which means everyone sleeps. This is where I camp. I actually unknowingly plop my tent right in the center of a sand patch being used for AA meetings. Next to me is a camper van all tricked out with a sink and a fridge, the outside painted checkerboard. It looks straight out of *Fast Times at Ridgemont High,* and it is occupied by, lo and behold, my friend Chris, who is out on his makeshift patio, smoking a lot of pot and triggering the substance-free campers. He's sharing his pipe with a lesbian named Mountain, who lives on a women-only commune in Oregon that has successfully integrated trans women into its home. It is, essentially, no big whoop. Life goes on, wimmin are still wimmin, they tend their organic gardens and print their lunar calendars and life is good. Mountain is one of those women who live for Michigan, and it's a real big deal that she's not there this year. She's here at Camp Trans, in solidarity.

Now people are scurrying around, full of excited purpose. Tonight is the big dance and performance, and the number of people on this land will rise with an influx of girls from the festival. Camp Trans's population, which hovers at around seventy-five, will shoot up above a hundred with the visitors. Which is nothing compared with the eight thousand or so women hunkered down in the vast woods across the way. Sadie is dashing around, all stressed out. She's got a sweet, kind face with sparkly eyes and short hair; her all-black outfits seem like military gear, especially with the big black women-symbol-raised-fist tattoo on her shoulder. She's still dealing with fallout from last night's sex party, and now she's just found a note from a Camp Transer looking to host a Camp Trans workshop inside the festival, where trans women can't go. There is a feeling that the action is spinning out of the organizer's hands, and she's upset that a so-called Camp Trans event would happen in a place where trans women aren't allowed. Sadie, needing a drink, bustles off with tears in her eyes.

SADIE CRABTREE

"One problem was that some festival attendees were unclear on the mission of Camp Trans, and didn't see it as a protest but rather as a part of their Michigan experience. Kind of a suburb of MWMF where fest attendees could go to hang out with hot tranny boys. That's another problem—the fascination with and fetishization of FTMs in some dyke communities makes trans women even more invisible. At least one fest attendee last year spoke openly about how she totally supported Camp Trans and loved trans guys but just didn't like trans women. We tried to solve some of those problems this year by having a very clear mission statement on all of the Camp Trans materials, providing suggested talking points for all campers, and having discussions about the experiences of trans women at Camp Trans. We had volunteer advocates whose job it was to listen to people's concerns—especially those of trans women—and help organizers plan solutions. Another thing we did was designate certain workshops and decompression areas "wristband-free zones" where fest attendees were asked not to go. Having a space to retreat from interactions with fest attendees was a need that had been expressed by trans women last year, but it also sent a message. It wasn't to stigmatize festival attendees, but to help people think a little more critically about what it means to give hundreds of dollars to a transphobic organization for permission to do activism inside, what it means to speak in a space where others' voices are forbidden, what it's like to have a space that specifically excludes you. When people asked about the wristband-free spaces, we offered them scissors. You have that choice. Some people don't."

LEMMY AND OTHER PROBLEMS

Another MWMF policy forbids male voices on the land, meaning no one is allowed to slip a Michael Jackson tape into their boom box and start moonwalking. Perhaps it also means the Porta-Pottie men take a vow of silence when they roar through the gate, who knows. This rule has been broken, or bent, with the rise of drag kings—female performers who costume themselves as men, both lampooning and celebrating masculinity in a sort of burlesque, often via lip-synchs. When, some years back, the Florida drag king troupe House of Ma took an MWMF side stage during a talent show, the audience was given warning that a male voice would shortly boom from the sound system. Offended women high-tailed it out of the vicinity, one step ahead of Neil Diamond. This of course is not an issue at Camp Trans, so the music is a little varied—better—on this side of the road. The dance party under way on the patch of sandy brown earth designated both "stage" and "dance floor" is shaking to Dr. Dre and the Gossip, Motorhead and Peeches, Billy Idol, Northern States, Ludacris, and Fannypack. I'm standing beside Benjamin, a genderqueer boy. Meaning he was born a boy and remains a boy, but he's gorgeous like a girl and does hella fierce drag. His hair is an architecture of multiple pieces that look like feather dusters protruding from his scalp in feathery pom-poms. "Everyone is so beautiful," he muses at the crowd, and he is right. Mostly young, like late teens and twenties, they are kicking up Pig Pen–size clouds of dust as they dance in their silver plastic pants and marabou-trimmed spandex, their starchy crinolines and pink ruffled tuxedo shirts, their neon orange nighties, push-up bras, and outfits constructed from shredded trash bags and duct tape. Everyone is gleeful, happy to be smashing the gender binary, to be partying down for a cause, to be part of a revolution of good-looking gender-ambiguous people. In the process of deconstructing gender identity, I muse, sexual preference may become obsolete. If you're an old-fashioned lesbian purged of transphobia, you'll be hot for the trans women. Bunches of dykes are already hooking up with trans men, and if you're dating trans men it's probably a good time to reckon with your bisexuality and attraction to the equally male, if perhaps less socially evolved, non-trans-men of the world. And that's pretty much everyone. Yeah. Maybe I'm just trampy, but I'm attracted to pretty much everyone here.

Showtime starts with an introduction by an organizer named Jess who instructs the crowd—part Camp Transers, part festie-goers—on proper behavior while in such an unusual space, a space where trans-people outnumber the non-trans. Because last year's visitors didn't understand how to act, pissing off a lot of trans women, this year we get a tiny schooling. Do not assume anyone's pronoun. There's really no way of guessing at who is a "he" and who a "she," and besides all that, there are gangs of genderqueers promoting the use of a third pronoun, "ze," which I am not going to conjugate for you. Others say to hell with pronouns altogether and dare us to be more creative in the way we refer to them. Also, Jess instructs, do not ask anyone rude questions about their bodies. If you're bursting with curiosity or just freaking out, please see an armbanded advocate. Last year Camp Trans was paid a visit by the weight-loss guru Susan Powter, who was greeted by an advocate named J. J. Bitch. "J. J. Bitch!" she shrieked, waving her arms around like a nut. "J. J. Bitch! I love that name! I want that name! I'm J. J. Bitch!" J. J. Bitch was stunned and delighted by the somewhat manic celebrity guest. Advocate work can be quite emotionally draining. It had to have been a lift.

First there are skits, one which demonstrates the simple cruelty of turning trans women away from the festival gates. Another enacts the traumatizing experience of having perfect strangers trot up and inquire about the state of your genitals because you are transgendered and are expected to answer this. Last-minute creations, the skits are shaky but effective. The audience ripples out from the spotlit performance area, sitting in the dirt, getting hopped on by grasshoppers and crickets and weird brown beetles with little wings folded beneath their shells. A moth as big as a sparrow keeps charging into one of the light dishes glowing up from the ground. A gang of women come out, all dressed in trash bags and duct tape. They are the Fat-tastics, and they deliver a smart performance about fat power and fat oppression, ending in an empowering cheer replete with pom-poms fashioned from more shredded garbage bags. A duo of transboys or genderqueers dressed like Gainsborough's Blue Boy enact a randy ballet. Nomy Lamm, an artist who has arranged a petition for artists who oppose MWMF's policy, howls heartbreaking songs into the warm night, accompanied by a honking accordion. The camp feels like some medieval village on a pagan holiday, bodies close in the darkness, being serenaded by a girl in striped tights and crinoline, harlequin eye makeup shooting stars down her cheeks. Benjamin is a total trooper when the CD he's lip-synching to keeps skipping and skipping and skipping. Eventually Julia Serano reads. Julia is a trans woman spoken-word poet. She's got a girl-next-door thing going on, with strawberry-blond hair and a sprinkling of freckles. She performs a piece about her relationship with her girlfriend. It's got sweet and honest humor, and it charms the crowd. Then she recites another, "Cocky":

> and if i seem a bit cocky
> well that's because i refuse
> to make apologies for my body anymore
> i am through being the human sacrifice
> offered up to appease other people's gender issues
> some women have a penis
> some men don't
> and the rest of the world
> is just going to have to get the fuck over it

Julia gets a standing ovation, everyone hopping up and brushing the dirt off their asses, brushing crickets from their chests, hooting and hollering at the poet as she leaves the "stage" and falls into a hug with her girlfriend and Sadie.

JULIA SERANO

"As part of Camp Trans, so much of our work is dedicated to convincing the women who attend MWMF that trans women won't flaunt their penises on the land, or that we won't commit acts of violence against other women. I have yet to meet a trans woman who has acted violently toward another woman and/or flaunted her penis in public, but I know I need to take the MWMF attendees' concerns seriously in order to gain their trust. At the same time, to borrow an analogy, it's like someone of Middle Eastern descent having to convince every person on a flight that s/he won't hijack the plane in order to be allowed onboard.

"Having talked to several festivalgoers, I was distressed at how often people centered the debate around 'the penis.' Everyone talked about the significance of penises being on the land, without much acknowledgment that these so-called penises are attached to women's bodies.

"Like most trans women, I have a lot of issues surrounding both my penis and the fact that I was born a boy. I have worked through too much self-loathing about these aspects of my person to allow other people to throw salt on my open wounds. It has taken me a long time to reach the point where I can accept my penis as simply being a part of my flesh and tissue, rather than the ultimate symbol of maleness. I find it confusing that so many self-described feminists spend so much effort propagating the male myth that men's power and domination arises from the phallus.

"It was surreal to have MWMF festivalgoers talk to me about their fear that transsexual women would bring masculine energy onto the land one minute, then the next tell me that they never would have guessed that I was born a man.

"I also found it distressing that so many women would want to exclude me (a woman) from women's space, under the pretense that my body contains potential triggers for abuse survivors. That line of reasoning trivializes the abuse that trans women face day in, day out. I have been verbally and physically assaulted by men for being who

I am. Like other women, I have had men force themselves upon me. In addition, I can't think of a more humiliating way to be raped by male culture than to be forced to grow up as a boy against one's will. Every trans woman is a survivor, and we have triggers, too. The phrase 'womyn-born-womyn' is one of my triggers."

I'm wiped out, exhausted, can't make it through the rest of the show. With my little flashlight I traipse through the scratchy, weedy terrain, locusts dashing away from my sneakers, toward my tent. My tent may be toxic. Earlier I dumbly spritzed a wealth of bug spray onto my body, fearful of West Nile Virus. I did this inside my tent, then had to quickly unzip the tent and let myself out, a step ahead of asphyxiation. The tent has aired out a bit but still retains its chemical tang. I eat a bunch of valerian, herbal valium, and crawl into my sleeping bag. The dance party has revved back up. I hear the shrieks of dancers over the thump of Outkast, and then I fall asleep.

DAY TWO

One thing I made damn sure to do before leaving civilization was to brew a two-liter container of coffee, and it is this I grab at when I wake up. My tent is already starting to bake as I scramble into some jeans, grab my toothbrush, and stumble out into the searing sunlight. I am the only camper—the only camper!—who did not camp in the shade behind the treeline. I camped in front of the trees, the scary trees that I imagined were dripping ticks, ticks poisoned with Lyme disease, the disgusting trees where many spiders live, the trees with their carpet of old leaves slowly rotting away, where mice no doubt burrow and any number of things that bite can be found. No, I arranged my borrowed tent right in direct sun. Not so smart.

The smart campers are emerging from their shaded glens, getting right into their cars and driving the fuck to the lake. There's a lake nearby and a creek, too, and everyone I speak to confirms that going to the lake is definitely part of this "Camp Trans Experience" I am hoping to document; they urge me to hop in for a swim. A fat caucus took place at the lake yesterday, as did an Attention Deficit Disorder caucus, though no one managed to stay very focused for that one. I am beyond tempted to ride along, to float in the lake in my underwear under the guise of journalism, but I am too scared of missing out on some crucial bit of drama. The vibe at Camp Trans is intense, flammable like the parched ground beneath our various feet. Something is bound to happen, and I can't be splashing around like a fool when it does.

I'm standing at the welcome tent when two festival workers show up. One is a femme girl with curly red hair, a cowboy hat, and glamorous sunglasses; the other is a butch girl in thick horn rims and a baseball hat. They carry a box of zines they've made, a compilation of the various opinions held by the women who work the festival across the road. The femme girl hands it off to the Camp Trans welcome worker. "It's our effort at having some dialogue," she says, or something like that. She seems a little shy, scared probably, and I have a few thoughts, watching the welcome worker accept the gift, a caul of skepticism on her face. I think the festies are brave to come over with a box of MWMF opinions, I think the opinions are probably already well known to Camp Trans campers, I think shit is going to hit the fan and these workers and their good intentions are going to get creamed. The two festival workers walk off to the side, lean against a parked car, light cigarettes, and hang out. I stick my zine in my back pocket and head over to a tent for the morning meeting.

I guess the morning meetings happen every morning, just a rundown of what's happening that day, a space for people to make announcements. A sort of exhilaration is blowing through the crowd as word of the zine, or the zine itself, hits them. People are hunched over, their faces stuck in the xeroxed pages, gasping. It doesn't look good. Simon Strikeback, a camp organizer, one of the activists who resuscitated Camp Trans after Nancy and company let it go, is facilitating the gathering. Like everyone here, he is very cute. He's got blond curls spiraling out from his baseball hat and is grimy in a fun way, like he's been playing in the dirt. He says yes, there can be a circle to process the zine. He announces some other events—a workshop called "Feminism and the Gender Binary," which I plan to check out despite its terrifying title. A dreadlocked white girl with facial piercings announces that she has anarchist T-shirts for sale and is looking for partners to hitchhike to Mexico for an antiglobalization rally. Someone else holds up a silkscreen emblazoned with a Camp Trans image designed by the cartoonist Ariel Schrag and asks for help screening T-shirts. I announce that I'm attending the festival as a member of the press. It's a good-faith thing I did at Sadie's request, so that everyone knows what's up and people who think it's terrible and exploitative that I am writing about their camp can glare at me from afar and not wind up, without their consent, in my story. I'm even wearing a dorky sticker that says PRESS in red Sharpie. At one point a boy walks up and presses it. "I thought something happened when I pressed it," he explains, perhaps disappointed. I try to remedy suspicious looks by volunteering to help clean up breakfast, over at the kitchen tent.

OVER AT THE KITCHEN TENT

There's not much to do until the water gets here. There are various pans with muck being swiftly baked onto them by this relentless sun of ours. There is a giant bucket of beets that people are wondering what to do with. I move it into the shade, sure it'll keep a bit longer. In another bucket a whole bunch of beans soak, plumping up for tonight's chili dinner. Culling the rotten vegetables from the vegetable boxes is what I'm told to do, so I join the others inside the tent. There is an abundance of vegetables, mostly donated from a co-op several states away: cardboard boxes of squash, zucchini, bulbs of garlic. I deal with a plastic bag filled with liquefying basil, pulling the top leaves, still green, from the blackening herb below. The stuff that's no good—the dried-up rosemary and yellowed cilantro, the split tomatoes and the peppers sprouting cottony tufts of mold—all get tossed into the compost. A woman is picking beets as large as a child's head and slicing off their wilting greens with a knife. When she discovers the mouse inside the beet box, she shrieks. "Oh, that's no good," says the person culling squash beside me. "You can get really sick. I ate food contaminated with mouse shit once, and I got really, really sick." We try to scare the mouse away, but it just burrows deeper into the beets. I leave the tent, walk behind it, and pull the beet box out backward, into the grass. The mouse leaps out and scrambles into the forest. We look for visible mouse turd, but everything is sort of brown and crumbly from the dirty beets. I decide not to eat a bite of the Camp Trans food while I'm there. I'm too worried about getting a tick in my armpit to take on the additional neurosis of hantavirus. I've got six energy bars stuffed in my suitcase, two packs of tuna, and a few cans of chili. That's what I'll be eating. Deciding that I saved the day by ridding us of the mouse, I retire from my cleanup duties. It's too hot; I need some tuna or I'll get heatstroke. I stop by Chris's stoner van to glob a bit of cool, refrigerated mustard into my tuna and listen to his instructions that I gulp down at least fifteen gulps of water each time I hit my bottle. That's the number: fifteen. "Till your stomach's all bloated," he advises. I do as he says. He does seem like an experienced camper, and the heat is killing people all over the globe, knocking them down by the thousands in France. His little dog, Poi, who looks just like Benji, has burrowed a cool hole beneath the van and lies there, panting.

BULLSHIT

I am very glad I didn't go to the lake. Now we sit in a ring, in a small, shaded clearing not far from where I've camped: a bunch of Camp Trans campers and the two festival workers who delivered the box of zines. The zine is called *Manual Transmission,* and people hate it. It's an anthology, essentially, of festival workers' opinions on the trans-inclusion issue. There is talk about throwing the box of them onto that evening's campfire, a good old-fashioned book burning. Ana Jae is set to facilitate the discussion, and Benjamin is by her side, "taking stack," which I think means keeping a list of everyone who raises a hand to speak, so that everyone gets to.

Excerpts from *Manual Transmission*:

> Let's be clear about what womyn born womyn means. It's not about defining a goddamn thing. It is about saying this is what I'm gathering around for this particular moment. It is saying that this festival, this period in time, is for women whose entire life experience has been as a girl and who still live loudly as a woman. Period. How is that defining you? Why do you think we are so ignorant as to not "get" that, to not figure out that we also have privilege for not struggling with a brain/body disconnect? But can you be so obstinate, can you be so determined to not understand that we have an experience that is outside yours? And that that experience, even though we have greater numbers, still entitles us to take separate space? Do you not see it as full on patronizing that you act as though these "thousands" of women's shelters can't make up their own minds and policies? Doesn't it make you sick to have the same objectives as the religious right? Why is it okay to totally ignore the need of women who do NOT want to see a penis? How and what world do we live in that you can completely divorce these things? Like being white and telling everyone your skin color doesn't matter because you are not a racist? Stop assuming our ignorance.
>
> Dicks are not useless signifiers. Even unwanted ones. You who I love and call my community of political bandits, you who grew up being seen as, treated as, regarded as boys (and perhaps miserably failing that performance), you did not grow as I. You did not experience being held out as girl and cropped into that particular box. You gotta understand, you are my sister, but you don't have that experience. And taking my experience and saying it is yours don't make it yours, makes it stolen.

"This is bullshit. In my opinion," Ana Jae states. The overall feel about the zine and its arrival is, first, "We know this already," and second, "How dare you bring it into this space that we are trying to keep free from such hurtful sentiments." People take turns expressing themselves.

Hitchhiking Anarchist Girl: takes issue with a passage defending MWMF's $350 entrance fee, calling it classist.

Simon: is frustrated, only open to discussing changing the policy, sick to death of back-and-forth arguing about penises and girlhoods.

Guy to My Left: generously concedes that the festie workers had good intentions but delivered a flawed product.

Festie Workers: admit they were rushed and that, though they specified no submissions degrading or attacking trans people would be published, they did not get to read all of the writings. They feel bad for the discord their zine has caused, but maintain that these are the opinions of workers inside the festival, like it or not: they didn't feel it was proper to censor anyone's thoughts—who can dictate what is right and what is wrong?

Sadie: maintains that, as an activist, it's her job to declare her views the good and right and true views; she is only interested in talking to people who agree and want to help further the cause.

Festie Workers: weakly remind everyone of their good intentions.

Girl to My Right, in Wheelchair: offers that she is hurt every day by people with good intentions.

Femme Festie Worker: cries; doesn't know how to help this situation.

Girl I Can't See: says that it's everyone's responsibility to educate themselves on trans issues.

Girl with Camouflage Bandanna: sympathizes with how painful the education process can be; urges please don't let that stop you from learning.

There's a lot of fear here, people afraid of each other, afraid of their own ability to do the wrong thing from simple ignorance, their own ability to bungle a peace offering, to offend the person they sought to help. It starts to rain. Light at first, and then heavy. The weather out here can turn violent in a finger snap, the dust suddenly flooded into muddy ponds, the sky cracking thunderbolts and sending threads of lightning scurrying across the cloud cover, occasionally touching down and setting a tree on fire. I run back to my tent and fling the rain cover over it, and by the time I get back to the circle it's over—the process, the rain, all of it. I talk briefly with a girl I know from my previous Augusts at the festival; she's usually been a worker. Last year she caught a lot of shit for taking a festival van over to Camp Trans for a date, so this year she's camping here, back in the trees where everyone seems to have gone. I go back to my tent to grab a notebook. Inside it is hot and smells strongly of sulfur, like hell itself. I take my notebook back to the now-empty clearing, sit in someone's abandoned camp chair, and write some notes.

HERE'S GEYL, THEN PAM

Geyl Forcewind is a lanky punk-rock trans woman with a red anarchy sign sewed into her ratty T-shirt. A good radiance sort of shines off Geyl. Her combat boots are patched with gummy straps of duct tape; she spits a lot and cracks jokes. She collapses into the chair next to me and asks how my "project" is going. She's teasing me, I think, but it's perfect that she's appeared because I wanted to talk to someone about the proliferation of trans men and trannyboys, and the small numbers of trans women or genderqueers who enjoy the trappings of femininity. I love girls, I love girlness, and though I love trans men—my boyfriend is trans—I wish there were more females around these genderqueer parts. The face of the transrevolution is, presently, a bearded one. "Riot grrrl made being a dyke accessible," Geyl reflects, "and now those people are seeing that they can be genderqueer and it's not so scary. There's none of that for MTFs." Pam, a trans woman who had been quietly strumming her guitar in the woods behind us, strolls up and joins our conversation.

177

PAM: Trans women get abused a lot more in our society.

She's right, of course. Because it's often harder for them to pass as women in the world, and because they're likely to get way more shit for it, lots of would-be trans women just don't come out.

GEYL: Being a girl is not as cool. I actively try to recruit.

PAM: Yeah, there must be something wrong with you if you want to be a woman.

GEYL: I tried to be really butch when I first came out.

MICHELLE: I tried to be really butch when I first came out, too. It seemed cooler and tougher, and safer, to be masculine.

Pam looks like just the sort of woman the music festival across the way embraces—smudgy eyeliner, long brown hair, rolled bandanna tied around her forehead, and that acoustic guitar in tow. She's even a construction worker, and isn't that one of the most feminist jobs a woman can work? After coming out as a trans woman, Pam's co-worker threatened to toss her from the very high building they were working on. When she complained, her foreman said, "You should expect that sort of thing." She was soon fired from the job, for "being late."

PAM: If I watch *Jerry Springer*, I don't want to come out.

GEYL: All the trans women on that show aren't really trans. They're a joke.

PAM: I think Jerry is a trannychaser. And I think he's resentful of it and wants to take it out on the community.

Soon we're informed that we're sitting smack in the middle of the space reserved for the "Feminism and the Gender Binary" workshop.

GEYL: I'll feminize your gender binary. If anyone quotes Judith Butler, I'll punch them.

THE RALLY

There's that girl Mountain again, on the mic this time, letting everyone know that if her feminist separatist farming commune can let the trans women in, anyone can. "I always have said that if I didn't go to the festival each year I'd die," she tells the crowd. "Well, I didn't go, and I didn't die, and I'm not going until they change the policy!" Everyone cheers. Sadie's on the mic, revving everyone up by insisting that we're going to change the policy. I guess it's impossible to engage in any sort of activism with a fatalistic view, and who knows, maybe MWMF will surprise us all and roll out the trans carpet, but I just don't see it happening. I remember glimpsing Lisa Vogel in the festival-worker area years ago, after Camp Trans had brought a protest onto the land. They'd been kicked off, of course, and a reiteration of the womyn-born-womyn policy was swiftly typed up, xeroxed, and distributed throughout the festival. Lisa was smoking, and she looked pissed. Someone told me that she saw it as a class issue and an age issue. Camp Trans was made up of a bunch of teenagers freshly released from liberal New England colleges, with their heads full of gender theory and their blood bubbling with hormones and rebellion. Lisa Vogel is loved the way that saints are loved by the women who attend her festival, and why shouldn't she be? She's provided them with the only truly safe space they've ever known. She's a working-class lesbian who built it all up from scratch, with her hands and the hands of old-school dykes and feminists, women who claim, perhaps rightly, that no one knows what it was like, what they went through, how hard they fought. It has taken a lot of work to create the MWMF that's rocking across the way, sending its disembodied female voices floating into our campsite. It's taken single-mindedness and determination. Lisa Vogel, I fear, is one severely stubborn woman.

Emily is speaking and she's saying things that could turn around some of the more stubborn festival women. Unfortunately, I don't think anyone has come over from the fest who wouldn't love to see the policy junked. Emily is preaching, as they say, to the choir. She's talking about her girlhood, how the girls all knew she was a girl like they were, and how powerful and life-saving it was to be recognized like that, your insides finally showing through. A young friend wished Emily would get a sex-change operation so she could come to her slumber party. It's a great response to the festival's insistence that trans women didn't have girlhoods. Anna speaks next. (Not Ana Jae—this is a brand new Anna, you haven't met her yet.) She's got big, dark eyebrows and wide lips painted red; she's holding the mic, and she's come to lecture the lesbians. For dating trans men but justifying this shades-of-hetero behavior by saying, "He's not really a guy." Sacrificing trans men's maleness so that their lesbian identities can stay intact. Sheepishly explaining, "He's trans"—again invalidating the real masculinity so as not to be confused with a straight girl. For fetishizing, as a community, this sexy new explosion of trans men, but remaining unwelcoming to trans women. It's all so true my frickin' eyes well up. I'd spent the first year and a half of my boyfriend's transition explaining to everyone—women on the bus, strangers in line at Safeway, people I sat next to on planes—that my boyfriend, he's trangender. So don't go thinking I'm some stupid straight girl, the confession implies. I'm *queer*. OK? It tended to be more information than anyone wanted. Everyone's uncomfortable, but at least no one thinks I'm heterosexual, and that's what counts. Oy vey, as my Jewish friends say. And I know lots of lesbians who date trannyboys but freak out if a trans woman enters their space. It's all so fucked up and heartbreaking and overwhelming. Or maybe I'm just really sleep-deprived from a night on bumpy ground, sleeping atop sticks and hard mounds of dirt. Before me are the Gainsborough Blue Boys, lying side by side on separate chaise longues, still in their wiggy tennis outfits. They clutch paper bags concealing what I assume are beers, and make out. Seriously—who are they? I love them. I wipe my soggy eyes, grab Anna as she shuffles past with her boyfriend, and thank her for her speech. I confess my past as a shameful tranny-dating lesbian; I heap upon her how sad and scared I get when my dyke friends start talking shit about trans women. I want Anna—beautiful, strong Anna with the microphone—to absolve me and also solve all my social problems. She seems so capable. I think I overwhelm her. She gives me her contact information, including her phone number and email address. "She loves being interviewed; it's her favorite thing," her boyfriend encourages. Of course she does; she's a genius. She walks away into the darkness, her beaded, sequined shoulder bag glinting in the night.

The rally is over, and everyone's dancing again. On the sidelines I find Carolyn, a writer and trans woman from Brooklyn. Carolyn must have found some way to construct a shower from rainwater and tree branches. Every time I see her, she looks really, really clean. Every night, before I sleep, I wipe a thick coat of grime from my body with some sort of chemical gauze pad called a Swash cloth. It's all I've managed to do, hygiene-wise, and I look mangled. Carolyn admits that others have commented on her cleanliness. "I don't know—I haven't showered for four days! I'm just lucky," she says modestly.

I HAD THE TIME OF MY LIFE

Two people—girls, trannyboys, genderqueers, I can't really tell in the light, so bright it turns them into silhouettes—are whirling across the dusty makeshift dance floor, doing a dance routine to a medley of songs from the movie *Dirty Dancing*. Here is my proof that this gender-smashing revolution is a generational thing: someone walks across the stage holding a cardboard sign reading NOBODY PUTS BABY IN A CORNER and everyone roars. I have no fucking idea what they are talking about. I was a moody death rocker when *Dirty Dancing* came out. This was back before Hot Topic in the malls, back when goth was a slightly dressier version of punk and wearing black lipstick and ratting your hair into a tarantula was a uniform that conveyed information such as "I am opposed to the dominant culture and movies such as *Dirty Dancing*." My little sister loved *Dirty Dancing,* and I ragged on her for it mercilessly. Patrick Swayze? Come on. But I like watching these two spinning into each other, knocking each other down and crawling all over each other. At the very end of their act, after dancing close, they pull apart and draw the audience in, and everyone responds; they move into the brightness, becoming silhouettes that dance and raise their hands into the light, and it's beautiful like a dark kaleidoscope, all the bodies coming together under the light. My eyes well up with tears again. Jesus. Chris asks me to dance, but I can't. I'm a mess. It's been such an emotional day, and I'm spent. A trans man is straddling the lap of a girl in a bright green dress, lap-dancing her on the folding chair. Two others are making out on the dance floor, and many bootys are being freaked. It's time for bed. I hike back to my tent, following the small spot of light my flashlight tosses into the weeds.

DAY THREE

"I asked you to dance and you disappeared," Chris complains. We're on his patio. He's making real hot coffee on his camp stove, but I had to swear I would tell no one about this luxury, because he's almost out of gas. He starts talking about how confused he was about Camp Trans, how he thought it was a bunch of trans men trying to get into the women's festival, and he wasn't down with that. "You gain a few privileges, you lose a few," he laughs. "Go cry on your own damn shoulder; get over yourself." Once he realized it was about getting trans women some women-only privileges, he was down for the cause. He's glad he's here. "I'm so comfortable," he says. "My tree keeps getting closer." He means the tree he pees on. Maybe he saw *Sleepaway Camp II* as well and is scared of the portos, maybe he's lazy, or maybe it's just such a rarity to be a trans person who can take a piss in the woods without fear.

THIS JUST IN

Excerpted email forwarded from Carolyn, from the D.C. Metropolitan Police Department's Gay and Lesbian Liaison Unit (GLLU), received three days after returning from Camp Trans:

> WASHINGTON, D.C. In the past week, the Transgender Community has been shaken by three shootings, two of which resulted in the deaths of the victims.
>
> On 8/16/03, Bella Evangelista (Elvys Perez) was murdered at Arkansas Avenue and Allison Street, N.W. Antoine Jacobs was immediately arrested and has been charged with First Degree Murder while Armed. The case has been classified by the Metropolitan Police Department as a suspected Hate/Bias Motivated Crime (Gender Identity).
>
> In the evening hours of 8/20/03, a black Male-to-Female Transgender individual was found near 3rd and I Streets, N.W. suffering from apparent gunshot wounds. The victim was transported to a local hospital, where she is in serious condition. The case has been classified as an Assault with Intent to Kill.
>
> In the early morning hours of 8/21/03, Seventh District officers discovered the body of a black Male-to-Female Transgender individual at 2nd Street and Malcolm X Avenue, S.E. The victim was unconscious and suffering from wounds by unknown means. Since there was no sign of life, D.C. Fire/EMS did not transport the individual.

Camp Trans is unraveling before my eyes. Cars and trucks are rolling out of the parking lot, which is just another part of the field we've all been living in. People wave out their windows as they pull onto the road. All day long the population shrinks. The planning meeting for Camp Trans 2004, which is happening beneath a tent, is repeatedly interrupted as vacating campers lavish good-bye hugs on their friends. I am sitting back and listening to participants who raise their hands and offer compliments on what they felt went well at this year's gathering, and what needs to be fine-tuned for next year. Everyone is generally pleased, and the renewed focus on trans women's needs and overturning the policy was a success. There are concerns about how white Camp Trans is, but no one is naive about seeking out token people of color to make themselves feel better. Instead, a resolution is made to make the event itself more welcoming to people of color, in hopes that the gathering will organically diversify. Geyl suggests travel scholarships for transpeople who want to come but can't afford the time off work or the travel expenses to the Middle of Nowhere, Michigan. People are happy about trans women being in charge, happy that there was essentially no rain in a region known for violent summer thunderstorms, and want greater accountability from women who say they are organizing within the festival gates. There will be greater fundraising this coming year, though Camp Trans did come out ahead by five hundred dollars. Incredible, really, since at the start of the week ziplock baggies had been duct-taped inside the portos asking for spare change each time you took a whiz. It cost the camp eighty dollars each time those monsters got cleaned.

Over at the welcome tent a few ladies from the festival have stolled in. They're older, in their fifties perhaps, from Utah. Probably they live for the festival and have never spoken to a transsexual in their lives, but they've come over, minds open, "to see what everybody's all 'ugh' about." Maybe because everyone at the welcome station is so burned-out on this, the last day, or maybe because I'm sitting closest to the two women, I wind up answering some of their questions, or rather countering their concerns. Their concerns are the usual ones: penises and girlhoods. So many women have been traumatized by a penis, is it really fair to force them to glimpse one at their annual retreat? I tell them that women need to find a way to heal from their abuse without displacing responsibility for it onto the bodies of trans women, who are also likely to have been abused. That a roving, detached penis didn't abuse anyone, but men with penises did, and those men are not these women. I tell them that trans women did in fact have girlhoods, girlhoods as rough and confusing as any girl's. One tiny conversation and I'm drained and frustrated. And this isn't even my life.

Everyone is called to help dismantle what's still standing of Camp Trans. Intimidated by the architecture of the tents and lean-tos that need to be torn down, I busy myself gently untying the neon plastic ribbons that have been knotted, for some reason, around a rusting cage that, for some reason, contains a stunted apple tree. Perhaps there's a hornets' nest in the crook of its branches. A large swath of our field has been roped off all week with that same neon plastic, to keep everyone away from a bur-rowing hornet encampment. That's being torn down now as well. I grab a trash bag and roam around the land, collecting debris. Part of what makes the Michigan Womyn's Music Festival is the land it takes place on. The trees are tall and cool; there's much grass and twining paths; the air smells fresh: it's nature, the real deal. And the women love it and care for it like a living thing, which it is. I try to arrange a similar mind-set about cleaning up Camp Trans, but I don't feel connected to this rather lousy scrap of national forest. Maybe if the event keeps occurring here for twenty-eight years it will become imbued with the specialness and familiarity that haunts the woods across the road. I snatch the torn corner of a bag of Chex Mix from the ground, some empty water jugs, balls of toilet paper, bits of shredded trash bag that blew off one of the Fat-tastics' pom-poms. I pull from the ground tiki torches that had been guiding nighttime revelers to the Porta-Potties all week. I leave to decompose back into the land some carrots, some tofu dogs, some onion skins. There are bullet casings and smashed clay pigeons scattered throughout the weeds, left behind by whoever was here last.

Over by the portos is a structure made of tarps that all week-end I'd thought was someone's wicked punk-rock campsite. Tarps spray-painted with anti-policy slogans, tied and duct-taped to stakes driven into the ground. I'd had a brief fantasy that it was Geyl's squat-like queendom. But as I pass it, Chris sticks his head out from the plastic, and asks, "Did you know there was a shower here?!" He is delighted. The shower is a little pump with a thin hose attached; it looks like the pesticide tank an exterminator lugs around. You pump the top like a keg, click a switch at the end of the hose, and a fine stream of water mists all around you. It looks like a feeble shower, but a great way to cool off. Later I'll help Geyl and a person named Cassidy—butch girl? genderqueer?—tear the whole thing down, and have great fun squirting myself with all the leftover water in the little tank. I pull stakes from the ground and untangle knots of rope, listening to Cassidy tell the story of Blane, the man who rents out the portos we've been peeing in. Blane lives on five hundred acres of land and raises beefalo. Beefalos are a crossbreed of cows and buffalos, and Blane is proud that he has been able to breed out their horns. Beefalo meat is lower in cholesterol then regular beef, and after his doctor warned him that his was shooting dangerously high, he took to farming the animals. He feeds them corn that he also grows on his land, and the corn is grown in compost made from the slurry in the Porta-Potties. All of our crap will be distributed throughout a nearby cornfield. It's incredible, slightly sickening.

"The birds of prey have come for us," Geyl says, pointing a long finger up to the sky, where some large birds are indeed circling. I've been trying to find a place to sit and read, but every patch of shade I see is inhabited either by creepy daddy longlegs or by intimidating cliques of remaining campers. There's a girl doing yoga in a growth of weeds; her legs become visible, then her butt, her head, her legs. A car is flung open—all doors, the trunk— and people load their belongings. X's "White Girl" leaks from the stereo, soon to be overpowered by a car blaring Tiffany. I settle down in what's left of the dismantled welcome station and try to read, but I'm distracted by the heat, the mosquitos, the loud sex noises howling out from the woods in front of me.

I hitch a ride into nearby Hart with a boy named Billy. Billy drives his big red truck into Hart every day, three or four times, to dump trash, redeem bottles, and fetch more water. It seems nuts that this duty has fallen solely on his shoulders, but he's a trooper about it. Especially considering how trashed the bed of the truck has become—gummy with spilled booze and moldy produce—and that he's been living in that same truck bed for the past seven months, traveling around the country. A lot of the campers at Camp Trans are part of what I've heard referred to as "travel culture" and "youth travel culture." The anarchist hitchhiker, or the many groups of people who are not going home from here but traveling onward to distant cities—New York, Chicago. Lots of people are heading to Tennessee, where a similar, though less politically charged event will be taking place on a patch of land owned and inhabited by a group of pagan gay guys known as the Radical Faeries. Billy pulls in behind the nearest gas station and I help him dump clanking bags of unredeemable glass and wobbly boxes heaped with vegetables gone bad. He grabs a bottle of whiskey, sucks the dregs, and tosses it empty into the Dumpster. Next Billy dumps me at a Mobil station, while he fetches water, so I can call my boyfriend from a pay phone and grab some snacks. After a few days of nothing but tasteless nutrition bars, dry tuna, and cold canned chili, the weirdest snacks look appetizing. I buy a giant bottle of Coke, a pack of Pop-Tarts, and a bag of potato chips with a mysterious flavor—Mustard and Onion "Coney" Chips, the bag proclaims. They taste just like hot dogs.

Next is Dave's Party Store, where an affable, Pauley Shore–ish dude hands over twenty-five dollars in exchange for a worn trash bag of sludgy bottles, and a literally rednecked white guy tells the cashier, in deep Ebonics, that he's going to join the traveling carnival. "That sounds like a great place for you," the woman says drily. Back in the truck we listen to Lil' Kim and cruise to Camp Trans, past the music festival and its vast parking lot still stuffed with cars. There's Blane the Porta-Pottie guy, vacuuming the ultimate grossness out from the portos, then loading the empty toilets onto his truck and driving them away. Now we'll all be peeing on trees. I use my rusty can-opener to peel the lid off another can of vegetarian chili and wander over to Chris's van. I find him inside, smoking pot with Andrew, a twenty-year-old trannyboy whose legend I'd already heard from Geyl, last night at the dance. How he'd never met another tranny, ever, until arriving at Camp Trans yesterday. How he learned he was trans from watching the film *Boys Don't Cry*, in which the actress Hilary Swank (who later won an Oscar for her performance) portrayed the young trans man Brandon Teena, who was raped, then murdered when the boys he'd been hanging out with learned of his situation. Andrew lives in Lansing and caught a ride down to Camp Trans—which he'd just found out about—from a couple of anti–Camp Trans ladies on their way to the festival. They'd already stopped by earlier, to curtly inform him that they were staying at their festival a little longer, to hang out and catch the last concerts. "I don't want to go back with them at all," Andrew says, and soon he has arranged to catch a ride home with the nomadic Chris, who plans to continue meandering through the country in his surfer van for a few more months. Andrew is cute: He's got the buzz cut of a young recruit and eyes that shift icily between the palest blue and green. He is stroking the soft skin on his jaw tenderly. "Do I have a bruise?" he asks, half to pose an honest question and half to brag. I don't see any marks, but soon we're hearing about the wrestling match he was part of last night. He tells us how someone walked right up to him and said, "Can I kiss you?" He'd never been approached so bluntly by an admirer, and he's surprised that it didn't make him feel weird, threatened, or unsafe. He felt like he could say a friendly no and the person would have backed off. But since he felt so safe he said yes. Andrew has a girlfriend who is on her own vacation, and who, from the sound of it, is familiar with the heightened sex vibes of queer gatherings. When she heard he was off to Camp Trans, she said, "Don't even try to be monogamous, you'll be miserable." What a great girlfriend, I compliment, impressed. Andrew is satisfied with last night's kisses and wrestling, and is anxious to get back to Lansing and be with his very modern paramour.

ADVENTURE

Jess is complaining that she needs an adventure on this, the last night of Camp Trans, when all who remain are among the camp's core organizers (Sadie's fled back to D.C.), a few people procrastinating their long drives home, Chris, and me. I have found an adventure, but Jess does not approve. In fact, Camp Trans does not approve. It is its policy to ask its campers to please not sneak into the Michigan Womyn's Music Festival, but it is this that I am setting out to do. To be fair, it's not exactly sneaking. Some exiting festies tore their rubbery blue bracelets from their wrists and gave them away. I've got one, and so does Calwell. Geyl has one, handed over to her by a woman who tearfully said, "You deserve to be in there." True enough, but Geyl isn't going to risk it. She gives the bracelet to a girl named Kelly, whose T-shirt reads KING SHIT OF FUCK MOUNTAIN. "We really don't want anyone going over there," Jess says earnestly. She is wearing a black slip and has a fake blue rose in her orange bob. Last year Camp Trans was accused of allowing, if not encouraging, bunches of campers to sneak into the gates. MWMF insist this is true because the amount of food eaten was higher than it should have been. "I don't know why they just didn't figure people were eating a lot," Jess shrugs. So far, this year, no one has sneaked over. Since we plan to do nothing but stroll through the woods, and maybe find a party rumored to be going on at "the dump," it doesn't seem like a drag on anyone's resources. Off we go.

Excerpt from "Welcome to the Festival!":

> Those Security Gals: The womyn in tasteful orange vests are here to answer questions, keep things orderly and promote safety. Unfortunately, it has also become an increasing part of their job to deal with the girls who decide to try to sneak into the Festival in various places along the route. Please help in their effort to ensure everyone takes that basic first step and purchases a ticket to the festival.

We enter the festival perimeter by strolling through an unmanned (unwomanned?) checkpoint. The lean-to is there; the

189

chair is draped with a security vest, but no worker. Calwell especially likes feeling that we are being sneaky, even though we've got
the bracelets. Kelly is hoping to stay the night, maybe find a lady
with a tent to get lucky in. Calwell wants to find the party at the
dump, and I just want something to do. So we look for the dump.
We do not find it. We find, instead, the RV campsite, where bunches
of women are hanging out in luxury: Winnebagos and campers,
patios set up with tables and mosquito netting. Someone even
brought a birdcage containing a live bird. Other women have set
up mannequins on their front lawns, or strung Christmas lights
over their vehicles. No one is naked, but some women are topless.
Hard as it is for some, the campers at Camp Trans are required to
cover nipples and pubic hair at all times, the land being national
forest and all. Which means lots of topless people with patches of
duct tape—ow!—slapped on their nipples. We find the acoustic
stage quite by accident. It is surrounded by hundreds of women,
lined up on the cool grass before an elegant wood stage on which
there's a white grand piano and an empty set of chairs. It feels so
strange to be on the inside of this compound we've been locked in
opposition against all week. It feels a little scary actually—which is
odd, because I've been on this land before, and I don't really believe
anything will happen to us, even if someone found out we half-
sneaked in. It's hard not to have an affection for these women,
comfortable, all hanging out with each other on a hillside. It's also
hard not to be wary of them, to feel conflicted. I think of Geyl,
Sadie, Carolyn, all the trans women I've met this weekend. You can
call it unjust that they can't come in, call it wrong, unfair, but
really more than anything it just seems absurd. We march out of the
acoustic stage area and down a few roads. We get royally lost in the
woods, the sky darkening around us. Good thing I brought my
trusty flashlight. The three of us crunch along paths that wind
through real wilderness, and we find ourselves in the infamous
Twilight Zone, where the women camp who practice SM sex. We
pass a campsite that is a collection of tarps stretched out and tied
together, enclosing a large area. I can see a campfire burning inside

the plastic barrier, a butch woman moving around, a bunch of chains rigged up to a tree. But that's all. It wasn't that long ago that the SM women weren't welcome at MWMF. Their presence was protested, boycotted, until this space on the outskirts of the festival was created for them so they could whip each other in peace without "triggering" the women who feel like it's just more of the patriarchy seeping in. The SM controversy perhaps peaked when the dyke punk band Tribe 8 were invited to play and were picketed by women holding signs accusing the performers of everything from domestic abuse to violence against children. I've heard a lot of people suggest that trans women be allowed to camp here, among the bondage practitioners and heavy partiers. At least they'd be inside the gates, but what if a trans woman doesn't want to camp amid such heavy sex play? I camped in the Twilight Zone my first year at the festival, and, like those around me, was drunk pretty much round the clock. There was puke in our neighboring bushes; beer cans, cigarette butts, and latex sex supplies littered the grass outside our tents; and we almost got kicked out for lighting fireworks. More than once, while stumbling around in search of a place to pee, I walked smack into the middle of pretty intense sex scenes. And each morning we were all awakened by the exaggerated sex cries of a woman camped down the path. To require anyone to camp in such an environment seems downright abusive.

It's calming to be away from Camp Trans. To be in such a political, tense environment for an extended period of time does some wear and tear on your head. Me and Calwell talk about being afraid of being judged, feeling like you could say the wrong thing and wind up ostracized and alienated. It's kept him quieter than normal. Same for me. I'd Like A Safe Space To Fuck Up, I say, and we laugh. A space where everyone recognizes that everyone is trying their best, imperfectly struggling, human. But perhaps that's not possible. Activism is, famously, "by any means necessary." People on both sides of this debate like to compare their stance to the struggle against racism, but it is true that, camping at Camp Trans these few days, I feel like I'm in the midst of the first swell of a new civil rights movement.

THE FIRE, LAST TIME

Back at Camp Trans the final campfire roars, with Cassidy—somehow an expert on the various ways wood can grow—strategically loading branches into the flames. Chris is burning marshmallows on a long stick, Simon is shaving pieces of potato and garlic into an aluminum foil pouch to be roasted. Someone passes around cold pizza, someone else passes around a bottle of Boone's Farm. It's the first time alcohol has been visible all week, though many revelers have been visibly under its influence. Another of the national forest laws. Max, a trans man who is part of the posse responsible for reviving Camp Trans in 1999, is telling the story of the lesbian curse. Actually, he's acting it out with the help of others who stand in as various characters—trans campers and angry lesbians, mostly. Geyl acts as "rain," hovering over them and flicking her fingers. It is the story of how Max awoke in his tent to find a coven of festie women flashing mirrors at their campsite. They were angry witches putting a spell on Camp Trans, and they did succeed in scaring the crap out of Max. Simon tells a story of his first Camp Trans experience, and the action he undertook with a trans man named Tony, a sixteen-year-old trans girl named Cat, and the transsexual author and activist Riki Anne Wilchins.

SIMON'S FIRST FESTIVAL

"First Tony went on the land, to put the womyn-born-womyn-only policy to the test. He identified as a post-op trans man, with bottom surgery (I forget the kind). He was saying that his dick was made out of the skin on his arm—I think that's a rhinoplasty?—anyway. He said, 'Hey, if my trans women friends are still men because they were assigned male at birth, then I must still be a woman.' So he went into the fest and took a shower. He asked consent of the women showering, telling them what kind of body he had. They said OK, but because the showers were public, new folks came in and freaked. By the time the ticket-buying action happened the next morning, the rumor was that something like six non-op trans women flashed their erect penises at the girls' camp. Gross, eh?

"The ticket-buying action: At noon on Saturday, Riki led a ticket-buying action at the fest. A bunch of the avengers [the Lesbian Avengers are a lesbian direct-action group that has prioritized fighting for the rights of trans women], myself included, bought tickets to the fest. The young trans woman who was with us also bought a ticket, though at the time she could have been 'read' other than a womyn-born-womyn. This was a great victory for us and there were certainly tears. Then the trouble began. A woman started walking in front of us, shouting, 'Man on the Land!'

"We did have some support from festie-goers who walked with us. We got to the main area, and it was very overwhelming. We were asked if we wanted to have a mediated discussion in the kitchen tent. Before that discussion, women were just coming at us from all over, some to be supportive, some to yell at us, and some to stare. There was very little middle ground, and it was very hostile. So we started this 'mediated' discussion and the setup was such: We (us avengers, maybe four of us, and Riki) were sitting on folding tables in the front, while seven rows of angry lesbians yelled at us, audience-style. I kid you not. People called us rapists, woman-haters, said we were destroying their space by just walking on it, that we had no respect for women, that we had no respect for rape survivors, etc. Three hours this lasted, and the mediation was so one-sided we didn't get out of there with any confidence that anyone heard what we had to say. That was my first festival."

I don't want to leave the circle, 'cause I know this is it. In the morning I will ride into Grand Rapids with a girl named Katina, a festie-goer who has spent basically all of her time over at Camp Trans, much to the dismay of the girls she's camping with. "You know how every time you leave Michigan, you think, I'm coming back next year?" she asks. "Well, this year it wasn't like that. I know

I can't come back next year." Katina's got hair that's bound up in bunches of braids, the ends secured with brightly colored elastics in different colors. She lives and works in Brooklyn, where she supplements her income selling Strawberry Shortcake dolls on eBay. Her trick is to search for the dolls right there on eBay, but to search for sellers who have misspelled the name of the toys, therefore getting fewer bids and selling their wares cheaper. After securing the dolls, Katina puts them back up on the site, with the proper spelling, and doubles her money. She's a smart cookie. Camp Trans is lucky to have her. All week she's been offering her cell phone, offering hummus and wine, and now she's driving me to the airport. I give her a big hug as I climb out of her car. We used to see each other at MWMF, hug each other good-bye, say See You Next Year. And now we say it again. ★

FRANKLIN BRUNO

IN PRAISE OF
TERMITES

DISCUSSED: *Labyrinthine Criticism, William Powell's Nose, Dog-piled
Edge-of-Grammar Transitionless Writing, Contemptuous Scare-Quoting
(and Capitalization), Lester Bangs, Wittgenstein, Elbowy Directors,
Doughnut Holes, Snake Diets, La Chinoise, Dancing Frogs
and Utter Futility, Mole People, Humanism*

At a 2001 panel on painter and film critic Manny
Farber, held at the New School for Social
Research and later transcribed in *Artforum,* Greil
Marcus had this to say about a passage from
Farber's *Negative Space*:

...Farber is complaining about some movie, and he says, "It isn't
sustained." Then there's a parenthetical that says, "But how many
movies since *Musketeers of Pig Alley* have been sustained?" What was
really scary to me about this line, and it's scary today, is that never
having seen *Musketeers of Pig Alley,* I didn't know if this was a joke,
or if, in fact, it's the only movie in eighty years that's been sustained.
I still don't know. So you can dive into this book, and, if you are like
me, you will never get out.

195

Marcus's enthusiasm, and his vertigo, will be familiar to readers for whom Farber's work is a touchstone. Blurbs aren't everything, but those on the expanded edition of *Negative Space,* published by Da Capo Press in 1998, suggest that the list of Farber's admirers is long, impressive, and heterogeneous. Who else could draw praise from Peter Bogdanovich and Jonas Mekas, *Newsweek*'s Jack Kroll and *October*'s Annette Michelson, Pauline Kael and Susan Sontag? Perhaps not all of these figures feel the book's pull as strongly as Marcus—but others do. As another New School panelist, *Salon* editor Stephanie Zacharek, put it, "I sometimes want to shake it or throw it against the wall, but I always want it close by."

Farber's writing career began in 1942 at the *New Republic,* where he succeeded Otis Ferguson as the magazine's regular movie reviewer. Stints followed at the *Nation* (after the death of friend and rival James Agee), the *New Leader,* and, decades later, *Artforum*; other work ran in less august periodicals, such as the forgotten *Esquire* knockoff *Cavalier. Negative Space* first appeared (from Prager) in 1971, as carefully winnowed as a volume of selected poems, favoring think pieces over weekly reviewing. (Farber's uncollected writing, including his pieces not even nominally about film, is forthcoming in a volume edited by Robert Polito.) The earliest inclusion is a 1943 defense of Chuck Jones cartoons; aside from an introduction, the latest are from 1969, on Samuel Fuller and that year's New York Film Festival. The arrangement is chronological, except when it isn't. The expanded edition, currently in print, adds seven pieces coauthored by fellow painter and wife Patricia Patterson in the 1970s, a three-way interview with Richard Thomson from 1977, a new preface by Robert Walsh, and a helpful index.[1]

Any edition—there is also *Movies,* an ugly but complete reprint of the 1971 edition—is worth celebrating for the same reasons as any collection of "practical criticism" that displays flair

---

[1] The shaded article heads on the newly included material, obviously designed at a later date, don't quite match the more distinctively marqueelike ones on the pages reshot from the older edition. This only bothers me because I imagine it bothering the detail-minded author.

and insight over an extended period: Jonathan Gold's *Counter Intelligence,* Robert Christgau's *Consumer Guides, The Complete Prose of Marianne Moore.* (Not to mention the collected film writing of Kael, Andrew Sarris, Renata Adler, Agee, and Ferguson.) But the book's singularity is not explained by the jar-of-cashews addictiveness common to its genre. None of the books just mentioned is merely a colloquy of freestanding aesthetic judgments; each determines a sensibility, if not a theory. But Farber's seems uniquely tensed between the particular and the general, between the sense that the object of critical attention is being wrestled with in all its specificity and the impression that one is about to receive some broader enlightenment. This never happens; or, when it does, the illumination is partial, and comes from unexpected angles. More often, pinpoint observations and word-by-word stylistic decisions provoke questions that repeated readings deepen: just what is it for a film to be sustained?

If there were a textbook on *Negative Space,* it would read: "Manny Farber's film writing has several distinctive features, the three most important being: (1) It is more concerned with form and composition than with performance, narrative, or theme; (2) it is most responsive to unpretentious B-film craftsmen (Samuel Fuller, Anthony Mann) and exceedingly pretentious 'structuralist' technicians (Chantal Ackerman, Michael Snow); (3) it is written in an irreverent style that shuns journalistic blandness and academic cant alike."

This capsule description shows why there is no such textbook. First, Farber's formalism is neither as abstract nor as single-minded as (2) suggests. He's terrific on actors' bodies: "[William] Powell, an artist in dreadful films, would first use his satchel underchin to pull the dialogue into the image, then punctuate with his nose the stops for each chin movement." He's equally adept at pointing out how faulty plot construction can fail a movie: "It is inconceivable that this high-glossed, ultrasophisticated drama [*Sweet Smell of Success*] hinges on a dope-planting act in a nightclub that is carried out with as little difficulty as water finding its way through a sieve." Later pieces, especially those also signed by Patterson, show heightened concern with what literary or politically minded readers are pleased to call a film's content. From "The Power and the Gory," their split decision on Scorsese's magnum opus: "What's really disgusting about *Taxi Driver* is not the multi-faced loner but the endless propaganda about the magic of guns."

None of which changes the fact that all Farber's writing is deeply informed by his parallel—in fact, much longer—career as a visual artist. His visual descriptions are bracingly acute. On the framing typical of late-sixties art-house cinema: "Antonioni must have invented it: the human future as an island silhouetted against a sharp drop of unsympathetic scenery. There are two or three delineated elements, none of which act as support for the other." His richest essays switch from film to painting and back as though it were beyond argument that art is art is art. (Sportswriting, jazz, and carpentry are also touched on, the last having been Farber's day job for many of his writing years; prose fiction and staged drama, hardly ever.)

Farber's best-known paintings, in turn, allude to favored films and directors, though not by aping their visual styles. A first-generation abstract expressionist who showed alongside Franz Kline and Philip Guston at Peggy Guggenheim's Art of This Century gallery, he turned to representation in the 1970s, around the same time he stopped publishing, and has never looked back; at eighty-five, he now paints full-time. But stating that Farber's painting and criticism are "deeply informed" by each other is more textbook boilerplate. Attending to About Face, a major (seventy-plus works) retrospective that originated at San Diego's Museum of Contemporary of Art, may help us do better. The show traveled to the Austin Museum of Art, and is on view at New York's P.S. 1 until mid-January 2005. (We'll get there, but not for a while.)

The bit of cinephilic erudition Marcus quotes is not entirely representative of Farber's method. In a 1999 interview with Edward Crouse, he admits (or boasts), "I never saw more than two or three movies a week, ever," far fewer than Agee, Kael, or Sarris, never mind the monomaniacs at *Cahiers du Cinema.* If Farber's judgments are forceful, even intimidating, it's not because he's seen more than you have, but because he's looked harder. The *Musketeers* passage, which occurs midway through a deflation of *Strangers on a Train,* is worth setting down in full:

> Nothing, even the pristine engineering of the bashful, uncomplain-ing Master, is sustained here (how many movies since *Musketeers of Pig Alley* have been sustained?). Walker's contaminated elegance, which suggests Nero Wolfe's classy, intricate hedonism, with om-elettes in a brownstone, dissolves into momma's boy brocade. Along-side a pretty block of husband-wife bickering in a record shop, its unusual use of glass partitions, sexual confidence and bitchiness in a girl with glasses, there are literally acres of scenes in elegant homes and tennis stadiums which could be used to stuff pillows if there were that many pillows in the world.

The argument is direct: despite his reputed precision, Hitchcock can't control the best elements of his film. What is more important is the detail of the examples, and the techniques with which they are rendered. The dog-piled, edge-of-grammar quality, achieved partly by the removal of transitions. The references to pop-cultural flotsam (*Musketeers,* Nero Wolfe) barely on most readers' radars, even at the time of writing; elsewhere, Farber praises Agee's similar facility with "stray coupons." The substitution of a spatial relation ("alongside") for an expected temporal one ("after"). The repeti-tion of a word ("pillow") as a design element on the page.

Other key strategies:

Get-it-over-with plot summaries: "*The Fox* (bleak outlands, two forbiddingly lonely women trying hopelessly to make a go of a chicken farm, an extremely willful hunter-soldier wants the stranger of the two girls) is…"

Scare-quoting (and capitalization) at its most contemptuous: "For this reason, many people, including the critics of *The New Yorker* and *Time,* think the movies are full of 'ideas'—'disturbing,' 'offbeat,' and even 'three-dimensional.'"

Metaphorical figures more vivid in their own right than as terms in a comparison: Agee makes clichés "sparkle like pennies lost in a Bendix"; an unnamed actor "shuffles around downtown like a coat sleeve looking for an arm to stick in itself."

Then there are the puns, often redundant with their surroundings. The coinages "Monica Unvital" and "Jeanne Morose" only reinforce a fuller critique of Antonioni's heroines of existential ennui. Cruelest is his treatment of British kitchen-sink queen Rita Tushingham (perhaps best known to many present readers as the cover star of the Smiths' single "Hand in Glove"). Like a schoolyard bully, he mocks her name repeatedly—"Tushless situation," "the Tush treatment"—throughout a decimation of her acting called, I'm afraid, "Pish-Tush." Even this cheapo stuff is part of the warp and woof of Farber's maximum-thread-count prose.

Throughout *Negative Space,* Farber observes exactly one (pre-New) journalistic convention. He shuns the first person, with telling exceptions—Jean-Luc Godard "is the filmmaker that most consistently makes me feel like a stupid ass"—and never enters a piece via personal anecdote. As Polito notes in his catalog essay for *About Face,* the sole mention of Farber's birthplace is just one more stray coupon: the main set of Howard Hawks's *Only Angels Have Wings* "might be good for a Douglas, Arizona, high-school production." (Farber's paintings display a stronger autobiographical impulse.)

In playing down the personal, he's miles away from Lester Bangs, his nearest equivalent in rock criticism. As Howard Hampton noted in "Let Us Now Kill White Elephants" (*The Believer,* September 2003), neither is a hypester or a flack, and both excel at arguing themselves past received positions. (Bangs's love-hate relationship with Lou Reed is a more tortured version of Farber's with Godard.) But if Farber ever staggered home from the Thalia vomiting Seconal before phoning his exes, we're not in on it, and not merely because the *New Leader* wasn't *Creem.* His language constantly calls attention to itself, but hardly ever to Manny Farber. It isn't that his writing pretends to objectivity; it's just that, in the formulation "*my* response to *this movie*," the emphasis falls squarely upon the second term. Farber wrote as he paints: as a modernist, with all the self-consciousness about the medium that label implies, but one whose concern with his chosen subject matter is no less serious than his interest in his own materials and methods.

Farber's impolitic tone has also led to the misconception that his writing is antitheoretical or, worse, anti-intellectual. Anti-*academic*, perhaps: no one is likely to mistake *Negative Space* for a scholarly work. The bulk of its content was written for a general readership, long before the disciplinary rise of film studies. Even in the 1970s, the jargon of the field is notably absent: I count one *mise-en-scène* and zero *suture*s. He rarely pauses to acknowledge that anyone had previously thought or written compellingly about movies, with his meta-review of *Agee on Film* and a swipe at high-toned populist Gilbert Seldes being notable exceptions. "The Subverters," Farber's 1966 *Artforum* debut, is patently his entry into the then-contemporary mêlée over the merits of the auteur theory: "One of the joys in moviegoing is worrying over the fact that what is referred to as Hawks might be [screenwriter] Jules Furthman, that behind the Godard film is the looming shape of [cinematographer] Raoul Coutard." (The notion that "worrying" is a "joy" is characteristic.) But it's only clear that Farber is siding, more or less, with Kael (and André Bazin) against Sarris (and François Truffaut) to readers who know that the battle is joined; none are named in the text.

In this respect, *Negative Space* resembles Wittgenstein's *Philosophical Investigations*—another curiously organized work, short on citations and professionalized vocabulary, from which some readers never escape. Wittgenstein had reasons of his own to cover his tracks, one being that his primary philosophical adversaries were those who made a dogma of his own earlier work. In Farber's case, though, there are indications that he might have written more systematically—not, one imagines, less vividly—under different circumstances. In the book's introduction, he grouses that "newspaper editors believe readers die like flies at the sight of

aesthetic terminology." Having any use for such terminology—
even if he has to invent it himself—is one thing that distinguishes
Farber from Kael, with her notorious inquiry "Is There a Cure
for Film Theory?" For all Farber's specificity, he is also (again like
Wittgenstein) a not-so-secret theory-builder whose biggest ideas
peek out from behind or around accumulations of details.

Getting down to cases: "Termite Art vs. White Elephant Art," published in 1966 in the relatively specialized *Film Culture,* is Farber's
most puzzled-over piece, for reasons we'll soon discover. As polemic, the essay opens straightforwardly, conducting a two-pronged
attack on a kind of cinematic "masterpiece" that strives to gather
reflected glory from European high-art models. One prong is sociological: the "gilt culture" aspirations of current filmmakers are
traced to their need to be viewed as great artists. (Another argument against the auteur theory is implicit: some directors believed
it, to the detriment of their practice.) The other prong is formal or
compositional, and not confined to movies. Farber argues that Cézanne's unfinished works, shorn of the burden of doing something
brilliant, or even professional, with every inch of space, are his most
exciting. He then accuses contemporaries "from Motherwell to
Warhol" of treating "art as an expensive hunk of well-regulated
area" before locating the same tendency in directors as different as
Antonioni, Truffaut, and Tony Richardson.

Similar negative judgments were already present in 1957's
"The Gimp" and 1962's "Hard-Sell Cinema": movies are at their
worst when they strain for effect, as though the director were
elbowing you to notice every cleverly chosen POV and camera
move. This also applies to psychology and plotting: in certain
"beautifully controlled Freud-Marx epics, the only things that
really move are the tricks and symbols." All these essays, "Termite
Art" included, can also be read as contributions to the culture-
versus-kitsch debates that centered, in their day, around Dwight
Macdonald and Clement Greenberg. As ever, our man's position is

tricky: he's not anti-pop, decidedly not anti-art, and nearly always more concerned with creators than audiences.

Against elephant art—"the iceberg film full of hidden meanings"—Farber sets termite art, or, at one point, "termite-tapeworm-fungus-moss art." Such work, in whatever medium, "feels its way through walls of particularization, with no sign that the artist has any object in mind other than eating away the immediate boundaries of his art, and turning these boundaries into conditions of the next achievement." Examples include John Wayne's "hoboish" performance in *The Man Who Shot Liberty Valance,* the "sober fact-pointing" of Raymond Chandler's letters (not his novels?), and exactly one scene in a Rod Serling's *Requiem for a Heavyweight.* Most of Farber's praise is reserved for parts or elements, rather than whole works; Kurosawa's *Ikiru* is the only film singled out, in the essay's abrupt closing paragraph, as entirely "buglike."

The termite/elephant distinction, then, is in part Farber's colorful way of expressing a preference for the unassuming over the grandiose, or for the human-scaled over the epic—but only in part. When it comes time to elaborate on individual films, it's remarkably difficult to unravel just what Farber takes to be the virtues and vices of, say, *Jules et Jim,* and the final diagnosis of the "flying out effect" of Truffaut's work is mystifying, an impressionistic image unmoored from the original distinction: "As the spectator leans forward to grab the film, it disappears like a released kite." This is an indictment of some sort, but not one supported by the established (so we thought) terms of debate.

The titular notion of "negative space," a phrase that appears only in the book's openly theoretical introduction, is just as slippery. After that comment about editors and flies, Farber plunges ahead in a mock-pedagogical vein—the one I swiped some paragraphs earlier:

> If there were a textbook on film space, it would read: "There are
> several types of movie space, the three most important being: (1) the

field of the screen, (2) the psychological space of the actor, and (3) the area of experience and geography that the film covers."

Types (1) and (3) involve space in a literal sense. The latter concerns what is represented; the former, how. Type (2) is where the trouble starts: no longer Morose, Jeanne Moreau "works in a large space, which becomes empty as she devastates it with scorn," while performers like Jane Fonda control an area that "extends about six inches to any side of their bodies, and anything else is uncontrollable, unattainable, and therefore hardly concerns them." He's not describing the size of an image, or even the relative scale of a presence or gesture within it, but something balanced on a thin edge between the physical and the psychological. The pages that follow scramble the picture further: while the third type of space "controls everything else—acting, pace, costume," all three interact in multifarious ways. In decades past, Farber railed against anything that smacked of symbolism (those "Freud-Marx" epics), but now he calls Orson Welles's use of space in *Touch of Evil* "allegorical," and not perjoratively.

Adding "negative" to "space" does not simplify matters. In any graphic (or photographic) arts course, you'll learn a neat definition of "negative space." It is the space that is not your subject; well-used, it has a compositional relevance of its own. Draw a doughnut. The region between the doughnut and the edges of the paper (the "contour") is negative space; so is the hole. Contrast this with one of Farber's attempts—there are several—to delineate the notion: "Negative space assumes the director testing himself as an intelligence against what appears on screen, so that there is a murmur of poetic action enlarging the terrain of the film, giving the scene an extra-objective breadth."

One thing is clear: we're not just talking doughnut holes here. Despite the straightforward example of "huge-seeming" figures in a glacial landscape (from *Alexander Nevsky*), formal, narrative, and imaginative elements are all in play. We're out of the realm of treating the screen as an easel, and into—what? No one doubts that all the features discussed, however categorized, contribute to a film's final effect. But if some kinds of space, negative or otherwise, are pictorial, others psychological, still others "allegorical," why call them all *space*?

Farber, I think, accepts the "flying out effect" of his own categories; he may even intend it. One suspects that he doesn't especially *like* the idea that his notions may be incommunicable; hence, his incessant attempts to exemplify and support them. But as he does, the framework he began with changes from an "either" or into a "well-and-but-yet," with the result that the object of criticism also looks more interesting that it did originally. Or, as he says in the interview that ends the 1998 edition of the book: "the thing becomes filigreed."

The introduction to *Negative Space* reaches another important conclusion. In 1960s film, Farber argues, "the illustrative naturalism that serviced Keaton's *Navigator* through Hawks's *Red River* simply broke apart." For decades the codes of framing, lighting, and editing that governed what film theorists usually dub "Classical Hollywood Cinema" were a spatial lingua franca. At his '40s–'50s tetchiest, Farber sometimes seems to be handing out penalty cards for overly conscious deviations from these norms. But after Godard, Pasolini, a reassessed Antonioni, the Tower of Babel has fallen. Henceforth, space is always a problem, one that every director—every film—is obliged to solve anew.

The directorial individualism with which Farber makes peace has implications for his writing as well. Now that "the space in film has been wildly and ingeniously singularized… it doesn't seem right that the areas for criticism should be given over so completely to measuring." That is: once, movies could be rated in accordance to some standard, established partly by reference to other movies; now that their strategies are incommensurable— "singularized"—the up-or-down assessments of the journalistic review are no longer adequate, or even meaningful. The same thought lies behind Farber's dismissal of "evaluation," again from the closing interview: "It's a derelict appendage of criticism."

Farber doesn't quit publishing immediately after making these remarks. But the introduction's final sentence, which returns to the termite/elephant distinction, gets at both the necessity of saying something and the increasing difficulty of saying anything:

> ...all the directors I like—Fuller's art brut styling; Chuck Jones's Roadrunners; the inclement charm Godard gets with drizzly weather, the Paris outskirts, and three nuts scurrying around the same overcast Band of Outsiders terrain—are in the termite range, and no one speaks about them for the qualities I like.

Farber's painting over the thirty-odd years since these passages were written should not be seen solely as a running illustration (or defense) of his criticism. But the degree to which he transfers energies and concerns from one medium to another is hard to miss.[2] The modestly scaled "Auteur Series" of 1976–78 is not the first figurative work Farber exhibited—arrangements of musty office supplies and forgotten concession-stand treats date from 1973—but these are his first paintings to reference particular films. In *Preston Sturges* (1976), which initiates the series, there's "negative space" aplenty, in the textbook sense of absence. The center of the picture is empty save for morsels broken off of the Tootsie Rolls that occupy the painting's rightmost edge. (Their wrappers poke up from the bottom of the frame.) The composition, a skewed frame around a void, makes no attempt to evoke Sturges's antic pace.

Instead, Farber simply writes his subject into the painting. Dominating its upper third, a yellow notepad reads, in critic-in-the-dark scrawl, "feeding four flies, a glass of milk, and one piece of white bread to a snake." This phrase describes the diet of the specimen

---

[2] Beyond the catalog essays for *About Face,* I recommend earlier accounts of the connection between Farber's bodies of work, one by Kevin Parker, one by Patrick Amos and Jean-Pierre Gorin, both in the catalog for a smaller retrospective (1985-86) at Los Angeles's MOCA. I regret that space forbids a discussion of Farber's nonfigurative painting.

kept by Charles "Hopsy" Pike (Henry Fonda) in Sturges's *The Lady Eve*. It is a close paraphrase of dialogue that occurs more than once in the film, but it is an almost-exact quote—originally, the snake was "rich, pampered"—from Farber's own 1954 essay on Sturges (co-written with one W. S. Poster, about whom I have discovered nothing). This clue resolves much of the surrounding imagery. A packet of pipe tobacco bears the image of an ocean liner, one of the film's main settings; the model trains that alternate rhythmically with the Tootsie Rolls refer to the characters' disastrous honeymoon; and so on. (As currently shown, the painting's title has been switched from the director's name to the movie's, possibly to avoid confusion with 1983's larger *Nix,* which refers to several Sturges films.)

Other works in the series—on Hawks, Mann, Fassbinder—present more intricate systems of reference, allusion, and response. Overlapping with Farber's withdrawal from criticism, they manifest the old impulses in a new way. Kevin Parker goes further: "Farber's painting and writing are the same thing." I'm not so sure—they're *about* the same thing, until explicit cinematic references trail off in the mid-1980s. The paintings' decentered, "all-over" look is a solution to the compositional problems of abstract painting, here given a figurative twist. But it is also a response to the difficulties of representing his thinking about movies—about anything—distinct from the compromises of expository prose. The reader of *Negative Space* might enter at an arbitrary point; the viewer of the paintings can hardly do otherwise.

The larger paintings that follow (variously on board, canvas, and mounted paper) are to the "Auteur Series" as his capacious late essays are to his single-film reviews. Even the titles indicate that the net is expanding: *"Other Men's Women," Etc.*; *Mostly "The Wild Bunch."* Half-legible scribbles on flopped-open notebooks and torn scraps of paper—always depicted, never collaged—appear frequently; so do model-railroad tracks, which both divide and connect. Visual puns abound: in 1981's *Roads and Tracks,* half a grapefruit rests on a head shot of James Cagney, as payback for his table manners in *The Public Enemy.*

This particular gag is no fresher than "Pish-Tush," but it indicates how the referential aspects of these paintings interact with their composition and technique. Farber's film paintings are all still lifes of a sort. A photograph of his studio in the *About Face* catalog shows a shelf of toy cowboys and other objects. From these, he makes tabletop arrangements that serve as his "model," though changes in scale and rendering complicate the completed paintings. Films of Farber at work show him painting on boards laid flat; thanks to the angle from which he approaches their surfaces, objects near the top edge come out elongated, and the whole takes on a just-off-bird's-eye perspective. The method is a literal-minded extension of Cézanne's famous device of tipping a surface toward the viewer at a steeper angle than what's on it. Still later, in circular where-do-I-look? paintings made between 1980 and 1985, spatial coherence is at most local. A typical detail, from *Rohmer's Knee* (1982): a whitish wedge of cheese floats free of a neutral black field; a metal ruler, rendered in a conflicting perspective, lies across its top edge at an impossible angle; the entire contraption is a see-saw for two tiny human figures, out of scale with others nearby. The depicted props interact as memories, words, images might, on the page or in the mind.

Arguably, another cinematic influence lies behind these paintings' surface action. Jean-Luc Godard's *La Chinoise* (1967) receives as much play in *Negative Space* as any other single movie, first in an essay that emphasizes the variety of "form and manner of execution" among the director's films, then in a double review with Buñuel's *Belle de Jour* (starring "Catherine Deadnerve"), and lastly in the introduction, where he dubs Godard "a cunning De Stijlist." It isn't that Farber thinks Godard's choppy anthropology of a Maoist cell is so terrific. The actors are "puerile," the politics, incredible: "The film actually sees itself as part of the movement to shake up the Establishment." But visually, *La Chinoise* sticks with him, with its shallow, sidelong camera moves and scenes "set-up like a first-grade primer," as student radicals spout dialectics "like fervid teachers against a blackboard." Much of the action (barely) occurs in front of broad swatches of primary color, studded with slogans and torn-out magazine pages that underscore the dialogue and complete the composition.

Painted fifteen years later, Farber's last explicitly movie-centered works play out against just the same kind of uninflected backdrop. Before the circular paintings just mentioned, Farber's earth-toned backgrounds were usually worked with visible brushstrokes or otherwise variegated. But from the mid-1980s forward, the ground is "sectioned" (Gorin's word) into equally sized hunks of flatly applied color, recalling both Mondrian and comic-strip panels. Other elements are set on or against—never "in"—this ground. In *"have a chew on me"* (1983), a cardboard stencil of the word *UP* sits on the border between a region with a yellow background, and an adjoining green one. Both colors show through the holes that form the word. (Remember our doughnut?) But the background itself is no more a depiction *of* something than a blank sheet of paper is; it can't be understood as representing the tabletop or any other real-world surface on which all else is arranged. This device, which allows the contents of a particular work to bump up against one another associatively or even "allegorically," as well as pictorially, is as close as Farber comes—closer, anyway, than his prose—to demonstrating what he might have meant by "negative space."

I've already noted that Farber stopped including easily traceable movie references in his paintings in the mid-eighties. (Not incidentally, he retired from teaching around the same time.) What supplanted them? Everything: food, chunks of pottery and metal, more handwritten notes-to-self (from phone messages to dream reports), renderings of art-book reproductions, and a great deal of vegetable life. *Domestic Movies,* an important painting from 1985, bridges the shift in his concerns. Though specific allusions are absent, strips of multicolored film leader run around and between the painting's Post-it notes, cereal bowls, and potted plants. In part, it's a painting *of* film rather than *about* film, weighing the artificial products of the cinema against the natural ones of his and Patterson's Southern California garden.

* * *

Cellulose may have trumped celluloid in his paintings, but Farber still has movies on the brain. The San Diego run of *About Face* was accompanied by four screenings—one short, one feature—curated by himself and Patterson. Farber attended all four, and briefly cointroduced two, one with Patterson, the other with Gorin. A typical juxtaposition: *Goodbye, South, Goodbye,* a distant, glacially paced film by contemporary Taiwanese director Hsiao-hsien Hou, and Chuck Jones's 1955 *One Froggy Evening.* (You know: "Hello my honey, hello my baby, hello my ragtime gal." Both films use get-rich-quick schemes as a metonym for the futility of human endeavor.) Other features included Samuel Fuller's *Pickup on South Street,* whose pickpocketing scenes *Negative Space* heretically rates above Bresson's, and Abbas Kiarostami's *A Taste of Cherry.* (Paired with Laurel and Hardy's *Two Tars,* this was the only one of the four I was obliged to miss.)

The first in the series paired Jean Renoir's *The Grand Illusion* (1937) with, of all things, *The Musketeers of Pig Alley. Musketeers,* it turns out, is a seventeen-minute proto-gangster film from 1912, just one of the numerous Biograph two-reelers turned out by what Gorin called "the Griffith-Gish machine." After seeing it, I'm still unwilling to speculate on the precise significance of "sustained," but one can sense the volume of thought pressed up behind the "How many films…" one-liner that scared Greil Marcus so.

The story is nothing. On what a title card terms "New York's Other Side," seamstress Lillian Gish and sister Dorothy become mildly entangled with "The Snapper Kid," leader of a gang of hoods who have, unbeknownst to her, recently mugged her violinist beau. The film's real interest is formal; with no camera movement within a shot, what narrative there is accumulates from rhythmic permutations among discrete camera setups. Here is a coldwater flat; here is a hallway with a staircase; here is the teeming street. Seen today, the short's rhythm and technical constraints are strikingly similar to those of Michael Snow's *Wavelength* or Chantal Akerman's *Jeanne*

Dielman, 23 Quai du Commerce, 1080 Bruxelles—radically stripped-down films Farber and Patterson championed in the 1970s.

The Grand Illusion, on the other hand, is not a movie to which you'd expect Farber to direct his attention, or ours. It's unmentioned in *Negative Space,* and one of the few references to its director is a sarcastic poke at film-festival "myth": "Renoir is deadly accurate on 'human passions,' hard-working folk, and the plight of the poor." Worse yet, this particular film is at pains to propound Big Themes, soppy liberal-humanist ones at that: the meaninglessness of war, and the essential nobility and comradeship of Men of Every Nation, Class, and Religion (and exactly one farmhouse fräulein). The single rose cultivated, and later snipped, by Erich von Stroheim's Nazi officer symbolizes—there is no other word—the Inevitable (and Not Entirely Lamentable) Demise of European Civilization. We already know Farber's more than capable of reorganizing his own critical categories. But isn't this movie the kind of pale pachyderm he's had in his crosshairs all along?

On the afternoon of the screening, after working through *About Face* for a few hours, and *Negative Space* for a few years, the choice made sense. Renoir's prisoners are a variant on the tight-knit bands of gangsters, cargo pilots, and newshounds that populate the Howard Hawks movies Farber doted on early in his critical career. Their bonding may be backed by rhetoric, but it's stitched together modestly, believably, from small exchanges of food, song, and physical contact, as when Pierre Fresnay washes Jean Gabin's legs. In scenes packed with the observational detail Farber prizes, the characters squander their energies in an ultimately fruitless attempt to burrow their way under and out of the camp, one coffee can at a time. (One subtitle reads, "Watch me play the mole.") If any figures in a movie can be said to eat away at their immediate boundaries, and turn these boundaries into conditions of the next achievement, it's this crew. Their termite-tapeworm-fungus-moss qualities are as bald as Farber's puns.

The film's closing moments can stand in for Farber's deliberate trudge from particular to particular, against the grain of two media and seven decades. Contrasting with Stroheim's brace-stiffened frame, Gabin and Marcel Dalio hunch diagonally across a snowy expanse as featureless as a just-primed canvas. Like the objects that lie over two adjoining sections of the late paintings, they've just crossed over an "unreal" line: the border between France and Germany. The scene depends in part on well-thumbed antiwar cliché, already pounded home by unbelievable dialogue: "You can't see the borders. They're man-made. Nature could care less." But Renoir again gives the idea dramatic and visual form. The line has no physical embodiment, but it's hardly illusory—once the pair makes it across, the German patrol, who can see them as clearly as we can, is duty-bound to hold their fire. Even in the final long shot, the effort of every step is distinctly visible. As figures in a composition, these forms organize the space that surrounds them. As subjects of a representation, they're interchangeable, indistinguishable. They could be anyone; they could only be human. *

(Note: Farber passed away on August 18, 2008)

A BRIEF TAKE ON GENETIC SCREENING

DISCUSSED: *Nucleotide Tea Leaves, The Narrative Art of Medicine, Marcel Proust, Sibyls, Genies, Majestically Sphinxlike Oracles, Stuart Dybek, Constraint and Possibility, Aristotle, Giving Shape to the Endless Middle That We Inhabit*

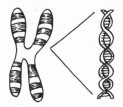

HISTORY OF CURRENT COMPLAINT:

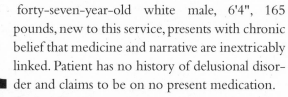 forty-seven-year-old white male, 6'4", 165 pounds, new to this service, presents with chronic belief that medicine and narrative are inextricably linked. Patient has no history of delusional disorder and claims to be on no present medication.

And then what happened?

From the earliest campfire fable, this question has united hearers and tellers, doctors and patients, readers and writers. And from the earliest diagnostic chart, our need to know *What happens next?* has slammed up against that classic source of dramatic tension: knowing what's coming does not shield us from living it.

We humans remember in story, anticipate in story, dream, explain, learn, and love in story. As patients, we grow ill and recover, rally and fade, all experienced as narrative excursions inside wider story frames. So it hardly diminishes the rigorous, empirical, and context-free nature of medical diagnostics to say that medical *practice* is a narrative art. From taking the history and conducting the physical to signing off on the postmortem notes, doctors read, and then help arrange, relevant clinical data into a series of causes and effects that forms a linear, time-driven story. Diagnosis and treatment are sometimes a detective novel, sometimes a domestic drama, sometimes a good old psychological character sketch.

Every decent plot consists of exposition, complication, crisis, and denouement. And those four points on the classic tension graph define three regions under the curve: Aristotle's old beginning, middle, and end. But as Frank Kermode points out in *The Sense of an Ending,* to our eternal, private, bodily dismay, we are each born in the middle of things, live in the middle of things, and die in the middle of things. To create a more satisfying story, we do everything in our power to read into the history around us a plot more harmonically tuned to our own. By imagining how things beyond us will end, we give shape to the endless middle that we otherwise inhabit. Life is the act of revising our lives.

So all good writing is rewriting. The art of medicine, too, must be a rewriter's art. Its chief goal is to open up the patient's story, to give new plot to possibility and new possibilities to the plot. But a patient's story *about* medicine sometimes risks imagining that its job is the elimination of all constraint. In good narrative, constraint is the mother of possibility, not possibility's opposite. When anything can happen, nothing tends to. It's only when we begin to consider all the places our own story cannot reach that we find the means to bring it where it needs to go.

At its best, predictive testing seeks to identify those plot complications and constraints that can be resolved in order to free up the patient's story and move it forward. But this is not always what we patients seek when turning to medical auguries. Something in us wants to read the determined future even as we race to write our alternatives. Today's genetic tests revive, in a rationalized, high-tech setting, the ancient obsession with divination. The same patient who has little use for such indisputable predictions as *Regular exercise and good diet will add to the quality of your life* may still crave a glimpse of the destiny written in his nucleotide tea leaves. Something in us seeks out ironclad prophecy—the stuff of Birnam Wood and the Ides of March, readings of our preinscribed, inescapable fate—if only as the first step in trying to escape it. Some incurable readers stand in bookstores, trying out the last pages of novels before they will plunk down good money for one.

Clinical medicine, then, can leverage its own narrative nature by beginning with an artful reading of what a patient is *really* seeking, when presented with the possibility of predictive tests. Patients who ask "What do my numbers say?" may really be asking the very different question "What will these numbers *mean* to the story I'm writing?" And as for meaning, medicine can have no definitive tests. *What happens next* is precisely what the doctor and patient together are about to find out.

The arguments for and against genetic tests are themselves part of an unfolding story. Medicine's powers continue to change rapidly in the run of time. Our roles as characters and as authors of our own lives are undergoing a radical transformation. We live at a dangerous moment, one when the gap between our ability to make a genetic prediction and our ability to alter it is widening precariously. For the present, our clairvoyance remains contingent. The results of a given genetic test may not be valid. When they *are* valid, they may still tell you nothing more definitive than a probability. When they *are* definitive, they may cost you your insurance, your job, or your comfort and ease with friends and family. They may plunge you into depression. They may leave you with no way of changing those parts of your plot that may then obsess you. They may blind you to your own continued ability to generate and understand meaning, even in the light of fixed events. The only fully healthy patient may be the one who hasn't been fully worked up yet.

Then again, tests and screens may save or extend a story. They may lift an impending sentence or indicate a lifesaving prevention or treatment. Everything depends on how well we engage, not with some invariable database of external facts, but with the constantly changing private narrative at stake. The tests we devise and undergo must submit to an act of *reading* that complements the patient's continuous act of self-writing. Interpreting a test result is not the same as interpreting a life, but like any twist of plot, it may serve to set in motion no end of useful interpretative developments. This is the key: genetic tests are not about escaping the story; they are about figuring how best to be in it. The story-*writing* component of medicine, similarly, remains the art of anticipating and identifying constraint, and getting that constraint to be the start of personal possibilities, not their end.

Proust writes: "We guess as we read, we create. So much begins in an initial mistake."

The patient often comes looking for palmistry. But the physician just as often has no more to offer than an informed weather prediction. *Here's a look at what might happen next.* Colder toward winter and as you head north. But as for tomorrow's temperature: it will fluctuate. Even when the physician can give a more definitive prophecy, the oracle tends to remain majestically sphinx-like until its words are lived through. In a *New England Journal of Medicine* a few years ago, Bernadine Healy, the former director of the NIH, with regard to routine clinical use of the BRCA1 and 2 mutation tests, invokes "a commonsense rule of medicine: don't order a test if you lack the facts to know how to interpret the result."

Even where the results are definitive and the interpretive apparatus is solidly in place, there is still the danger of conflating prediction with explanation. Tests may read the future, but they cannot write it. Plot does not determine meaning; readers do.

The literature of prophecy constantly hinges upon a cautionary trope. The oracle or sibyl or genie will tell you an ironclad answer to the question *What will happen to me?* But you won't understand the answer until it comes true. This is the source of power and pleasure in the eternal genre of prophetic drama. How will the fulfillment of the inevitable still manage to deliver one more surprise in the working out? How will an ambiguous prophecy dupe the subject into fulfilling it? Even with foreknowledge, the future remains recalcitrantly the future.

As the world's oldest writings put it: We live our lives as a tale told, somewhere between our next heartbeat and forever. The act of reading the world is the act of writing ourselves. So, too, with predictive medicine: even when we've jumped ahead to skim the pages yet to come, we must still read them in order, in order to say what the story means. Theodore Roethke's open-ended villanelle refrain makes the point in perfect, multiply parsable pentameter: "I learn by going where I have to go."

However powerful clinical prediction will still become, it best serves us not in revealing what is to come but in suggesting how our stories have not yet been written. We tell the tales of our lives only by living them. The present's medical model is predicated on the conviction that our futures need not merely happen to us, that we reserve the right to compose what happens next. But to the extent that it really matters—in the tale's understanding—such has *always* been the case, even before the vast increase in medicine's ability to alter the material plot. For the story lies not in what happens; it lies in what the characters *do* with what happens. Tests that increase a patient's ability to write her own life are deeply desirable; tests that decrease the patient's ability to write her own life are not. Which tests do which depends upon their taker.

It pays to keep in mind that the *denouement* is not the tying up: the word means, quite literally, "untying."

In Stuart Dybek's story "Chopin in Winter," a five-year-old white male, sickly and short, presents with severe pneumonia. He asks his doctor if he is dying.

And then what happened?

"Dr. Shtulek… put his stethoscope to my nose and listened. 'Not yet.'"

This seems to me the great story-advancing, possibility-launching refrain of medical narrative, the thing that we have no choice but to test and to know: "Am I dying?" *Yes, but not yet.*

And to the question *How long do I have?* every genetic prediction ultimately returns some variation on the same answer: *Not long.* The end will come, but that fact, far from finishing off the meaning of the middle-bound Story So Far, serves to begin it. ✶

RICH COHEN

THE SINATRA DOCTRINE

DISCUSSED: *"White Christmas," Ventriloquism, Las Vegas,*
Buying Melodies, Vietnam's Long-haired Crazies, Preemptive Strikes,
Senator Jacob Javits, Train Rides, Lincoln's Funeral Procession,
E. E. Cummings, Pop-Star Disease, Prophetic Opening Lines,
Parting the Red Sea, Dialectics, Mikhail Gorbachev, The National Anthem

P aul Anka was born on July 30, 1941, in Ottawa,
Canada, a son of Lebanese immigrants. When he
was fourteen, he cut his first record at a local studio.
The song was called "I Confess." When he was fifteen, he went to Los Angeles, tried to make it in the
recording business, flopped, went home. When he was sixteen, he
went to New York, tried to make it in the recording business, succeeded, and became known as the writer and performer of "Diana,"
which, within a few years, had sold twenty million copies. (This was
1957, three years after Elvis Presley recorded "That's All Right.")
"Diana" was, for many years, the second-best-selling single ever released, outsold only by "White Christmas." It had been written for
Anka's babysitter Diana Ayoub, whom he loved but who did not
love him back. When he was seventeen, he went on tour with the

Caravan of Stars, a showcase that included Bobby Darin, Fabian, Buddy Holly, and Annette Funicello. Chuck Berry was also on the Caravan of Stars but refused to ride the bus, instead following in his pink Cadillac. In these months, Anka fell in love again, this time with Funicello, for whom he wrote "It's Really Love." Years later, stripped of lyrics, this became the theme of *The Tonight Show Starring Johnny Carson,* a turn that, all by itself, brought Anka eight hundred thousand dollars a year in residuals.

Anka has written more than nine hundred songs, including three number ones: "Diana," "Lonely Boy," and "You're Having My Baby." He had five songs in the top twenty before he turned eighteen. These include "Put Your Head on My Shoulder," "You Are My Destiny," and "Puppy Love." He has also had hits in French, Spanish, and Italian. His score for the movie *The Longest Day,* in which he also acted, was nominated for an Academy Award. He has five children, all girls whose names begin with the letter *A,*[1] one of whom married the sitcom warhorse Jason Bateman, which makes Paul Anka Jason Bateman's father-in-law. He owns the Ottawa Senators of the NHL but has become a naturalized U.S. citizen. In his living room, he has, according to *Cigar Aficionado* magazine, a wall with four TV sets, an echo of the basement room in Graceland where Elvis watched three TV sets, showing Westerns, usually, simultaneously. According to a guide at Graceland, Elvis borrowed this habit from LBJ, who used to watch all three network newscasts simultaneously. A pillow on the couch in Anka's living room is embroidered with the words BE REASONABLE. DO IT MY WAY.

Paul Anka is, in other words, one of the most successful songwriters of all time, having had hits before the Beatles and after Nirvana, having survived the British invasion, disco, metal, hip-hop, grunge. And yet he has no public identity. His aura is everywhere, his personality nowhere. Try to imagine his face: you can't, can you? Because he's a ventriloquist, a cipher. His career has been about

---

[1] Amelia, Anthea, Alicia, Amanda, Alexandra.

giving the audience whatever it wants, about locating the mood of the moment, then expressing that mood in song. Inhabiting the psyche of other artists, finding words of self-expression they could never find themselves—that's his talent. It's the lost voodoo of the Brill Building, where chain-smoking songsmiths turned out tunes the way other, happier people turned out costumes for Broadway. (It's a world that was largely destroyed when Bob Dylan began performing his own material.) In the 1950s, Anka wrote "It Doesn't Matter Anymore" for Buddy Holly, but his greatest work was done in the late 1960s, when he wrote "My Way" for Frank Sinatra, a song that would come to represent a whole style of manhood.

By the mid-1960s Anka and the rest of the Caravan of Stars had been pushed out of the spotlight by the various turns in popular music. Anka was making his living in the casino showrooms of Vegas. It was in this way that he first came to know Frank Sinatra. This was the Sinatra of the middle years, miraculously back from oblivion, having nearly been destroyed by his affair with Ava Gardner, throat polyps, surgery, miscues, and flops, including a duet he recorded with a howling dog.[2] He had been made large by experience, by his entourage, by his association with mobsters, by the violence, real or threatened, that surrounded him. His voice had deepened, and his eyes were as blue as a stinger, a favorite drink of the Rat Pack. He was still handsome, but had been knocked off his game by the tremendous success of rock and roll. This Frank wanted to be respected, but feared he wasn't, or not always, or not by everyone. This Frank tried to stay current by recording songs by the Beatles and Stevie Wonder. Depending on whom you ask, this Frank and his entourage either owned Vegas or were owned by the gangsters who actually ran the town.[3]

---

[2] Following that session, Sinatra turned to Mitch Miller, his producer at Columbia Records and said, "Mitch, out!" Decades later, Miller approached Sinatra in a hotel in Vegas. By this time, they were both old men. Sinatra said, "Fuck you. Keep walking."

[3] In the 1960s, a wiretap captured a gangster asking Sam Giancana to hit Sinatra and members of his circle as a way to retaliate against Sinatra's friend Robert Kennedy, then attorney

Frank took special notice of Anka in these years. He looked at him as a millionaire rancher might look at an especially lush piece of grassland.

One night, after Anka had performed at the Fontainebleau Hotel in Miami Beach, Frank and members of the Rat Pack stopped by his dressing room to pay their respects. You cannot overemphasize what it meant to get such a visit from Sinatra. It was like an audience with the King, if the King could sing and drink and ace a screen test. Sinatra said he was planning to retire. This was 1969. The hippies had taken over. An entertainer in a fedora faced certain obstacles. It was time to leave the stage, but Frank wanted to do it his own way, with a big show, and one last hit that would sum up the entire journey. Could Anka write such a song? It was like the Pope asking you to paint the roof of the Sistine Chapel and tell again the story of God's sojourn on Earth. But Anka had to be careful. "He kept teasing me about writing something," Anka said. "Well, I wasn't going to give him 'Puppy Love' or 'Lonely Boy.' He'd have tossed me out the window."

Anka turned the problem over in his head, then remembered a rock-and-roll song he had heard on TV in Paris called "Pour Mois" by Jacques Reveaux. Later reworked by Claude François and Gilles Thibault, it was released as "Comme D'Habitude." Anka did not love the words of this song ("The lyrics were very French," he told *Cigar Aficionado*. "'I get up in the morning, I drink coffee, your armpit smells, I love you'") but was intrigued by the melody. When he called to inquire about the publishing rights, the man at the company said, *You want it, take it.*

"As simple as that," Anka said. "I mean, we weren't buying the pyramids here."

---

general, who was waging a war on the underworld. "No," Giancana said, "I have other plans for them." Thereafter, Frank and members of the Rat Pack often performed in Vegas for free. "Frank lent himself and Dean and Sammy and Eddie Fisher as bait to bring in the high rollers, while Sam and the boys fleeced them," Peter Lawford said. "I guess it was either that or die." This was reported, among other places, in the *New York Times* by William Safire (September 29, 1986).

He ran the melody through his mind as he meditated on Frank, the meaning of Frank, the essence of Frank, playing with words and phrases. "I was back in New York, it was after midnight, it was raining," he said later. "I started thinking about this French song and playing it on the piano, and making it less rock-and-roll, and the whole time thinking about Sinatra, about how great it would be to write a song for Sinatra. That was one of the eighteen times he was going to retire, so I'm thinking about this and I walk to the typewriter and I type: 'And now, the end is near.' When I started getting to 'Eat it up and spit it out,' I knew I had it. It wrote itself. I finished it at five in the morning."

Anka called Sinatra's musical director and said, "Don, I think I've got something."

A few days later, he flew to Vegas, where Sinatra was perform-ing (for free?) at Caesar's Palace. Sinatra read the song between sets. "In those days, if Frank said *kooky*, that meant he was really excited,"[4] said Anka. "Well, he was crazy for it."

A month later, Anka got a call from Sinatra's agent. He first heard Frank's version of "My Way" over the phone. It showcases the deep, expressive voice Frank came into—as some people come into money—in his middle years, after the heartbreak and string of failures. It seemed to contain all the experience of an eventful life. "It was Ava [Gardner] who taught him how to sing a torch song," Nelson Riddle, who arranged some of Sinatra's best songs, said later. "That's how he learned. She was the greatest love of his life, and he lost her." As Anka listened to his lyrics filled with Frank's life he "started crying," he later said. "It was the turning point of my career."

---

[4] In *His Way: The Unauthorized Biography of Frank Sinatra,* Kitty Kelley helpfully supplies a glossary of terms and phrases regularly used among members of the Rat Pack. Women, for example, were "broads"; God was "the Big G"; Death was "the Big Casino"; anywhere but Vegas was "Dullsville, Ohio"; a good time was "A little hey hey"; the male sex organ was "a bird." A common greeting was "How's your bird?"

When Frank wanted to leave a party, even a party where, say, Joey Bishop was having a great time, he would say, "I think it's going to rain."

Sinatra first sang the song publicly on June 13, 1971, at the Los Angeles Music Center in what, he announced, would be his last show.[5] The audience included Ronald and Nancy Reagan, Henry Kissinger, and Spiro Agnew. Taken together, the songs Frank performed that night were meant to tell the story of his life—it was a musical autobiography. He opened with "All of Me," the big hit from his early years with Tommy Dorsey, then sang "I've Got You Under My Skin," "I'll Never Smile Again," "Nancy," cowritten by Sinatra for his first wife, "Fly Me to the Moon," "The Lady Is a Tramp," and "Ol' Man River," on which he changed the line "Darkies all work on the Mississippi" to "Here we all work on the Mississippi." He closed with "My Way." By the time he reached the last stanza, the arena was filled with sobbing power brokers who believed Frank had just told their story.

Here are the words:

> *And now, the end is near*
> *And so I face the final curtain*
> *My friend, I'll say it clear*
> *I'll state my case, of which I'm certain*
>
> *I've lived a life that's full*
> *I've traveled each and every highway*
> *And more, much more than this*
> *I did it my way*
>
> *Regrets, I've had a few*
> *But then again, too few to mention*
> *I did what I had to do*
> *And saw it through without exemption*

---

[5] This was the first time Sinatra publicly announced his retirement, though he would do so many times in the future. In fact, he did not play his last show until 1996, shortly before he died, by which time he was forgetting words onstage.

I planned each charted course
Each careful step along the byway,
But more, much more than this,
I did it my way

Yes, there were times, I'm sure you knew
When I bit off more than I could chew
But through it all, when there was doubt,
I ate it up and spit it out
I faced it all and I stood tall
And did it my way
I've loved, I've laughed and cried
I've had my fill; my share of losing
And now, as tears subside,
I find it all so amusing

To think I did all that
And may I say—not in a shy way,
No, oh no not me,
I did it my way

For what is a man, what has he got?
If not himself, then he has naught
To say the things he truly feels
And not the words of one who kneels
The record shows I took the blows
And did it my way!

Of course, the irony is that this song, meant to tell the story of Sinatra, set him above the trends, and make him timeless, rooted him more firmly in time: the great man who has seen his greatness flicker, who has entered his decline in a moment of social upheaval. To me, it sounds less like a fight song than like the complaint of a wounded animal, the old man making his case on the edge of the abyss. It mirrored the protest songs then dominating the charts, the rants of all those angry young men, fake Dylans who wanted to tear down the system. "My Way" is the protest of an angry old man, or a man of any age who knows he's on his way out. Meant to be a credo, it nonetheless says less about how you should live than about how you should die. The choice of this material, even if meant ironically, should be taken as a danger sign.

It's no coincidence that the singers who define "My Way" (Frank Sinatra, Elvis Presley, Sid Vicious) almost never wrote their own material. All these men were actors, investing someone else's words less with authenticity than with attitude, a pose, a way of dressing, a way of living, a way of dying. "My Way" is just a script— it comes to life only when inhabited by someone like Frank,[6] the guy who follows you outside, threatens you, or asks his bodyguard, the Crusher, to crack you because you made Frankie feel bad. "My Way" plugged into Sinatra's boundless sense of self-satisfaction and self-pity.

What's more, it plugged into the self-satisfaction and resentment of that entire generation, which is why it was such a hit. This was 1971, Vietnam had already gone wrong, and the streets were filled with long-haired crazies. "My Way" was blowback, a counterattack in a generational war. It was a big fuck-you from the boss. A song of former glory or imagined glory. It might seem strange that Sid Vicious had a hit with this song, but it's natural. "My Way" is driven by the same defiance that drives punk and hip hop, which is why there have been both punk and hip-hop versions[7]—it's the anthem of the powerful man who has seen, with fear, the arrival of an ignorant new generation. In 1974, Marion Javits, whose husband, Jacob, a child of poverty who went on to become one of the

---

[6] Here's how Sinatra described this process on television, as quoted in a profile of the singer written by John Lahr in the *New Yorker* (November 3, 1997): "You begin to learn to use the lyrics of a song as a script, as a scene." He also said, "I try to transpose my thoughts about the song into a person who might be singing that to somebody else. He's making the case, in other words, for himself." He also said, "An audience is like a broad. If you're indifferent, Endsville."

[7] Jay-Z released a stunning hip-hop version in 2002.

most powerful senators in the history of New York, told a reporter from the *New York Times,* "[Jacob] just loves it when Frank Sinatra sings, '(I Did It) My Way.' Every time he hears it, he cries."

In 1953, Elvis was the sort of gawky teenager that other teenagers avoid in the high-school hallway. In 1955, Elvis was the world's first true rock star, singing *those nigra* songs and playing *that nigra* music, dressing like a pimp, shaking his hips, and wearing eyeliner. In 1958, Elvis was stationed in West Germany, his hair shorn, a foot soldier in America's army of occupation. At times, he wondered if anyone would remember him. In 1960, soon after he got back home, he boarded a train for Miami, where, in his first public performance in more than two years, he would sing on a TV special called "Frank Sinatra's Welcome Home Party for Elvis Presley."

In other words, it was time for "a little hey hey."

The arrangements had been worked out by Colonel Tom Parker, the former circus advance man who had taken over Presley's career before he went into the army. Elvis would be paid $125,000 to sing two songs, the most ever paid for a TV appearance, which was especially impressive considering Sinatra's earlier position on Elvis. In 1955, when Elvis was breaking big, Frank, as if spotting the approach of a Comanche war party, fired off a preemptive barrage. "Rock 'n' Roll smells phony and false," he wrote in a music magazine. "It is sung, played, and written for the most part by cretinous goons and by means of its almost imbecilic reiteration, and sly, lewd, in plain fact, dirty lyrics... it manages to be the martial music of every sideburned delinquent on the face of the earth."

I suppose it was decent of Sinatra not to name names, but everyone knew who it was he had in mind.[8] This article offered a perfect example of an older generation reacting to its successor. Elvis would respond in the same freaked-out way to the Beatles a

---

[8] When a reporter asked Elvis to comment, he said, "I admire [Sinatra]. He has a right to say what he wants to say. He is a great success and a fine actor, but I think he shouldn't have said it. He's mistaken about this. This is a trend, just the same as he faced when he started years ago. I consider it the greatest in music." He then said, "You can't knock success." As reported by Peter Guralnick in *Careless Love: The Unmaking of Elvis Presley.*

few years later. (If Elvis was having a bad day, he would say, "My mouth feels like Bob Dylan's been sleeping in it.") But Sinatra had misread the situation. Elvis did not want to overthrow Frank. He wanted to become Frank. They all wanted to become Frank, and still do. That's how cool Frank was when Frank was cool.[9] Sinatra quickly realized he could not hold back the wave, so he decided to ride it, hosting the TV party for Elvis, because Elvis meant ratings.

Elvis was traveling south by train, accompanied by a few musicians, most notably Scottie Moore, whose Chet Atkins–like guitar solos haunted those early records. At each stop, crowds stood along the tracks. This had been arranged by the Colonel, the advance man, who had gone up and down the line, spreading the word: ELVIS IS COMING. It must've been like flashing through a tunnel of eyes. "It was unreal," Scottie Moore later said. "The only thing I can relate it to was reading about Lincoln's body going back to Springfield or seeing movies of Roosevelt—his body coming out of Georgia after he died. Every little crossroads, every little town; you just can't imagine—they were lined with people."

It's perfect that Scottie Moore compared the trip that Elvis took to Miami after he returned from the army to the most famous funeral processions in American history. Because it *was* a funeral procession: the Elvis that lit up the country in 1955 was already gone. The story of that trip is the story of the decline retold in symbols. It's the story of how the androgynous cracker turned into Frank Sinatra. Think of a train leaving a tiny country station at first light, the engine starting to fire, the towns wandering by, Elvis in back in a flame-red suit, music drifting in from the joints, Sonny Boy Williamson singing "Bring It on Home," the harmonica imitating the clack of the iron tracks, Elvis ducking out, drinking in the afternoon, mobbed by girls, his picture plastered to every post

---

[9] Here's Bruce Springsteen in a televised tribute talking about Frank's appeal: "It was a voice filled with bad attitude, life, beauty, excitement, a nasty sense of freedom, sex, and a sad knowledge of the ways of the world. Every song seemed to have as its postscript 'And if you don't like it, here's a punch in the kisser.'"

in every town, and the sky clouds over, and it rains money, and in the fields beyond the last house an old carnie gets on, and he has a coat full of flyers, and he says, "Call me the Colonel," and then it's night, and Elvis has been awake for years, and the train is moving so fast the towns just blur by, and there is no music, just the sound of the engine steaming into a big, nameless city where Elvis is onstage with Frank.

It makes me think of the E. E. Cummings poem about Buffalo Bill:

> Buffalo Bill's
> defunct
> who used to
> ride a watersmooth-silver
> stallion
> and break onetwothreefourfive pigeonsjustlikethat
> Jesus
> he was a handsome man
> and what i want to know is
> how do you like your blueeyed boy
> Mister Death

Here are some ways Elvis came to resemble Frank:

Like Frank, he spent more and more time in Las Vegas, moving mostly by night, surrounded by his entourage. Like Frank, the most important woman in his life was his mom. Like Frank, his voice deepened and his body thickened. (Unlike Frank, this increase did not convey the authority of experience—Elvis just got fat.) Like Frank, he collected houses, women, and cars. On a visit to Grace-land, you see Cadillacs, motorcycles, dune buggies. But one car does not fit: a steely European roadster that is sophisticated in a different way from the others. If you ask the guide, she will tell you, "That's because it was special made for Frank Sinatra. Elvis saw it and liked it so much he bought it before it could be delivered." Like Frank, Elvis had affairs with Natalie Wood and Juliet Prowse. At the time Elvis was filming *G.I. Blues* with Prowse, the actress was said to be Frank's unofficial fiancée. Between scenes, Prowse and Elvis would hole up in a trailer until the PA shouted, "Here comes Frank!"

It therefore makes perfect sense that, in 1976, when he was drugged out and almost done, Elvis decided to record "My Way." He had taken Frank's car and Frank's girl; he would now take his world-weary tone. Elvis had not earned this tone, but, then again, neither had Frank. It was a con. But Elvis was too naive to understand that.[10] His interest in "My Way" should've been taken as a danger sign. It was like blood on the handkerchief, or the elevated white-cell count that warns of trouble. It was a symptom of that deadly pop-star disease, fame. Frank could handle it; Elvis could not.

The arrangement on Presley's "My Way" is almost identical to the arrangement on Sinatra's. The song opens, builds, crashes, and rebuilds in the same epic fashion. Only the voice is different. It's as if Elvis had slipped inside Sinatra. In fact, the whole performance feels like karaoke. "That's All Right" was Elvis's first single; "My Way" was among his last. He sang it at every show on his final tour. Perhaps he cut it just so he could sing it, and tell himself again each night that he was his own man, that he took the blows, that he ate it up and that he spit it out, not that every steak had been cut into small, manageable pieces by the Colonel. Elvis deteriorated visibly in the course of that tour, but no one seemed to care. Not his fans, not the Colonel. The drummer on the tour said Elvis seemed asleep much of the time. "An eerie silence filled the hall when he sang, 'And now, the end is near,' the opening line to the Frank Sinatra favorite 'My Way,'" a reporter from Long Beach, California,

---

[10] The following is from a George W. S. Trow story published in the *New Yorker* in August 1977. It ran unsigned and is my favorite thing written about Elvis: "He didn't know what he was about, but he was protected for a while by his naïveté and by his simple energy. He cut through gruesome layers of self-consciousness, although they closed in on him later. But they didn't close in on him completely, you know. Whatever there was toward the end of his life which was grotesque was probably the result of an attempt to keep his integrity and his cool—as he, imperfectly, understood the nature of his integrity and his cool. And he was cool up to the end."

wrote at the time. "It was like witnessing a chilling prophecy." One of these performances was captured on film and later included in the movie *This Is Elvis*. "In a scene whose irony is both too broad and too enormous for this film to contain," Janet Maslin wrote in the *New York Times* in 1981, "the pitifully deteriorated Elvis sings 'My Way,' barely remembering the words."

On August 16, 1977, Elvis was found dead in Graceland—on the toilet was how I first heard it, the King on his Throne—but in fact he was on the floor of the bathroom, his gold pajama bottoms down around his ankles, his face in a pool of vomit. In the hours before his death, he had taken Seconal, Valmid, and Demerol. As Springsteen later sang, "They found him slumped up against his drain, a whole lotta trouble, hey, running through his veins." Elvis liked to read in the bathroom, and on this last trip he had taken a book about the Shroud of Turin.[11] Within hours, news of his death had spread around the world. If you are old enough, you probably remember where you were when you heard he was gone. I was at Camp Menominee in Eagle River, Wisconsin, on the strip of grass between cabins 15 and 16, watching the swimmers come up the hill from the waterfront.

Punk rock, which turned up in dive bars in London and Manhattan around this time, was a protest against the direction of rock and roll or, to put a face on it, against what had happened to Elvis—how he had been declawed and tamed and fattened, and turned into Frank.

In the spring of 1977, Sid Vicious, nineteen, was drinking at the 100 Punk Club in London, heckling the band because they were not the Sex Pistols. Because they were still not the Sex Pistols, he threw a bottle at the singer, which missed but shattered on a wall. A piece of glass lodged in the eye of a girl near the stage. She lost the vision in that eye, and Sid was taken to jail. By the time he returned to the club a few nights later, he was a legend, the pure punk, the

---

[11] Elvis consumed books about conspiracy and the occult. At the time of his death, he was also reading *The Passover Plot* and re-reading *The Warren Commission Report*.

kid who would do anything.[12] Malcolm McLaren, the guru of the scene—he dreamed up and recruited the Sex Pistols—then asked Sid to join the band. He wanted to capitalize on Sid's reputation but also on his looks: until the end, when his teeth started to rot, Sid was handsome in a picturesque, waifish way that never goes out of style. His favorite book was *Helter Skelter.* Quoting Charles Manson, he often said, "Everything is nothing, nothing is everything."[13]

Sid's first performance as a Sex Pistol came on April 3, 1977, at the Green Cinema in London. He had taken over for Glenn Matlock, the band's original bass player, who held a grudge for years. Here's the joke: Sid could not play bass or any other musical instrument. On records, someone else played his part. At shows, they let him stomp around but turned off his amp.[14] But he had the perfect face for the mission, which was to return rock and roll to its original spirit, to make it again, as Sinatra had said, "the martial music of every sideburned delinquent on the face of the earth"—that is, to get its Elvis back. Sid was a train wreck in concert and would do anything, so the people lined up. And you must know that music! Each song was a revolution that lasted two minutes. "God Save the Queen," released in 1978, hit number one in the U.K. As it was considered offensive, the title was omitted from the charts, so, in *Billboard,* a blank space appeared next to the number.

The Sex Pistols burned, then were gone. Members of the band blamed the breakup on Sid's girlfriend Nancy—"Sid came to hate everything but heroin and Nancy," their road manager said—but there was no way the band could've sustained that level of energy for long. Nor did they need to. The Pistols were engaged less in a

---

[12] His real name was John Simon Ritchie. He took his punk name from Johnny Rotten's hamster, Sid, who bit Ritchie and drew blood. See *Vicious: The Art of Dying Young,* by Mark Paytress.

[13] Here's something else Sid liked to say: "I've met the man on the street, and he's a cunt."

[14] A punk guitarist named Jimmy Zero later told Paytress, "It seemed to prove what I felt in my heart: that rock n roll was dead. You had finally reached a point where the art form was so decadent the poster boy doesn't know how to play it. I thought, 'This is actually perfect.'"

war than in a commando raid or a suicide mission. They recorded their video—*We are the Sex Pistols, we do this because we want Elvis back*—then, in essence, blew themselves up. The final break came on January 14, 1978, during a concert at the Winterland in San Francisco, when Johnny Rotten, the front man, walked offstage in the middle of the show. And that was it. In the ensuing weeks, Sid collapsed into a haze of drug abuse and self-pity. Seeming to prepare himself for death, he was actually preparing himself to record "My Way."

Sid and Nancy moved to Paris in 1978. They lived in a succession of hotels, staying until they were kicked out for shooting up in the hallway, puking in the lobby. In one room, they smashed all the mirrors.[15] Malcolm McLaren was pushing Sid to make a solo record. His French label wanted him to cover Edith Piaf's "Je Ne Regrette Rien," but Sid hated the song. He recorded "My Way" instead. The session ran two nights, April 3 and 4, 1978. At Nancy's suggestion, Sid rewrote the lyrics to reflect his own journey. Some of the new phrases include: "I shot it up," "I ducked the blows," "I killed a cat," "I ain't no queer." It's been described as a punk-rock assassination.[16]

Sid's "My Way" was released in 1978. It climbed the charts. It reached the *Billboard* Top Ten in Britain. By that time, Sid and Nancy had moved to New York and were living in room 100 of the Chelsea Hotel. Mostly they walked around, went to shows, scored drugs, took drugs, and fought. Sid was an icon in the East Village. He had become Elvis, who had become Frank. A friend of Sid and Nancy's said, "I remember going out on the corner to watch them, and everyone parted like the Red Sea as they walked by."

---

[15] In *Vicious,* Paytress quotes journalist Nick Kent, who, in describing Sid's limitations, sums up his life in these months: "If you're a hopelessly absorbed person, whose idea of nirvana is sitting on the toilet [this brings us back to Elvis] for an hour while listening to the Ramones and reading about yourself in the *New Musical Express,* you're never gonna have a very fulfilling life."

[16] Here's Anka commenting on Sid's version in the *Chicago Sun Times:* "I never thought I'd hear Sid Vicious and the Sex Pistols doing 'My Way.' Come on. Were they supposed to do it? But he put himself into a song he believed in and did it *his way*." (My emphasis).

On October 12, 1978, Nancy was found dead in a bathroom in the Chelsea Hotel. She had been stabbed. Sid was charged with the murder, which he did not deny committing, because he couldn't remember one way or the other. A few weeks before, in one of his last performances, he, like Elvis, forgot the words to "My Way." That winter, while staying at his girlfriend's house on Bank Street, he took an overdose of heroin scored by his mom, who had come to New York to take care of him. She was in the apartment when he shot up. Later, when she looked in, she said his body was glowing. He was dead by morning. And so the story of "My Way" comes full circle: Act One, Act Two, Act Three. Or, as the dialecticians would say: Thesis (Frank), Antithesis (Elvis), Synthesis (Sid).

For a song that presents itself as a personal anthem, and was written as such for Sinatra, then recorded as such by Elvis and again by Sid, "My Way" has been covered by a surprising number of artists. On April 12, 2004, to celebrate the song's thirty-fifth anniversary, thirty-five thousand radio stations played the song simultaneously. The list of recommended covers included versions by Tom Jones, Nina Simone, Shane MacGowan, the Gipsy Kings, Kanye West, Robbie Williams, and Julio Iglesias. In other words, the song that started inside the French armpit has grown into an institution. In 1989, as the Soviet Union was coming apart, the Kremlin announced new rules whereby the Warsaw Pact countries would be left, for the first time in decades, to go their own way. Mikhail Gorbachev's spokesman called this policy "The Sinatra Doctrine."

In a performance at Madison Square Garden, Sinatra introduced the song by saying, "We will now do the national anthem, though you needn't rise."[17] It was a joke, I guess, but the song does capture something fundamental about the American character, the anger and defiance, the propensity for self-importance and self-satisfaction. It plugs into the self-pity people can feel when they are

---

[17] It can be heard on the *The Main Event,* an excellent late Sinatra record.

on the other side of something big. Sinatra, Presley, Vicious—each artist recorded it near the end of his public life, and in each case it became associated with the artist's decline. It's as if this song were a highly contagious virus, or else the virus is some invisible pop-star disease and the song is a symptom of a terminal illness.

With the death of Sinatra in 1998, "My Way" returned to Anka, who performs it about 150 times a year.[18] Most telling are the shows done at corporate getaways—these pay around three hundred thousand dollars a pop. It's amid the shrimp cocktails and Cobb salads and PowerPoint presentations that the song really does become the national anthem. After running through his catalog, Anka, launching into the song, jumps offstage, wanders past the peons and nobodies, drops to one knee before the CEO, spreads his arms, and sings, "The record shows *you* took the blows, and did it *your* way!" ✶

---

[18] Anka recently released his 120th record (*Rock Swings*), on which he covers several rock songs, including "Smells Like Teen Spirit," by Nirvana, itself a bastard descendant of Sid's "My Way." Anka sets it to a swinging beat and sings it before a seventeen-piece orchestra—written for Frank, played by Elvis, stolen by Sid, it has now been stolen back and rehabilitated by Anka.

DAVID ORR

HOW FAR CAN YOU
PRESS A POET?

DISCUSSED: *Seamus Heaney, Philip Larkin, Rare Birds,
Creative Exhaustion, Throwaway Jottings, Obsessive Morbidity,
Figure Skating, Faux-Naïf Virtuosos, Flippant Eulogies, Office Cats,
Algernon Charles Swinburne, Emily Dickinson, The Theory of the
Objective Correlative, Frank O'Hara, Gertrude Stein*

How far can you press a poet?
To the last limit and he'll not show it
And one step further and he's dead
And his death is upon your head.

or most poets, craziness is a virtue; silliness a mortal
risk. After all, true craziness is a serious thing, and
if there's one thing that unites the contemporary
poetry world, it's the desire to be taken more seriously than, say, the world of PEZ-dispenser collect-
ing. This attitude isn't entirely new, of course: English-language poetry has been busily defending itself since Sir Philip Sidney enjoined
the art's Puritan assailants "no more to scorne the sacred misteries
of Poesie" over four hundred years ago. Yet something different—

something plaintive—has crept into the usual rallying cries over the past century. Seldom these days do poets and critics get to fight the good fight against accusations of indolence or blasphemy; instead, they tend to find themselves addressing an infinitely less gratifying question best phrased as the title of an influential essay by the critic Dana Gioia: "Can Poetry Matter?" This state of affairs isn't necessarily a bad thing (sometimes a little self-doubt can do an art form a world of good), but it can make life difficult if you're the sort of writer who likes to draw cartoons of cats, dress up in schoolgirl clothes, and begin poems "The Cock of the North / Has forgotten his worth / And come down South/ In a month of drouth." At the very least, this kind of behavior is going to make your fellow poets, many of whom are trying to be taken seriously, inclined to forget you exist.

Which brings us to Stevie Smith, the cartoon-drawing, school-girl-dress-wearing, near-doggerel-spouting British poet who died in 1971 at age sixty-nine. It's probably fair to say that of all poets generally considered to be "serious," Stevie Smith ranks among the silliest, both personally and poetically. As to the former, this was largely a matter of presentation—in addition to her eccentric wardrobe, Smith was known for warbling her poems during readings in a manner that Seamus Heaney once characterized as a cross between "an embarrassed party-piece by a child… and a deliberate faux-naïf rendition by a virtuoso." As for the poetry itself, well, Stevie Smith is a willfully ridiculous writer—or, as some have preferred, "eccentric" (Heaney), "completely original" (Philip Larkin), and "a rare bird" (Clive James)—which means, more or less, that nobody has a clue as to how to describe her. You could talk about the peculiar rhythm of lines like "All the waters of the river Deben / Go over my head to the last wave even." You could mention the clowning, idiosyncratic rhyming ("Under wrong trees / Walked the zombies"), which makes many of her poems sound like badly translated ballads. You might pause over the patently ludicrous asides ("May we inquire the name of the Person from Porlock? / Why, Porson, didn't you know?") with which she interrupts poems that examine creative exhaustion and the longing for death. You could dwell on her bizarre habit of including throwaway jottings, not to mention amateurish cartoons, beside her most accomplished pieces. You could discuss her obsessive morbidity ("I cannot help but like Oblivion better"), her piercing humor ("This Englishwoman is so refined / She has no bosom and no behind"), or her fearful tenderness ("I can call up old ghosts, and they will come, / But my art limps,—I cannot send them home"). You could do all of this and more. But something would still be missing.

In fact, the best description of a Stevie Smith poem is not a description of a Stevie Smith poem at all, but rather an account of one of her public readings by the art historian Norman Bryson that appears in Frances Spalding's enjoyable *Stevie Smith: A Biography*. Here's what Bryson witnessed:

> The performance was unnerving because it was so excessive... The meaning of the words was set aside in the performance. And the *motives* for this were entirely unrevealed: this seemed almost the main point. It was as though what was being dramatized was a state of being so pent up, so much without outlet, that emotions couldn't have, any longer, appropriate objects... Nothing in the world could focus them or make them cohere, or earn them or deserve them.

This is almost (but not quite) a description of pure song, and it is almost (but not quite) a description of pure silliness. What Bryson's account captures is the way in which Smith's poetry seems both ferociously concentrated and utterly arbitrary—as if the poet were a figure skater who, over the course of her seemingly purposeless meanderings around the rink, somehow managed to cut into the ice the figure of a hanged man. To read through Smith's *Collected Poems* is to be amused, amazed, confused, and disconcerted; most of all, though, it is to wonder how something so alarming could seem so natural.

But how, exactly, does she create this unique effect? What does it look like on the page? It's often the case that a poet's best-known poem is neither typical nor particularly good, but not where Smith is concerned. The perennial Stevie Smith anthology piece is "Not Waving but Drowning":

> Nobody heard him, the dead man,
> But still he lay moaning:
> I was much further out then you thought
> And not waving but drowning.
> Poor chap, he always loved larking
> And now he's dead
> It must have been too cold for him his heart gave way,
> They said.
> Oh, no no no, it was too cold always
> (Still the dead one lay moaning)
> I was much too far out all my life
> And not waving but drowning.

Is this sad? Funny? Both? Neither? The nominal subject—a plea for help mistaken for a salutation—practically embodies the dominant theme of twentieth-century lyric poetry; that is, the agony of the insulated, isolated self, which keeps straining and failing to metamorphose into language. But Smith pushes things to the border of parody—the "dead one" is somehow "still moaning" (and moaning an unpoetic "Oh, no no no" at that), his life is flippantly eulogized by the phrase "he always loved larking" (*larking?*), and the simultaneously fussy and tub-thumping rhyme on "They said" in the second stanza puts a weirdly comic spin on the spectacle of a man's heart giving way. One reaches for the word *tragicomic,* but it doesn't seem adequate; as in many Smith poems, we seem to be getting too much information, and not enough.

Which, for Smith, often seems to be the point: as she writes in "The Donkey," "No hedged track lay before this donkey longer / But the sweet prairies of anarchy." Smith encourages this sense of incongruity by changing registers within and across poems with calamitous speed; her voice often seems to be arriving belatedly and inappropriately at images her mind's eye has already passed over. Consider, for example, "Do Take Muriel Out," which, like many Smith poems, begins in a childlike singsong ("Do take Muriel out / She is looking so glum"), but then ends in an altogether different key:

> Do take Muriel out
> Although your name is Death
> She will not complain
> When you dance her over the blasted heath.

This poem would be unusual enough on its own; it's even more peculiar when you notice that the final, apocalyptic stanza is followed a few pages later by an unrepentantly trivial homage to Smith's office cat. In each Smith collection, the pattern seems to be this lack of pattern. No sooner has the poet rhymed "pinkie" and "thinky" in one poem than she serenely announces in another:

> Would that the hours of time as a word unsaid
> Turning had turned again to the hourless night,
> Would that the seas lay heavy upon the dead,
> The lightless dead in the grave of a world new drowned.

No "pinkies" here, thanks (though there's probably some Swinburne). The weightiness of Smith's "serious" lines only intensifies the absurdity of her "silly" poems; the result is that the poetry on the whole can seem half-cocked. That, at any rate, is what Seamus Heaney seemed to argue in a review of Smith's *Collected Poems* that appeared about five years after her death. Heaney suggested that Smith's tendency to wander (or "wobble," as he put it) between the profound and the nonsensical revealed a fundamental flaw in Smith's poetry: her "literary resources are not adequate to [her] somber recognitions." Though he admired certain poems, Heaney ultimately found in Smith's poems "a retreat from resonance, as if the spirit of A. A. Milne successfully vied with the spirit of Emily Dickinson."

So arise, Tigger, and get thee gone. In phrasing his concerns in

241

this way, Heaney seems to have had in mind an old theory of literary emotion best expressed by T. S. Eliot in his essay on *Hamlet*. This is the idea that in a good poem, emotions match up with their contexts in more or less the way that certain elements, when combined, always form the same compounds. As Eliot tells us,

> The only way of expressing emotion in the form of art is by finding an "objective correlative"; in other words, a set of objects, a situation, a chain of events which shall be the formula of that particular emotion… The artistic "inevitability" lies in this complete adequacy of the external to the emotion…

If a poet wants to express, say, a "somber recognition," she should develop an "objective correlative" for somberness and build it into the poem; otherwise, we don't know whether we're supposed to be sad, or annoyed, or just confused. Like Heaney, Eliot is suggesting that poems can be divided into what we're meant to feel and what the poet means to say, and furthermore, that those two things should correspond in some way that makes reasonable sense. According to this theory, Smith's quirks can be explained as deficiencies—not only does her work rarely stand still long enough to be much of a correlative for anything, but as noted above, her poems are always accompanied by her cartoons. And while nobody knows exactly what a "somber recognition" looks like, the odds are good that it doesn't resemble a scribble of a tap-dancing cat. Does this mean that Heaney is right? Is Smith's poetry ultimately unsatisfying because it "wobbles"? Because it's silly?

Before drawing any conclusions, it's helpful to remember that Eliot used his objective correlative theory to claim that *Hamlet* was "most certainly an artistic failure." Perhaps hoping for a comparable failure, our better poets have tended to ignore Eliot's advice and create effects not through correspondence but through a compelling *lack* of correspondence. Consider John Ashbery's "Pleasure Boats":

Wash it again
and yet again.
The equation drifts.
Wallowing in penguins,
she was wallowing in penguins.
With fiendish cleverness,
the foreground was closing in.
The four-leaf clover loses.

Whatever this poem may do or not do, it certainly isn't playing by the rules Eliot described. More assertively avant-garde poets
go even further—in Christian Bök's book *Eunoia,* to pick one of
many examples, the poet allows himself only one vowel per chapter, leading to lines like "He engenders newness wherever we need
fresh terms." To seem properly objective, an objective correlative
would probably need to buy more vowels than that. If the poetry
world has room for things like *Eunoia,* you'd think it would have
no trouble whatsoever with Stevie Smith. And indeed, when an
author's customary critical label begins to peel, it's always tempting to argue for the opposite description—to insist, for example,
that a writer previously thought of as anti-romantic was "really"
a romantic all along. In Smith's case, the temptation is to say that
her frivolousness is "really" sophistication, that she's a calculated
lounger along the lines of Frank O'Hara or a studied rebel like
Allen Ginsberg—at heart, an avant-garde poet.

The problem, though, is that Smith doesn't really fit into any
of the avant-garde traditions (an oxymoron, but a fair one) any
better than she does into Heaney's more conventional formula-
tions. She's too earnest about God ("O Lord God please come /
And require the soul of thy Scorpion"), too pleased to be English
("Time and the moment is not yet England's daunt"), and far too
committed to the traditional subjects and themes of lyric poetry
(hardly a page of her *Collected Poems* goes by without making a
point about love, death, or justice). Most of all, though, she's just
too ridiculous. That may sound odd, considering that the heirs

of Gertrude Stein have long made outrageous wordplay a central part of their practice. But *practice* here is the key word: For contemporary experimental writers, the ridiculous is generally part of a method, a system intended to "make new" or to "subvert" or to "reexamine"; it is a ridiculousness that is underwritten by theories, argued over in journals, and justified with footnotes. It's a ridiculousness that isn't silly.

For Stevie Smith, however, ridiculousness means:

Aloft,
In the loft,
Sits Croft;
He is soft.

Or if that seems too willful to be truly silly, how about:

Oh my darling Goosey-Gander
Why do you always wish to wander
Evermore, evermore?

What makes Smith distinctive—as opposed to coy, or clever, or conventionally unconventional—is that her silliness *is* silliness. It exposes her; it makes her seem vulnerable. And that's exactly why it seems to work.

In this sense, Smith's poetry complicates an old question about technique: To what extent can we separate being something (like an artist) from doing something (like writing sonnets)? Most people would agree that great art transcends technique—which is related to saying that you can learn to write pretty good iambic pentameter, but you can't learn to be Elizabeth Bishop. But no one would say that technique is irrelevant to great art. For one thing, accepting a writer's distinctive style requires an act of faith from readers, and we usually like to know that someone can shoot a bow and arrow before we put blindfolds over our eyes and apples on our heads. Yet with her absurd titles like "Hippy-Mo," her public singing, and her doodles, Smith not only declines to demonstrate recognizable mastery, she refuses to give us any justification for her failure to do so. (Stein, by contrast, had the literary-political savvy to proclaim her genius to anyone within earshot.) The same quality that makes Smith's poems convincing—their naturalness—can make them seem slight, as if Smith's technical achievement consists of little more than, well, being Stevie Smith. Can she be great if she's just being herself?

With this question in mind, it's useful to take a closer look at how one of Smith's characteristic "wobbles" affects one of her better poems, "Thoughts about the Person from Porlock." The Person from Porlock is the anonymous figure who supposedly interrupted Coleridge as he was writing "Kubla Khan," and whose visit (according to Coleridge) caused the poet to lose the fragments of his vision "like the images on the surface of a stream," leaving him unable to finish the poem. The anecdote is often taken as a metaphor for the eternal incompleteness of art, the fleeting nature of inspiration, the tragedy of... you get the idea. Smith is skeptical of all this:

> Coleridge received the Person from Porlock
> And ever after called him a curse,
> Then why did he hurry to let him in?

> He could have hid in the house.
> It was not right of Coleridge in fact it was wrong
> (But often we all do wrong)
> And the truth is I think he was already stuck
> With Kubla Khan.

The wit is sharp, but the tone is slightly unstable, even for Smith—the oddest thing is the repetition of "wrong," which appears again as the first section's closing couplet, "It was not right, it was wrong / (But often we all do wrong)." What's so wrong about making an excuse? Smith doesn't answer that question for us immediately, instead "wobbling" into what seems to be patent nonsense:

May we inquire the name of the Person from Porlock?
Why, Porson, didn't you know?
He lived at the bottom of Porlock Hill
So had a long way to go,
He wasn't much in the social sense
Though his grandmother was a Warlock,
One of the Rutlandshire onces I fancy
And nothing to do with Porlock,
And he lived at the bottom of the hill as I said
And had a cat named Flo,
And had a cat named Flo.

Smith once described this section as a parody of academic inquiry, but if so, it's an amazingly unconvincing one. Since Smith proves in other poems to be a deft satirist (read one way, "Not Waving but Drowning" is a wicked rewriting of Eliot's "Prufrock"), it probably makes more sense to interpret her remark as an attempt to justify in more conventional terms what she knew might strike many readers as a flight of pure foolishness. But foolishness, like love, is a many-splendored thing—and here it's curiously strained and repetitive. The third stanza (if you could call it that) seems to be winding down, as Smith repeats herself ("as I said"), and then repeats herself again ("And had... / And had...")—the effect is like a slowing nervous twitch. Is there some reason for this, or is the poem just badly written?

Smith gives us a hint about the answer to that question in the next section:

I long for the Person from Porlock
To bring my thoughts to an end,
I am becoming impatient to see him
I think of him as a friend...
...
I am hungry to be interrupted
For ever and ever amen

O Person from Porlock come quickly
And bring my thoughts to an end.

"I am finished, finished," Smith has Coleridge cry as the poem begins, and now we understand that his cry is hers—the agony involved in finishing a masterpiece has become the agony of simply living life. Like Emily Dickinson, Smith is forever taking long walks in the moonlight with Death, who as she puts it here, "comes like a benison." Generally these references are too stylized to take entirely seriously (as Clive James memorably observed, Smith had "an ostentatiously suicidal *Weltschmerz* that for most of her long adult life made it seem unlikely she would get through another day without trying to end it all under a bus"). But here the pressure seems genuine. Not because Smith seems to be more "serious" or "adequate," but because her repetitions ("a cat named Flo") and hiccups ("as I said") seem increasingly *in*adequate as the poem progresses—less like flights of fancy than worried muttering.

These mutters become clearly audible as, in her conclusion, Smith turns away from Death and toward the subject that has underwritten the poem from the beginning:

These thoughts are depressing I know. They are depressing,
I wish I was more cheerful, it is more pleasant,
Also it is a duty, we should smile as well as submitting
To the purpose of One Above who is experimenting
With various mixtures of human character which goes best,
All is interesting for him it is exciting, but not for us.
There I go again. Smile, smile, and get some work to do
Then you will be practically unconscious without positively
having to go.

Philip Larkin said that Smith's poetry "speaks with the authority of sadness," but what it more frequently speaks with is the license of despair. And Smith's despair isn't the wild despair of grief or defeat, but the hushed despair of drudgery and isolation, of a quicksilver mind ground down again and again in repetitions that stack up like unfinished chores: "We all do wrong... There I go again... As I said... and had a cat named Flo... Bring my thoughts to an end... Bring my thoughts to an end..." Smith matches her plate-juggling absurdity—her "wobble"—against this pressure, and absurdity loses out in the mechanical flatness of the final line, "Then you will be practically unconscious without absolutely having to go." Recall Bryson's description of Smith's public reading: "It was as though what was being dramatized was a state of being so pent up, so much without outlet, that emotions couldn't have, any longer, appropriate objects." This is a fair sketch of idiosyncrasy run amuck, but it's also a compelling portrait of mental and spiritual extremity. Though biographical details generally tell us much less about writers than we suppose, it's worth noting that Smith entered secretarial school around the age of eighteen and spent much of her life in a clerical job that was dull at best, crushing at worst ("Dark was the day for Childe Rolandine the artist / When she went to work as a secretary-typist"). It should come as no surprise that one of Smith's most passionate admirers was the equally beleaguered, if differently situated, Sylvia Plath.

But where does this leave the question of Smith's technique? Is there a method to her melancholy? The best answer is no, not exactly, not unless we're willing to say that the lack of technique is itself a technique—which is both tautological and uncharitable to Smith, given that her great accomplishment in poems like "Thoughts about the Person from Porlock" is to change our perception of what constitutes a poetic accomplishment in the first place. In his appreciative, if slightly puzzled, review of Smith's work, Larkin concludes that her "successes are not full-scale, four-square poems that can be anthologized and anatomized, but occasional phrases or refrains that one finds hanging about one's mind." Larkin was clearly on to something, but his critique inadvertently undercuts itself by substituting one form of anthologizing for another—instead of poems, now we're to single out "occasional phrases." Better, maybe, to single nothing out, to say instead that

Smith is not so much a poet of poems as a poet of sensibility. And as such, she needs to be read whole.

All poets write poems with varying degrees of polish, and for most poets, the unfinished poems are exactly that: not finished. In Smith's work, though, poems aren't a series of objects, they're movements in an atmosphere—and to ask why Smith can't be more serious is like asking why the wind can't be squarer. As Larkin intuited, she can't be selected into perfection, because she doesn't appear in pieces. That observation is true of poetry in general, of course, but it isn't true of all poets to the same degree. In particular, it isn't true of poets like Heaney or Eliot, whose bodies of work are acts of self-conscious authority, and whose poems bear the master's seal on each enjambment. Smith, on the other hand, demands total devotion rather than sampling; she will either have the reader who will listen to her in all her falling-down absurdity, or she'll scorn readers altogether and vanish across the gray sands. This desperate posture forces her poetry to the very edge of speech, where a poem could just as easily have been a cartoon, or a snatch of song, or a flick of the wrist, and what emerges from the chill of this leveling aesthetic transcends conventional notions of ambition.

This is why poets determined to show us their "mastery" struggle to match this writer in the extreme terrain she favors. Consider these stanzas from Robert Lowell, a poet much praised for both his ambition and his ability to translate intense emotion:

> One dark night,
> my Tudor Ford climbed the hill's skull,
> I watched for love-cars. Lights turned down,
> they lay together, hull to hull,
> where the graveyard shelves on the town....
> My mind's not right.
>
> A car radio bleats,
> 'Love, O careless Love....' I hear
> my ill-spirit sob in each blood cell,

as if my hand were at its throat....
I myself am Hell,
nobody's here—

Now set Lowell's lines, with their careful, Miltonic echoes ("I myself am Hell") and self-conscious poetic flourishes ("my ill-spirit"), against Smith's "Dirge":

From a friend's friend I taste friendship,
From a friend's friend love,
My spirit in confusion,
Long years I strove,
But now I know that never
Nearer shall I move,
Than a friend's friend to friendship,
To love than a friend's love.

Into the dark night
Resignedly I go,
I am not so afraid of the dark night
As the friends I do not know,
I do not fear the night above,
As I fear the friends below.

Lowell's lines are more complex, more erudite, and more obviously ambitious. They are also profoundly less effective. "There's more enterprise / In walking naked," Yeats tells us, and Smith has stripped herself of nearly all defenses, including her identity as a poet, if not as a writer of poetry. Left bare is the essence of the lyric.

Smith pays a price for this exposure, of course; the same arbitrariness that gives her poems their anarchic intensity also denies her the comforts of "adequate" language. An art of pure chance creates a temporary shelter, not a home, and Smith is a writer whose understanding of loneliness is greater even than that of Wallace Stevens. Her isolation could only have been exacerbated by the critical underestimation her poetry has often received; an underestimation of which Smith herself was well aware. Her late poem "The Poet Hin" addresses the issue with equal portions of self-mockery and self-defense:

> I am much condescended to, said the poet Hin,
> By my inferiors. And, said the poet Hin,
> On my tombstone I will have inscribed:
> 'He was much condescended to by his inferiors.'
> Then, said the poet Hin,
> I shall be properly remembered.

Having made light of her ambitions for herself ("You know the correct use of *shall* and *will*. / That, Hin, is something we may think about"), Smith quietly asserts her ambitions for her poems:

> Yet not light always is the pain
> That roots in levity. Or without fruit wholly
> As from this levity's
> Flowering pang of melancholy
> May grow what is weighty,
> May come beauty.

Levity is light, of course, but it's also cold and scattered, changeable and cutting. Considering the time that Stevie Smith spent cultivating this unforgiving territory in solitude, the least that serious poets and serious readers can do is give thanks for the great harvest with which she returned. ✷

TAYARI JONES

SYMBOLISM AND
CYNICISM

DISCUSSED: *Black History Month As Cultural Segregation,*
McDonald's As a Purveyor of African American Literature,
The Effectiveness of Symbolic Resistance, Lagniappes, Tokenism,
Carter G. Woodson, "Black" Work v. "Universal" Work, Countee
Cullen, Hallucinated Childhoods, Camden Joy, Intricacy

The invitations start around Thanksgiving: *Greetings,*
Ms. Jones! I am events coordinator for the Mayberry Pub-
lic Library and we are delighted invite you to be our
Black History Month speaker! About ten years ago,
when I was struggling to make a name for myself
as a writer, I greeted these requests with an uncomplicated delight:
my handful of short stories and essays had reached an audience and
had earned me a place not just as a spokesperson on black history
but as example of black excellence. These invitations usually came
without honoraria and I often shared the docket with three or four
other "emerging" writers. Some of my peers who are not black
writers grumbled a bit about the idea that I could score invitations
"just" for being black. And I must admit that at that stage of my life,
I did think of this as lagniappe, just a tiny leg up. Since then, I have

published two novels and have begun to chafe a bit at these invitations. Like many black writers, my schedule is frequently packed during February, but comparatively lean during the rest of the year. If February is Black History Month, is the rest of the calendar reserved for white people?

Countee Cullen was not the first to declare that he wanted to be a "writer" rather than a "Negro writer," and Percival Everett certainly will not be the last. The politics surrounding Black History Month have made the decision to accept or refuse an invitation far more complicated than matters of scheduling. There are writers who adopt an unnuanced stance, flat-out refusing to read during Black History Month. When their in-boxes start to fill in November, they request dates in March. If the sponsor agrees, fine. If not, not. Other writers ask for the March 1 booking, as a test of the sponsor's politics: if the sponsor agrees, the writer will backtrack, accepting the February date. This dance is just a part of the ongoing conflict that black artists struggle with as we wonder if we are being used as symbols or tokens. I have been asked to read at institutions in February and I have been fairly confident that I would not have been asked were it not Black History Month. If my schedule allows, I accept the booking anyway, although I know many who would refuse.

Writers turn down dates in February to take a stance against tokenism, to smite those who believe that good behavior during the shortest month of the year makes up for eleven months of exclusion. The writers believe their participation in these Black History Month programs endorses this cultural segregation in pursuit of exposure and, of course, the honoraria.

The cynicism of our age has taken Black History Month far from the idealism of its founder, Carter G. Woodson, best known for his book *The Mis-education of the Negro*. In 1926, he instituted Negro History Week (also known as Negro Achievement Week) primarily for the benefit of black Americans who were unaware of their contributions to American history. He also imagined this week to be a weeklong PR campaign to improve race relations by improving the estimation of black folks in the eyes of white America. Of course, like many other American institutions, Black History Month has been appropriated by corporations. There is something obscene about McDonald's restaurants in the greater Washington, D.C., area handing out copies of *A Raisin in the Sun* while they push unhealthy foods on African American children. Although universities are not seeking to make a monetary profit from Black History Month, I am sometimes uneasy in the moments before my talk when the organizer professes a commitment to diversity and tolerance and then invites me to the stage as defense exhibit A.

The irony is that those who would opt out of Black History Month share the goals of its founder. Although many black people grumble that it is not their responsibility to educate white people about our worth, most would agree that racism stems largely from ignorance, the antidote to this is obviously education, and somebody's got to do it. The question is whether refusing the invitations serves any purpose besides giving the writer a sense that she is doing something to address the problem. This, of course, brings in a second irony: performing a symbolic action to critique the symbolism of another equally symbolic action. This quiet act of "resistance" vibrates no further than the consciousness of the writer in question.

The flip side of the complaint—"The only time they invite me is in February"—is to imagine the scenario from the point of view of the audience: "The only chance I get to see these writers is in February." This idea is even more compelling when you consider that audiences during Black History Month are disproportionately African American, many of whom live off the usual black book-tour circuit—D.C., Atlanta, Chicago, Detroit, etc. They arrive for these February events in excited groups—sometimes they are members of book clubs, other times they are families.

This is not to say that my experiences during Black History Month have been entirely positive. For example, in Raleigh, North Carolina, I was asked, "What percentage of your work is black, and what percentage is universal?" One benefit of that encounter was that the man who asked me that will never pose such a question to anyone again, ever. I do not look back at that event as one of my best moments on the road, but writers shouldn't travel just to be feted. We travel for the same reason that we write: to bring attention to the stories and truths that matter to us.

One February, I read from *Leaving Atlanta,* my first novel, a recollection of growing up during the Atlanta child murders, when at least twenty-nine African American children—two of whom were my classmates—were murdered in 1980. The reading, at a junior college in my hometown, was well attended by students of all ages and races. During the Q&A, I received the usual comments from the students and even the faculty that they had been previously unaware of this aspect of our recent history. Then a black woman about my age raised her hand. "Thank you for writing this book. It's like nobody remembers what happened to us. Before hearing you talk, it was like I had hallucinated my whole childhood."

After the Q&A was over, I pushed through the crowd looking for her. I tapped her shoulder, and when she turned around, we hugged, grateful to have found each other. There has been no more rewarding moment for me in my life as a writer. That it occurred courtesy of Black History Month doesn't diminish the significance of the experience.

Although this may seem a bit feel-goody, it would be dishonest to omit this recollection in the interest of making a larger point about the implications of cultural segregation. The woman in the audience who affected me so profoundly had never heard of me or read my work. She saw my black face on a flyer and figured that my talk would be as good a way as any to earn credit for her English class. When I walked to the podium, I didn't care much what motivated the students to attend. I was naive enough to imagine that they were dedicated readers of my work, that they were there because of who I am. I was invited because I am black and much of the audience attended because I am black. I don't care. What matters is not so much why the people filled the room but rather what happened when we were there together.

This is not to dismiss the problematic aspects of Black History Month invitations. However, the invitation itself is just the catalyst for an experience that will likely fall within the range I'd have at readings during any other month of the year. It's naive to think that potential organizers and attendees notice my race only in February. Similarly, it's foolhardy to assume that the most significant interaction during these February events happens between the black writer and the white members of the audience. Finally, it's cynical to presume that the motivation behind the planning of the event is more important than the writer's contribution, the audience's reaction, and, of course, the power of the work itself. ✳

LET US NOW KILL
WHITE ELEPHANTS

DISCUSSED: *Punk-Rock Romantics, Lesteroids, Creem Magazine, Screwball Heroism, Myth-cum-Brand-Name, Corrosive Material, Patti Smith, Guerilla Class Warfare, Deliverance, Vintage Naked Lunch Box Slogans, Cameron Crowe, Masturbation, Sid and Nancy, Camden Joy, Intricacy*

Sui generis critic and painter Manny Farber stated, "I can't imagine a more perfect art form, a more perfect career than criticism." Such a declaration must sound nuts if your points of reference pattern their careerism after such fast-growing fields as termite control, postmodern interior decorating ("This edgy Radiohead end table will perfectly complement your fabulous featherette Björk recliner"), and buzzword processing (every speck of expression forced though the finer-than-thou filters of a proper Esperanto machine). On the other hand (sporting half a *Night of the Hunter* tattoo), if you think of contentiously addictive voices from the past like the now-retired Farber or the late Lester Bangs, you may recall a time when such notions were self-evident. The fearless, heady, armor-piercing vernacular of "Carbonated Dyspepsia" or "Let Us Now Praise Famous

Death Dwarves," "Hard-Sell Cinema," or "James Taylor Marked for Death" amounted to more than off-the-rack jobbery, gushing politesse, consumer guidance counseling. Each new piece was an adventure in thought, language, feeling, and sensibility: meeting art and life on equal terms, it was the kind of writing that opened up whole underground vistas of tough-minded possibility.

"He was a romantic in the gravest, saddest, best, and most ridiculous sense of that worn-out word." So said Nick Tosches, no lightweight as a critic himself, eulogizing his friend and comrade Lester Bangs: romantic in a punk-rock/*Naked Lunch* sense of the term, the kind who thought the only love worth having was one where all parties involved saw exactly what was on the end of every fork. He was the rock critic as simultaneous true believer and loyal apostate, someone who wanted to save rock 'n' roll, Blank Generation youth, and the world at large from themselves. His rambunctiously free-associating first-person prose has spawned a host of Lesteroids over the last few decades (less recognized is the way his insistence on the intimately personal as the political helped pave the way for more assertive, irreverent female voices in rock criticism). But as with Pauline Kael, his followers have tended to latch onto the more obvious and narrow aspects of his style, centering around no-bullshit attitude and an amped-up canon embracing the guilt-free pleasures of "trash." (Brian De Palma/Iggy and the Stooges serving as the standard-bearing yardsticks of their respective aesthetics, but instead of shaking up well-bred folks from within the venerable confines of the *New Yorker*, Bangs found his calling as writer and editor for *Creem* magazine—under his aegis, a cross between *Hit Parader*, the *National Lampoon*, and the *Partisan Review* if Susie Sontag had only been a glue-sniffing headbanger.)

Since his death, in 1982, at age thirty-three, his notoriety and stature have gradually outgrown the strict insider status of rock cultdom: the posthumous 1987 collection *Psychotic Reactions and Carburetor Dung* (Knopf), edited by Greil Marcus, has become a modern touchstone that ranks with *I Lost It at the Movies*, *Negative Space*, *Mystery Train*, and *Studies in Classic American Literature*. Think of it as "Studies in Beautifully Unreasonable Noise," for *classic* is too stately a word for its Garageland environs and outlying districts, not merely launching pads for the best pure rock criticism ever written but criticism as pure rock 'n' roll. That this hardy truism has become the bedrock cliché in the Legend of Lester—and no less accurate for it—has been helpfully nudged along by Jim DeRogatis's reverent but unflinchingly detailed keeper-of-the-flame Bangs biography *Let It Blurt* (2000) and in particular by Philip Seymour Hoffman's deeply affectionate portrayal of Bangs in Cameron Crowe's rapt valentine to early seventies rock, *Almost Famous*. The mystique of his writing and persona hasn't worn thin with the passing of time; that tightrope sense of writing without a safety net retains its capacity to move and amaze. Resolutely human-scale yet larger-than-life, Bangs's work had a warts-über-alles, kitchen-sink candor that made every tumultuous wrestling match with the high and low mucky-mucks of rock (right along with his own tag team of highly personalized demons) into a form of screwball heroism. A Shadows-of-Knight-errant Quixote and Sancho Panza rolled into one logorrheic typewriter junkie, he tilted at white elephants, sacred cows, boredom, and rampant mediocrity with a ravenous mixture of perception and bloodshot glee.

The publication of *Mainlines, Blood Feasts, and Bad Taste: A Lester Bangs Reader* (Anchor) finally provides the long-overdue follow-up to *Psychotic Reactions*. The book positions itself as a logical extension of its predecessor, but as the slightly self-conscious title indicates, there's also a wish to play to the red-meat, Wild Man aspects of the Bangs myth-cum-brand-name. (Hey, Kids! It's the Amazing New Pocket Lester! Now with Extra Nova-Expressionism & Twice the Gonzo Scrubbing Bubbles of Hunter S. Thompson!) Given its bitter ruminations on the mortality of music as well as all things human, *Death May Be Your Santa Claus* might have been a better title, one belonging to a magnificent old Mott the Hoople rant (prevailing inarguable sentiment: "You're all too fuckin' slow") that Lester took for the headline of his exclusive 1976 interview with a very late Jimi Hendrix. ("Because one thing I learned while killing myself," Jimi ruminates from beyond the grave, "was that a hell of a lot of that shit was just sound and fury kicked up to disguise the fact that we were losing our emotions, or at least the ability to convey them.")

Mainlines features a good deal of corrosive material that can stand with the best of the earlier collection, along with a wider, more uneven spectrum of workaday pieces ranging from inspired to autopilot-entertaining to a few genuflecting, all-too-human duds. But even his much-too-solemn and dewy-eyed review of Patti Smith's *Horses* is a useful object lesson, a testament to the unavoidable occupational hazards of the profession: the awful, honest temptations of hyperbole and needful thinking, especially in barren times like the mid-seventies (or now), though many have made whole highly respected careers out of far more egregious, uninspired treacle. Compare this Joan of Art treatment to his "Jim Morrison: Bozo Dionysus a Decade Later," about the great Doors Revival: it's not that he was initially off the mark about Smith's soft parade of pent-up ambitions and influences, only that he glossed over the half-cocked, loony-tune tendencies that made Miss Smith as much the provocateur-clown-headcase second cousin to Valerie Solanas as noble heiress to Rimbaud or the Ronettes. (Of course, she was also a friend he happened to have a hopeless crush on, but even factoring that in this seems more a case of giving in to the savior fantasy: she was a better conceptual fit for him than Bruce Springsteen, the other big, street-angelic candidate for Rock Messiah circa 1975.) Taken all in all, though some of editor John Morthland's choices will doubtless be "heatedly debated," by encompassing the respective Babylons of Bob Marley and David Johansen, impassioned testimonials on behalf of Black Sabbath ("Bring Your Mother to the Gas Chamber!") and the Weimar-era Comedian Harmonists (take the A train!), the undersea world of Eno and *The Marble Index* of Nico, some inspired Dylan and Beatles debunking, plus naturally more of his running battle with spiritual godfather Lou Reed, no Bangs fan is going to feel cheated by *Mainlines*.

As the kind of incendiary book that could make a person want

to become a critic, or remind one why he became a critic in the
first place, it is also meant to separate the initiated from disinterested
observers and intellectual dilettantes. Like *Psychotic Reactions*, and in
the great cultural tradition of "Sister Ray," these *Mainlines* are dares
drawn in the sand: emphatically not nice little slices of music appreciation nor Dean's List honors seminaries nor funhouse slumming
for squeamish gentlefolk who require a formal introduction to *Raw
Power*. ("I say, Jeeves, these Iggy and the Stooges characters really
are dashed clever fellows." "Indeed, sir?" "Just listen to this corker:
'I am the world's forgotten boy/The one who's searchin' to destroy.'" "If you say so, sir.") Bangs practiced criticism as a hilarious
form of guerrilla class warfare, the revenge of the starving underclass
(as much in existential as economic terms) against the proudly oblivi-
ous Overclass, the bourgeois-boho-yoyos, the Middle-C brows fur-
rowed in rigid anal-retentive concentration, and indeed the High
ideals of Class itself, understood as a plumy nexus of ego-massaging
rationalizations, humorless self-importance, affluent pretensions,
good table manners, solid musicianship, starched professionalism,
and an insatiable appetite for respectability at all costs. Discomfit-
ing the comfortable and afflicting the affected was what he lived
for—"You cannot kick intentional cripples awake," but gee, Officer Krupke, it sure is fun to try anyway—but there was something more at stake than just being a gadfly freelancing boils or a
chaotic court-jesting nuisance. (Dear me, what'll that darn Lester
say next?!) The guiding suspicion behind his work was that the
language of assurance and reassurance most art is couched in was
a way of insulating audiences from their own lives: by substituting
overdetermined pseudo-emotions and numb, freeze-dried ideas
for precarious human exchange, the next thing you knew you'd
wind up in a Keir Dullea pod, slippery-sloping into Kubrick's re-
make of *The Incredibly Strange Creatures Who Stopped Living and Became Mixed-Up Zombies!!?*, with music by Kraftwerk and "emetic
narcissism" by Stevie of Bel Air (a manicure worse than the disease). Hence Lester Bangs's writing contains more scar tissue and
stealth vulnerability per square inch than anything this side of Mo

Tucker singing "After Hours" to finish the Velvet Underground's third LP: "Oh, but people look well in the dark."

Somewhere over the slough of despond, *Mainlines, Blood Feasts, and Bad Taste* includes his debut review for *Rolling Stone* in 1969, dismissing the MC5's *Kick Out the Jams* (he later famously reversed himself on the album, but in Bangs such diametrical opinions weren't self-canceling: they were Polaroids of the running love-hate argument with music and life that constantly went on inside his head) and the Canned Heat review that got him bounced from its yellowed pages. Fittingly, too, there's the last piece published in his lifetime, "If Oi Were a Carpenter," sizing up minuscule punk offshoots. The book starts with a few instructive chunks of wrought-up teenage angst, rites-of-passage pieces drawn from his unpublished autobiographical tome, "Drug Punk": "A Quick Trip Through My Adolescence" et al lay out a picture of early influences, tantrums, and formative traumas. In "Two Assassinations," William Burroughs looms larger than any of the other Beats as an influence. (Kerouac would show up in his more fulsome and tender paeans.) Young Lester incorporates a vintage naked lunch-box slogan—"Fuck 'em all, squares on both sides, I am the only complete man in the industry"—to serve as a nineteen-year-old hipster's holy grail, but the facade is already being undercut by his own grievous sense of estrangement, isolation, and doubt. When the kid from El Cajon gets cozy with the San Diego Hell's Angels and winds up as a passive, guilt-stricken bystander at one of their come-one-come-all rapes, the horror kind of takes the bloom off the whole outlaw-rebel pose for Lester. Hipster cool held an immense attraction for him, but his determination to break through that attitude of reptilian detachment and reach for some kind of human connection no matter what is what would ultimately make him an indelible writer.

There's also a tour through what *Mainlines* designates as the "Pantheon" (an I. M. Pious wax museum perhaps better left to

Madams Sarris and Christgau), which includes four pieces on the
Rolling Stones (about two and a half too many—dutifully forcing
himself to muster a response to the supremely indifferent likes of
Black and Blue) and a couple nice exercises in ambivalence devoted
to Miles Davis's queasy-listening electric period ("Kind of Grim"
and "Music for the Living Dead," funk in both senses of the word).
A long profile of Captain Beefheart does veer off into awestruck,
witch-doctor hagiography, but a good Kierkegaard-laced review of
Public Image Ltd. (belying Bangs's anti-intellectual rep) counteracts
such tendencies. There's achingly fervent, can-I-get-a-drowning-
witness testimony on behalf of Nico's *The Marble Index*, as well as
"Deaf Mute in a Telephone Booth" on Uncle Louie entering his
Scrooge McFucked decline, and an epic, positively wistful evocation of Black Sabbath. Encountering Ozzy back in 1972, when
The Osbournes was not even a gleam in the all-seeing TV Eye, the
piece is at once a completely sincere, mostly convincing attempt to
find the humanist impulses secreted in "War Pigs" and "Children of
the Grave," and a disarming visit with a Prince of Darkness who is
already halfway to his shrewdly befuddled husband-and-father persona, right down to the wholesome sitcom wackiness when Ozzy
sans Harriet attempts to avoid the breathy clutches of a chick who
calls herself the Blow Job Queen.

Here you catch a glimpse of the Lester Bangs who befriended
a barely teenage Cameron Crowe and offered cranky encouragement to Crowe's alter ego in *Almost Famous*: while he positioned
himself as the enemy of the whole scene-making "I am a Golden
God" rock-star trip, Bangs had his own streak of wayward idealism and sentimental tenderness. It was more likely to express itself
in a communing sing-along to "Ballerina" or "Beside You" rather
than "Tiny Dancer," but so much of the rage and despair in his
work came from a sense of possibilities betrayed, hope deferred or
destroyed, good things turned into breathtaking travesties of themselves. (Crowe's adolescent chivalry toward beatific distressed dam-
sels reflects an aspect of the romantic in Bangs as well.) It's not hard
to imagine an alternate version of *Almost Famous* in which Lester

is the star, emerging from a far grungier, more stifling background, with a Jehovah's Witness mother and no prospects of an interesting, bearable life at all—his autobiography written in the albums he discovered and the books he found, which were signs not only of another world but another self he would construct from the traces they left. Music—and writing—was his deliverance, hence the desert-island album essay included in *Psychotic Reactions* about Van Morrison's *Astral Weeks*:

> It was particularly important to me because the fall of 1968 was such a terrible time. I was a physical and mental wreck, nerves shredded and ghosts and spiders looming and squatting across the mind. My social contacts had dwindled almost to none; the presence of other people made me nervous and paranoid. I spent endless days and nights sunk in an armchair in my bedroom, reading magazines, watching TV, listening to records, staring into space. I had no idea how to improve the situation, and probably wouldn't have done anything about it if I had.

The big epiphany voice-over would go something like this:

> But in the condition I was in, it assumed at the time the quality of a beacon, a light on the far shores of the murk; what's more, it was proof that there was something left to express artistically besides nihilism and destruction. (My other big record of the day was *White Light/White Heat*.) It sounded like the man who made *Astral Weeks* was in terrible pain, pain most of Van Morrison's previous albums had only suggested; but like the later albums by the Velvet Underground, there was a redemptive element in the blackness, ultimate compassion for the suffering of others, and a swath of pure beauty and mystical awe that cut right through the heart of the work.

There was always that alternating current in him that oscillated between destructive-nihilist character traits and the deep-seated beauty-awe component, a tension that was easier and more salutary to manage in writing than a life of self-mocking, self-medicating excess. *Lester the Movie: Almost Bilious* would therefore traverse

circumscribed beginnings handing out *The Watchtower* in El Cajon, his humble start sending record reviews to *Rolling Stone* (*The
Watchtower* redux), the glory days in Detroit as the conscience and
soul of *Creem*, his move to New York, where he submerged himself
in CBGB's burgeoning lemming-demimonde (Richard Hell and
the Voidoids more or less serving as his Stillwater) and freelanced
for the *Village Voice*. (Though in order to survive, he wrote for
anyone who'd take his byline: *Stereo Review, Musician, Rolling Stone*
once again, *New Wave, New York Rocker, Music and Sound Output,
Contempo Culture, Back Door Man*—publish or perish wasn't an
idle threat, but an imperative on several distinct levels.) The movie
would brim with obligatory romance and heartbreak up the wazoo
(cf. *Psychotic Reaction*'s love-as-absurdity classic "New Year's Eve"),
but Lester's most lasting lifelong relation outside of music was with
masturbation, so there'd have to be one of those gauzy memory
montages of the way we wanked: from early boyhood stirrings before the telephone-book-size Sears catalog (ladies' undergarments
section) on to Hef's plasticine Playmates to Runaways album covers to the pastoral nostalgia of *Celebrity Skin*. But besides sentimental journeys, you'd get action 'n' adventure (remember "Jethro Tull
in Vietnam"?—our correspondent goes upriver to get the skinny
on a Kurtzian pied piper), rockin' intrigue (remember "Screwing
the System with Dick Clark"?—I see Michael Douglas doing a
perfect cameo as Mr. American Bandstand), and even Lester's in-
gratiatingly mortifying attempt to become a singer himself. (Andy
Kaufman and the Blues Brothers had nothing on our boy.)

Only the last reel would have to be rewritten: overdosing
on Darvon after getting relatively straight and sober is by far
the worst cliché he ever perpetrated and his one unforgivably
corny stunt, going out in what he would have surely mocked
as a shamelessly cheap career move. (The old die-and-become-
immortal routine—the stalest joke in the book.) Maybe a *Twilight Zone* finish would be more in order: since Bangs has already
entered cinema's nether realm of cultural fantasy alongside such
luminaries as Sid and Nancy, Valerie and Andy, Charles Bukowski,

Naked Lunch's William Lee, Jim Morrison, Hunter S. Thompson, Kaufman, John Belushi, and *24 Hour Party People*'s Tony Wilson and Ian Curtis, why not convene a round table of the living and the dead, a meeting of the minds and the mindless. Have P. S. Hoffman's Lester and Lili Taylor's Val and the Thompson twins (Bill Murray and Johnny Depp) and the rest of 'em hash out the liberties taken by film biographies, the consolations of philosophy as spelled out in the Sex Pistols' version of "No Fun," the perils and ecstasies of nostalgia, and the nigh-unto-insurmountable task of not turning into the very thing you despised, especially once you've been projected onto the silver screen as some kind of suitably iconic/ridiculous figure. One minute you're the Elephant Man on stampede ("I am not an animal!") and the next you're another shiny white death-mask on display in a showroom window: Smile, says the plaster caster, you're on *Candid Camera*! But Lester is unfazed: he goes into bemused Rod Serling mode and addresses the camera as a battle-of-the-stars melee erupts behind him (Andy has Val in a headlock, Bukowski's holding a pillow over Morrison's big mouth) and calmly intones, "Is there a happy ending? I don't think so." Roll credits as the mandolins play and Mott the Hoople's "I Wish I Was Your Mother" serenades you out of the theater humming a pretty epitaph.

No matter how you look at it, with all the exuberance and crazed comic poetry and hot/cold running insight of *Psychotic Reactions* and now *Mainlines*, there's an aura of sadness beyond simple untimely loss (as a wisegal said to me, "Whaddayouwannaliveforever?"): the unremitting sense beneath all that beautifully overwrought manic desperation of how fragile and futile the constructs underpinning art and life really are, a rising awareness of the steep toll of all that persistent grappling with the inadmissible. No surprise then that Lester Bangs wrote some of the best obits in the business, his own dress rehearsals: for Elvis (whom he didn't much care for, and wrote all the more movingly about what that disconnection meant), Peter Laughner (a musician and writer who if he hadn't self-immolated trying to live out a fantasy-camp version of alcoholic-druggie nihilist stupor might have grown up to surpass either Lou Reed or Bangs himself), "Bye, Bye, Sidney, Be Good" (for punk rock and all its slam-bam illusions, his own most of all). In addition, he invented the preventive obituary in his Lou Reed opuses and "Richard Hell: Death Means Never Having to Say You're Incomplete," bait-and-switch tracts which attempted to lure/jolt their subjects out of downward-spiraling self-hate with a carrot of praise or a cattle prod to their numb genitalia. (His answer to the Clash's "Ya need a little dose of electrical shockers," I expect.)

And then there were those reconnaissance flights that were hard to tell from kamikaze missions, diving into a record as he does on *Mainlines*'s "Your Shadow Is Scared of You: An Attempt Not to Be Frightened by Nico." Which is about trying to get past all the baggage of Pavlovian-dinner-bell art, chic dehumanization, overweening significance, cheap thrills, working instead toward a definition of art as something as personal as the most intimate, wrenching flesh-and-blood encounter. Clearing away the distractions of secondhand fashion and vicarious kicks, he then elicits a long string of Joycean dictation from an old love over the phone, a séance which ends with the woman comparing doomstruck chanteuse Nico to "Beckett's play *Breath*, she's trying to find the last breath so she can negate breath, love, anything. A soft look would kill her." Then he hunkers down with the vast hosts of the dead he hears on the album:

> She's quite a rock critic, that old girlfriend of mine—sometimes she scares me even more than Nico. But then, I'm scared of everybody— I'm scared of *you*. My girlfriend's eloquence was one reason I loved her almost from first sight, but not why I had to get halfway around the geographical world to write a song that said how much I loved her. It was because of something obviously awry in me, perhaps healing, at least now confronting itself, which is one way to perhaps not rot. There's a ghost born every second, and if you let the ghosts take your guts by sheer force of numbers you haven't got a chance though

probably no one has the right to judge you either. (Besides which, the ghosts are probably as scared of you as you are of them.)

Now most critics, whether good, bad, or humdrum, are usually doing their level best to suppress or deny such feelings, gloss over the awkwardness, the groping, the fear that John Cale may have said was a man's best friend but you wouldn't ever know it from *them*. After all, that terror is weakness which in turn is a form of need, which is just a shade removed from psychic disintegration and nervous breakdown—one slip on the stepping razor's edge there and it's back to the bedroom armchair, counting the spiders and staring into space forever, or worse. The difference between what Bangs is doing here and an equally personal (albeit in a more baroquely literary manner) writer, Camden Joy, is doing in his latest collection, *Lost Joy* (TNI), comes down to risk. Not formal risk, idiosyncratic experimentation in structure and fantasy and syntax, which Joy's work has in rhetorical abundance after a manner that suggests Fernando Pessoa's *The Book of Disquiet* remodeled as rock fan's mash notes to his own delicious sensibility. Bangs's work feels at risk in the same way the work it lauds is—in danger of coming apart at the seams, devouring its author and sucking its audience into the pit of disgust or hopelessness or fear with it. Joy's approach has a disembodied, art-project halo: as though instead of listening to "The Greatest Record Album Singer Ever" (Al Green) or "The Greatest Record Album Ever Told" (Frank Black's *Teenager of the Year*) or "The Greatest Record Album Band That Ever Was" (Creedence Clearwater Revival), you visited a gallery where they had been turned into ironic-obsessive-compulsive installations. Everything (performer, music, album jacket) becomes a pretext, each moved behind several layers of brilliant distancing devices; you marvel at the intricacy and thoroughness of every conceit, but they remain conceits, art for artifice's sake. Bangs was convinced the only worthwhile purpose of music and criticism was to break through that artifice. If it didn't implicate you, as coconspirator or shamed silent partner, then it wasn't doing its job: It was just providing a glass-bottom service to gawk at the colorful creatures of the deep from a nice dry vantage point. The world as he saw it wasn't so much divided between the hip and the square ("Fuck 'em all") or even between the haves and the have-nots so much as between those who had to live in whatever drowned world they'd been consigned to or made for themselves (if it was even possible to tell the difference) and the tourists who watched the show and then put on their warm coats and went back home.

In *Mainlines*, there's a terrific 1976 piece called "Innocents in Babylon," on the lures and traps of such tourism, going to Jamaica in search of Natty Dread while waiting for Bob Marley's Godot at the Sheraton Hotel. (The Clash could have cribbed notes for "Safe European Home" from it.) There's a glimmer of utopia that looks a little like prophecy:

> All the singles have an instrumental version on the B side, so the deejays can flip them over and improvise their own spaced-out harangues over the rhythm tracks. Since Jamaican radio plays so little reggae, most of the deejays come off the streets, where until recently you could find, periodically, roots discos set up. Out of these emerged deejay-stars like Big Youth and I-Roy, and along with producers like Lee Perry and Augustus "King Tubby" Pablo they have pioneered a fascinating technological folk art called dub. An album by I-Roy can thank six different producers on the back "for the use of their rhythms." Don't ask me where the publishing rights go. Don't ask anybody, in fact. And, don't ask how musicians might feel who play on one session for a flat rate, only to find it turn up on one or more other hit records. The key with dub is spontaneity, the enormous creative sculpting and grafting of whole new counterpoints on records already in existence. And this sense of the guy who plays the record as performer extends down into the record shops, where the clerks shift speakers, tracks, and volume levels with deft magicianly fingers as part of a highly intricate dance, creating sonic riot in the store and new productions in their minds: *I control the dials.*

But the reality beneath the pipe dream turned out to be predictably messier: exploitation, greed, racism, violence, lunacy, enough delusion to go around for everyone involved, the writing on the wall no one wanted to read.

The era Lester Bangs belonged to was unlike the present one in a key respect: A lot of people hadn't learned the rules of the game yet. All garage bands like the Count Five and the Troggs and uncounted no-hit wonders were too dumb to know any better: they didn't have a dainty neo-primitive paint-by-numbers instruction manual to work from. Punk was, briefly, a smarter free-for-all: anyone could join, and nobody had the slightest clue where it was going, oblivion or taking over the world as equally plausible consummations devoutly and simultaneously being wished. Then people internalized the rules or were assimilated by them—a process that was well under way before Bangs's death and so turns the later pieces in *Mainlines* into the sound of a man tired of losing the good fight, and certain that the worst was yet on its way. The book is Lester's Last Stand against the march of the lumbering artistic behemoths, Old Home Week back in the human wilderness: or as the girl on the phone once asked in the dead of night, "What good is music if it doesn't destroy you?" ✶

PAUL LA FARGE

DESTROY ALL MONSTERS

DISCUSSED: *Basements as Dungeons, Middle-earth, War Games, Moral Clarity, Vin Diesel, Biological Determinism, Death by Misadventure, Freaks and Geeks, Tom Hanks, Castration Anxiety, Satanism, The Pantheon of Cool Dangers, The Buck Rogers Fortune, Cthulhu Calamari, Tom Waits, The Holy Scriptures, Orson Welles*

NOTE TO THE READER

This article is divided into two parts: a manual and a scenario. The first part, the manual, is an exposition of the game Dungeons & Dragons: what it is, how it's played, how it came to be, and how it came to be popular, at least in certain circles. If you once played D&D yourself (no need to admit that you played a lot, or that you still play), you may want to skim the manual, or turn directly to the scenario, which is an account of a trip my friend Wayne and I took last spring to Lake Geneva, Wisconsin, in order to fulfill a wild and uncool dream: to play D&D with E. Gary Gygax, the man who invented the game (more or less: see below). If it isn't immediately clear why this would be an interesting, or, to be frank, a fantastically exciting and at the same time a curiously sad thing to do: well then, you'd better start with the manual.

THE MANUAL
1.0 OUTSIDE THE CAVE

You are standing outside the entrance to a dark and gloomy cave. If you are anything like me, you have been here many, many times before. It isn't always the same cave: Once it was a "cave-like opening, somewhat obscured by vegetation," which led to the mystical Caverns of Quasqueton; another time it was the Wizard's Mouth, a fissure in the side of an active volcano ("This cave actually seems to breathe, exhaling a cloud of steam and then slowly inhaling, like a man breathing on a cold day"). Once it was a passage from the throne room of Snurre, the Fire Giant King, "extending endlessly under the earth." Once, memorably, the "cave" was made of metal: it was the outer airlock of a spaceship that had crash-landed in the crags of the Barrier Peaks.[1] You don't know what lies in that darkness, but you have heard rumors: there are troglodytes, dark elves, a long-dead wizard, terrible creatures, treasure. You are here to learn the truth. So strike a light: you're going in.

---

[1] How many of these entrances do you recognize? The fourth is from *Module S3: Expedition to the Barrier Peaks;* the third is from *Module D1: Descent into the Depths of the Earth;* the second is from *Module S2: White Plume Mountain,* and the first is from *Module B1: In Search of the Unknown.* In the spirit of the game, you might want to use your score on this quiz to assign yourself a Reading Level, from 0 to 4, which will correspond, roughly, to your familiarity with old-school D&D. If you like, you can even give yourself a title:

Reading Level [i.e., # of caves recognized]	Title
0	*Novice*
1	*Dabbler*
2	*Player*
3	*Campaigner*
4	*Fanatic*

I'll key further remarks in the notes to these reading levels. Which means, you novices and dabblers, that you will be drawn into the cave, willy-nilly.

If you are not between the ages of eighteen and forty-five, or if you happen to be a woman, you may not know what Dungeons & Dragons is, exactly, or why you would want to get involved with it, even in the context of an essay in a respectable magazine such as this one. This introduction is for you, although, as it turns out, neither question is easy to answer from outside the cave. TSR Hobbies, the company that used to make D&D,[2] once wrote a brochure for hobby-store owners, in which it tried to explain what it was selling:

> While one of the participants creates the whole world in which the adventures are to take place, the balance of the players—as few as two or as many as a dozen or more—create "characters" who will travel about in this make-believe world, interact with its peoples, and seek the fabulous treasures of magic and precious items guarded by dragons, giants, werewolves, and hundreds of other fearsome things. The game organizer, the participant who creates the whole and moderates these adventures, is known as the Dungeon Master, or DM. The other players have personae—fighters, magic-users, thieves, clerics, elves, dwarves, or what have you—who are known as player characters. Player characters have known attributes which are initially determined by rolling the dice.... These attributes help to define the role and limits of each character.... There is neither an end to the game nor any winner. Each session of play is merely an episode in an ongoing "world."[3]

This is what the cave sounds like when it speaks to outsiders: its diction is erudite and occasionally awkward ("treasures of magic"); it uses game terms as though their meanings will be obvious (what are *attributes*?); it raises as many questions as it answers. You who

---

[2] **Note for Level 0–1 Readers:** D&D is now published by Wizards of the Coast, a division of the toy manufacturer Hasbro.

[3] TSR Hobbies, *Understanding Dungeons & Dragons,* 1979. Quoted in Gary Alan Fine, *Shared Fantasy: Role-Playing Games as Social Worlds* (Chicago: U Chicago Press, 1983), about which more later.

have never played could be forgiven for asking, what are the rules of D&D? If no one wins, how do you know if you're playing well? Where's the board? OK, listen up: there is no board. You play a character, as in theater, though you don't usually act out your character's words or deeds. Rather, you communicate *about* your character with other players and with the Dungeon Master, whose job is to speak for the world. You tell the Dungeon Master what you do; someone rolls some dice; the DM tells you what happens. Together you tell a story: a fantasy epic à la Tolkien or whomever you will; or rather, given that the game has no natural end, maybe we should call it a fantasy soap opera. Imagine for a moment that Adam and Brian are players, and Charlie is the DM. Their story might go like this:

> CHARLIE: OK, you guys have just entered the mystical Caverns of Quasqueton. You're in a ten-foot-wide corridor, which leads to a large wooden door.
>
> ADAM: I'm going to open the door.
>
> CHARLIE: Just like that?
>
> ADAM: OK, maybe not. Brian, have your elf check the door.
>
> BRIAN: Don't tell my elf what to do. [*Pause.*] My elf checks the door.
>
> CHARLIE: [*Rolls dice.*] It appears to be a normal door.

What may remain obscure, even now, is *why* people would choose to play D&D, all night, night after night, for years.[4] Why intelligent human beings would find the actions of imaginary fighters, thieves, dwarves, elves, etc., as they move through a space that exists only notionally, and consists more often than not of dimly lit

---

[4] **Note for Level 0 Readers, to which Level 2–4 Readers will probably object:** Especially given that the actions described by the players (and taken by the characters) tend to be repetitive: walking down corridors, opening doors, fighting monsters, looting corpses, etc. A very great variety of actions are possible in the game: your character could gather wildflowers on the mountainside, or go back to town and start a dry-goods business. In practice, however, the players and the DM usually agree to keep their play within the bounds of the scenario the DM has prepared: an underground dungeon, a nasty spot of wilderness, etc., where there are monsters to be fought and treasure to be found. Although see note 27, below.

corridors, ruined halls, and big, damp caves, more compelling than books or movies or television, or sleep, or social acceptance, or sex. In short, what's so great about Dungeons & Dragons?

2.0 THE HARLOT ENCOUNTER TABLE

The appeal of D&D is superficially not very different from the appeal of reading. You start outside something (Middle Earth; Dickens's London; the fascinating world of mosses and lichens), and you go in, bit by bit. You forget where you are, what time it is, and what you were doing. Along the way, you may have occasion to think, to doubt, or even to learn. Then you come back; your work has piled up; it's past your bedtime; people may wonder what you have been doing.

Once you set foot inside the cave, however, you see very quickly that D&D is quite different from a book, or movie, or soap opera. For one thing, there are a lot more rules. I remember opening the Basic D&D rulebook—I was eight years old—and coming to the "Table of Bonuses and Penalties Due to Abilities," which begins,

Prime requisite 15 or more	add 10% to earned experience
Prime requisite 13–14	add 5% to earned experience
Prime requisite 9–12	no bonus

By reading the accompanying text, I figured out that my character's abilities—his strength, his intelligence, his wisdom or lack thereof, and so on—were each determined by rolling three six-sided dice, and that the "prime requisite" was the ability my character needed to do what he did (a fighter's prime requisite is strength; a magic-user's is intelligence, etc.). It would be several pages before I understood that "earned experience" referred to the experience points a character earns for killing monsters and amassing treasure, and which regulate his promotion to ever-greater levels of power and ability. And I remember how, as the meaning of these terms became clear, my bewilderment yielded to delight. The rules guaranteed the reality of the gameworld (how could anything with so many rules not be real?), and, if they were hard to understand, at least they were written out, guessable and debatable, unlike the implicit, arbitrary, and often malign rules that people live by in the actual world.

D&D is a game for people who like rules: in order to play even the basic game, you had to make sense of roughly twenty pages of instructions, which cover everything from "Adjusting Ability Scores" ("Magic-users and clerics can reduce their strength scores by 3 points and add 1 to their prime requisite") to "Who Gets the First Blow?" ("The character with the highest dexterity strikes first"). In fact, as I wandered farther into the cave, and acquired the rulebooks for Advanced Dungeons & Dragons, I found that there were rules for everything: what kind of monsters you could meet in fresh water, what kind you could meet in salt water, what wise men knew, what happened when you mixed two magic potions together. If you happened to meet a harlot in the game, you could roll two twenty-sided dice and consult a table that told you what kind of harlot it was.[5] It would be a mistake to think of these rules

---

[5] I reproduce it here in full as it appeared in the *Dungeon Master's Guide:*

THE HARLOT ENCOUNTER TABLE

01–10	slovenly trull
11–25	brazen strumpet
26–35	cheap trollop
36–50	typical streetwalker
51–65	saucy tart
66–75	wanton wench
76–85	expensive doxy
86–90	haughty courtesan
91–92	aged madam
93–94	wealthy procuress
95–98	sly pimp
99–00	rich panderer

What, you may ask, is the difference between a "brazen strumpet" and a "wanton wench"? I don't know, and it doesn't matter; this is a rule that exists purely for its own sake.

Here you have one reason why D&D appealed more to boys than to girls: it just wasn't written with girls in mind. But I hope you can also see a good reason why boys might have found it interesting: not only, DM willing, did you get to meet harlots; you got to meet *words*. I don't think I knew what a *panderer* was before I read the *Dungeon Master's Guide*, not to mention a *dweomer* or a *geas*, words that Gygax more or less introduced into modern English. Look them up.

as an impediment to enjoying the game. Rather, the rules are a necessary condition for enjoying the game, and this is true whether you play by them or not. The rules induct you into the world of D&D; they are the long, difficult scramble from the mouth of the cave to the first point where you can stand up and look around.[6]

2.1 THE INVENTION OF DUNGEONS & DRAGONS

D&D gets its appetite for rules from war games, which have been around for thousands of years. The modern war game began in the late eighteenth century, when a certain Helwig, the master of pages to the German duke of Brunswick, invented something called "War Chess": instead of rooks and knights and pawns it featured cavalry, artillery, and infantry; instead of castling it had rules for entrenchment and pontoons. The Prussians adapted Helwig's game to train their officers; the French learned the value of war games the hard way in 1870. In 1913, when the Prussians were again rattling their sabers, the British writer H. G. Wells came up with a game called Little Wars, which was played on a tabletop, with miniature lead or tin soldiers. Then, in 1958, a fellow named Charles Roberts founded the Avalon Hill game company, and published a board game based on the Battle of Gettysburg. Gettysburg and its successors were wildly popular; all over America, college students and other maladjusted types began to re-create, in their dorms and basements and family rooms, the great battles of history.

One of these enthusiasts was a high-school dropout named Ernest Gary Gygax. In the late 1960s, Gygax was living in Lake Geneva, Wisconsin, where he worked as an insurance underwriter.

---

[6] When players want to conjure up the atmosphere of the game, they often do so by reference to a widely known or infamous rule. Consider, for example, the T-shirts sold to gamers, which read JESUS SAVES / EVERYONE ELSE TAKES FULL DAMAGE, a reference to the "saving throw," the die roll a player must make to determine if he is affected by poison, magic, dragon's breath, etc. (Not to mention the even more obscure JESUS SAVES / EXCEPT ON A NATURAL 1, which I won't get into here.)

He was married to a Lake Geneva girl and had four children, but he remained an active gamer: together with a couple of friends, Gygax founded the grandly named International Federation of Wargaming, the Castles & Crusades Society, for medieval war-gamers, and the Lake Geneva Tactical Studies Association, which met weekly in his basement. In the course of these meetings, he became friendly with a hobby-shop owner named Jeff Perren, and they coauthored a set of rules for medieval miniatures combat,[7] called Chainmail, which was published in 1971.

Meanwhile, up in Minneapolis, a student named Dave Arneson was running Napoleonic miniatures games in his parents' basement.[8] Arneson got a copy of the Chainmail rules; only it turned out that medieval miniatures combat wasn't very exciting,[9] and Arneson and his fellow gamers looked for a way to spice it up. A fellow named Dave Wesley gave each player a personal goal: now the figurine on the table represented Sir So-and-So, and he had a rudimentary personality. This was the dawn of tabletop role-playing. Then Arneson issued a *Star Trek* phaser to a druid, much to the disgust of the other players: this was the dawn of tabletop fantasy role-playing, although no one seemed to realize it yet.[10] The phaser wasn't enough; Arneson spent a weekend eating popcorn

---

[7] **Note for non-war-gamers:** Until computer games came along, there were two main kinds of war game: board games and miniatures games. Board games, as their name implies, are played on a board, with plastic or cardboard counters. Miniatures games are played with miniature soldiers (or tanks, or elephants, or what have you) on a sand table or some other model terrain. Miniatures gamers tend to look down on board gamers, who can't achieve as high a degree of historical accuracy as the miniatures gamers can. Board gamers, on the other hand, tend to regard miniatures gamers as fussy collectors.

[8] Basements keep coming up in the story of D&D. I wonder if the dungeons where most early adventures took place are fantasy versions of the basements of the Midwest?

[9] E.g., imagine simulating a long siege.

[10] Gygax made similar modifications to the game: "After a while, though, the guys got tired of playing. I decided one day that we were going to play a little variation of medieval combat. I secretly told one side, 'OK, you guys have a wizard in your group and here's what he can do: he can throw a fireball,'" etc.

and reading *Conan* novels, and at the end of it, he had an idea. The next time the Napoleonic miniatures people showed up in the Arnesons' basement, they found a model of a castle on the sand table. They thought it was going to be someplace in Poland, which they would storm or defend. Then Arneson told them that they were looking at the ruined castle of the Barony of Blackmoor, and that they were going to have to go into the dungeons and poke around. The Napoleonic miniatures people weren't thrilled; they would have preferred to storm the castle. But they agreed to poke around. And around, and around.

In the fall of 1972, Arneson visited Lake Geneva and introduced Gygax to Blackmoor. Gygax liked the game, and he and Arneson worked together to develop a publishable version of the rules. The first edition of Dungeons & Dragons appeared in 1974. Gygax and his business partners, Don Kaye and Brian Blume, assembled the sets by hand in Gygax's basement:[11] they put stickers on the boxes, collated the rulebooks, folded the reference sheets. Even so, they didn't know what they had on their hands. They called D&D "rules for fantastic medieval wargames," and Gygax hoped to sell fifty thousand copies, that being the approximate size of the war-gaming market. At first, D&D seemed unlikely to meet even these modest expectations. It took eleven months for Tactical Studies Rules, which is what Gygax, Kaye, and Blume called their partnership, to sell out the first thousand copies. But news of the game was traveling by word of mouth, from hobby shops to college dorms, from dorms to high schools. People called Gygax in the middle of the night to quiz him about the rules. The second thousand copies, also hand-assembled, sold in six months, and from then on sales increased exponentially. In 1975, Tactical Studies Rules incorporated and changed its name to TSR Hobbies; in 1979, the company sold seven thousand copies of the D&D Basic Set each month. Their gross income for 1980 was $4.2 million.

---

[11] See note 8, above.

3.0 I'M A FIFTH-LEVEL DARK ELF
WITH A +2 SWORD[12]

What set D&D apart from its cousins, the war games, was, first of all, the thrill of "being" someone else. In *30 Years of Adventure: A Celebration of Dungeons & Dragons,* a volume published in 2004 by Wizards of the Coast, celebrity gamer Vin Diesel remembers his twin brother selling him on D&D with the line that "[it's] a game that allows you to be anyone you want to be…." Games designer Harold Johnson heard from a friend: "It's a fantasy game. You get to play knights and wizards, clerics and thieves." The appeal isn't hard to understand, especially if "being" yourself isn't all that much fun: if you are, say, a bookish adolescent male with few social skills and no magical powers to speak of.[13] What's more, D&D offers its players a moral clarity rarely found in the real world: your character has an *alignment;* he or she can be good or evil, lawful or chaotic. Most players choose good; the paladin, a virtuous knight with magical powers, is a perennial favorite, although the evil-leaning dark elf is also popular.

In practice, though, the transformation of player into character often turns out to be cosmetic: the fearless paladin and the sexy dark elf both sound and act a lot like a thirteen-year-old boy named Ted. And what Ted likes to do, mostly, is kill anything that crosses his path. It's little wonder that Dungeons & Dragons was uncool

---

[12] This is classic cave-speak. *Fifth-level* refers to the notion of *experience levels,* which are based on experience points (see above). A fifth-level elf kicks more ass than a newly created first-level elf, but considerably less ass than a superheroic eighteenth-level elf. *+2 sword* denotes a magic sword, which gets a bonus of 2 on its dice rolls to hit a foe, and to do damage.

[13] Not everyone is drawn to the role-playing aspect of Dungeons & Dragons. Glenn Blacow, in an article called "Aspects of Adventure Gaming," describes four types of gamers, a taxonomy that has come to be known as the "Fourfold Way." The types are: war-gamers (who seek to dominate the game by means of superior strategy), "power gamers" (who seek to dominate the game by exploiting the rules to maximize their characters' power), role-players (for whom character is paramount), and storytellers (who get their kicks from the narrative aspect of the game). Of these groups, however, only the war-gamers may be immune to the pleasure of being someone else—and even they must have some sense that their characters are *kewl.*

in the 1970s and '80s. Under the guise of role-playing, the game condoned behaviors that would get you ostracized (or worse) if you tried them in the real world. The dungeon adventures that were the game's mainstay in the early '70s had only two objectives: destroy all the monsters, and get all the treasure.[14] Circa 1978, Gary Gygax wrote and published a series of adventures with a narrative arc: the characters begin by taking on a hill giant, and they are gradually drawn into the underground world of the Drow, or dark elves, one of Gygax's best-loved creations. The story was compelling to the people who played the adventures, but this may have had less to do with its complexity than with the fact that there was a story at all. In any case, the ins and outs of Drow society only slightly mitigated the game's bloody-mindedness; instead of destroying *all* monsters, the wise course now was to destroy *some* monsters.[15]

Women in the game—female players, female "nonplayer characters" who turned up in bars and dungeon cells—fared little better. Gary Alan Fine, a sociologist who in 1983 published a book-length study of fantasy role-playing games, reported that "in theory, female characters can be as powerful as males; in practice, they are often treated as chattels." Indeed, one of the players Fine observed[16] reported that he didn't like playing with women, because they inhibited his friends' natural tendency to rape the (imaginary) women they met in-game:

> Because a lot of people I know go in and pick up a woman and just walk off.... Some people get a little carried away and rape other

---

[14] Strangely, these seem to be more or less acceptable behaviors in the real world circa 2006, which raises an interesting question: Was D&D uncool because it catered to people who liked to express their aggression and greed in fantasy, rather than in reality? Or has the world become more like D&D?

[15] Level 1–4 readers may now recall another category of adventures, exemplified by the horrifically difficult *Tomb of Horrors:* those adventures in which *few* monsters could be destroyed, and your goal was mainly to keep the monsters from destroying you.

[16] In a public Minneapolis gaming group, if you're curious.

people.... Well, I've seen a lot of players just calm down because of [females].[17]

You will not be surprised to learn that, in one 1978 survey of fantasy role-playing gamers, only 2.3 percent of respondents were female; in another, only 0.4 percent. Nor did TSR, in the early days, do much to remedy this situation (I recall a print ad for D&D in which a tweenage girl is pictured playing with some boys, and enjoying herself: now *that* was a fantasy, I thought), perhaps because Gygax is a self-avowed biological determinist who believes that "women's brains are wired differently... the reason they don't play is that they're not interested in playing."

3.1 THIS IS B.A.D.D.

In 1979, an average of 6,839 young men were picking up Dungeons & Dragons each month: sooner or later there was bound to be trouble. And sure enough, that same year, a Michigan State student named James Dallas Egbert III disappeared after a game of D&D. The thing was, Egbert and his friends weren't just rolling dice and moving lead miniatures around on a card table; they had been acting out their characters' exploits in the university's steam tunnels. It seemed possible that the game had gone too far, and that Egbert had been killed, or died by misadventure. A few weeks later, Egbert turned up in Morgan City, Louisiana, and revealed

---

[17] And this is to say nothing of the player whom Fine observes playing Empire of the Petal Throne, another fantasy role-playing game published by TSR:

> Later in the game, when we meet another group of Avanthe priestess-warriors, Tom comments: "No fucking women in a blue dress [*sic*] are going to scare me.... I'll fight. They'll all be dead men.
>
> JACK: Men?
> ROGER: Is that your definition of a woman, a dead man?
> TOM: A *dead* man.

It's hard to know what to make of this, but the phrase *castration anxiety* certainly comes to mind.

that D&D had nothing to do with his disappearance, but the case caused a sensation. The private investigator hired to find Egbert published a faintly lurid book called *The Dungeon Master,* which inspired a lurid novel called *Mazes and Monsters,* which inspired a made-for-TV movie of the same name, starring Tom Hanks. Meanwhile, in Washington State, a seventeen-year-old boy shot himself in the head. Witnesses said that he had been trying to summon "D&D demons" just minutes before his death. Was Dungeons & Dragons a blood sport? Was it a gateway to Satanism? A woman named Pat Pulling, whose son, a D&D player, had also committed suicide, started an organization called Bothered About Dungeons and Dragons, or, yes, B.A.D.D., and before long D&D had joined a pantheon of mostly cooler or at least more authentically dangerous phenomena that were said to be corrupting America's youth: marijuana, rock and roll, free love, LSD, heavy metal.

Even from the point of view of a teenage boy who would have liked nothing better than to be corrupted by any of the phenomena listed above, if *corrupted* meant meeting girls or even just getting out of the house, the furor over D&D was hard to understand. Didn't the grown-ups understand what losers we were? That all we did was roll dice and shout and stuff our faces with snacks? Evidently not: in 1989, Bill Schnoebelen, a reformed Milwaukee Satanist, wrote an article called "Straight Talk on Dungeons and Dragons," which can still be found on Chick Ministries' website.[18] He listed the "brainwashing techniques" that D&D uses to lure its players into the devil's world, among which are:

> 1. Fear generation—via spells and mental imaging about fear-filled, emotional scenes, and threats to survival of FRP [fantasy role-playing] characters.
> 2. Isolation—psychological removal from traditional support structures (family, church, etc.) into an imaginary world. Physical

---

[18] Chick Ministries being, of course, the fundamentalist Protestant group responsible for all those tracts in cartoon form: there's one about the end of the world, and one about how the Jews are going to hell, and, yes, there's one about role-playing games.

isolation due to extremely time-consuming play activities outside the family atmosphere.

3. Physical torture and killings—images in the mind can be almost as real as the actual experiences. Focus of the games is upon killings and torture for power, acquisition of wealth, and survival of characters.

4. Erosion of family values—the Dungeon Master (DM) demands an all-encompassing and total loyalty, control, and allegiance.

Most of which is, of course, true, though I'd quibble at Schnoebelen's emphasis on torture—usually it was enough for us to kill the monsters without torturing them first—and at the logic of no. 4: the DM could *demand* total loyalty as much as he wanted, but he was unlikely to get it from us; we were too busy finding ways to reduce his creation to rubble, or eating ice cream. But the mention of "spells" in no. 1 is bizarre. Did Schnoebelen think that the players were actually capable of working magic? Further study of his article suggests that he did. "Just because the people playing D&D think they are playing a game doesn't mean that the evil spirits (who ARE very real) will regard it as a game. If you are doing rituals or saying spells that invite them into your life, then they will come—believe me!"[19] This was every player's fantasy: that the magic in the game would work, that we would become our characters, for real, and be rid once and for all of our lowball ability scores, our pathetic skills, our humdrum real-life equipment. If wishing, or talking, or even praying could have made it so, then there would have been a *lot* of dark elves out there, brandishing their +2 swords, and—perhaps the people at Chick Ministries will find this reassuring—a lot of paladins, too, curing us of our diseases, protecting us from evil within a ten-foot radius.

---

[19] Schnoebelen also reports that in the late 1970s, two TSR employees came to speak with him in his capacity as a Satanist, to make sure the rituals in the game were authentic. "For the most part," he assures us, "they are." This assertion must have alarmed people who had never read the D&D rulebooks, in which, to the best of my knowledge, no rituals are described. Nor do I remember a player ever "saying" a spell. Mostly people said, "I zap the troll with a fireball," or "Let's see if my sleep spell will work on these orcs."

Despite a near-total absence of evidence linking D&D to Satanism, or magic, or anything, really, except obesity and lower-back pain, Pat Pulling and Gary Gygax appeared on a special investigative episode of *60 Minutes,* which left viewers with the impression that there was "strong evidence" that Dungeons & Dragons could inspire teenagers to kill themselves, or each other. Gygax started getting death threats in the mail, and he hired a bodyguard. Yet notoriety had its advantages: in 1981, with the Egbert case still fresh in the public's mind, TSR's revenues quadrupled, to $16.5 million.

3.1.1 A FURTHER NOTE ON RITUAL

As silly as Schnoebelen's fears may sound to us now, he did get one thing right: Dungeons & Dragons is not a game. The French anthropologist Claude Lévi-Strauss notes that "Games... appear to have a *disjunctive* effect: they end in the establishment of a difference between individual players or teams where originally there was no indication of inequality. And at the end of the game they are distinguished into winners and losers." Which is, as noted above, not true of D&D: "There is neither an end to the game nor any winner." But if D&D isn't a game, then what is it, exactly? One theorist of fantasy role-playing games proposes, following Lévi-Strauss, that D&D is, in the strict sense of the term, a ritual. "Ritual, on the other hand," this is Lévi-Strauss again, "is the exact inverse: it *conjoins,* for it brings about a union... or in any case an organic relation between two initially separate groups...."[20] D&D conjoins: this is not the first thing you notice when you enter the cave; nor is it

---

[20] The theorist in question is Christopher I. Lehrich; his essay "Ritual Discourse in Role-Playing Games" can be found at *www.indie-rpgs.com/_articles/ritual_discourse_in_RPGs.html.* Specifically, Lehrich says, D&D is like a rite of passage by which a boy is inducted into manhood: the boy is removed from his familiar surroundings; he is made to wear strange costumes and utter strange sounds; at ritual's end he is received into the community in his new status. Actually, it might make more sense to think of D&D as an anti-manhood ceremony: having undergone trials by rules and by role-playing, the initiate is guaranteed immunity from growing up.

mentioned very often by the game's recruiters (or by its detractors), who prefer to talk about killing and money and other things the uninitiated can understand. And yet it is an essential feature of the game—ritual—whatever you want to call it. Adam's fighter may be more powerful than Brian's elf, but if the fighter kills the elf, or even pisses him off seriously, who will find the secret door? In order to get very far in the cave, the players need to work together.[21] Which would make D&D not very different from any other team sport, if there were another team; but there isn't. The remarkable thing about D&D is that *everyone* has to play together. Even the DM, who plays all the monsters and villains, has to cooperate; if he doesn't—if he kills the entire party of adventurers, or requires players not to cheat on life-or-death dice rolls—the chances that he will be invited to run another session are small.

Here I am tempted to advance a wild argument. It goes like this: in a society that conditions people to compete, and rewards those who compete successfully, Dungeons & Dragons is countercultural; its project, when you think about it in these terms, is almost utopian.[22] Show people how to have a good time, a mind-blowing, life-changing, all-night-long good time,[23] by cooperating with each other! And perhaps D&D is socially unacceptable because it encourages its players to drop out of the world of

---

[21] Even nominally evil player characters (see §3.0) often cooperate; they do their evil only to the nonplayer characters, who aren't in a position to resent them when the game is over. As Skip Williams, who for many years wrote the "Sage Advice" column in *Dragon*, a D&D magazine, puts it, "Evil characters tend not to act like evil people in real life. It's more of a hat you wear."

[22] Not unlike the New Games, which emerged circa 1966 as a mode of resistance to the Vietnam War (which was a "game" conditioned by the zero-sum mentality of the Cold War, but which, in the instance, both sides seemed to be losing), and persist as a way of encouraging kids to think cooperatively. It's a pity that New Games are even less cool than D&D these days.

[23] The resemblance of this description, to, say, an old-school rave, experienced by a person or persons under the influence of ecstasy, is not unintentional. Actually, a rave is one of the few things I know of that's as massively and necessarily cooperative—and as fun—as a really good game of D&D.

competition, in which the popular people win, and to tune in to another world, where things work differently, and everyone wins (or dies) together. You will object that a group of teenage boys slaughtering orcs and raping women doesn't sound like utopia. Granted. But among teenage boys whose opportunities for social interaction were otherwise not great, D&D was like a door opening. Forget for a moment that behind the door there were mostly monsters and darkness. For us, for the people who played, what waited behind that door was a world, and the world belonged to us. We could live in it as we really were; we could argue about its rules; we could learn how, by working together, to get the better of it. For some of us it was a lesson: the real world could, on occasion, and by similar means, be bested. For others of us, who never really left the game: at least we had a world.

In fact, the ability to function in another world may be the game's most important legacy. D&D provided a conceptual framework for some of the most popular computer games of the 1980s: *Wizardry, Ultima,* and *Zork* all involve poking around in dungeons and slaying monsters. *Wizardry* begat *Wolfenstein 3D, Wolfenstein* begat *Doom, Doom* begat *Quake,* and *Quake* begat *Halo:* it may be an exaggeration to say that these games could never have existed without Dungeons & Dragons, but D&D certainly showed a lot of people what kind of fun they could have by participating in a virtual reality. The game's influence is even clearer on the massively multiplayer online role-playing games: *Everquest, Ultima Online, World of Warcraft,* and *D&D Online,* which made its debut early this year. Almost every aspect of the old tabletop game has been re-created in these pretty, expensive beasts, except the pleasure of being in the same room with other human beings. Perhaps the people who spend thirty hours a week playing *World of Warcraft,* the people who used to buy and sell *Everquest* magic items for real dollars on eBay, and the people who buy online characters that have been "leveled up" by workers in the Third World, don't miss the companionship. D&D taught us to live in an imaginary place—a literal *utopia*—and if that place is engrossing enough, what does it matter if there are other people in your living room or not? And yet it sounds lonely to me. The great thing about old-fashioned, paper-and-pencil D&D was that it straddled the virtual world and the real one: when the game was over, the dungeons and dragons went back to their notebooks, but you got to keep your friends.

4.0 DADDY NEEDS A
NEW SWORD OF WOUNDING

Even now, more than thirty years after its invention, people are still playing Dungeons & Dragons. Not quite the game I played as a child: a Second Edition appeared in 1989; it tidied up the hodge-podge of rules that Advanced D&D had become, stripped the paladin of many of his powers, and was duly reviled by most old-school players. By then, Gygax had lost control of TSR; he was replaced by Lorraine Dille Williams, the heiress to the Buck Rogers fortune.[24] Williams was not generally beloved by those who worked under her; nonetheless, the company managed to publish some good material: the Gothy Ravenloft campaign setting, the killer Return to the Tomb of Horrors, and a number of successful fantasy novels. But the market for the game had stopped growing. Everyone who was going to buy the rulebooks had already done so; in order to keep selling its products to gamers, TSR had to come up with new rulebooks. Thus we got, among other things, *The Complete Book of Gnomes & Halflings,* 127 pages on "The Myths of the Halflings," "A Typical Gnomish Village," etc.

Meanwhile, TSR spent a lot of money pursuing licensing deals and starting lawsuits, several of them against Gygax, to protect its copyrights. Changes in the bookselling industry further eroded the company's revenues; TSR went deeply into debt, and in 1997 Williams sold the company to Wizards of the Coast, which was best known for a collectible card game called Magic: The Gathering. In

---

[24] For the long version of this story, see the Scenario, below.

2000, Wizards published a Third Edition of Dungeons & Dragons, which systematized what had been erratic or arbitrary in the first two editions. Reactions to the Third Edition have generally been positive, although some players grumble that the rules are now *too* consistent. William Connors, a designer for TSR and, briefly, for Wizards, says that with the Third Edition, "the heart and soul of the game was gone. To me, it wasn't all that much more exciting than playing with an Excel spreadsheet."[25] A gamer I talked to in a Manhattan hobby shop says that he's afraid the Third Edition is for "power campaigners": people who exploit the rules to make their characters as powerful as possible, at the expense of role-playing plausibility or narrative interest. Nor has the proliferation of rulebooks been checked. Wizards of the Coast publishes about two dozen official rulebooks for D&D, not counting dozens of supplementary books by other publishers; and the Third Edition rulebooks have already been superceded by Edition 3.5.

Meanwhile, a stranger transformation has taken place: D&D is no longer uncool. In part, this is because the game has become more sophisticated, more narrative-based, less single-mindedly devoted to the destruction of monsters. A live-action role-playing game[26] called Vampire: The Masquerade introduced members of the goth subculture to gaming; some of them switched over to D&D, with the result that there are more women gamers now, and they are in a position to make their own version of the game.[27] Also, some of the people who create mass culture now were once themselves gamers. There are graphic depictions of D&D in *The X-Files* and *Freaks and Geeks* and *Buffy the Vampire Slayer;* Gary Gygax has even made

---

[25] Connors was speaking to Monte Cook, a designer who has interviewed many of the TSR personnel. The interviews are available at *montecook.com,* an invaluable resource for anyone who wants to know more about the history of Dungeons & Dragons.

[26] I.e., a game where people act out their characters theatrically: costumes and running around are often involved.

[27] One female gamer reports, "I have been a player in an all-female game where we spent all session shopping." Is that a Prada Cloak of Disappearing?

a cameo appearance on *Futurama*. Vin Diesel admits happily to being a gamer; Stephen Colbert admits to having been one. Mostly, though, D&D has become acceptable because people get used to things. As John Rateliff, who has worked on the game since the early '90s, puts it, "It's kind of like rock music. All it takes is time for people to get over their fear of the new and find out whether it's something they might actually enjoy trying themselves."

The question is, are new people joining the game? According to a recent survey, there are four million D&D players in the United States, and that number hasn't changed much in the last few years. The majority of the players are between eighteen and twenty-four years old, then you have the twelve-to-seventeen-year-olds and the twenty-five-to-thirty-four-year-olds, who play in roughly equal numbers; then the thirty-five-to-forty-five-year-olds, and finally the eight-to-eleven-year-olds, very few of whom play D&D, or have even heard of the game. The survey notes cheerily that a third of these tweenagers expressed interest in learning about D&D, but whether Wizards of the Coast can translate this interest into sales—and players—remains to be seen. Last summer I visited Gen Con, a gaming convention that has been held annually since 1968, when Gary Gygax and his friends rented out the Lake Geneva Horticultural Hall.[28] The convention has grown to about twenty-six thousand attendees annually, and it has moved from Lake Geneva to Milwaukee and now to Indianapolis, where it occupies the convention center downtown, between the state house and the football stadium. I didn't see many twelve-to-seventeen-year-olds, and the ones I did see were gathered in the Xbox area, blowing each other away in *Halo 2*. The people who filled the gaming rooms and prowled the Exhibit Hall were men and women in their twenties and thirties, some of them in doublets and hose, some in goth regalia, most in shorts and T-shirts and jeans and sneakers and sandals. If they had dispersed into the streets of Indianapolis no one

---

[28] **Note to Level 3–4 Readers:** It turns out that Gen Con predates Dungeons & Dragons; in fact, Gygax and Dave Arneson met for the first time at Gen Con 2, in 1969.

would have known them for anything but citizens, if it weren't for their convention badges and the fervent light in their eyes. Of course, these were the people who loved gaming enough to travel to central Indiana and spend several hundred dollars on entrance fees, game tickets, hotels, and restaurants, which, incidentally, were serving special game-themed meals: whatever else gamers may be, they are apparently willing to spend money on almost anything game-related.[29] You wouldn't expect a fifteen-year-old to turn up here on his own—except that in the early days of Gen Con, you heard stories about kids who did just that. They came by bus and hitchhiked to the convention center; they gamed all day and slept in the hallways at night because they couldn't afford hotel rooms.

I didn't play much D&D while I was at Gen Con, in part because the Third Edition rules are too different from the rules I grew up with, and in part because tournament play isn't my cup of tea: it's goal directed, without much emphasis on role-playing.[30] However, according to the same survey, the largest group of D&D players are just my age: thirty-five-year-old men make up almost 10 percent of the D&D-playing population (twenty-two-year-olds are next, at 7 percent, then thirty-two-year-olds, at 5.5 percent). These are the people whose adolescence corresponds to the peak of D&D's popularity, the ones who were in college when the Second Edition came out and the game's popularity surged again. At the risk of drawing false conclusions, I will venture to speak for my demographic: we were hooked early, and the hooks went deep

---

[29] Among these dishes was the Cthulhu Calamari, which I have to confess I ordered. It turned out to be a half-size portion of rubbery deep-fried squid in an oversweet sauce: one of the worst foods I've ever eaten, which, I guess, serves me right.

[30] Also, I got sucked into a game of Call of Cthulhu, a role-playing game set in the universe of horror writer H. P. Lovecraft. This is basically another story, but as I may not have the chance to tell it in print elsewhere, I will note that in one round of the game, we role-played the highest echelon of the current administration: Bush, Cheney, Rumsfeld, Rice, Porter Goss, and Michael Chertoff. The really eerie thing about this round was how *plausible* it all seemed, even when we were herded into a bunker where Cheney shot Bush and Rice and Rumsfeld, and I shot Cheney, and Cheney shot me. (Goss had already committed suicide under mysterious circumstances.) It could happen, I tell you.

into us. Few of the people I talked to or read about, who have been involved with gaming since the early '90s or longer, show any sign of wanting to quit. John Rateliff says, "If I'm still alive [at seventy-five], I'll still be playing. Why not? I intend to still be listening to the music I like and reading the books I like at [that age], if I'm still able. Why shouldn't I still be enjoying my favorite hobby?" Skip Williams, who has been working on D&D since First Edition days, has left Wizards of the Coast, but he can't seem to leave gaming; right now he's sprucing up a bunch of "classic monsters" for a new monster book. Even Brian Blume, who left TSR after a bitter struggle with Gary Gygax, and seems unlikely to have fond memories of those days, was recently roped into a game of Boot Hill, the Wild West–era role-playing game he cowrote in 1975. "I was at a games convention in Des Moines, and a fellow was running a big barroom shoot-out, and I got involved. It was a big nostalgic moment." Apparently the referee begged Blume to play the sheriff, the toughest role, because usually in those situations the sheriff is the first one to be shot. "Were you shot?" I asked. "I role-played it a little," Blume said, and chuckled. "I got about halfway through, and I'm happy with that."

If Wizards of the Coast can't find a way to make Dungeons & Dragons compelling to children, then the day will come when D&D is the equivalent of bingo or shuffleboard, played by forgetful old men in retirement homes, community centers, and, yes, church basements. "I'm an elf of some sort," one of the players will say. "Where did I put that character sheet?" But the best hope for D&D's future currency may be that we thirty-five-year-olds will overcome our geekdom for at least long enough to start families. "My kids are coming tomorrow," said one Gen Con visitor, a thirty-six-year-old man who had been playing D&D for twenty-four years. "They've never played before, but I thought I'd give them the chance to try it out." There's no reason to think that children have lost the desire to become elves, warriors, wizards, and thieves. If we're lucky, they'll be willing to play with their parents.

THE SCENARIO, OR, WAYNE
AND I MEET THE WIZARD
BACKGROUND INFORMATION

We are far enough into the cave now that I can tell you that I have mixed feelings about Dungeons & Dragons. I played fantasy role-playing games more or less incessantly from 1978, when my father brought home the D&D Basic Set, until 1985, when I changed high schools and fell out of constant contact with my gamer friends. I played so much that it's hard for me to understand in retrospect how I managed to do anything else, and the truth is that I *didn't* do anything else. I was a mediocre student; I didn't see hardly any of New York City, where I lived; I knew less about girls than I did about the Gelatinous Cube (immune to cold and sleep; takes normal damage from fire). I played at friends' houses; I played in the school cafeteria; I played in the hallway between classes; I cut class to play in whispers in the library. I hesitate to say that I was addicted to role-playing games only because I never knew what it was like to go without them; in D&D I had found something I loved more than life itself. Then a number of things happened, and for fifteen years I didn't think about D&D at all. I was living in San Francisco, where *dungeon* referred to something entirely different, and life seemed mutable and good, like a game. In December 2001, I moved back to New York, and soon afterward I began to think about D&D again. It turned out that my agent's office was a block from the Compleat Strategist, the hobby shop where I used to buy my role-playing games. I wasn't eager to revisit that part of my life, which I thought of as a dangerous mire from which I had miraculously escaped, but I slunk into the store. Nothing had changed: *nothing*. The same pads of hex paper[31] stood in the same racks by the door, their covers bleached by twenty years of sunlight. It was as if the place had been preserved as a museum to the

---

[31] Like graph paper, but printed with hexagons instead of squares. Commonly used for large-area and wilderness maps.

heyday of tabletop role-playing games; it was as if someone had set out to demonstrate that you *could* go home again. Maybe I wanted to come home; maybe I had never really left that mire; maybe I needed to own up to an old love—an old habit—in order to make my life whole. *This thing of dorkness I acknowledge mine.* All I knew was that I had to do something about Dungeons & Dragons: put it behind me once and for all, or return to its warm, embarrassing embrace. For a long time I did neither. Then one day, when my friend Wayne and I were talking about our gaming days, he said, Why don't you interview E. Gary Gygax? It made sense. Gygax was the source of Dungeons & Dragons, the wizard who cast the original spell.[32] Perhaps by going to see him I could get the spell lifted at last. And besides, as Wayne was quick to point out, how cool would it be to meet Gary Gygax? Not to mention, he said, the possibility that we could convince him somehow to play D&D with us. *We,* he said, because of course it had to be both of us. You need three people to play D&D; besides, Wayne was under the spell, too.

LAKE GENEVA

Gary Gygax still lives in Lake Geneva, a resort town about two hours northeast of Chicago. Incorporated in 1844, it has a cutesified little downtown and a historical museum in which a street from Old Lake Geneva is haphazardly re-created, down to the Indian arrowheads, barber poles, and photographs of former firemen. There's an excellent video arcade, with a vintage *Robotron* console still in good working order. There's a place that sells Frozen Custard

---

[32] Well, Gygax and Arneson, anyway. But Gygax's has always been the name to conjure with. Perhaps because it's such an excellent name: *Gygax.* It sounds alien, as though E. Gary Gygax were the point of tangency between the ordinary world and the world of dragons and magic. (Actually, it turns out that Gygax is a Swiss name. It comes, Gygax says, from the Latin, *gigantus,* meaning "gigantic," which suggests that Gygax's ancestors must have been extraordinarily large. Gary Gygax himself is only 5'11", so either the race has fallen off, or he's telling me tall tales. Which, in fact, he has a habit of doing; maybe that's what *gigantus* really refers to. But I'm getting ahead of myself.

Butterburgers, two distinct Midwestern delicacies, I hope. There's a big lake, which freezes in winter; people build a shantytown on the ice and go fishing for bass and cisco. Gygax was born in Chicago, but he grew up here, and he returned to Lake Geneva in his mid-twenties to raise his family. It's not hard to see how Dungeons & Dragons would come out of a place like this, a place where, on a fine spring night, you can find the town's youthful population walking up and down Main Street, from the ice cream parlor to the arcade, from the arcade to the lake. If you grew up here, you would need to dream of *something*.

Gygax and I agreed to meet on a Saturday in May. I said I'd come at eleven; he said, come at nine, I'll make you breakfast. So Wayne and I found ourselves outside his big yellow house one gray morning, wondering if we were worthy to meet the Wizard. Then he let us in. Gygax does not look unwizardly: he has a long white ponytail, a white beard, and fierce black eyebrows, like Gandalf. He is shorter than Gandalf, however, and stouter, and more cheerful: picture him as a cross between Gandalf and Bilbo Baggins.[33] A lifelong smoker, Gygax sounds a bit like Tom Waits, especially when he laughs, and he laughs often. He had a mild stroke in 2004, and his doctor ordered him to quit cigarettes; now he smokes Monterrey Black and Mild cigarillos, one after the other. He led us to a table at the corner of the screened porch, which was cluttered with a long life's worth of wicker furniture and floor lamps. In the center of the table lay a big pleather-bound copy of the Holy Scriptures: maybe it was there by accident, or maybe Gygax wanted to reassure us that he wasn't a Satanist. I had told him that I was writing for a magazine called *The Believer,* after all. As we sat down, his wife appeared from within the house, saw us, and cried,

---

[33] **Note to Level 3–4 Readers:** For a portrait of the youthful E. Gary Gygax, consider the cover of the original *Players Handbook*. The face of the thief who's prising a gem from the eye of the idol is Gygax. Actually, the thief who's helping him is Gygax, too, and so is the fighter cleaning his two-handed sword in the lower foreground, and so are all the people on the back cover. Apparently the artist, D. A. Trampier, wasn't good with faces; he learned how to draw Gygax and stopped there.

"They're two hours early!" Gygax excused himself and conferred within. Then he came out as if nothing had happened; he lit a cigarillo and began to speak.

E. Gary Gygax was born in 1938. His father, Ernst Gygax, came to America from Switzerland; he settled in Chicago, and one summer he went to a dance in Lake Geneva. There he met Almina Emilie Burdick, the daughter of an old Lake Geneva family, married her, and returned to Chicago, not necessarily in that order. Ernst wanted to play the violin, he put himself through music school and for a time he played with the Chicago Symphony Orchestra, but when he saw that he would never make first chair he gave it up and sold clothes instead. He was, Gygax says, an attentive father, and he must have been a permissive father also, because Gygax's childhood was marked by a disregard for rules and obligations. He went to school half a block from his childhood house in Lake Geneva, but he was rarely to be found there. "It was just dull and stupid," he says, "and you know, I had so many other things I wanted to do. I had a day full of active going out with my friends, playing chess, hanging around, trying to pick up girls, usually without any success whatsoever. What? Sit home? Do schoolwork? Unthinkable." Instead he threw firecrackers at the chief of the waterworks, shot .22s down empty streets, and haunted the abandoned Oak Hill Sanatorium, a five-story brick building that overlooked Lake Geneva. He played make-believe with the kids next door: he was a cowboy named Jim Slade, and he got the drop on his friends so often that they quit in disgust.

Easygoing as he sounds, Gygax likes to win; there is in him more than a little of the Ernst who would be first violin or nothing. You can hear it in the way that he talks about the invention of Dungeons & Dragons. Gygax and Dave Arneson are credited equally as authors of the original game, but as Gygax tells it, Arneson had at most a minor role in the process. When I asked him whether Arneson ran his Blackmoor campaign before the D&D rules were written—a fact which seems beyond doubt, and which establishes Arneson's involvement in the creation of the game—

Gygax answered evasively, "Um, he was up in Minneapolis, and he ran a lot of game campaigns. He was using my Chainmail rules for a campaign and I think that was called Blackmoor." Arneson, for his part, claims that he scrapped the Chainmail rules early on, in favor of a more complex system derived from Civil War–era naval simulations.[34] And the gloom thickens: Arneson sued TSR more than once for royalties and a coauthorship credit on the Advanced Dungeons & Dragons rulebooks; the court decided in his favor, but as far as I know he never got the credit.[35] Arneson is legally enjoined from discussing the matter, and Gygax doesn't like to talk about it either, perhaps because it reflects badly on him, or perhaps because he is at heart a Midwesterner, and so not disposed to speak ill of his fellow man. As we talked, though, it became clear that Gygax thinks strategically about more or less everything. He mentioned that his son Luke had served in the first Gulf War: "I told him when he was over there for Desert Shield, I said, 'Well, here's what's going to happen. The [Coalition's] left flank is gonna come around and pocket all those dummies!' And that's exactly what they did. I couldn't believe it, you know? Boy, Saddam Hussein's not a general." Wayne asked Gygax what he would have done in Saddam's place. Gygax thought about it, then answered, "I would have gotten right out of Kuwait....You'd have to slow 'em up and you'd try to fight a guerilla war." He conceded that against Allied airpower, the Iraqis would have lost anyhow. But it didn't stop him from figuring out how to make the best of a weak position.

Gygax's own position at TSR had become weak by 1982. In order to finance the publication of D&D in 1974, he and his partner Don Kaye had brought in a friend named Brian Blume, whose father, Melvin, was willing to invest money in the company. Kaye died in 1976, and Brian got his brother Kevin named to TSR's board.

----

[34] **Note to Level 1–4 Readers:** From which D&D essentials like *armor class* and *hit points* are derived.

[35] My copy of the *Monster Manual*, one of the contested volumes, reads "By Gary Gygax" on the cover.

Gygax was the president of TSR, but the Blumes effectively controlled the company; to keep Gygax further in check they brought
in three outside directors, a lawyer and two businessmen who knew
nothing about gaming but always voted with the Blumes. So Gygax
moved to Los Angeles and became president of Dungeons & Dragons Entertainment, which produced a successful D&D cartoon, and
set out to produce a D&D movie. This was, to put it mildly, a strategic retreat. Gygax rented King Vidor's mansion, high up in Beverly
Hills, with a bar, a pool table, and a hot tub with a view of everything from Hollywood to Catalina. He had a Cadillac and a driver;
he had lunch with Orson Welles, though he mentions with Gygax-
ian modesty that "I find no greatness through association."[36] Here a
whiff of scandal enters the story. Gygax had separated from his first
wife, the mother of five of his six children; he had not yet married
his second wife, Gail.[37] In the interim, well, it was Hollywood, and
Gygax was in possession of a desirable hot tub. Gygax refers to the
girlfriends who used to drive him around—he doesn't drive; never
has—and to a certain party attended by the contestants of the Miss
Beverly Hills International Beauty Pageant. But he also mentions
that he had a sand table set up in the barn, where he and the screen-
writers for the D&D cartoon used to play Chainmail miniatures.
This is perhaps why Gygax, unlike other men who leave their wives
and run off to L.A., is not odious: his love of winning is tempered
by an even greater love of playing, and of getting others to play
along. He ends the story about the beauty-pageant girls with the
observation that Luke, who was living with him at the time, was in
heaven, seated between Miss Germany and Miss Finland.

---

[36] Which didn't stop him from recruiting Welles to play the villain in the Dungeons &
Dragons movie, a part which Welles apparently accepted. If only Welles had lived a little
longer, and the movie had been made, instead of the dismal D&D movie that *was* made in
2000, starring, mysteriously, Jeremy Irons and Thora Birch.

[37] The same wife who was dismayed to find Wayne and me sitting on her porch early one
Saturday morning. About halfway through our interview, she came out of the house again
and asked, incredulously, "Is he still talking?" He was. "He doesn't have that much to say!"
she exclaimed, and left without another word.

Gygax spent a lot of money in Hollywood. According to Brian Blume, he paid the screenwriter James Goldman, best known for *A Lion in Winter,* five hundred thousand dollars for the script of the would-be D&D movie, but a movie deal remained elusive. Meanwhile, TSR had other problems: believing that it would continue to grow indefinitely, the Blumes had overstaffed the company; they invested in expensive computer equipment, office furniture, a fleet of company cars. But TSR's growth spurt was over. By 1984, the company was $1.5 million in debt, and the bank was ready to perfect its liens on TSR's trademarks: in effect, to repossess Dungeons & Dragons. Gygax got word that the Blumes were trying to sell TSR, and he returned to Lake Geneva, where he persuaded the board of directors to fire Kevin Blume and published a new D&D rulebook to raise cash.[38] At the same time, Gygax looked for people to invest in the company. While he was living in Los Angeles, he'd become friends with a writer named Flint Dille, with whom he collaborated on a series of Choose Your Own Adventure–type novels. Flint arranged for Gygax to meet his sister, Lorraine Dille Williams, who, in addition to the Buck Rogers fortune, had experience in hospital and not-for-profit administration. Gygax asked Williams to invest in TSR; Williams demurred, but agreed to advise Gygax on how to get the company back on its feet.

In May 1985, Gygax exercised a stock option that gave him a controlling interest in TSR; he named himself CEO, and hired Williams as a general manager. And here the darkness of the cave becomes so great that almost nothing can be seen. Some time in the summer of 1985, Williams, impressed by the potential value of TSR's intellectual property, decided to take control of the company. She bought out the Blume brothers, who wanted to quit anyway; but first she got Brian Blume to exercise *his* stock option,

---

[38] *Unearthed Arcana,* if you're wondering. The book is a miscellany of rules, spells, and character classes; it introduced to the game the gnome race, the seldom-played cavalier, and the beloved barbarian, along with spells like Withdraw, Banish, and Invisibility to Undead, which may or may not have expressed Gygax's feelings toward the Blumes.

which meant that Williams ended up with a majority of the shares of TSR. At this point, Brian Blume says, "ugly things happened." Blume says that Gygax tried to fire Williams and hire Gail Carpenter (the future Mrs. E. Gary Gygax) in her place. Gygax says that he wanted to fire Williams when she was still only a manager, but was advised not to, and didn't, until it was too late. Flint Dille speculates that Gygax wanted the company for himself. "Gary was interested in running TSR again. He was going to replace the board with his then-girlfriend, family members, and pets. And Lorraine said, You can't do that. We don't want to replace one tyranny with another."

For nearly a year after we met Gygax, Wayne and I entertained various wild theories about what had really happened, and why. Then I found Lorraine Williams. She has kept silent about TSR since she left the company, in 1997, but she agreed to talk with me for some reason, perhaps because I didn't sound like a hard-core gamer, or because even keeping silent no longer seems important to her after all these years. I hoped for something extraordinary from our conversation: a revelation, a glimmer of light in the dark heart of the cave. I was disappointed. "There's no great, hidden story," Williams told me, "as much as people would like there to be one." She saw the potential for TSR to move beyond the sluggish market for role-playing games: "If you look at the track record of what has been published by TSR, and how many people in the fantasy and science-fiction area got their start publishing with TSR, it's impressive. And I found that exciting. I also saw an opportunity that we were never really able to capitalize on, and that was the ability to go in and develop intellectual property." She moved in. "And it was my intention at that time," she said, "and I really thought that Gary and I had actually worked out the deal, that he would continue to have a very strong role, a leading role in the creative process, and I would take over the management. But that didn't work for a bunch of really extraneous reasons." Williams declined to say what those reasons were, but her brother speculates, plausibly, that they had to do with the Los Angeles operation: basically, Gygax didn't want to give up King Vidor's mansion, not when a movie deal could come through any day, not when he was having so much fun.[39] Gloom, gloom.

When Gygax learned that Williams had bought the Blumes' shares, he tried to block the sale in court. He lost. Lorraine Williams had outmaneuvered him, and she would continue to do so through the 1980s and '90s, thwarting his attempts to create games that were, in her eyes, infringements on TSR's intellectual property.[40] Gygax succumbed to the business equivalent of air superiority. In 1986, he became the chairman of the board of directors of a company called New Infinities Productions, which published the Cyborg Commando role-playing game, which has been utterly lost, like most of the role-playing games published in the 1980s. Not even the Compleat Strategist stocks it anymore.

King Vidor's mansion has been torn down; Gary Gygax is back in an old, cluttered house a few blocks from where he grew up. He has sold or renounced his rights to Dungeons & Dragons, and the money he made in TSR's fat years seems mostly to be gone, too. He continues to write D&D supplements with names like *Gary Gygax's Fantasy Fortifications,* but the market for such work is small: a third-party D&D title is doing well if it sells five thousand copies. Gygax is still designing his own games, too. He worked for a while on a fantasy role-playing game called Dangerous Journeys, and now he's working on one called Lejendary Adventures, a rules-lite alternative to the behemoth that Dungeons & Dragons has become. I haven't

---

[39] And indeed: while Wayne and I were talking to Gygax, his son Luke called to say that he was moving to Monterey, California, which prompted Gygax to list some places where he would have liked to live—New Orleans, San Luis Obispo—"But I said, fuck 'em, they won't let you smoke, and, land of fruits and nuts, bah." He concluded, "You know I'd still be up there on top of Summit Ridge Drive if it was my choice."

[40] The decision to keep fighting Gygax must have made business sense, but when you look at how much it cost TSR, and how little the company gained by it, in the long run, their victory seems Pyrrhic. For the company, at least: Williams says she did fine by the sale of TSR in 1997, and her brother Flint suspects that she came out ahead. Which makes her the winner in this story, I guess, by any real standard.

played Lejendary Adventures, but to judge from the rulebook the game seems to be haunted by the specter of copyright infringement: characters are called *avatars;* classes are called *orders;* experience points are called *merits;* the elf has been renamed the *Ilf.* This despite the fact that *elf* is uncopyrightable: it's as if Gygax were still dodging Lorraine Williams after all these years. And yet he doesn't seem to feel much rancor, or much regret. Perhaps that's because, win or lose, Gygax has made a whole life of playing games; and he is still playing. He has a weekly game of Metamorphosis Alpha, a science-fiction role-playing game, with Jim Ward, the game's author. He plays old-fashioned D&D regularly with his son, Alex, and Ward, and sometimes with fans who make pilgrimages to Lake Geneva. And no one ever comes to ask why he isn't in school! No wonder he laughs so often.

THE TEETH OF BARKASH-NOUR

Wayne and I took Gygax to lunch at an Italian restaurant on the outskirts of Lake Geneva: an expensive place, Gygax warned us. Our sandwiches cost six or seven dollars each. After lunch, we returned to his house to play some Dungeons & Dragons. Wayne and I felt curiously listless; it had already been a long day of talking; Wayne wasn't sure he remembered how to play; I would have been happy to go back to our motel room and sleep. This happens to me often: I decide that I want something; I work and work at it; and just as the object of my quest comes into view, it suddenly comes to seem less valuable, not valuable at all. I can find no compelling reason to seize it and often I don't. (This has never been the case, curiously, in role-playing games, where my excitement increases in a normal way as the end of the adventure approaches. Which is probably another reason why I like the games more than the life that goes on around them, and between them.) I wonder if we would have turned back if Gygax hadn't already gone into the house and come back with his purple velvet dice bag and a black binder, a module he wrote for a tournament in

1975. This was before the Tolkien estate threatened to sue TSR, and *halflings* were still called *hobbits*. So I got to play a hobbit thief and a magic-user and Wayne played a cleric and a fighter, and for four and a half hours we struggled through a wilderness adventure in a looking-glass world of carnivorous plants, invisible terrain, breathable water, and so on. All of which Gygax presented with a minimum of fuss. The author of Dungeons & Dragons doesn't much care for role-playing: "If I want to do that," he said, "I'll join an amateur theater group." In fact, D&D, as DM'ed by E. Gary Gygax, is not unlike a miniatures combat game. We spent a lot of time just moving around, looking for the fabled Teeth of Barkash-Nour, which were supposed to lie in a direction indicated by the "tail of the Great Bear's pointing." Our confusion at first was pitiable, almost Beckettian.

> GYGAX: You run down northeast along the ridge, and you can see the river to your north and to your northeast. So which way do you want to go?
>
> PAUL: The river is flowing south.
>
> WAYNE: Which is the direction we ultimately want to go, right?
>
> PAUL: We have to wend in the direction of the tail of the...
>
> PAUL, WAYNE: "Great Bear's pointing."
>
> PAUL: But we have no idea which way that is.
>
> WAYNE: Tail of the Great Bear's pointing. Maybe we should go north.

The sky clouds over; raindrops fall; the clouds part and the light turns rich yellow. The screen porch smells of cigar smoke. I want to go outside, to walk by Lake Geneva in early May, to follow the beautiful woman Wayne and I saw walking by the shore, to meet a stranger, to live. But I can't get up. I roll the dice. I'm not tired anymore; I'm not worried about making a fool of myself in front of Gygax, who obviously couldn't care less. And something strange is happening: Wayne and I are starting to play well. We climb a cliff by means of a magic carpet; we bargain with invisible creatures in an invisible lake. We steal eggs from a hippogriff's nest; we chase away giant crabs by threatening them with the illusion of a giant, angry lobster.[41] The scenario was designed for a group of six or eight characters, but by dint of cooperation and sound tactics (basically, we avoid fighting any monster that isn't directly in our path) we make it through, from one page of Gygax's black binder to the next. So we come to the final foe, the Slimy Horror, which turns our two spellcasters into vegetables; my hobbit thief and Wayne's fighter don't stand a chance against it. "That was pretty good," Gygax says. He lets us read through the scenario, noting all the monsters we didn't kill, all the treasure that was never ours. The Teeth of Barkash-Nour are very powerful: one of them increases your character's strength permanently; another transports you to a different plane of existence. We were so close! So close, Wayne and I tell each other. We did better than we ever expected to; in fact, we almost won.

POSTSCRIPT

I would like to tell you that playing D&D with Gary Gygax lifted whatever spell I was under, and that when we left Lake Geneva, I embarked on a new life, unhaunted by the past. But here, outside the cave, things are rarely so simple. I still eye my weatherbeaten copy of the *Players Handbook,* with Gygax's face all over the cover, and think about how much fun it would be to go in one more time. Wayne has moved to another city, but he and I are talking about meeting up at Gen Con this summer. In the meantime, we both have work to do. Maybe that's all the peace you can make with the past: you agree that it can come back, but you make it meet you for just a weekend, at a convention center in a city far from your home. Or maybe that's just my way of making peace.

I talked to Gary Gygax again in March of this year, to ask, among other things, if there was any truth to the rumor that he was diagnosed with stomach cancer in the early 1980s, and that he

---

[41] We acted out the illusion, waving our arms and making lobster noises, which alarmed Gygax.

moved to L.A. because he didn't want to spend the last six months of his life fighting with the Blume brothers in Lake Geneva. "No," he said. "I have an abdominal aortic aneurysm, though." He told me that he'd found out about it in January; the doctors tell him it's inoperable. One day it will rupture and that will be the end. "I'm in no hurry," he said. And indeed, here he was, telling me about Elastolin plastic miniatures, and a hobby-shop owner named Harry Bodenstadt, who used to run a game called the Siege of Boden-burg, in order to sell miniature castles to war-gamers in Wisconsin in the 1960s. From which you could conclude, I guess, that games are everything for Gygax, or that everything is a game; but I don't think that would be quite right. I think that he has found a way to live. ✱

Thanks to Michelle Vuckovich and Jennifer Estaris for their help researching this article, and of course to Wayne, for being a part of it. Gary Gygax died on March 4, 2008. We miss him.

WAITING FOR
THE BAD THING

DISCUSSED: *Pre-9/11 Prophecy, Corgis, Apocalypse Now, The Celebrity Circuit, Prurient Brinkmanship, The Attraction/Revulsion to Retail, Esalen, Bourgeois Notions of Good Taste, Assuming Responsibility for Your Protagonists, Coffee Drinks, Post-Humanist Partying, The EU's Constitution, The Possibility of an Island, Scotch Tape*

Any minute now Michel Houellebecq, the bad boy of French literature, is going to do something very, very bad. It's true I've been on the road with him all week and his behavior has been impeccable, but something's got to give. There's too much history. What about his purported obsession with sex clubs and prostitutes? What about his penchant for hitting on female journalists, explaining that only one night with him will guarantee the real story? What about the time he called Islam "the stupidest religion"? Surely, the man's going to bust out with something reprehensible, and now, in his smoke-filled semi-suite at the Bel Age in L.A., is as good a time as any. He flies back to Europe tomorrow.

Houellebecq, forty-eight, is a slight man, fragile-seeming, handsome in his way. There's a boyish gleam to him that calls to mind that terrible disease where children age rapidly. I have to stop and remind myself that he's just a forty-eight-year-old man. Right now he slouches in a swivel chair while a woman he's met tonight, a well-known book critic, kneels before him. They speak in low tones about the possibility of love in a loveless universe, or something like that. I'm sitting on a sofa with a few other people drinking beer and whiskey and waiting for the bad thing. Maybe he'll denounce Allah while pissing on a Gideon Bible, assuming the Bel Age provides them. Maybe he'll curl up on the sofa and weep and curse liberal democracy. Maybe he'll demand the lot of us blow him. Maybe he'll do all of these things, but I doubt it. He's been a perfect gentleman since San Francisco. A sleepy gentleman, at that.

Still, I can't leave. I might miss something major. What if he orders up racist transsexual escorts to fist him while he questions the validity of monotheism? There's another journalist in the room, Brendan Bernhard from the *LA Weekly,* and I can't leave him here to witness any badness without me. Brendan wants to go home, too, but it's a stalemate, a sad case of prurient brinkmanship. So we wait here in the not-so-enfant-terrible's room and watch him get wooed by the kneeling book critic and we crack some jokes with Sylvie, the French cultural attaché (who also wants to go home), and wait some more. Any minute now…

I've been a Houellebecq fan for a while. I even wrote an essay about him for this magazine a few years ago, but it never occurred to me I might get to meet him, let alone take a trip with the man. Margaret Atwood once wrote that wanting to meet a writer because you loved his book is like enjoying some pâté and wanting to meet the duck. But when I think about it, there is a part of me that wants to meet a duck, and so when the call came asking if I'd like to have a public conversation with Houellebecq in L.A. at the Hammer Museum, and spend the preceding week with him driving down the Pacific Coast Highway, which was his condition for the tour, I looked around at my toy-infested Queens apartment, my wailing, food-encrusted eleven-month-old son, my sleep-deprived wife, and said, "Sure."

It's been a long week for me. For Michel Houellebecq, it's been a long life. Born on the island of Réunion in the Indian Ocean, raised by a grandmother after his parents ditched him, Houellebecq was a morphine addict at eighteen and has spent some time in psychiatric clinics. His first book, an extended essay called *H.P. Lovecraft: Against the World, Against Life,* whose English-language publication (by Believer Books) has brought him out here to California, begins: "Life is painful and disappointing." He's been exploring that theme with increasing pungency and sales ever since.

While Houellebecq had gained a certain notoriety with his first two novels, it was Houellebecq's third, *Platform,* that made him more than just a famous writer. The novel revolves around the sex-tourism trade and ends with a Muslim terrorist attack. His lover killed, the narrator resigns himself to lonely bitterness, his only joy news of Palestinian deaths on the Gaza Strip. "It meant one less Muslim," he observes. Houellebecq, refusing to hide behind the brutal generalizations of his protagonists (that the main ones tend to share his first name makes it difficult), concurred with some of them when he told *Lire* magazine that "Islam" is the "stupidest religion." A few weeks before 9/11 Houellebecq appeared on the cover of a Moroccan newspaper beneath the headline: THIS MAN HATES YOU. The Houellebecq Affair became a touchstone for debate in France and Europe, perhaps a way to broach certain subjects—the changing demographics of Europe, the struggle over the forging of a European Union identity—at a safe distance, while heaping a complex web of catastrophes and misunderstandings at the feet of one slightly dweeby novelist. (Houellebecq, in his former life, debugged computers for the French Ministry of Agriculture.) Some French Muslim groups hauled him to court for libel, where the judge asked him if he was familiar with the French legal code pertaining to the case. No, Houellebecq replied under oath, but he imagined it had a lot of "boring passages."

Houellebecq was acquitted and the controversy died down,

though 9/11 did give the book a prophetic mystique. Still, the rancor has never really gone away. Houellebecq has lived in semi-exile in Ireland with his wife and dog, and, more recently, in Spain.

I'm hoping to spend a few hours decompressing after the flight from New York, but in the elevator of the Hotel Nikko in San Francisco I chance upon my contact for the trip. Or she chances upon me. When the elevator doors open, a woman I've never laid eyes on before shouts my name and embraces me. Dorna Khazeni was born in Tehran but has lived in California most of her life. She's an attractive and worldly translator who speaks French, Farsi, and English. It was her godfather, the movie producer Tom Luddy, who first gave her the idea to translate Houellebecq's Lovecraft book into English.

"Follow me," she says, and the next thing I know we're at Enrico's, a café in North Beach, with the Bad Boy of French Literature himself.

Maybe it's his jet lag, but Houellebecq seems to be the master of a kind of heavy-lidded stare that says, "Anytime You Want to Shut Your Stupid Mouth I'll Be Quite Delighted." He drinks a string of double espressos and sucks on his Philip Morris cigarettes, holding them between his middle and ring fingers, gnawing on the filter tips. The nicotine stain on his fingernail seems to possess a mysterious power.

We talk a bit, with long silences in between, about his flight, the perils of translation, his love for his corgi (later he'll confide that he "wouldn't survive the death of his dog"). His English is quite good, though he mumbles and pauses a lot. (Of course, being a monolingual American, I reserve the right to comment on the English of non-native speakers, and the fact that I don't have a driver's license makes my role in this enterprise even more suspect.) We talk about movies for a while. He's very up on the latest in serious cinema, though he also mounts a passionate defense of the latter two *Matrix* movies. Is it this kind of counterintuitive thinking that has set the Continent ablaze? I order a drink as we discuss where to go for dinner, and then

I begin to describe the Hearst Castle, where I've been several times and which I suggest as a stop on our impending drive. As I hear the word *Rosebud* tumble out of my mouth more than once, I watch his eyelids lower again, those slightly milky blue eyes bearing down on me. I recall reading somewhere that Houellebecq is not such a sucker for that old-time Tinseltown glamour as some of his countrymen. Shut your stupid mouth.

After dinner, we get lost driving back to the hotel. Houellebecq snores in the backseat. Three (or maybe it was nineteen) double espressos will do that to you. Only a true provocateur, I think, would drink so many double espressos. Who knows what might happen next?

We've been in San Francisco less than a day, but a drive out to Napa Valley seems like a nice idea. Things are getting weird here. Today I hit Mason Street in a good mood until a passing construction worker turned and called, "Hello, faggot!" Not a moment later, an older black man with a cane approached me at the crosswalk.

"Why are you smiling?" he said. "Don't smile. You stick out, man. Look around you. Nobody is smiling."

Some idiot's homophobia is one thing, but I will never smile in San Francisco again. Now we're heading to Francis Ford Coppola's winery in the big luxury Chrysler we've rented for the week in accordance with Houellebecq's request for an "American boat." Tom Luddy, who's with us, is Coppola's friend and longtime collaborator, and there's a chance Francis will be on the grounds. Soon the land turns pretty and Houellebecq seems to relax. He's had a revelation he's ready to share. Smoking bans have kept him off international flights in the past, but now that he's flown business, the amenities, he's decided, almost compensate for the patches and nicotine gum.

Still, he muses, "Do they let the prisoners about to be executed in America smoke?"

None of us are sure, though I offer up something inane like "It goes state by state."

I'm suddenly reminded of a man I met the night before, when I left the hotel for a quick drink at the dive bar across the street. He was a Mexican optician named Frank who told me that if he were president he'd send death-row inmates into battle in Iraq and give them a chance to win their freedom through valor.

"There are some bad motherfuckers on death row," he informed me.

Frank, I decide, who said he moonlighted as a heavy-metal bassist and that he'd turned down a chance to become a cop in Mexico because he knew he'd be corrupt, would probably let the doomed men smoke. He'd certainly make them the offer he made as we said our good-byes: to hook me up with some cooler glasses.

I'm snapped out of my reverie by a new tension in the car. Apparently a few publications want to do extended photo shoots with Houellebecq later in the week.

"No," says Houellebecq. "As soon as there's a photograph it's all over." I assume he means the tour, or the presence of any press on the tour, but I can't help thinking he means it in a deeper philosophical sense, as well.

The Niebaum Coppola winery sits on some lovely acreage in the heart of the valley. If I knew anything about soil or grapes I'm sure I'd be impressed. After a visit to Coppola's movie-research library and sound-editing center we stroll over to the museum and gift shop. There is a great deal of Coppolalia on display, including the *Tucker* car and Kilgore's surfboard from *Apocalypse Now.* There is also, in the gift shop, tons of food and wine and knickknacks bearing the Coppola name, from olive paste to leather-sheathed thermoses. Houellebecq and I sample some merlot and I ask if he's ever looked into these kinds of branding strategies. He seems to grow excited at the prospect, and decides he will launch his own line of cigars. Perhaps to celebrate, he buys a cigar cutter, the cheapest one they've got.

Francis isn't around, but maybe on our drive down south we'll drop in on Clint Eastwood. Tom Luddy appears to know him, too, and I'm not surprised. As we cruise back to San Francisco I stare out the window and take in the rolling hills while Tom fields a call from Andy Garcia and places one to his old buddy Werner Herzog. I fiddle with my cell phone so that it maybe seems Andy Garcia might call me in a moment, too, but the only message is some free-form babble from my son and a quick "We miss you" from my wife. I miss them, too, and I'm a little worried that I'm not really witnessing the bad boy being bad in America, but hey, the week is young. He may seem courtly and reserved now, but by the end of our trip, when he's shoving a magnum of Veuve Clicquot up his ass (or mine!) and denying the Holocaust, I'll have a hell of a story.

Back in the city limits we pass some low brick buildings that Tom says are leather bars. We pass an OfficeMax and I make a dumb joke about that being the biggest leather bar of all. Houellebecq's eyes light up but not for any obviously pervy reason. No, like many writers, yours truly included, stationery has a nearly pornographic appeal, and besides, he appears to possess a Frenchman's revulsion/ attraction to big-box retail. We pull over and head into the store. He assures me he's an "efficient consumer" and once inside he does seem to know exactly what he needs: erasers, folders and, most intriguingly, Scotch tape. It's this final purchase and an earlier comment about how he planned to work in his room tomorrow that sets my mind racing. What's the Scotch tape for? What's he working on in his room? A collage? I've been on book tours before, and even bought stationery in foreign cities, but never Scotch tape. That must be the genius of Houellebecq.

It's Wednesday afternoon and there's trouble in the air. Tonight is Houellebecq's big to-do at Foreign Cinema, a San Francisco restaurant where he'll have a publicly attended chat with novelist Daniel Handler, better known as Lemony Snicket, followed by a feast for fifty hosted by San Francisco gallerist Martin Muller. This morning Dorna told me she'd happened upon a website calling for a protest against Houellebecq. Phrases like "anti-Muslim" and "the new face of Nazism" appeared in the announcement. I get a little giddy at the prospect of street action. Besides, won't this move units?

Most of the others involved don't share my enthusiasm. I guess I'm just a little burned out driving around this city and hearing so much French, waiting for snippets to be interpreted, or else barging into the conversation to shift it to English. I feel caught between things, not quite in my world but not really in Houelle-becq's, either. At one point, when I'd asked him what he thought of San Francisco, he'd said it was no different from "any other Anglo-Saxon city." Tell it to Frank the Optician, I wanted to say.

By the next morning I'd broken through my funk. Maybe the threat of a protest was lifting my spirits. I was picturing barricades, mounted riot police, tear gas. And then, later, a top-notch meal.

The extra security turns out to be unnecessary, though they look sharp in their dark suits and Kangol hats. Houellebecq and Handler talk in a large, packed room, mostly about the travails of Lovecraft and his horror-fiction legacy. In his book, Houellebecq says that Lovecraft wasn't really literary. This is a compliment. The idea of "bad taste," or at least opposition to bourgeois notions of "good taste," is important to Houellebecq, still a way forward. The talk goes very well. They even get a few laughs, which is pretty good for a discussion about perpetual fear and the pointless agony of life. I begin to worry about how it'll go in L.A., when I have to do the talking. I'm afraid I lack the smoothness of Mr. Snicket. Then again, once you have millions of children under your thumb, what's one quasi-nihilistic French novelist?

At dinner I meet another duck, this one braised, delicious. We're all outside at one long table in the restaurant courtyard. Martin Mul-ler, dapper, Swiss, intense, sits beside me. He's Diane Von Furstenberg's stepbrother and he's been showing art at his Modernism gallery since 1979, including works by Warhol, Crumb, and Russian giants like Malevich. Another of his artists is here in the flesh, painter Mark Stock, a big man with magic hands. He's got a deck of cards, and his tricks, including one where your card somehow winds up in his shoe, are strictly old-school, but amazing, at least to me. I can't even shuffle cards. Meanwhile Muller chats on beside me. He tells me how the Bohemian Club, and its annual two-week camp for the rulers of the planet in nearby Sonoma, has gotten a bad rap over the years. It's not just a place for CEOs and ex-presidents to traipse around pissing on the redwoods. "They don't care if you've got money as long as you have ideas to bring to the table," he says.

Dinner stretches through a few more glorious courses and everybody seems in a good mood. Maybe I'll join the Bohemian Club. I've got ideas. Houellebecq asks for his customary double espresso and seems very content, or bored. They might be equivalent states for him. I've had a little wine and I can't stop babbling about the Scotch tape. I'm still obsessed with the Scotch tape. Some of the guests give me a pitying look.

Later I'm back at the hotel again. No protest, and still no bad-boy antics. I haven't even seen Houellebecq drunk. Just very tired.

Still, tomorrow we hit the road.

We're a few hours out of San Francisco coasting down the PCH. Houellebecq is up front, his permanent place of honor. The door on my side is broken so every time we stop Houellebecq has to open it for me. It's nice having a world-famous novelist as your valet.

Beside me is Sylvie Christophe, deputy cultural attaché to the French consulate in Los Angeles. The consulate has kicked in some money for this tour and she's flown up to ride back down with us. I assume she's here as a sort of minder, to make sure that Houellebecq doesn't do anything too embarrassing, or to provide instant damage control if he does. We make jokes about how she's really a spy, but if she's not a spy, Chirac is making a big mistake. Sexy and stylish like all the official French people in California, Sylvie's also quite funny. But there's a levelheadedness to her that can almost unnerve. It's not hard to picture her lounging by a pool as she calls in coordinates for a Mirage jet air strike on Hamburger Hamlet.

I try to keep her amused by teaching her Americanisms, some of which I make up.

The weather is beautiful and we stop off for lunch in Carmel. We drive up to the Mission Ranch, co-owned by Clint Eastwood, where we have instructions from Tom Luddy to pass a note to Clint and see if he'll join us. I lean over the seat into Houellebecq's ear.

"Are you a Clint Eastwood fan?" I ask.

Houellebecq pauses for a long time, squints into the passing landscape.

"I don't know," he says.

The restaurant is closed and nobody is around except for an older gentleman on some kind of motorized tricycle. We tell him we're passing through, friends of friends of Clint's. How would we get a note to him?

"Send it to Paramount Pictures," the gentleman says.

So much for the celebrity circuit.

We eat pizza at an Italian joint, or three of us do. Houellebecq says he never eats lunch. We talk about the film he wants to direct, and some research he did in Pattaya in Thailand. He talks about the many Americans who go there and, when their funds run dry, commit suicide.

"Just Americans?" I ask.

"Usually, yes," he replies, a tiny smirk growing on his becalmed face.

We walk down to the beach and sit on the sand, which Houellebecq fondles and remarks upon for its softness. Then an older man, who turns out to be a Danish dentist traveling alone, takes our picture. He points excitedly at the photo in the digital viewfinder.

"You see, you see, I got all of your feet, too. I do not believe in photographs of people that do not show the feet. Without the feet you have nothing."

I want this to mean something, some corollary to Houllebecq's remark about the photo shoots, but I have a feeling it's just the ravings of a Danish dentist. Still, for the record, Houellebecq wears expensive-looking leather loafers on his feet, no socks. They work well with his light trousers, usually red or beige, buckled with a very skinny belt at the belly button, and the hint of turquoise wife-beater beneath his sedate striped shirt. It's sort of an insane taste-mocking look, but it works beautifully on the guy. Besides, it jibes perfectly with his literary aesthetic, which he describes at one point as the "brutal attack."

We drive a few more hours and Houellebecq seems to nap through a lot of it. He has this uncanny ability to appear asleep and then rise up out of his slumber with some bon mot, as though he's been listening to the conversation the whole time. It's his M.O. in a wider sense, too, this disheveled, seemingly discombobulated man, an establishment outsider who looks like easy pickings until he opens his mouth (or laptop) and starts hurling thunderbolts. It's hard to tell whether it's all a big game or he's some kind of narcoleptic savant. I'm beginning to think it's a bit of both, but that his glue is a sometimes charming, sometimes grating, semi-autistic geekiness. He's not a conversationalist, and he's none too curious about anything or anybody that doesn't directly feed his observational mechanism. He may be an artist for our age, but he's got none of the media-ready gabbiness or false compassion that goes with it. Even his narcissism doesn't seem to stem from the usual brew of selfishness and insecurity. It's a cold, glittering thing. Life is painful and disappointing. And then you die. He may be a major writer, I tell my friend on the phone one night from my hotel, but you wouldn't want him, say, running a country.

"Are you kidding?" says my friend, a Houellebecq fan. "You wouldn't want that guy running the local gas station."

Our next stop may have been my idea: Esalen. Founded in 1962 on the cliffs near Big Sur as a center for the exploration of "human potential," Esalen, with its New Age cant and hot springs and encouraged nudity, became for many a symbol of all that is false and annoying about this part of California. Now, of course, it's more your usual spa destination, but I figured we should stop here because it's mentioned in *The Elementary Particles* as the model for the colony in France which Bruno's stepfather runs, the site of the young protagonist's formative sexual humiliations. We have a day pass, courtesy of Tom Luddy, of course.

It's near dinnertime when we arrive. We decide to skip the meal and simply stroll the grounds, better to take in the majestic sunset and maybe peep at some naked folk. Houellebecq wanders off, perhaps to ruminate on the failing dream of the European Union. I sit on a bench and watch a woman in spandex and headphones dancing on the edge of a cliff. If she had Rollerblades on we could be in Washington Square Park, but there's something eerie about the same self-absorbed gyrations here. It must be the cliff.

I spot Houellebecq at a balcony and join him. Below us, moving in and out of a warren of stone bathhouses, are tiny naked people.

"What do you make of it all?" I ask.

His eyes sweep up the hill past the dining hall across the grounds to the main entrance.

"There's a lot of parking," he says.

"I guess I mean given that you wrote about this place," I say.

"I never wrote about this place," says Houellebecq.

We walk up to the garden and sit on a bench surrounded by lush and highly organized vegetation. Houellebecq lights a cigarette. I ask him if he's ever tried meditation and he says not really. I mention some monks I saw on television who could raise or lower their body temperature at will.

"I'd rather put on a coat," he says.

The sun is down and our momentous visit to Esalen has come to an end.

There is no time for Hearst Castle. There is time for elephant seals, though. At dusk we pull over to watch them wallow on the beach. They huddle together by the dozens, great gray tubular hulks, most asleep, a few bellowing on the margins of the herd like prescient and despised artistes.

We drive to a seafood joint in Morro Bay, eat some fish, and drink a few bottles of Riesling. Houellebecq unwinds with some stories about his last trip to the U.S., to New York. He's speaking mostly in French but Sylvie and Dorna interpret the choice bits, as when he notes that the "barmaids" in New York tend to be "big-titted, ambitious bitches," or that one of his middle-aged, long-haired American editors resembled a "rock music producer in his comeback phase."

Finally, I'm thinking, release the bad boy!

But next thing we're checking into our motel rooms in San Luis Obispo, saying good night. I sit up watching *Dune* on television until I get to the scene where Kyle MacLachlan has to put his hand in the pain box. Many have tried to write a compelling piece about Michel Houellebecq, I picture the old intergalactic sorceress/glossy magazine editor telling me, or Kyle, or both of us.

"Tried and failed?" Kyle and I ask, trembling.

"Tried and died."

In the morning we set off on the final stage of our Tour de Cali. But first it's breakfast at the Madonna Inn. The Madonna Inn, for those who've never been, is an irresistible tourist trap specializing in bizarrely furnished rooms—the rock room, basically a cave with light fixtures and a bed, is a favorite—and Southern German kitsch. The waitstaff uniform is pure *Heidi,* and the men's room has a waterfall for a urinal. The food is terrible, and though he appreciates the urinal, Houellebecq doesn't seem overly impressed. He says he's been to places in Bavaria where the kitsch is much more elaborate.

"Yes," I say, "but this is California."

Houellebecq seems to concede my point, and through this small victory, I feel we've forged a strange new bond. Later, at a gas station in Los Angeles, when he gives me a sip of his Frappuccino, I'll know I was right.

Now that we're in L.A. it's hard to believe the road trip is over. Our merry band was just getting into the spirit of things, even if Houellebecq slept through a good deal of this drive he insisted on taking. As it turns out, the pristine beauty of the California coast wasn't really what he had in mind. "I was thinking of Colorado or something," he tells me. At any rate, now it's time to greet the wider world. There's a radio interview with the king of book-talk in L.A., Michael Silverblatt, and there's still the photo-shoot question. Houellebecq agrees to a few pictures but no formal shoot.

Finally, a celebrity has been secured. Oliver Stone would like Houellebecq to join him for dinner. I'm invited, but against every journalistic instinct I decline. They will be speaking in French for one thing, and for another I want to visit an old friend instead. Shortly after his dinner with Houellebecq, Stone is pulled over and arrested for drunk driving and drug possession. Houellebecq is not in the car and I'm immensely relieved. It all belongs to somebody else's bad-boy story. When I ask Houellebecq how Oliver seemed, he replies, "Agitated."

Saturday Houellebecq stays in his room until the late afternoon. Maybe he's finishing up the collage. Late in the afternoon we take a drive to a nearby PETCO, where Houellebecq shops for dog toys. He's also in the market for a GPS tracker that will fit on a collar, but that's a little high-tech for this place. I suggest he implant a chip in his dog's head. He's not at all amenable to that idea. The day before, watching a pit bull go by, he'd remarked how awful it was to breed animals for killing. What about humans? I asked. The eyelids lowered once again, this time not from fatigue, and it occurred to me that I was speaking with the writer who put the phrase "post-human" on the literary map. It's too late for us, but maybe not the pit bulls.

Later we go to a drugstore and Houellebecq buys an expensive facial mask. Should I be buying one, too? That night a group of us go to Mel's, the popular burger joint. Talk veers geekily toward *The Lord of the Rings,* and Houellebecq notes that part of its draw is the way people can imagine themselves as different beings from Middle Earth.

"What would you be?"

There's an almost dreamy cast to his face as he answers my question.

"An elf."

And now something truly magical occurs. A stranger approaches our outdoor table and hovers incredulously over Michel Houellebecq, world-famous novelist.

"Holy shit," he says. "Is that a quadruple espresso?"

It's Sunday afternoon, showtime at the Hammer Museum, with *show* being the operative word. Neither I nor the hundreds of people who've shown up at the Hammer are quite prepared for the Velvet Hammer, no relation, a burlesque troupe that's been hired to warm up the crowd. An MC charges out onstage and tells bad Vaudeville jokes while a drummer hits post-ironic rim shots. Next up are the strippers: the pretty one, the fat pretty one, and the tiny pretty one. The tiny pretty one is named Bobi Pins and she's very tiny. Circus tiny. Some of the older museum subscribers gasp as she twirls her pasties.

It's a strange act to follow, but Houellebecq and I make the best of it. We're a good team. I stammer and he mumbles into a bad microphone. We talk about Lovecraft, cosmic fear, and the pointless suffering of life, not to mention the French referendum, in which the people of France have just voted down the EU constitution. "You can't have direct democracy if the people won't obey," says Houellebecq. Not even the local gas station, I think.

So now, after the wine-and-cheese reception, after one more long dinner, here we are in Houellebecq's room for the final stand. The book critic is a new addition. She's seems smart, if a little loony, and Houellebecq seems glad she's here. I'm glad he seems glad. It's been a frustrating week from a journalistic standpoint, often from a human, or even post-human, standpoint, but I genuinely like the man, especially when he gets a little goofy, showing off his kung fu moves, as he did earlier this evening, or mixing up English words, declaring himself not an honor to but an "otter of" France.

Houellebecq opens his laptop and shows us the cover for his new book, *The Possibility of an Island*. It's a photo of a sultry woman submerged in water. The book critic pooh-poohs it, says the image is beneath the dignity and importance of his work, but Houellebecq stares rapturously at the cover model.

"I want to go to North Dakota," he declares. I strongly believe this is apropos of nothing.

We start talking about planes again, and travel. I quote the Austrian writer Thomas Bernhard.

"It makes no difference," Bernhard wrote, "whether I go from New York to London, or London to New York."

"Yes," says Houellebecq, "but Bernhard did not smoke so he would rather be on the plane."

"And if you didn't smoke?" I ask. "Would you rather be on the plane?"

"I think so, yes."

"Look, Michel," I say. "I need to ask you something."

"Yes, Sam?"

"What's with the Scotch tape?"

The answer is so mundane I want to cry. He's been using it to fasten some loose caps onto his pill bottles. And that's the true genius of Houellebecq. He just goes about his business, buys his Scotch tape. It's what the rest of us invest in his every gesture and utterance that keeps the Houellebecq balloon afloat. Without our slavering he'd be an important writer, for sure, but he wouldn't be Houellebecq. And it's now that I turn to Brendan Bernhard, the *LA Weekly* guy, and say, "Why don't we both leave? Then nobody misses the big scoop." Brendan takes a last look at Houellebecq and agrees.

There will be no bad-boy antics tonight, no scabrous words for the prophet Muhammad, no child hookers, no home porn. The bad boy of French literature is growing sleepy. Or maybe not. The book critic who was just speaking to him about the possibility of love is possibly spending the night. ✶

WHIRL

DISCUSSED: *Jim Crow, Gangsta Rap, Gutbucket Blues,*
Wayward Preachers, Pruitt-Igoe, Carlos Fuentes, Jesse Owens,
William H. Gass, Duke Ellington, The Ten Commandments,
Sawed-Off Shotguns, Vietnam, Cecil B. DeMille, Molotov Cocktails,
Mario Vargas Llosa, The Dallas Cowboys, Drug Lords

He appeared as a guest on *The Arsenio Hall Show* in
1989. Seated rigidly on a purple sofa, the lights
beating down, sweat forming on his forehead, he
did not in any way appear to belong there, in a
place, more often reserved for NBA athletes or
rap stars of high commercial visibility. A careful dresser, he wore a
navy-blue worsted suit, a shirt with red candy stripes, a red neck-
tie, and a white pocket-square. Onto his feet he had slipped a pair
of two-tone red-and-white spectator shoes. He was seventy-nine
years old, small and spry and bandy-legged. He had hair white as an
empty page. Upon being introduced—"For over fifty-one years,"
Arsenio Hall announced, "our next guest has published the wildest
newspaper, I think, in the country"—Ben Thomas parted the curtains and stepped onto the stage as if from another century.

Although the studio audience applauded and whistled and, as they were prone to do on *The Arsenio Hall Show,* whoop-whooped, it was quite unlikely that many of those present, or watching on television, had ever heard of either Ben Thomas or his *Evening Whirl,* an eight-page weekly newspaper, a one-man operation, that had covered crime, scandal, and gossip in the black neighborhoods of St. Louis since 1938. Thomas looked a bit dazed, and throughout long portions of his conversation with Hall he maintained a wide, mute smile on his face.

To Thomas's friends and relatives watching the show in St. Louis or in the studio, this performance by the editor might have been peculiar, if not exactly worrisome. It could simply have been a case of nerves. Or, seen in retrospect, it could have been the first symptoms of senile dementia, for within four years of Thomas's television appearance, stories in the *Evening Whirl* would begin repeating themselves verbatim in back-to-back weeks, the names of cops would sometimes get confused with those of the perps, and finally, in 1995, Ben Thomas's dotage would force his retirement.

But no one foresaw that now. Both on the page and in life, Ben Thomas had a domineering presence—he was a fearful disciplinarian with his sons and a taskmaster with his assistants. He commanded attention; he had the gift of authority. Possibly this characteristic had resulted from a professional five decades spent publishing a newspaper in which his voice alone prevailed. His editorial predilections ran toward such subjects as lovers' quarrels gone homicidal, preachers who spent their free time pursuing sex on the St. Louis stroll, the 1970s heroin dealers who ruled over the housing projects in this border-state river town—not North, not South, not quite the Midwest—or any person who got on the editor's bad side. He'd put your face on the front page.

Although the *Evening Whirl* covered crime and scandal in St. Louis, the word *covered* when applied to Thomas and his paper suffers from some imprecision. Concerning a territorial war between rival gangs in 1978, for instance, Ben Thomas wrote:

There is a rumor around the town
That one of three will be cut down
The Petty Brothers or Dennis Haymon
Will join the soap man, Mr. Sayman.

The city wonders who it will be,
Just take it easy, you will see;
Guns will roar and rip like hell,
And how the Evening Whirl will sell.

The *Evening Whirl* had a singular design—mug shots, both in profile and obverse, were wainscoted two deep below the headlines. Pictures of the perps, Ben Thomas knew, sold newspapers. The faces were almost always black. Eight columns of triple-decker tombstones declaimed the week's crimes and scandals, usually involving a killing, a cutting, a robbery, a rape, or some piece of local gossip. The lead story of nearly every edition was annexed with verse, built of four-line stanzas rhymed *a-b-a-b*. The meter of the lines approached the iambic. Headlines and pictures were sometimes cockeyed. Captions and advertisements were occasionally handwritten. With its shabby appearance and neighborhood scuttlebutt and atmosphere of danger, the *Evening Whirl* had the look and feel of an old, dark corner-saloon metamorphosed into a newspaper.

People likened Thomas to a Wild West newsman, an X-rated Walter Winchell, a blues lyricist. In later years he was also called an ancestor of gangsta rap. But he considered himself none of these things—in his own eyes he was a crusader against crime, an exposer of wrongdoing, and he had absolute confidence in the righteousness of every word that he wrote. His persona in print was that of a hanging judge; he thought of his paper as a public service. But the man also liked to sell newspapers. At its peak, in the 1970s, it had newsstand sales of fifty thousand. Thomas relied not on advertising but on circulation—the popular vote—and at a time when black business success came rarely, people around St. Louis referred to the editor as a "black millionaire."

By the time Thomas came to Hall's attention, however, the editor had entered the twilight of his career, and the health of the *Whirl* had begun to erode. Circulation had declined substantially. People had begun to think of the *Whirl* as a relic of another era, as a particularly offensive anachronism. Controversy and animosity had always surrounded the newspaper, and it arrived from two socioeconomic directions—from the criminals it brazenly attacked, and from the black bourgeoisie, whose sexual peccadilloes and petty connivings Thomas sought to expose whenever he could get the dish.

Nearly every issue of the *Evening Whirl* included lists of curious blurbs that appeared under the heads WHY and WHO. They were bits of crime news posited in the form of a question, as in:

WHY

didn't Primus Oden, 18, of 3916 N. Florissant, pick up a gun and mow down the robber that invaded the P.M. Gas Wash at 3720 N. Kingshighway and robber the place of $250 cash? Make yourself valuable and useful.

and:

WHO

was the charming woman that had a flat tire in front of 1500 N. Union and was offered assistance by a stranger, and of course she accepted, but was fooled by the man who said, "Come and go with me to get a new tire," and he then led her into an alley at gunpoint about midnight where he robbed her of $5, her watch and raped her too? A dog! Beware of strangers.

Thomas sprinkled these WHOs and WHYs throughout his pages. Readers ran across them like police-blotter Easter eggs. They implicitly articulated the theme of his publication, a theme that Thomas, in his *Evening Whirl* creed, stated in this way: "*The Evening Whirl* is a weekly newspaper dedicated to the exposure of crime and civic improvement. Our chief aim is to keep the public well informed of the interesting happenings in our community from week to week. Our aim will always be to help, but never to harm, and let the chips fall where they may regardless of class or culture or status in life."

In his editorials Thomas expressed his opinions rather more bluntly. They read like apologias. He was responding to his critics. "We know that all good christians [*sic*] and decent citizens love the *Whirl* for its daring exposure of crime and attempt to lessen it by mere exposure. Our chief aim is to let the people know what is happening in St. Louis. We print the good and the bad news. That is what it takes to make a newspaper. Even a preacher doesn't always preach about the good things in life. He tells you of the vice and varied types of crime happenings. Then he tells you how to live a decent life and serve God. The *Whirl* does exactly the same thing." As time went on and his critics grew more vocal, Thomas's apologias appeared more frequently, and followed an opposite course in delicacy. "The Whirl has preached PURITY and condemned CRIME. Those who don't like it can kiss our behind."

Over the course of his career Thomas survived Molotov-cocktail firebombings and drive-by shootings. He suffered libel-suit claims amounting to millions of dollars and an attempted boycott of his newspaper organized by the president of the St. Louis chapter of the National Association for the Advancement of Colored People. And yet, despite this constant flack, despite the vehemence of his opposition, Ben Thomas survived long enough to wind up on Arsenio Hall's purple sofa.

I first heard of the *Evening Whirl* while a graduate student in creative writing at Washington University in St. Louis. A professor of mine named Charles Newman, a writer of elusive novels and a founder of *TriQuarterly* magazine, suggested the *Whirl* as a possible story idea. Among a handful of the university's literary academics—most prominently William Gass—the *Evening Whirl* had long been a favorite. Gass even gave copies of the *Whirl* to visiting writers as a kind of going-away present. Evidently, Mario Vargas

Llosa and Carlos Fuentes were particularly taken by Thomas and his paper. In Gass's explanation, the Latin American writers, so attuned to the structures of race and economic class, found in the *Whirl* something familiar.

When Ben Thomas died, in 2005, he left behind a body of work comprising some three thousand editions of his newspaper and untold millions of words. It has all largely gone missing. Most African American newspapers have been poorly collected, and, perhaps not surprisingly, the *Evening Whirl* has been collected more poorly than most. No library in St. Louis, university or municipal, owns even a single copy. Scattered issues lie here and there in scattered institutions around the country. The newspaper repository at the University of Texas at Austin, for example, owns precisely two copies. Howard University has an eighteen-month run from the mid-1970s with a four-month lacuna. But these are not hard copies; all are microfilmed, and many of the images are warped and whitewashed in the manner of poorly shot microfilm. Nonetheless, relative to any other library, the Howard collection is unequaled in its breadth.

But by far the largest number of *Whirl*s amassed in one place belongs to a private archive. Stored inside three plastic mail crates, one stacked atop the other, they sit in a closet in the basement of a house in St. Louis not far from the boyhood home of T. S. Eliot. Anthony Sanders, the owner of the house and the current editor-in-chief of the *Evening Whirl,* uses the basement as his newsroom. Along with Barry and Kevin Thomas, the founder's sons, who have lived in Southern California since their boyhood, Anthony Sanders took control of the *Whirl* in December 1995. A few months earlier, the Thomases had moved their father, deemed senile and incompetent, out of St. Louis for good. Despite his failing health, Thomas did not want to relinquish his throne. Under some duress, his sons brought him to California, where he had long owned vacation homes, first in the Mid-Wilshire district of Los Angeles, and then near the ocean in Laguna Beach—examples of what the *Evening Whirl*'s income could buy you. But these properties had lately been sold by the boys. And so, for the ten years between his retirement and his death, at the age of ninety-five, Ben Thomas resided in the Los Angeles exurb of Valencia, first at Kevin's place and then in a nursing home, while halfway across the continent his legacy moldered, as shopworn as its creator.

Shortly after arriving in St. Louis in the summer of 2000, I sought out Sanders, who escorted me into his basement and introduced me to the mail crates. The *Whirl* editions were yellow and fragrant with age. Brittle at the edges, they shed flakes like confetti, and after several hours spent parsing through the pages I had to wash my hands. Water from the faucet ran black with ink. The dates of the newspapers stretched from July 1971 up through Ben Thomas's final days, with major gaps impeding the way. They constituted the disordered, incomplete record of a career, of a life.

He was born in 1910 in Pine Bluff, Arkansas, raised by maternal grandparents who were born into slavery, and educated in the early 1930s at Ohio State University, where he claimed he ran on the track team with Jesse Owens. (For the rest of his life he would ceaselessly tell stories of his exploits on the team with Owens, especially when in conversation with single women.) By the time he arrived in St. Louis in 1934, Thomas was already purged of his country-rube beginnings. As an undergraduate he worked as an OSU campus correspondent for a black weekly in Pittsburgh, and when he settled in his new city, he found a job at the St. Louis *Argus*, which in those Jim Crow times was the newspaper of record for the city's black community. (The mainstream dailies, which wouldn't hire black reporters in the first place, covered black neighborhoods only infrequently.)

Despite the Depression and Jim Crow, St. Louis hit its cultural apex in the 1930s. The Swing Era was in full sway, and Thomas became the *Argus's* lead entertainment and music reporter, a post he held for a little over three years. Whenever big acts visited town—

Duke Ellington, Fats Waller, Cab Calloway, Louis Armstrong—Thomas became part of each one's entourage. For a brief time in the mid-1930s he dated Billie Holiday. His nickname was "The Baron," which he often used in the *Argus* as his byline. Always entrepreneurial and trolling for new hustles (he was also a jazz and nightclub promoter), Thomas eventually decided to apply his talents to his own weekly publication. He titled it the *Night Whirl,* and for the first year of its life, in 1938, it covered music, nightlife, and local celebrity gossip—the social whirl of black St. Louis.

But less than a year later, Thomas caught wind of another kind of story that had nothing to do with jazz acts or club owners. Two high-school teachers had escorted a group of boys on a picnic to the country; pedophilia was the allegation. No other paper in town had the temerity to print the scoop. In 1991, Thomas conducted an interview with an archivist and oral historian from the University of Missouri-St. Louis. He recalled in his steady baritone, "So I changed the name from *Night Whirl* to *Evening Whirl*"—it was, the editor believed, a newsier title—"because right then and there I was through with amusement news… And sweetheart? I had no idea that they were gonna keep runnin' me back to the press to print more papers. I put that paper out, and I went back to the press for the third time before I could satisfy Saint Louis. It's been a crime sheet ever since."

Thomas sold fifty thousand copies of that first crime issue, at a nickel apiece, several orders of magnitude beyond his normal *Night Whirl* circulation. If he had wanted to make a dollar by hustling newspapers, this, Thomas discovered, was how.

Never simply a crime newspaper, the *Whirl* stuck close to its roots as a scandal and gossip sheet, and however adamant Thomas became in later years about his anti-crime crusade, he relied upon titillation as his most powerful newspaper-selling tool. Always economical, the resulting headlines told the entire story. They read like abstracts:

TEACHER PASSES OUT AFTER TORRID SEX WITH ANOTHER TEACHER IN
MOTEL; SHE DRESSES AND LEAVES HIM; HIS WIFE COMES, GETS IN BED
WITH HIM; HE AWAKES MAKING LOVE TO WIFE AND HAS HEART ATTACK

Almost always Thomas appended these tales with verse, often
in the form of dramatic monologue:

Pearl there's one thing I want you to know,
You're nothing but a husband-stealing hoe;
Your ears may quiver and your hips may shiver,
If you have Max again I'll throw you in the river.

Respectable burghers were *Evening Whirl* favorites. They were
the success stories of the black population, coveted examples of
racial uplift, and yet Thomas attacked them anyway. The *Whirl*
stood in complete opposition to one of the traditional and well-
established projects of the mainstream black press—that is, to
print whenever possible only the positive doings of the African
American community as a way to encourage its rise up the socioeconomic ladder.

For his part, Thomas felt he was being democratic. "The average man, be he a preacher, a schoolteacher, a doctor, a lawyer—
whatever, they like to get out and get around sometimes," he told
a reporter from the *Chicago Tribune* in 1989. "And when they get
caught, that's when I cash in on them."

In graphic, salacious detail Thomas chronicled scandals picked
up from the police or whispered over the telephone by anonymous sources or confided over drinks in dark barrooms by trusted
informers. Lawyers caught cuckolded, doctors who had sexually
harassed their patients, churchmen busted by streetwalkers who
suddenly presented badges, political leaders discovered to be
homosexual—potential targets such as these would say prayers of
mercy, and open that week's *Whirl* with trembling hands.

In 1979, for instance, a lawyer was caught in flagrante delicto
with another man's wife:

PROMINENT ATTORNEY CAUGHT IN BED IN HOTEL WITH HIS LOVER AS
HER HUSBAND ENTERS WITH GUN, HE KNEELS AND PRAYS

Thomas spared no invective. He also seemed in awe.

> Many women have described [the lawyer] as one of the sexiest sex-
> men his age. They say he deals heavily in sex. Many sex stories about
> the great lover have been revealed, but not printed. But this time an
> arrest and police report were in evidence.

The married couple of the story had evidently come upon
hard times. The husband, who "had reasons to suspicion the fidel-
ity of his wife," trailed her and the lawyer to their hotel room and
"smashed through the door like a football player on the Dallas
Cowboys Football Team. And there they lay buck naked in the bed
all absorbed in a love duel. Trysting time had come around and [the
wife's] paramour was functioning." The occasion inspired seven
stanzas. Thomas prefaced his verses by explaining that they were not
his. Instead, they were part of an extemporaneous song sung by the
wife while in bed with the lawyer. A portion of the poem read,

> Daddy, oh daddy, I love your stroke,
> You conjure my soul with every poke;
> Love me this morning till the cows come home,
> Carry on fool; you're real gone.

> I'll quit my husband if you quit your wife,
> And be your woman the rest of my life;
> I'm a good rocking mama night and day,
> We will have only the devil to pay.

It was hard to tell, as the story went on, whether Thomas's purpose was to condemn or defend the actions of the lawyer. Thomas
concluded the article:

> Since the door was smashed in and [the husband] was holding the
> nudists at bay with a gun, the hotel manager begged of him not to
> kill his wife and her lover of renown. [The husband] was staging a

talk show and the lovers were forced to listen, look and keep still in their imposing pose that would tear any husband's mind asunder. [The lawyer] was not allowed to plead this case. He was on trial. The judge was his woman's husband....

[The lawyer] feels guilty of nothing. He realizes that he hasn't broken The Ten Commandments. He did not covet his neighbor's wife because they didn't live in the same neighborhood. There is no law against two grown sexists fornicating. Millions do it every day. That includes preachers, teachers, business executives, nurses, lawyers, bankers, electricians, plumbers and laymen.

One cannot know, of course, whether Thomas achieved the pun of the story's last word deliberately, but the result is nothing short of masterful. Like this particular attorney, Thomas felt guilty of nothing in printing such pieces, and his neighbors in St. Louis came to expect this. Around town people would often say to each other, as a kind of half-joking, good-luck good-bye, "All right, now, we don't want to read about you in the *Whirl*."

Though Thomas had an eye for the absurd and the comic, his voice in the *Evening Whirl* also contained heavy doses of anger. In the 1960s and '70s, Thomas watched as poverty, drug addiction, and gangland violence increased in the black neighborhoods of his adopted hometown. The social whirl of St. Louis now involved more gunfights than jazz acts. Sixty percent of crimes committed in St. Louis in 1973 were perpetrated by blacks against other blacks. It all must have seemed particularly nasty to Thomas, who had reached retirement age, and whose memories of youth involved heavy nostalgia and idealization for that Jim Crow/Swing Era period of music, parties, and a tight-knit community supporting and insulating itself against the wider white world, with its subtle and not-so-subtle oppressions. Whatever the broader political and economic reasons behind the problems of the current moment, to Thomas it seemed as if the black community of St. Louis was responsible for destroying itself. His frustration set to boil, Thomas became consumed with outing the symptoms of the collapse—and he came to see this as his noble crusade, his life's purpose.

Thomas's anger was particularly evident when one of the last remaining gang lords of the 1970s, a man named Nathaniel Sledge, was murdered early in 1980. Thomas felt obliged to sum up the '70s with a kind of retrospective:

> The decade that ended December 31, 1979, was the bloodiest decade for, by and with blacks in the history of the city of St. Louis. Hundreds of black men and women died each year from 1970 to 1980 by the slashing and plunging blade or by the smoking bullets. It is a disgrace to our race to have so many murders within the race.
>
> One might blame the white man for leaning toward segregation and discrimination, but he certainly doesn't destroy our lives with bullets and knives. We are our own worst enemy. Even blacks slay more whites than whites slay blacks. We seem to be attuned to murder as a pastime.

Later in the piece, Thomas wrote that Sledge "went at it wholesale killing 2, 3, 4 and five at a time. Why did he remain free and never go to prison for these massive slayings?" Thomas responded to his own question by invoking the character of the Intimidated Witness. "Many known killers have gone free and scores of persons knew they were guilty. Their knowledge without application is fruitless and worthless." It seemed as though Thomas had taken it upon himself to provide the service that intimidated witnesses wouldn't—to take on, via the ink of the *Evening Whirl,* their collective civic duty.

In terms of newsstand sales, the *Whirl* didn't really start gathering momentum until the 1950s. Not coincidentally, it was during that decade that the city's black street gangs first developed a certain entrepreneurial élan. "Crimes were happening and reports of them appeared in the dailies in about 3 inches of space unless a white person was involved," Thomas wrote in a short history of his career, printed in the *Whirl* in 1984. Coverage of black neighborhoods by the big mainstream newspapers virtually didn't exist. And those African American papers that were in operation, including the *Argus,* tried to avoid any news that might have cast a negative light on blacks. Thomas and his newspaper, therefore, filled the gap. By the 1970s, the circulation of the *Evening Whirl* reached its peak, estimated by Thomas's sons at anywhere from thirty thousand to fifty thousand issues.

Among the reasons people bought the *Evening Whirl* was that it detailed the doings of the community's most mythologized figures. Within their poverty-stricken confines, St. Louis's black drug lords and career criminals achieved folk-hero status. And because the *Evening Whirl* told their stories over and over, and in such gut-bucket style, Thomas played a major role in that mythmaking. A *Whirl* headline, 1972:

VICELORDS T.J. RUFFIN AND "FATS" WOODS TO RUN FOR MAYOR OF CITY

The story's lead:

> Two representatives of the underworld came to the Whirl Office by appointment Thursday evening at 5:30 p.m. very nattily dressed. They said they came to announce the entry of T.J. Ruffin, 47, of 3920 Beachwood, a ruthless gunman and killer deeply wedged in the heroin traffic, and the impossible "Fats" Little Al Capone Woods, 25, of Cass Avenue, as candidates for the mayor of St. Louis. Both said neither Cervantes nor Poelker [the city's legitimate mayoral candidates] would have a chance at the lofty position. They reasoned that the two crime overlords had taken over the city anyway and were running it as they saw fit with a few cooperative police and their own men.

Even when he used satire to make a point, Thomas succeeded at the same time in creating antiheroes.

During the first half of the 1970s Thomas directed much of his rage—and myth-forging influence—at a group of heroin dealers led by James Harold "Fats" Woods and Earl Williams Jr. Based in an apartment located several blocks from the massive Pruitt-Igoe housing project (perhaps the worst public-housing fiasco in the history of HUD), Woods and his group were arguably the city's most powerful black gangsters of any decade. Earl Williams served as the gang's lead assassin. Between 1970 and 1973, he beat murder raps on three separate occasions. Over the previous decade he had collected a total of twenty-six arrests. A jury had yet to convict him. In the fashion of the day, he wore wide-brim hats and jawbone-length sideburns. He had learned his trade with a high-caliber rifle as a Marine Corps sniper in Vietnam, but for his work stateside he preferred, a bit self-indulgently, sawed-off shotguns. He lived on the first floor of a high rise in Pruitt-Igoe, but in order to reach him, and offer one's regards, it was necessary to pass through a platoon of armed sentinels. He had ensconced himself in the projects like a *nazir* in his tents.

Enraged by Earl Williams's ability to beat the rap, Thomas published this headline in August 1970: COMMITTED MURDER 3 WEEKS AGO; COMMITS ANOTHER AND HE WALKS THE STREETS FREE. He led the article by saying, "If I, Benjamin Thomas, were to be a judge in the circuit courts of St. Louis I would retire in shame." He went on to relate how authorities had released Williams for lack of evidence despite the fact that the hit man had shot two of his rivals to death. "This newspaper viciously condemns such court action and suggests that our court system be abolished and replaced with a court of honor that would protect the innocent and the worthy citizens who detest crime. I hope I am elected to the State Legislature. I will do something about this horrible situation and do it fast for the safety of decent human beings." The editor noted that 282 people were murdered in St. Louis in 1969, and that in 1970 so far 161 had met the same fate. "The year," he wrote portentously, "is only half gone."

Thomas did indeed run for Missouri state representative, in 1970, with crime curtailment and gun control constituting the whole of his platform. He made sure to play up his *Evening Whirl* credentials, not that he needed to. The name recognition was built in. Ultimately, though, his campaign failed; he lost in the Democratic primary by a wide margin. The incumbent, a woman named

DeVerne Lee Calloway—the first black woman to hold elected office in Missouri—focused not on crime but on liberal welfare reform. She went on to a fifth term in the House. Thomas the politician was unable to compel the electorate as well as his newspaper could compel his readership. When separated from the pages of the *Evening Whirl,* his message lost a good portion of its power. Though he never again stumped for office, though he never again took the podium to deliver an anticrime harangue, each week in the *Evening Whirl* Ben Thomas continued to preach his gospel.

At the Delmonico Diner, on Delmar Boulevard in north St. Louis, a coterie of Baptist ministers gathers each morning before work. They eat breakfast, read through the local papers, and conduct heated political debates, exercising their wits in preparation for Sundays at the pulpit.

One cold December morning before Thomas died, I arrived at the Delmonico to discuss the *Evening Whirl* with two preachers: the Reverend Earl Nance Jr., the head of the St. Louis Clergy Coalition and pastor of the Greater Mount Carmel Baptist Church, and the Reverend E.G. Shields Sr., pastor of the Mt. Beulah M.B. Church, another big local congregation. With jokes and handshakes, the preachers greeted almost every other diner at the Delmonico. After a leisurely interval, they sat down. Men still desiring an audience walked over to the table and lowered themselves to whisper into the preachers' ears. Examining the day's *Post-Dispatch,* Shields and Nance dissected the latest Jesse Jackson scandal, in which Jackson had admitted to fathering a child out of wedlock, but soon, and more than a little appropriately, the preachers' conversation turned to Ben Thomas and his *Evening Whirl.*

"I don't think you'll find too many ministers who will admit to reading the *Whirl* on a regular basis," Rev. Shields said. "It was a scandal sheet. Ben was always looking to put something about ministers on the front page."

This was an understatement. Aside from murderers and maybe

hookers, stories on wayward preachers amounted to the *Whirl's* most fertile genre. Everywhere in St. Louis, it seemed, "prayermen" were cultivating harems or fleecing the faithful with healing roots or instigating with their "dictatorial" ways "unglorious battles" with their congregations. There was the clergyman who had acquired four wives, and, in defense of his polygamy, was quoted by the *Whirl* in a monologue: "All of us are God's chillun, and we can marry as much as we want to... When I moved out it was the next sucker's job to take over, 'cause he'd be the one sleeping with her and enjoying her." There was the pastor who, according to a 1984 *Evening Whirl* headline, begged MOTHER AND DAUGHTER TO BE HIS BABES; HE ASKS THEM TO INDULGE IN ORAL SEX; HE'S JAILED. The pastor was quoted as saying to the daughter, "If I have to put you to sleep to make love to you, I will do so. Do you know how to put lipstick on my dipstick? Amen! Glory! Now you have heard my story." There was the preacher who allegedly beat his children with "tree limbs and electric cords," and who, Thomas continued, "badly needs his own ass whipped until he can't sit down on it on a pillow without crying like a baby and meowing like a pussy cat." There was the "renown" reverend who had allocated seventeen thousand dollars a year to his gay lover out of the congregation's tithings. "He is like a hound dog after and with this man whom he describes as his husband and wife and thrill of his life."

Not surprisingly, preachers around town grew ever more wary, and weary, of Ben Thomas's scribblings. The Reverend Nance said, "Oh yeah, they printed rumors. Preachers were always feeling the heat from that kind of thing."

The Reverend Shields said, "Between the both of us, we knew any number of ministers who were written up in the *Whirl*. I was kind of glad when he stepped down."

(Neither Nance nor Shields ever saw their faces on the front page of the *Whirl,* it bears remarking.)

Though the *Whirl's* preacher reports undoubtedly grew out of Thomas's desire to attack the hypocrisy of the serially sinning cleric, the editor also seemed to have a preternatural compulsion to undermine the provinces of power, wherever they existed. The church was (and arguably still is) the most influential institution in black America, and had been since before the Civil War. Hundreds of churches did business in St. Louis, and for Thomas they were, on the whole, just that—commercial enterprises masquerading as spiritual. Obviously Thomas had no problem with commerce; it was the masquerade he attacked. Wherever a minister abused his station, whenever he drove around town in a fancy car or enticed young women with his congregational pay stub or lorded over the laity with an iron fist, Thomas was there to report it, substantiated or not. More than once an irate minister sued the *Whirl* for libel, and more than once the *Whirl* lost.

The money Thomas made by printing these stories mitigated the occasional legal obstacle. Indeed, as with all of Thomas's journalistic endeavors, his true motivations were ambiguous, for he waged his crusade against the city's profligate clergy for reasons of cash flow as much as principle. Like copy on gangsters, accusatory headlines about churchmen sold newspapers, and sold them fast. Both gangsters and preachers, at least when they appeared in the pages of the *Evening Whirl,* were exploiting a class of the vulnerable—poverty-stricken addicts in the one case, the poor devout in the other. Barry Thomas says of his father, "Even if preachers were quote-unquote good or honest, that a preacher would ask for money—it looked dishonest to my father. He'd say, 'Why take money from poor people?' And then you'd see preachers driving around in big Cadillacs while all of their members were destitute."

As the Reverends Nance and Shields discussed Ben Thomas at the Delmonico, a man walked into the restaurant. He was older, perhaps in his early seventies, tall and broad-shouldered, with graying hair and a thin mustache. After a round of hearty good-humored greetings with Shields, Nance and almost everyone else in the restaurant, he sat down at the table and removed his leather gloves. Without a word passing between him and the waitstaff, food appeared in front of him. Nance apprised the newcomer of the discussion at hand. Instantly the man's face changed shape.

"The *Evening Whirl*! That was the dirtiest, lousiest evidence of lies about the truth about a people I'd ever seen! What angered me about it, you could find it in Clayton."

The man's name was James F. DeClue; Clayton was an affluent, mostly white suburb of St. Louis, where for decades a local newsstand had sold the *Evening Whirl*. DeClue sketched a hypothetical scene. A white father, on his way home from work, buys the *Whirl* at the Clayton vendor, and later that evening his kids get hold of it. They spread the paper wide across the dinner table for a gander at the doings of the black race in St. Louis. Mug shots among the brussels sprouts. "Children's minds would be infected with the idea that this is how these people live," DeClue said. "But nobody would fight him. It must've been some kind of mob hookup."

In the mid-1980s James F. DeClue was pastor of the Washington Tabernacle Baptist Church, for years the most important black church in the city. During the same period he was also president of the St. Louis chapter of the NAACP. Sometime during his tenure there, DeClue became fed up with Ben Thomas and the *Evening Whirl,* and in his capacity as president, he took the extraordinary step of attempting to organize a boycott of the newspaper. The seriousness of this is not to be underplayed, for according to NAACP rules, any boycott of a business requires the permission of the national office, in Baltimore. DeClue's gambit, however, never made it that far.

"Mostly I was just trying to find someone who would join me in a fight against him and his paper," DeClue said. "I tried to convince my members to boycott it, to not buy it. I wasn't successful. For one thing, it was a popular magazine, and the level of pride in the community was such that they didn't think it was a problem. No matter whom we talked to, groups of ministers, businessmen, there seemed to be some kind of fear. Maybe they were afraid they'd end up in it."

"What's the saying?" Rev. Nance said. "'Don't get into a brick fight with the man who owns the brickyard'? Or, 'Don't hit the king unless you can kill him.'"

*   *   *

On the concrete driveway of a suburban house in Southern California, a ninety-year-old man stood with his hands behind his back, surveying the scene. The day was bright and dry and warm, November 2001. Hills the color of khaki loomed in three directions. In their arid crooks and gorges, at about the time of Ben Thomas's birth, Cecil B. DeMille had staged his Westerns. But now, two superhighways, the 5 and the 210, coursed through the canyons like paved-over riverbeds, and rising above the valley's racket of corporate parks and shopping malls and palm trees tall as freeway streetlamps, vast neighborhoods—stucco, Spanish tile—were cambered to fit the hills. This was Valencia, set down and let loose in the once-wild chaparral of the Santa Clarita Valley, about forty miles north of downtown Los Angeles.

"Right now," Ben Thomas said, "if you asked me what city I was in, I'd be guessing."

"Take a guess," said Barry Thomas, who stood beside him.

"I lived in Columbus once. Am I in Ohio?"

"You're in California."

"California! Well. I wouldn't have guessed that."

Earlier that morning Thomas had dressed carefully in 1970s chic: brown polyester trousers, a silk shirt with wide purple stripes over a red turtleneck sweater, burgundy patent-leather shoes. His eyes were still intense, their color extraordinary—deep brown surrounded by a band of cobalt blue. Photographs of Thomas taken just five years earlier showed a man with broad shoulders and an almost corpulent face. Now his ankles and wrists were bone thin and he weighed only 145 pounds. Still, considering his age and despite his frailty, Thomas moved nimbly. He looked athletic and fit, a little, huggable man.

In Valencia, Thomas was not altogether aware of what status he had with regard to the *Evening Whirl*. A pencil always peeked out of his breast pocket. In explanation, he responded, "Well, I'm a newspaperman." Sometimes he believed he was on short-term leave, and that he'd would soon be back making the rounds at police headquarters. At other moments the old vitriol over his contentious retirement would loosen his synapses. Once, informed of the paper's new ownership, Thomas, his voice pitched with disgust, said, "When I get back to Saint Louis, I'm going to clear out the entire staff." He was reminded that he had retired and therefore had no staff.

"Well, I'll come *out* of retirement then! No one can stop me. I own that paper. I can do anything I want. There's not one person alive," he said, holding his thumb and forefinger a quarter inch apart, "who owns *this* much of that paper!"

In Thomas's bedroom at his son's house, old photographs covered the tops of a dresser and a bookshelf—an ornate photobiographical collage. More than half were pictures of girlfriends. The shelf also held a half dozen spiral notebooks and yellow legal pads. Out of them stuck envelopes, scraps of paper, dog-eared pages. They contained hundreds of poems, all of which Thomas had composed since his move to California: "Lonesome," "Puzzled," "Forever," "Whenever," "On the Ball," "Get Up and On the Go," "Day and Night," "I Am Ready," "Screaming in My Sleep." Thomas would sometimes take a notebook, seclude himself in his room, and write for hours. One poem, called "Confused," has this last stanza:

> Nothing special was on my mind.
> Was there something I had left behind?
> Somehow I twisted and I turned,
> The more I did it, the more I burned.

In July 1995, in a wood-paneled auditorium at Washington University, the Greater St. Louis Association of Black Journalists convened its annual Hall of Fame awards ceremony. The headlining inductee was Benjamin Thomas. Three months later he would be in California, never to return to St. Louis. Needless to say, it came as a surprise to many that the *Evening Whirl* had, in the year of its editor's retirement, received this tribute from its peers, especially from a group as archly mainstream as the Association of Black Journalists. It was cofounded by Gerald Boyd, a former St. Louis *Post-Dispatch* reporter and—until it was discovered that Jayson Blair had burned his master's house by composing some dubious copy of his own—the managing editor of the *New York Times*. A debate within the association's board had preceded its decision to induct Thomas. Gregory Freeman, a columnist for the *Post-Dispatch* and a member of the board, explained to me, "The question we asked was, 'Is this journalism? Is this something we should be honoring?' Ultimately this guy has been around since 1938. At one time it was the best-read black weekly in Saint Louis. And in that sense, he was deserving of the award."

At the ceremony, Gregory Freeman introduced Thomas with perhaps five minutes of remarks, after which the editor slowly ambled to the podium. He accepted his Hall of Fame prize and turned to meet the camera flashes. The crowd applauded—some people stood, some did not—and when Ben Thomas returned to his chair to watch the rest of the night's presentation, he fell asleep. ★

STEPHEN ELLIOTT

THE SCORE

DISCUSSED: *Burning Man, Andy Warhol, Michael Jordan, Bill Clinton, Nike, Eddie Murphy, Harold Washington, The San Fernando Valley, Jim Morrison, Ronald Reagan, Public Mental Hospitals, Crack Cocaine, Graduate School, Jean-Luc Godard, Theo van Gogh, The Rise of Militant Islam*

1.

issette told me she was never very sexual with her husband. "In fact when we were first together we only had sex maybe twice a day."

I'll let the absurdity of the statement stand for itself. You just have to remember how fragile she is. I have to always remember it, and how fragile I am. We met in a café in Berkeley fifteen months ago, when she was still married. She was reading a fantasy book and I wasn't reading anything. We loved each other with one foot out the door. Or we loved passionately, recklessly. We loved like we didn't care if we lived or died or what the world looked like a week from tomorrow. And then we woke up bored, looked around for who else might be in the room. And she whispered softly in my ear, "We're doomed. It will never work."

2.

This is not an essay about breaking up with my girlfriend. I was leaning against a closed restaurant when I started to write this. Lissette wasn't even home yet; she was still out in the desert celebrating the Burning Man festival. I was reading a book about Theo van Gogh, the filmmaker killed by an Islamic fundamentalist in Amsterdam. I had quit taking speed for the most part but only because it didn't work anymore. I couldn't focus and I was running out of money and I kept making plans and then giving up. I checked out war zones and interviewed celebrities and politicians but none of it mattered.

This is right now I'm talking about.

Around this time I was in New York and I got in bed with a twenty-three-year-old volunteer with long, thick red hair. I thought she was Russian but she said she was Spanish. She was just very pale. I couldn't figure out what to do with her breasts. We were in bed half-naked and it was like this dead end. It was 2006, two months before the midterms. I could have gone for the belt on her jeans but I had no intention of doing that. I had wanted her but I had no idea what I wanted from her. I kept asking myself what all of it meant but you can't ask yourself a question like that and expect any kind of answer.

Around this time I saw a woman walking down Valencia Street in San Francisco wearing a purple nightdress. She was limping, holding the hand of some punk rocker, staggering past the coffee shop. She was almost glamorous except I was in the Mission and in the Mission nobody is glamorous except the kids in the street gangs with their smooth brown skin and blue scarves hanging out of their back pockets.

Around this time I went to dinner with a woman, a sex worker, someone I used to date, someone I dated briefly. I always date briefly and I always date sex workers because they're the only ones who understand desire without sex. Real desire. Raw and unattainable and without purpose. Desire that ends there, all-consuming, for nothing. We ended up at the back of a restaurant called Delfina and I told her I was having money problems and couldn't afford a fancy dinner.

She said, "Don't worry."

This particular woman had been raped by her father and one day a client came to her. The client looked just like her father. She tied the client to a wooden cross, screwed clamps onto his nipples, and beat him until his back was bleeding. The man begged to see her again but she refused. Or something like that. I told her I have dreams about my father where I'm holding his ears and screaming in his face. My father's old and crippled now. I haven't spoken to him in years. She said another time, earlier, she was in Florida and she was crying and her husband threw her in the closet with a shotgun and locked the door. She should just kill herself, he said. That's when she knew it was over between them.

I held her hand under the table. She has hard palms, strong fingers. She had one more client so I walked her back and we laid on her couch for a couple of minutes.

I was just back from Connecticut, where a bunch of true believers were working eighteen hours a day to elect a businessman worth $300 million to the Senate. They were against the war and he was against the war. I thought, This man has hired and fired people. That's not a statement on his character so much as a basic truth. Win or lose, they would all be disillusioned, particularly if he won. They would go home crying.

This was at least half my problem. I was jealous of these people. Their youthful idealism. Even the ones who were older than me. I've worked for politicians. I've been a believer. They've never failed to make a fool out of me and break my heart.

And that's what I was thinking about, the intersection of the half-naked girl, the sex worker with the dark past, and the new politics. But the only place these things met was at me and I was sitting against what used to be a Kentucky Fried Chicken trying to figure out what to do with my life. I was tired of having breakdowns, bored with perpetually standing at the edge of a panic attack. This is now I am talking about. I was going to have to do something but I wasn't sure what.

3.

When Burning Man was over Lissette called me from Reno. Not immediately, a couple of days later.

She said she didn't want to come home. She was having such a good time. She had that desert voice. The *I don't care about you* voice. It was like a challenge. "I had such a good time," she said. She said she met a guy who is going to teach her how to weld and blow glass. She said she met a guy who is coming to San Francisco to work in the prison and told him he could live with her for a couple of months in her studio in the Tenderloin.

She told me all this from inside a hotel room where she was staying with one of her clients. A client had driven her out to the desert and another client was driving her home. Lissette worked as a dominatrix. In San Francisco they pay $150 an hour for her attention, plus tip. On the open roads of Nevada, littered with the occasional casino, they had her all to themselves for the price of gas. They were happy for her time but I was less excited. I felt pushed away by this idealized version of herself. This insistence on being happy, even if it was true. She had made promises to herself out on the playa. Promises that included making more art, spending more time with her son, and worrying less about what I thought. She promised herself she would be happy, forgiving, and carefree. Then she danced in front of the fire.

When I saw her she wore a T-shirt she'd just bought at Target and black underwear and sat at her desk with one leg tucked beneath her. Her windows were frosted and closed but from the top of them I could see some of the buildings in Union Square.

"I wish I had been at Burning Man with you," I said, and she called me a liar.

We talked about her happiness. How she had never been happy with me since we got back together. How we never did anything together. We had been dating for over a year now. I asked her if she'd fucked anybody in the desert and she said no. She'd had a platonic boyfriend out there and at one point they'd sat near the end of the playa, where the mountain rises suddenly, and talked about what might have been.

I thought of how last year New Orleans had flooded during Burning Man and people had been dancing in the desert while Jefferson Parish was guarding its bridges with shotguns and people were dying in the New Orleans Convention Center.

Lissette said she decided to break up with me while she was in the desert. She was staying in a tent village when she made her decision. To make sure she didn't go back on it she fucked three men and then took two hits of ecstasy and acid. This was different from what she had told me earlier, but I guess she was waiting for her moment.

We were lying in her bed. "I'm waiting for you to talk me out of it," she said.

"How would I do that?" I asked.

"I take it back. I don't want to break up with you. I love you."

"Do you take back fucking those other guys?" I asked. Her leg was over my leg and she'd pulled my shirt off. I kept grabbing her ass, squeezing. She has the greatest ass I've ever seen. Even when I thought about her fucking other men all I saw was her ass jiggling up and down and how good that looked.

"Just give me a month," she said and I asked her why she thought that would work and she said she needed people to suffer for her and if I would do this then she would know I was suffering and then she would love me and I would feel safe and then I wouldn't be distant from her anymore and everything would be fine.

I told her I didn't know. I told her I needed to think about it. I wanted to have sex then. She started playing with my nipple, biting me. I reached between her legs, slid a finger inside her. "Tell me you'll see me again," she said. It was totally unfair but fair had nothing to do with it. I thought it had to be possible for me to have a real relationship. The kind people have in magazines, that "fulfill" and "facilitate." This had to be open to me though I'd never experienced anything like it.

I almost said yes but I didn't. I said, I don't really care who you fucked out in the desert. The desert is the desert. I know about the music, the lights, and the pills. I'm glad you had a good time. It was probably the greatest display of disposable art ever assembled. Fuck whoever you want. But then I thought, I am in bed with a crazy person and she tried to hurt me and she would try again. She was aiming an elephant gun at my heart. So I said give me a day to think about it and that's how she knew it was over.

"You're breaking up with me," she said.

"That's ridiculous," I said.

When I left her apartment the Tenderloin was full of fog. It floated near my kneecaps. The air was cool and wet and it wasn't totally dark. There were drug dealers and college students in front of the red and green flag of the taqueria. Forty thousand people had gone to the desert carrying art to burn and pills. A spontaneous, impermanent city.

She would call and say it was over. She would send me a note detailing all the time we'd been together and she had felt alone. Sitting on a bar stool later that night I felt the floor shift beneath me. I felt profoundly fucked up and sad that I hadn't spent the night with her. I wanted to tell my friends about it. I would build up to the punch line: "And then she fucked three guys just to make sure she didn't go back on it. And then, get this, she tried to go back on it anyway."

Would I tell them that? Would I mention that she had actually told the men why she was fucking them and they had fucked her anyway?

4.

I think everybody has an Andy Warhol story. I grew up in Chicago. When I think about Andy Warhol I think about the Kelly house on Sacramento Street. The father was dead and the oldest of three children had moved out. The younger son was trying to destroy himself and the daughter was wrecked by the loss of her father. The place was filled with junkies and house thieves, people I had known all my life. It was like a contained plague. There was shit coming up over the rim of the toilet. There was also this vicious dog that had to be kept locked in the daughter's room upstairs. People were sleeping everywhere and some of the people were very beautiful. Particularly Justin, who slept with everybody, boy or girl.

There was also Maria, Justin's girlfriend and my first love, who was beautiful and tragic. Her grandmother had kept her locked in the closet and sent her door to door begging for heroin money when she was only ten or eleven years old. She used to call me crying, saying she had been masturbating with the vacuum cleaner and she couldn't stop and her thighs were all bruised. Or she would tell me she had walked down to the gas station at night in her underwear and heels. Everything about her screamed "rape me." I loved her but I didn't know what to do about it. We had met in the group homes when we were just fourteen. We had tried for years to find some meeting point where we could comfort each other but we both wanted basically the same things and what we needed was someone who wanted something different.

Sometimes I would sleep with Justin, too. He would wrap around me so tight, like an octopus. I think he slept with everybody that way but I never knew if he was doing it for my benefit or his own. He had long black hair and wiry arms. When he wore makeup he looked like a dragon woman.

When everything was really going down at the Kelly house I had already left for college 150 miles south of the city. But I couldn't stay away. I came up every weekend. I wasn't even getting high then,

I spent six years clean and sober, I just didn't want to be alone. And that's what the Kelly house was really about. It was about not being alone. The filth and the drugs were secondary.

It was just like Warhol's factory in New York, except it was on the North Side of Chicago, the drugs were cheaper, and nobody was ever going to be famous.

I recently met Ted from the old neighborhood. He was just walking down the street. Turns out we live in the same neighborhood on the edge of San Francisco. I'm pushing thirty-five now and he's pushing forty. He asked what I was up to and I almost started crying. I didn't have a good answer. Of course I was up to things; I was writing *this* essay for example. I was also working on a screenplay and an oral history of myself. So that's what I told him. But I got kind of choked because it also wasn't true. I wasn't doing anything. The true answer would have been something like: "I'm drowning." Or, if I was feeling optimistic, I might have said, "I'm recovering." . Same thing really. He asked if I would be getting on the campaign. There were all these races coming up, elections to be held. I said no, not this year. What else could I say about it? I didn't want to leave the city. I didn't want to see another town, another strip mall, another campaign office. I didn't want to be anywhere where I was unfamiliar with the public transportation. In fact, I didn't want to go anywhere that wasn't directly on the route between where I lived and where I worked.

I first met Ted at least fourteen years ago when he was bartending in the Heartland Café and I was just out of college starting to shoot heroin and strip in the gay bars. Back then he was directing plays at this small storefront theater. He was older than I was, not part of my social group, and seemed to have his shit together. He was basically slumming. He came from a good family. His father was an airline executive and owned a penthouse in New York with an atrium. He had been to NYU for dramatic writing. A friend of the family had made a phone call to get him in. One time he slept with my friend Angel's girlfriend and when Angel asked him why he did it Ted responded he did it because he was a writer and Angel punched him in the face.

Now he's the literary director of a large theater in San Francisco but we never see each other. I've been in San Francisco eight years already and we've seen each other maybe five times. His wife, he said, was at home working on a children's book. They owned their own house and had a dog.

He told me they were really happy and I didn't doubt it. We didn't talk for long. I was on the way to get some nails; I wanted to hang a painting. My ex-girlfriend's slave had made it for me as a housewarming present. I had just moved into a cheaper apartment in a neighborhood where there were a lot of dogs and children and I was trying to make it livable. I kept thinking, It's OK, I'm not that far away from things.

How about it all, I thought. What was I up to, he had asked.

5.

After the Kelly house had come and gone, when I was just out of college, the world revolved around Michael Jordan and the Chicago Bulls. There was no politics. Bill Clinton was president and all I knew about him was that he was against welfare and he was putting a lot of people in jail. I would meet my friend Angel at the Beachwood and we would watch the games on the small TV there with Lisa the social worker and Pat the mailman. The bar owner lived in two rooms attached to the bar.

It was the 1990s. It was Wicker Park. The junkies still shot on Milwaukee Avenue but the neighborhood was changing. Occasionally Angel and I did heroin, or stayed up all night snorting coke at Lisa's apartment down the street, where she lived with her twelve cats and her broken mirrors. But what was really important was the Chicago Bulls.

They could do anything and if things were really bad MJ would launch six three-pointers and score thirty-five points in the half.

One season we won seventy-two games. They played incredible defense. They would swarm you, knock you off balance, smack the ball away. Scottie Pippen with those long arms and that crossover dribble. B. J. Armstrong with his boyish good looks. He actually got voted onto the all-star team just because he had the fortune of passing the ball to Michael Jordan. There was Coach Phil Jackson and Tex Winter with his fabled triangle offense. Then Dennis Rodman came along pulling down fifteen rebounds a game and covered in tattoos. They had to take Dennis's image off the facade of a building because it was causing traffic jams on I-94. I would see Dennis on Sunday nights when Liquid Soul played at the Double Door. He would lean against the wall near the stage. His birthday party was invitation-only at the Crobar. He fucked Madonna and married Carmen Electra during a Las Vegas bender. He was crazy. A couple of years earlier he was caught sitting in a truck in the stadium parking lot with a loaded shotgun under the seat.

In the mid-'90s everything clicked. We beat Detroit and Portland and Phoenix and Utah and Orlando and New York and Houston. There were all these great players that were never going to wear the rings: Charles Barkley, Karl Malone, Patrick Ewing, and Clyde the Glide. There were all these teams that were good enough to win the championship but we wouldn't let them. We won every year except when MJ left basketball to play minor-league baseball and even that year we did good. We built a new stadium on the South Side with a statue of Michael in front. It was called the United Center but there was a petition to name it after Jordan's father, who had been killed in a carjacking in North Carolina.

Then I left Chicago for Los Angeles and basketball didn't matter in the same way. Even though the Lakers now had Shaquille O'Neal, in the bars they left the music on. You could watch the game but you couldn't *hear* it. People sat at tables talking over the music, explaining the screenplay they were writing or the film they were producing or the pilot they were acting in. There's a lot of room in Los Angeles. The bars weren't crowded enough. And then I stopped caring.

Later I would decide that politics was the only game for adults, only to realize it wasn't any different from a schoolyard, just a bunch of hurtful insults, character destruction, power grabbing, and co-alition building. Meaningless, but with consequences. The worst of human nature on display under glass. But early in the new millennium I would follow it just like I had followed basketball. Reading charts, comparing scores, discerning who was on the rise and decline, remembering the stats, and rooting crazily, passionately, for my team.

Later still I met Phil Knight, the man who founded Nike and revolutionized the celebrity endorsement. He tried to introduce me to Michael Jordan but I had to go on the radio that day to talk about the upcoming presidential election. I was just a friend of a friend but we hit it off. When we went out to dinner I would make jokes about picking up the tab and he would try to hand me the bill but I never took it.

It's only recently, when I'm reevaluating everything, that I realize somewhere in there I made a bad trade. Now I sometimes watch sports with friends but I get bored. They all have fantasy teams and they're mostly only interested in how their own players do. I used to read the statistics in the newspapers but now it's just guys in uniforms on a TV set. Most of the uniforms have a Nike swoosh.

I'm jealous of my friends who follow sports. They read about football while I read about the war in Iraq. Of course they read about the war as well but they don't follow events the same way. But I'm tired of the war in Iraq and the more shadowy war on terror. The propaganda and the *he said, she said* of the daily news cycle. I want to watch the athletes, the very essence of human ambition, gladiators in the stadium, the bright green turf or the smooth wooden slats. I want to see their long bronze arms extending, fingers reaching from somewhere inside that great huddle of men, all of them leaping in the air, grasping heroically for the ball. And I want to care about the score.

6.

I have more to say about my time in Los Angeles. Hollywood is an awful place and I wasn't even in Hollywood, I was in Granada Hills, just off the Ronald Reagan Freeway. One day we had a bachelor party. There were strippers with an Indian bodyguard there, and an actor from *Seinfeld*. One of the strippers was drunk and she grabbed my hair and pulled my head back between her breasts and asked me to tell her she was beautiful. I told her she was and that possibly I was in love with her.

Later the actor was doing shots off the woman's chest. I remember wondering what he was so happy about. He was big and handsome and full of life and we were in this crappy house in the San Fernando Valley where everything was just awful dirt and smog. I was staying there, sleeping on a mattress on the floor and jerking off to a forced-feminization magazine someone had left in the bathroom. The magazine was filled with cartoons and stories of men being kidnapped by their girlfriends and fed hormone pills. There were dogs and I was always stepping in puddles of urine. The actor rented a house in the Hollywood Hills so things were nicer for him but I still couldn't get it. He had just landed a part in the next *Batman* movie. I wished I could be happy like that.

At some point the bridegroom got upset and then there was violence, the Indian rushing the strippers out the door, the rest of us hanging on to the groom by his limbs. What did anybody expect from us? Violence was all we knew. That guy from *Seinfeld* never came around again. Everybody else left Los Angeles or got into porn. The ones that stayed pushed barbells in strip malls and worked on their cars in front of pale ranch houses and their lawns filled with so many tools and parts soon you couldn't see the grass. They folded into the smog and the landscape and disappeared.

I thought about Granada Hills watching the news the other night. A reporter had done an exposé on a real estate developer and he was back to do a follow-up. First the wife came and threw water at the camera. Then the developer arrived. He went right to the reporter and hit him in the face. He pulled back as far as he could and let go with this enormous swing. The reporter had his arms crossed and didn't even try to block it. He was obviously a coward. They fell to the ground and the cameraman just kept filming. When it was over the reporter's face was swollen and covered in blood and the police were taking the real estate developer and his wife away in handcuffs. That's what it's like in Granada Hills, even though this happened in San Diego. Maybe it's the same, all those low houses and so much sun.

7.

In better times, Lissette used to cut me. She would slice elaborate patterns into my shoulders and stick me with needles. My breathing would slow down when the pins went through me. It was like being on a raft. Everything would be OK. When we were first together she dug her keys into my back and carved a series of *Ls* in my skin. The letters were deep and the cuts were ragged and for a while it didn't seem like they would heal, but they did.

I still have scars from my girlfriend before Lissette, who left three marks on my side with a scalpel. Before that I just had marks from a woman in Michigan who burned me with a cigarette on the back of my hands. Lissette decided to make an *E* out of the scars on my side, the first of ten letters. She kept a knife by my bed, a present from a client. It had a grip handle. She would tie me up and hold the blade against my throat. One time I was blindfolded and my chest was bleeding and I tried to kiss her, pushing up against the knife, which she held to my jugular.

"You have no sense of self-preservation," she said.

It wasn't true. I had a fantastic sense of self-preservation but it had left me for a while. I wasn't sure if it would come back.

Lissette used the knife to carve *possession* in my side but she spelled it wrong. She used only one *s*. When I told her I asked her not to be mad. "It's ruined," she said. Then we broke up. Then we got back together. She recut me, tried to fix it.

It was such an obvious metaphor for our relationship I didn't even want to think about it. It was like Jim Morrison dying in the bathtub or Ronald Reagan's tax cuts. It meant exactly what you thought it meant.

Between the cutting and the beating and the sex I could barely move. We would lie in bed for days until the sheets were covered in blood and lube. She would go home to her husband but she would be back before I ever recovered. I would try to keep her entertained so she wouldn't leave without giving me my next fix.

I thought of my friend who broke his leg playing football when we were younger and he was sitting on his bed in the hospital when they came in and wheeled him into the psych ward. His mother had him committed. I used to visit him. They had him in Northwestern, a nice hospital on the lake, much nicer than the place they put me when I was found with my wrist slashed sleeping in a hallway— a public hospital with shit smeared on the walls. That's what it was like with Lissette. Like being locked in a room. I almost never went out. I missed my friends. I felt like there was nothing I could do.

This is all I know about love.

After Lissette and I broke up I had to come to terms with my depression. For two years, ever since George W. Bush was reelected, I had been waiting for the right time to kill myself. When I thought about it I got so sad.

The first time in my life I was really suicidal was when I was thirteen. My mother had just died and I was living on the streets and slashed my wrists. Then I did it again. I made about seven suicide attempts that year before I was locked up. I don't think I would have been locked up but when they found me they asked where my parents lived. I said I didn't know. My father had moved to the suburbs. Actually I had seen him that morning. He caught me sleeping in the house I grew up in, the house he still owned, the house he was trying to sell. When he found me he beat me up and shaved my head.

Things got better after that. The state took custody. There was the mental hospital, then the group homes. I was completely divorced from culture in those days. In the group home we would watch Eddie Murphy movies and listen to house mixes, which didn't interest me at all. I didn't watch television. I read *The Catcher in the Rye* and thought it was the worst thing I'd ever seen. Who cared about Holden Caulfield? Who cared about rich people who stay in boarding schools and don't know what to do with their lives? That wasn't my environment.

Of course, culture affected me more than I knew. Those house mixes would change music forever. There was a war on drugs going on and marijuana was getting more expensive. While Joan Didion was in El Salvador, crack was moving into the inner city with the help of the CIA and the administration's ties to the Nicaraguan contras. It just appeared one day. Hard candy. Cocaine was out of our range but crack was the drug of the people. We would smoke the rocks in pipes made from pressure gauges and burn our lips.

This was Harold Washington's time, the first black mayor of Chicago, and all sorts of construction was going on in the South Side, where I lived. There were ribbons in front of buildings and blue and white signs with the mayor's name. Washington actually lived in the same neighborhood as the group home, just closer to the lake. When he was reelected, a staff member who dealt drugs on the side took seven of us over there in the house van and we watched the mayor come out of his building and make a speech.

This wasn't what concerned me. I didn't care about the mayor. Farrakhan was making his move at this time, coming down on the Jews, and his mosque was nearby. So were Jesse Jackson and the Rainbow Coalition. I was beat up in the Garfield train station by people wearing Adidas suits. They stole my gym shoes—Nikes—and I walked home in socks. It all came back to me in the waves of violence and social change that occur in the lowest strata of society, beneath the antennae of mainstream media coverage. We were as important as sand at the bottom of the ocean. We didn't understand that it was the paths of the planets that control the tides. We were too far down to see anything but a thick, dark sky.

8.

The second time I was suicidal I was twenty-three years old and I'd just gotten out of the hospital following a massive heroin overdose. I'd gone from college to graduate school and made up with my father. When I came home to the room I rented near the university, the walls were all yellow and the ceiling was very low.

I was in film school and we watched Godard and Truffaut. We saw Chaplin falling across the stage and the final frame of *The 400 Blows* and Crazy Pierrot trying frantically to put out the fire after he's wrapped his head in brightly colored dynamite sticks and lit the wick.

"How did you find me," Anna Karina asks.

"It was an accident," Pierrot replies.

We discussed Sissy Spacek and Martin Sheen in *Badlands* and who was the real criminal in *M*. The murderer, after all, couldn't help himself. But what excuses the rest of us?

I had spent eight days in the hospital following my hot shot. I'd had a stroke, or a seizure. There were strange boils all over my body. I'd been unable to move. I left the hospital late at night walking with a limp.

I planned to kill myself the same as Kurt Cobain had two years earlier, with a gun in my mouth. I lost thirty pounds after I got out of the hospital. I wanted to kill myself at the lake but I was afraid the cold water would keep me alive. Instead I went back to the hospital crying. It was after midnight. I had been out of the hospital a month. I didn't have anybody else I could cry to. My friend who had been in the room with me when I overdosed had turned me over and left me to die.

A resident at the hospital gave me some Klonopin. The next day I enrolled in a drug treatment program. In the program I could cry every day. Nobody cared.

Later that year I was hauling cameras in Seattle, working on a docudrama about Prefontaine starring Jared Leto. Prefontaine was the original Nike hero. A long-distance runner from the University of Oregon and a protégé of Bill Bowerman's. A statue of Pre stands in the Nike headquarters.

It was just after the grunge movement and I was living with a girl from a good family who was giving up everything—including me—to service a cocaine addiction. Cobain was dead. Mudhoney never made it. Pearl Jam was out of town. Alice In Chains was nowhere. Soundgarden had broken up. It was summer in Seattle but there was nothing except rain.

There's still speculation that Cobain's suicide was a murder. People said, "What an idiot. He had everything." But obviously he didn't have everything. Obviously he was profoundly sad. Others said a person has no right to kill themselves once they have a child. But I thought, They can take everything else but you always have that. There's an escape clause built into every social contract.

9.

I sent a letter to my friend Heathen. I said, "Gosh, you know." I said I wanted to be somewhere safe but public. I wanted to be on a leash or have a bit in my mouth. I didn't want to be expected to speak. I had been in the papers recently for a book I'd written. My father had responded by sending letters to the editors insisting there was nothing wrong with me. I hadn't been abused, I was just spoiled. He complained to one reporter, "He's not damaged. My son is a success." He told anyone who would listen that those group homes were actually very nice places.

I told Heathen I was just finishing an essay that would combine everything I've ever seen and end with a man standing in front of a chasm, preparing to jump. But I didn't want to jump. I wanted to be naked and available and wanted. I didn't want to know who was doing what. I didn't want to engage with the politicians, the missing ballots in Prince George. I thought about Daniel Pearl saying, "I am a Jew. My mother is a Jew." I thought about Theo van Gogh, Mohammed Bouyeri stepping from the shadow. Theo begging for mercy. "Don't do it. Don't do it." First a bullet, then several more.

Then Bouyeri slits his throat, pins his manifesto to Theo's chest with a dagger, and Amsterdam is never the same again.

I lived in Amsterdam. It was 1992 and I was a barker for a live sex show called the Casa Rosso. I was dating a hooker from Australia and then Miriam, a Surinamese cabaret dancer whose husband was in jail for murder. It was the first time a woman ever took me home, tied me up, and slapped me without me paying for it. I didn't know anything about the world in 1992. It would be thirteen years before I fell in love.

In my letter I told Heathen I wanted to be penetrated and pierced and laughed at and pulled along by my hair. I wanted to be objectified. I wanted to be restrained and suffocated. I wanted to be slapped and talked down to. I had just come back from Israel, seen the smoke rising from the Lebanese villages beyond the hills, stared into the muzzle of a tank, witnessed the jet hovering still in the sky while Caterpillar D9s churned the soft red soil along the border. I walked along the fence watching for snipers, clenching my fists and pressing them against my head. I spoke with residents in deserted towns terrified to walk down the street. Realized for the first time that war is not about destruction, it's about fear.

I told Heathen I'd lost my girlfriend to the new sexual politics. I said I wanted a strap-on forced in my mouth while the girl wearing the strap-on spoke with her friends. I wanted pictures to be taken and posted everywhere. I didn't want to have sex but I wanted to be penetrated. I didn't want to go down on anybody but I wanted to be sat on by people wearing clothes. I wanted to be the only one naked.

There was a war going on between cultures. There was a new Crusade but the weapons were bigger. I apologized for being selfish. It had nothing and everything to do with the controversial Dutch filmmaker. The great conflict of the new century had moved into direct and violent contact with the outer limits of the Enlightenment. One man—deranged, on the edge of society, an immigrant's son, discriminated against, lacking opportunities, caught in the World Wide Web of militant Islam. The internet Jihadist Pornstore filled with dirty videos of beheadings, throat slittings, a boot pressing into a woman's stomach while a geyser of blood erupted from her neck, martyr glorification, bearded men holding guns and smiling for the camera before leaving to seek their deaths. All of these found on a short stack of DVDs in Bouyeri's apartment. And the other man, the one he killed, a minor celebrity, an attention seeker, a Dutch Bill O'Reilly. A man full of hate and convenient ideologies, a nationalist, a xenophobe, a grand-nephew of one of the greatest painters the world has ever known.

A woman screamed at Bouyeri as he reloaded his gun—"You can't do this!"

"Yes, I can," he replied.

That was 2004.

This was 2006. It was two years after Theo van Gogh's ugly murder. My girlfriend was fucking three men in a tent, in a city that had sprung up in a week with forty thousand naked wanderers, all of them covered in a thin film of white dust, looking to get high. A dry mecca of disposable art. They would burn everything.

"That's when I decided to leave you," she said. I don't think she had ever heard of Theo van Gogh, though I'm sure she attended the Van Gogh Museum as well as the Anne Frank Huis.

Later, Lissette would leave a brief note and a small pile of my possessions on my doorstep. Inside of these things, in a white box, would be a plastic Baggie and inside of that a sugar cube full of acid and a capsule full of ecstasy. She hoped I would see what she saw. The pills and the sugar would help me understand, like Rex Hofman, who drinks a cup of tea in order to find out what happened to his wife, who disappeared three years earlier, and wakes up in a coffin, buried alive.

Later, I would send a note to Heathen explaining everything I wanted in the current political climate. I told her I wanted what everybody else wants, it's just the details are different. I see connections everywhere I look. It's not that it doesn't make sense, it makes perfect sense, just that lives are fractured. I can easily keep this many balls in the air. This is who I am. This is the world right now.

I finished the note by saying I wanted to be afraid and I wanted to cry with someone who's not afraid to make me sad, who doesn't stop just because I'm crying.

Heathen wrote me back. She said she wanted the same thing. ✶

JONATHAN LETHEM

THE AMERICAN
VICARIOUS

DISCUSSED: *Humble Pleas for Moral Advice, Lightly Hardboiled
Surfaces, The Extension of Dada-Drunk Sophistication, Antagonist
Editors Named Shrike, Cults, Idiomatic Violence, Unsympathetic Novels
About Sympathy, Elevator Shafts, Desert Landscapes Littered with
Arbitrary Architectural Monstrosities, The Inadvertent Death of
Retail Clerks, F. Scott Fitzgerald in the Fetal Position*

1.

H alfway through *Miss Lonelyhearts,* Nathanael
West's eponymous protagonist blurts out:

Perhaps I can make you understand. Let's start from
the beginning. A man is hired to give advice to the
readers of a newspaper. The job is a circulation stunt and the whole
staff considers it a joke. He welcomes the job, for it might lead to
a gossip column, and anyway he's tired of being a leg man. He too
considers the job a joke, but after several months at it, the joke
begins to escape him. He sees that the majority of the letters are
profoundly humble pleas for moral and spiritual advice, that they are
inarticulate expressions of genuine suffering. He also discovers that

his correspondents take him seriously. For the first time in his life, he is forced to examine the values by which he lives. This examination shows him that he is the victim of the joke and not its perpetrator.

The passage, so disconcertingly clean and direct that it could remind you of a Hollywood "treatment" (the mercenary form in which West would come to specialize, a few years later), perhaps represents the book West suspects he ought to have written, or the book he suspects his reader thinks he ought to have written. That's to say, a coherently tragic narrative grounded, under an urbane, lightly hard-boiled surface, in comprehensible "values." The story is the sort that might have been nicely handled by a novelist like Horace McCoy, whose *They Shoot Horses, Don't They?* might be considered a temperamental cousin to West's, with its metaphor of the dance marathon forming a lucid indictment of the failure of popular imagination to encompass the Great Depression's dismantling of the American Dream.

Certainly this embodies a part of West's intention. *Lonelyhearts* was inspired by access West was given to real letters written to a real advice columnist, and its setting, a persuasively scoured and desperate early-'30s Manhattan, is rendered with the scalpel-precision that was West's prose standard. No doubt, one measure of Nathanael West's singular value is as a uniquely placed historical witness, a bridge between literary eras. His was a sensibility that extended the Paris-expatriate, Dada-drunk sophistication of '20s literary culture to the material and milieu of Steinbeck, Tom Kromer, Edward Dahlberg, Daniel Fuchs, and other 1930s writers (some explicitly tagged as "proletarian")—that is, to poverty's social depredations, with all the accompanying lowered sights, deluded daydreams, and susceptibility to cults, fads, and games of chance.

Yet hardly anything in this context prepares us as readers for the plunge into the nihilistic, hysterical, grotesque-poetic frieze that is the fifty-eight-page "novel" we know as *Miss Lonelyhearts*. For what that inadequate synopsis implies ("for the first time in his life, he is forced to examine the values....") is an approach to depicting fictional characters that West couldn't ratify: psychologically rounded, and capable of making and recognizing a traditional "mistake," of making a hero's progress through a typical plot, even if it is to be a tragic one. This isn't West's way. The journalist known to us only as "Miss Lonelyhearts," like his antagonist-editor, Shrike, indeed, like every human creature he encounters (including those "profoundly humble" authors of the advice-seeking letters), is a species of chimera, in many ways a mystery to him- or herself. If West's characters are human, it is only unfortunately so: trapped in a grossly prominent physical form, a creature lusting and suffering in bewildering simultaneity. As far as their "values," or *personalities*, these are glimpsed only fleetingly against a screaming sky full of borrowed and inadequate languages and attitudes—commercial, religious, existentialist, therapeutic, criminal.

West's characters mostly don't engage in conversation. In its place they toss blocks of rhetoric, of elegant mockery or despair, at one another like George Herriman's Ignatz Mouse chucking a brick at Krazy Kat's head. The comparison of *Lonelyhearts*'s form to a comic strip isn't mine, but West's, who intuited that for all his grounding in Dostoyevsky and T. S. Eliot he needed to find some version of vernacular form to embody his insight that "in America violence is idiomatic." The novel's short, sardonically titled chapters persistently end in morbid slapstick and cumulatively take on a slanted, compacted quality, like crashed cars exhibited bumper-to-bumper. Dislodged on the very first page from traditional identification with the travails of *Lonelyhearts*'s protagonist—in one ear by the horrific chorus of the advice-seeking letters themselves, in the other by the preemptive mockery of Shrike—the reader finds any possibility of redemptive self-pity brilliantly undermined. (A critic explained—or complained: "Violence is not only his subject matter, but his technique.") Nathanael West's masterpiece is a mercilessly unsympathetic novel on the theme of sympathy.

2.

New York is vertical, Los Angeles horizontal, as well as three thousand miles farther from any grounding in European historical consciousness. The difference between West's New York novel and *The Day of the Locust,* his Hollywood apocalypse, mimics these contrasts of cultural geography and form. *Lonelyhearts* is defined by stairwells and elevator shafts and basement speakeasies, *Locust* by the littering of a desert landscape with arbitrary architectural monstrosities, with random and flimsy quotations of varied building styles, whether for use as temporary movie sets or (barely more permanent) dwellings. Lizards scurry across this baked ground. In place of *Lonelyhearts's* claustrophobic compression, in *Locust,* West's savage attention flits from character to character, leaving more oxygen and sunlight between the tragicomically lumpen human operators—though eventually they'll crowd together and swarm this landscape like lemmings. Acutely conscious of the double-edged myths of Progress and Manifest Destiny (the diffident Jew Nathan Wallenstein Weinstein converted himself to the imperially urbane "Nathanael West" because, he joked, he'd heard Horace Greeley's call to "go West, young man"), West defines Los Angeles as the place where the American (Egalitarian) Dream has ended up, first to replicate itself in the synesthetic cartoons of the motion-picture industry, and then, under the exposing glare of sunlight, to die.

Of course it is also six years deeper into the Depression, and no one in *Locust* would bother, as does Shrike in *Lonelyhearts,* to puncture unattainable fantasies of luxurious Bohemian escape. The inadvertent Californians in *Locust* have made their last, weary migration, and in this zone of shoddy historical facsimiles history itself seems to have ground to an end. The aspiring painter Tod Hackett, the book's best hope for reader-surrogate (and West's best shot at such a thing, in any of his four books), a protagonist-watcher who dares both to dream of love and to attempt an artistic encapsulation of what's before him, can only plan a canvas depicting the gleeful burning of Los Angeles by its cheated residents: in destruction, they might make it their own.

West depicts the film industry from its margins, the lame cast-off vaudevillians and extras, the aspirants and show-biz parents, grasping intuitively that these figures articulate the brief continuum between manufacturing and merchandising bogus dreams, and lining up to buy them. The pathetically wishful movie scenarios dreamed up by the wannabe-starlet Faye Greener, Tod Hackett's tormenting love-object, are hardly less viable than the sorts of films that West himself ended up dashing off during his stints as a studio writer—the point seems to be not simply that anyone could dream such stuff up, but that everyone did, simultaneously. Most were buyers, not sellers.

West's diagnosis of the American Vicarious anticipates both reality television (where Andy Warhol's quip about everyone gaining fifteen minutes of fame became a drab processional) and the overturning of the "Death Tax" (where politicians aroused a righteous populist indignation in favor of the inheritance of fortunes, just on the chance every American would acquire his rightful own). West wouldn't have wondered *what's the matter with Kansas;* he knew the problem wasn't limited to Kansas, or Los Angeles, or the 1930s. In a 1967 article on West, Gilbert Sorrentino discerned that *The Day of the Locust* predicted Ronald Reagan's future presidency, and this book, a sun-blazed Polaroid of its moment, seems permanently oracular.

3.

West's ultimate subject is the challenge (the low odds, he might insist) of negotiating between, on the one hand, the ground-zero imperatives and agonies of the body and, on the other, the commoditized rhetorics of persuasion, fear, envy, guilt, acquisition, and sacrifice (those voices that George Saunders has nicknamed "The Braindead Megaphone" of late capitalism) in hopes of locating an intimate ground of operation from which an authentic loving gesture might be launched. That he identified this as a baseline

twentieth-century American dilemma as early as he did granted
West a superb relevance to the future of American literature—its
ongoing future, I'd say.

In the weeks while I've been re-reading his novels, the unfolding of a global financial collapse has many speaking of a "second
Great Depression," the public mechanics of which will certainly be
subject to the same forces of transference, denial, and fantasy that
West made his obsessive motifs. Last year in suburban Long Island,
on the day nicknamed "Black Friday" for its hopes of pushing retail
accounts into the black of profit, a tide of bargain-fevered shoppers
trampled to death a retail clerk attempting to manage their entry
into his store. The newspaper business has almost dissolved beneath
a willful tide of "authentic" voices demanding to be heard; its response is nearly as neurotic as Miss Lonelyhearts's. Which of West's
contemporaries can we imagine weighing in intelligibly on blog-
ging, or *American Idol*? (Picture Ernest Hemingway's thousand-
yard stare—and he lived a quarter-century longer than West—or
F. Scott Fitzgerald in a fetal position.) By applying the magpie
aesthetics of surrealism and T. S. Eliot to the "American Grain,"
by delving into the popular culture and emerging not with surrender or refusal but a razor-cool critique, West became the great
precursor to Heller, Pynchon, Philip K. Dick, George Saunders,
and so much else, likely including Bob Dylan's "Desolation Row."
West died at thirty-seven, with his wife, in an automobile collision
while returning to Los Angeles from a hunting trip in Mexico.
His biographer Jay Martin gives evidence of the many books West
had sketched out to write after *Locust,* surely the greatest shadow
oeuvre in American fiction. ✶

JOE HAGAN

TRANSIT BYZANTIUM

DISCUSSED: *Bob Dylan, The Everly Brothers, Big Star, The Grand Cooley Dam, Woody Guthrie, Elliott Smith, M. Ward, Cleveland, The Mice, Guided By Voices, The Cleveland Museum of Art, Ronald Reagan, KCRW, Reggae on Public Radio, McGruff the Crime Dog, The Beachland Ballroom, The Revelers, Dirt, North Olmsted, Big Chuck and Little John, The Book of Revelation, Seymour Stein, Aztec Archaeology*

Can beauty cause cardiac arrest? "That's what it felt like to me," my wife says. "Cardiac arrest or maybe a lightning bolt to the sternum."

This is how it started: She worked in town but lived in the country, requiring a long, solitary drive home that gave her time enough to wonder why she was spending her twenties alone in a Vermont farmhouse. Disquieted, reaching no good answer, she hit SCAN on her radio. A change in frequency, a change in thought. And there he was: One man and one guitar. A circular melody, a high, lonesome voice, lyrics of plaintive confession.

Hold the bell
I carry news that I have got to tell
Hold your head out and you can hear the sound

Of my baby crying
Peter and Paul
Stare at the sky and wait for Jesus to fall
The only sound that they can hear
Is my baby crying

Her lungs filled with words. Her breath stopped. Who was this? The blue of the sky and the yellow flash of passing fields were now tuned to this sweet and sandy voice. Was everyone within broadcast range in the same paralytic awe? Was she, perhaps, not alone? An anonymous bard, plucked from a pile of CDs by a university student in nearby Burlington, sang through her '88 Toyota Camry and broke her heart for three and a half minutes. It was the only sound she could hear.

My baby crying
My baby crying...

She pulled over, waiting for the DJ to identify the singer: Bill Fox.

That was 1998. We met a year later and she introduced me to Bill Fox's two albums. The music slowly overtook me, like water rising in a room. Here were familiar accents and phrasings borrowed from Bob Dylan and the Everly Brothers, Big Star and Woody Guthrie, antique references to "tender Ophelia," a "brown-skinned lover in Santa Fe," and the Grand Cooley Dam. But in the cottony aura of low-fidelity tape, Fox smudged familiarity into something intimate and modern. You could hear a TV set playing behind his exquisite homemade finger-picking. Harmonica, piano, his own overdubbed harmonies, all stitched to this dusky voice that strained with emotion. Later it became clear to me why musicians like Elliott Smith and M. Ward were so influenced by him, why they pursued the same hermetic, sepia-toned sound.

Bill Fox is now barely locatable among the hordes of Google-able Bill Foxes: the insurance adjuster, the law enforcer, the financial executive. He doesn't have a website. He isn't listed in the phone

book. No record label has his number. He disappeared. Vanished—
poof. A troubadour and rocker from Cleveland, Ohio, a leftist, artist,
and idealist—information I'd surmised from the lyrics and a nine-
year-old bio on the internet. I know he once fronted the Cleveland power-pop band the Mice, who rocked the clubs of Akron
and Kent in the late 1980s. His fifteen-year-old brother, Tommy,
played drums with the savage intensity of Keith Moon. Their records heavily influenced Robert Pollard, the Dayton schoolteacher
and beer-fueled front man for Guided By Voices, who frequently
praised the Mice after they broke up, in 1988. A decade later, Fox
quietly reemerged with two albums, *Shelter from the Smoke* (1997)
and *Transit Byzantium* (1998). After *CMJ,* the college-rock magazine that set the alternative-music agenda in the late 1990s, called
Fox "one of the most important artists of our day," he evaporated
from the public record.

By now, I'm accustomed to instant knowledge. I Google and
get, reflexively unearthing mysteries. It's a modern rhythm: question, click, answer. Absent new information on Fox, I started feeling
like a pre-internet teenager again, continually studying liner notes
for clues to imagine what the singer must be doing now. Without
an update in nearly a decade, I was left to study the blurry living-
room photo on the cover of *Transit Byzantium,* the hypnotic pattern
of its red velvet couch. Fox leans forward, stares off camera, his left
thumb in his right fist—vulnerable, even anxious. In an old press
photo for the Mice, I notice the idiosyncratic details that peg them
as hopelessly provincial: the square-jawed Tommy sports a Love
and Rockets mullet, but also boat shoes; Fox wears a sweater pulled
over an oxford, hands crossed in front of him like a choirboy being
photographed for the yearbook. With the leather-clad bass player,
they stand in front of a tall marble statue of a cherub playing a violin.
I realize they're in an art museum, probably the Cleveland Museum of Art. *They believe in art!* Of course they do: Ronald Reagan is
in office and the Mice are teenage romantics who sing a charging
pop anthem called "Not Proud of the USA."

The photo triggers a strange nostalgia, as if I had once been a part of his life in Cleveland and just remembered it after years of denial. I can smell the antiseptic hallways of his high school and imagine the dirty jokes his friends told. I wasn't there, but I lived in rural Ohio in the early 1980s for four miserable years, starting at age ten. I got beat up a lot in Ohio. I went to Cleveland on a sixth-grade field trip, visiting Sea World and the Cleveland *Plain Dealer,* where we saw the newspapers rolling off the presses. I moved in 1984, the year the Mice formed. If I had stayed, no doubt I would have heard them. I would have connected with their yearning, tear-your-heart-out choruses drenched in garage guitars. When I hear Fox's later folk songs, I imagine the shape of a life that I escaped—the feeling of isolation and longing I knew years ago but left for Bill Fox to keep feeling, the same one my wife felt in the car that day. It's as if he's my eyes and ears in another life.

> *Here in the flats there's a cattle call*
> *Of drunks out in the night*
> *Girls dressed up so fancy and all*
> *Their boyfriends they just want to fight*
> —"Lonesome Pine"

Last summer, searching deep in the folds of the internet for signs of Bill Fox, I discover the Holy Grail: an appearance on L.A. radio station KCRW from 1998. He sounds giddy, his speaking voice more high-pitched and boyish than I'd imagined. He pronounces his album "*Transit Biz-ant-ium,*" flattening the *-ant* with a Midwestern accent. He says he bought a 4-track recorder from his boss for a hundred dollars and just started recording in his living room. He plays "My Baby Crying." Then host Nic Harcourt asks him about his days in the Mice. "We played basically in the Ohio region," says Fox, "with a couple of occasions back in '88, we broke out and we went to Kansas City and Cincinnati and we went up to Toronto and then we disbanded."

HARCOURT: What were you doing in the ten years after the Mice broke up?

FOX: Just hanging out. Writing songs. Working, trying to pay the bills.

At the time of the interview, Fox had been on tour for three weeks. Los Angeles is the farthest from Ohio he's ever traveled. "I'm ready to go home, ready to roll on back home to Cleveland," says Fox. "Cleveland, Oh."

Then he clears his throat and starts making big, clanging chords on his guitar. His boyish talking voice expands and levitates as if an entirely new person had taken over, winging strange new words like magical incantations. It's a song without a title, one he never put out: the last recorded sounds of Bill Fox.

Last year, M. Ward, the indie singer-songwriter from Portland, Oregon, tried to contact Fox. A friend had once pressed *Transit Byzantium* on Ward, and the Yeats allusion hooked him. After hearing Fox's pop version of the early American folk ballad "Mary of the Wild Moor" and his urgent folk-rocker "Bonded to You," Ward "fell for it," he told me in an email.

> i had a u.s. tour planned last year and wanted to ask musicians who i
> didnt necessarily know but whose music had been an inspiration to
> share the stage with me: freakwater, mike watt and victoria williams
> responded but we never got a response from bill fox... i figured he
> didn't like what i was doing, or he didnt like what he was doing...
> anyway, wherever you are bill thanks for the music.

I first contacted Bill's brother, Tommy, in the fall of 2006. At thirty-seven he's a reggae DJ on a public radio station in Cleveland and plays percussion in a reggae band. He's cheerful and friendly, but he also levels with me straightaway about his brother. "Not to sound like a party pooper, but I can guarantee you right now, Bill's not interested," he says. "He's dropped out of music and shuns his musical past."

I've already heard rumors from a record executive about Fox, the temperamental recluse who never returns phone calls. But the story Tommy tells stuns me. Bill Fox now works as a telemarketer for the National Crime Prevention Council, selling advertising space in McGruff the Crime Dog brochures.

Tommy tells me that at night Fox hangs out in bars, that he doesn't even own a guitar anymore. He's a diagnosed manic-depressive with a history of hospitalization. Fox told Tommy he voted for George W. Bush in 2000. Tommy paints a portrait of a crabby loner and contrarian who barely makes ends meet and re-fuses to talk about his music with anyone, especially a reporter. He imitates his brother's response to an interview request in a harsh, tough-guy voice: *I don't want to fucking talk to him. Why the fuck do I want to talk to him for?*

"That's Bill," he says, with a thick-skinned laugh that I feel is oddly unsympathetic. "You've got to, you know, laugh or cry."

"Sounds rough," I say.

"Try being his brother."

Having just started to look for Fox, I wonder: who am I to try and coax him out of self-imposed exile? Then again, Fox's plight only deepens the call of his music, burnishing it with further mys-tery and sadness. I'm confused: how can he abandon this amazing gift? How could he make this music and then leave it behind, or-phaning people who wanted more, people like me?

I write him a long letter, which Tommy agrees to deliver. It takes me two weeks to write. I tell Fox about my wife hearing "My Baby Crying" on the radio in Vermont. His brother suggests I in-vite him out for a drink, so I do. I wait a month for a reply. Finally, Tommy tells me he asked Bill about my letter over the holidays in 2006. "Hoping Bill would be true to expectations, I said to him, 'Yeah, I told this guy that you wouldn't talk to him,'" recounts Tommy. "And in true Bill fashion, he replies, 'Why did you tell him *that*? What if I want to talk to him?' So, I don't really know. He might get hold of you…"

I'm hopeful, but months pass and Fox doesn't respond. I ac-quire his number at the telemarketing office and finally get up the nerve to call him one afternoon. I figure he'll say yes or no to an interview, but at least I'll hear his voice. I'm anxious, like I'm calling a girl I'm in love with for the first time. I'm about to bridge these songs to the singer. A man with a deep, gravelly voice picks up the phone. It's his boss, a guy named Jim. "He was in here this morning and then he left for lunch and I don't know if he's coming back," he says. "Bill kind of makes his own rules."

I call back two hours later, hoping Fox has returned. "He came in for about a half hour and he said he was not interested in talking to you," says Jim, flatly. "Have a very nice day."

> Some kind of twist
> Is tumbling down
> It finds me here in Cleveland Town
> And oh far away, far away is my love
> —"Song of a Drunken Nightingale"

From the airplane, Cleveland looks as glum and brown as an overripe banana. The tallest building, the Key Tower, pokes above the city in a way that seems to say, "Eh." It's the lazy beacon of a town that can't be bothered. But down below, somewhere in the gray March drizzle, among the sprawl of row houses, is Bill Fox, the lost bard of Ohio.

Maybe he'll change his mind.

My host is Tim Rossiter, a forty-year-old computer programmer with long hair and John Lennon spectacles who was Bill Fox's manager and his closest friend during the years Fox was making music. It was Tim, I was told, who knew Fox better than anyone and could tell his story, though the two have spoken only rarely since Fox dropped out of music in 1998. Without even knowing me, Tim invited me to stay with him and his wife. We would end up spending the next two days together, two strangers with one connection: we are haunted by Bill Fox.

That night, Tim invites me to the Beachland Ballroom to see

the Revelers, a garage-rock band who were reuniting for a rare club gig after breaking up in 1999. All of Fox's old friends would be there, including brother Tommy, who played drums for the Revelers, and some of Fox's barfly buddies who still see him socially. There's an off chance that Bill Fox might show up.

A reviewer once said that Tommy played drums like he had "a thousand ants crawling on his back." Skinny, bespectacled, and bearded, Tommy is a flurry of arms, a sweat-spraying machine backing two electric guitars and soaring, feel-good choruses that send the drunken crowd roaring with joy. *Shim-sham-shimmy, we're gonna get happy!* The energy spikes. People keep handing me beers.

Ten years ago to the day, the Revelers moved to New York to try and make it in the music business. "That shit beat us down," says the singer, Andrej Cuturic, between songs. Guitarist Joel Kaufman adds, "That's what you get for dreaming."

This sums up the spiritual condition of Cleveland, of growing up in a town whose name is a national punch line, where people's hopes have been shuttered along with the steel mills. Here they turn the desire to forget into an intense and sweaty three-chord clang. Rock and roll is what they have. "Existence sucks and if you can just eclipse it for forty-five minutes..." says Andrej afterward.

"I love Cleveland, but Cleveland is a loser town," Joel tells me. "That's what's so beautiful about it." He moved to Washington, D.C., eight years ago to work at the Library of Congress, digitizing Walt Whitman manuscripts.

That night, I meet the guy everyone calls Dirt, a land surveyor by day, sometime musician, and erstwhile music promoter who has known Bill Fox since the late eighties. I'm told he's one of Fox's regular drinking buddies. I want to meet somebody who has spoken to him recently. When I tell him I'm doing a story, he says, "Good luck," and takes a big gulp of beer.

"He's not mysterious," he insists. "He's just Bill. He's just this guy we hang out with."

Dirt never returns my calls that week. Fox doesn't show up that night, either. I've flown all the way to Cleveland, Ohio, hoping I'll run into him or have one of his friends tell me everything there is to know. I'd feel like a stalker, except Tommy and Tim both seem happy to see me. And Tommy has already told me much of Bill's story. I'm just here for the rest of it.

The Fox brothers grew up in a middle-class Cleveland suburb called North Olmsted. Their father was a dairy products technician, their mother a schoolteacher who quit work to raise four kids (the other two Fox siblings are sisters). Bill Fox got his first dose of fame at age fifteen when he appeared on the local TV program *Big Chuck and Little John* to perform "Yankee Doodle Dandy" in amazingly refined hand farts. In 1984, at seventeen, Fox managed to save up enough money working at Burger King to record his first single with the Mice, called "Can You Walk on the Water, Baby?" b/w "Little Creatures." Both were bright, buoyant pop numbers that could have come off the *Yellow Submarine* sound track. They had five hundred sleeveless 45s made. Tommy, thirteen, played drums.

That year Fox's parents divorced. Bill moved in to the basement of his father's chemistry lab, and Tommy went to live with his mother and her new husband, whom Bill distrusted. The divorce "really freaked him out," says Tommy. Not that he got along any better with his father. His dad came to the Mice's first concert at a club called the Phantasy, and they ended the set with "Not Proud of the U.S.A.," wherein Fox addresses his father directly, singing, "Dad! You're so proud of the U.S.A. / It moves you in many ways," before declaring America an arrogant, dying empire comparable to Rome and Babylon. Fox's dad was a Korean War veteran whose foot was blown off in combat. "For my dad to hear that, he didn't like that," says Tommy.

By nineteen, Fox was wielding an amazing talent for a pop hook. Most of the songs were earnest squalls of love and infatuation, like the melodic bubblegum punk of "Bye Bye Kitty Kat," which Superchunk would cover in the 1990s. But there was also the unabashed idealism of "Public Television," another bristly song aimed at his dad.

The White House calls it a communist threat
But Dad ain't seen the last of it yet
Because I got this goddamned cerebral contraction
I can't get no satisfaction, I need… public television!

By 1988, the Mice were rock sensations in Ohio, mainstays of JB's Down Under, a club frequented by students at Kent State. They put out two vinyl LPs and toured the Midwest. But being away from Cleveland made Fox unusually anxious. He often stayed awake for thirty hours at a time while the band was on the road. Tommy would give him pot and beer in hopes that he'd nod off, but when they'd awake in the morning, Bill would still be up, pacing around, restless and bugged out. The morning the Mice were set to go on a tour of the U.S. and Europe, Fox broke up the band. For days, he didn't answer his doorbell or return phone calls. Tommy didn't talk to his brother for two years.

"I was supposed to be a very wealthy man by now," Tommy says, only half-joking.

The day after the Revelers show, I sit in Tim Rossiter's two-story house on Cleveland's West Side, where he plays me outtakes from some early 1990s studio sessions that Fox recorded with money his father left him after he died of cancer, in 1991. One is called "Man of War," a distinctly Dylanesque polemic with beautiful harmonica and a melancholy refrain.

Long as I been free
I wished I could be
As sure as a man of war

Fox was so upset by the Gulf War he moved to Canada. He lived in Toronto and busked for money. But he had a hard time making ends meet. He pined for Cleveland and wrote a song called "Up Here in Canada Today," about how much he missed black people. "I miss that jivin' shit that you talk," he sings. "Ain't nothin' in Canada I find to compare / Your breath of freedom in the air."

In April 1993, Fox was back in Cleveland living with his sister, Molly. One night the neighbors saw him on their doorstep: naked, covered in blood, and raving loudly. They were so terrified they called in the Cleveland SWAT team to apprehend him. WOUNDED MAN WAVES KNIFE, SHOUTS ABOUT THE ANTICHRIST, went the headline in the *Cleveland Plain Dealer* the next day.

The story says Fox "held off police at his West Side home for two hours," although Tim says that was exaggerated. When Fox saw the police approaching the house, "he went into a rage, shouting incomprehensible messages about the antichrist." Images of Fox looking like a madman were broadcast on the news that night. Fox was released without charges. He had only cut himself, harmed no one else. His family admitted him to a mental hospital.

Nobody seems to know what set Fox off, although a friend says he'd been drinking heavily and reading the book of Revelation. He left the hospital a few weeks later, diagnosed with manic depression, and briefly took lithium to control his moods. He stopped using it because the drugs made him feel like a zombie. Fox was deeply embarrassed. He went out in public less and less. By then, he was already telemarketing to support himself.

Soon after, Fox heard Guided By Voices' first album, *Vampire on Titus,* which was recorded entirely on a 4-track. He loved it. The concept of home recording was a major epiphany: he could make music alone, in his own living room, without ever involving another soul.

At a GBV concert in Columbus a few months later, front man Robert Pollard sought Fox out beforehand, proclaiming his love for the Mice. "How do you write songs?" he asked. "How do you do it?" In the middle of the show, he convinced Fox to climb onstage and play the Mice song "Little Rage."

*   *   *

"Do I want to do a 7-inch?"
Somebody asked me from the deacon's bench
And I tell him, "Pick any track, man, you know that it's yours"
But I'm thinking of you

—"Thinking of You"

Tim drives me around Cleveland and points out local sites, explaining obscure historical events, like the time Ohio almost went to war with Michigan over Toledo in the early 1800s.

Bill Fox is alive but his ghost is everywhere. Here is where he stood on the cover of *Shelter from the Smoke,* inside the West Side Market, where Slavic immigrants sell fresh produce. And there stands the clock tower seen on the inner sleeve, rising over the market. The cherub statue in the Mice photo is indeed in the Cleveland Museum of Art, five miles away.

We park in front of an apartment building on West 101st Street, where Fox recorded the two solo albums in his living room. It's a perfect brick box, two gray and brown stories on a nondescript block. I stare at the closed white curtains in the perfectly square windows. Later that day, I read a 1997 *Chicago Tribune* record review describing the lyrics of Fox's jangly "Let In the Sun" as painting "a picture of a man so despondent he can barely rouse the energy to open the curtains of his darkened room."

From 1994 to 1997, Fox wrote and recorded one hundred songs in that room. Tim helped Fox self-release the fifteen-song *Shelter from the Smoke* in 1997 and worked the phones to get publicity for it. One day he called an editor at *CMJ.* "Yeah, we listened to it," the editor said. "We're putting it on the cover." The excited reviewer would urge readers to "pick up a copy of this record and discover for yourself why Fox is one of the most important artists of our day."

In 1998, the Revelers, brother Tommy's band, got signed to spinART, an indie record label in New York. The Revelers' bass player gave spinART a tape of Bill Fox songs, thinking they might like it. They did—a little too much. Joel Morowitz, the label's founder, was so blown away he signed Fox and began focusing more on him than on the Revelers. Suddenly, Tommy's brother was back from his years-long hiatus, eclipsing Tommy's biggest hope of making it since the disbanding of the Mice.

Fox then attracted the attention of music industry legend Seymour Stein, the head of Sire Records who discovered acts like the Ramones and was immortalized in a Belle & Sebastian song. Stein bought him an Amtrak ticket to New York so Fox could play a few songs in his office. The performance, by all accounts, was phenomenal. "He was channeling right at him, looking him right in the face," says Tim. "Just channeling all that animosity about the record industry."

"Oh my God, he's wonderful!" said Stein afterward, according to Morowitz. He told Morowitz to develop him for a possible Sire album.

On the train back to Cleveland, Fox played Dylan songs in the lounge car and got everyone singing along, from the café bartender to a fat businessman smoking a cigar.

By then, Fox depended on Tim to handle his business affairs, take care of him on tour, and keep him steady (he was with him in the KCRW studio). But just as things were ramping up, Tim was finding less and less time to take care of his charge. His marriage was falling apart and he was partying heavily. So Fox told him he'd start handling business himself. Things turned sour quickly. At Stein's suggestion, the record executives had asked Fox to make his third album in a Nashville studio with backup musicians. Fox declined, making it in a Kent studio without accompaniment. Spin-ART didn't like the results. "Wow, that is so Dylan, it hurts," recalls Morowitz. "It was like, maybe we shouldn't release this. Critics are going to slay it."

That year Fox was scheduled to headline at the CMJ Music Festival in New York, along with the Revelers. He didn't show up. He stopped returning anyone's phone calls. The record label never heard from Fox again. The third album was never released. They've since lost the tapes. When I call Stein, he apologizes and tells me he doesn't remember Bill Fox.

I'll be in the flats, tipping pints with bureaucrats
There's too many poets, there's too many songs
No voice can erase the wrongs
And oh far away, far away is my love
    —"Song of a Drunken Nightingale"

Tommy and his brother were driving home from their mother's house after Christmas last year when Bill Fox's car began smoking and broke down on the side of I-71, the highway that runs through Cleveland. They got out and called a friend to pick them up. Fox never returned for the car, leaving it sitting on the side of the road.

"That's Bill," says Tommy.

Why did Bill Fox stop playing music? It's the question I ask about fifty times in two days. "I wish I knew," Tommy says. "Fear of failure?"

Tim says the record business was simply too hard on Fox. He didn't like touring and selling CDs while holding down a day job. "He was not into it, the life of trying to make it in music," he says. "Scraping by. His dignity was called into question."

"Just because someone has a talent doesn't mean they in any way at all have to exploit it," Tim reasons, although he's deeply conflicted. While rifling through an old box of promotional material, reviews, and letters, going through pictures of their big New York trip to see Seymour Stein, Tim becomes overwhelmed with emotion, his eyes wet with tears. "This is really difficult for me," he says. "When I put that stuff on now, I just hear... pain. Maybe it's because I know Bill, but it's just obvious to me."

By now, I've spent almost forty-eight hours with Tim, a guy I hardly know. But he feels like a lost friend from an earlier chapter in my life. When we run out of Foxiana, we drink coffee and talk politics. We both admit that we secretly want to "save" Bill Fox, pull him out of seclusion to play again. As we sit in his living room, I imagine that Fox is probably in his own living room right now, just a mile or two away. But Tim is afraid to disclose his phone number, out of respect for Fox's privacy. I understand—*I'm not a stalker!*—but the clock is ticking and I have to fly home eventually. I convince him to call Fox and let him know I'm in town, in case he changes his mind. Tim is extremely nervous about it. He hasn't seen Fox since 2000. But he eventually gets up the nerve and dials. Fox doesn't answer, and Tim leaves a message. Then he insists we sit in his apartment for another hour just in case Fox calls back. He never does.

Before I leave, I meet up with Tommy, who calls Tim O'Malley, an old friend of Bill's. Tough but jovial, with a salt-and-pepper beard, O'Malley sees Fox fairly regularly in bars. With two hours before my plane takes off, he agrees to meet us at a watering hole near the airport. "If I'm looking to go for a beer, he's on the short list of people I call," explains O'Malley of their relationship. He tells me he tried calling Fox four times that week but hasn't heard back. He's not surprised. "That's Bill," he says.

O'Malley calls Fox again to invite him out for a drink with the reporter. Fox doesn't call back. But O'Malley reveals that my letter to Fox sat on Fox's desk for a month and that the two discussed for an hour whether he should do an interview. *He read my letter.* O'Malley urged him to do it, too, telling him that I seemed "earnest."

Fox's response: "Man, I don't want to be on the internet."

Bill Fox's friends accept that he's through with music, but it isn't because they don't want him to play again. *Everyone* wants him to play again. They just don't hold out any hope—or they try not to hope so maybe one day they'll be surprised. That's Cleveland for you. But once in a rare evening, when Fox is drunk, he can be coaxed to perform a song or two. "He'll just start playing something," O'Malley says. "You don't know if it's Woody Guthrie or something he's working on."

I sit up in my seat. It happened as recently as December, O'Malley says, during a drunken jamboree led by Dirt. Fox was handed the guitar. He sang "My Baby Crying." Afterward, Fox idly told Dirt, the promoter, "I'd like to go out and play." Everyone was stunned. Recalls O'Malley: "I don't even say a fucking word. Don't scare the bird!"

By now, I'd thought a lot about "My Baby Crying." I'd listened to it hundreds of times and even learned the chords, although I never did figure out how he picked it. At first, I wondered who inspired it. Fox wasn't known for holding down lasting relationships with women. As with everything else, he tended to suddenly pull up stakes for reasons no one could discern. Perhaps his "baby" isn't a woman at all but an expression of his own loneliness, a muse so sensitive the mere exhalation of "trivial facts" can smother it.

> *Sometimes I feel like a lover in vain*
> *I fail to protect her from the forces of pain*
> *That so silently pierce her tender heart…*

After we meet, O'Malley writes me a long, heartfelt email imploring me to protect Fox. When they'd talked about my letter last year, he explains, Fox worried he'd come off as a "circus freak." "Don't make Bill look an ass," says O'Malley. Fox isn't proud of his current life, he explains. He's forty-one years old with a dead-end job and no car. He doesn't own a computer. "We all balance our day-to-days with our long-dark-nights in our own ways," writes O'Malley. "And communicating to a reporter about all that is like… *Okay, somebody's going to publish something about me on the internet or in a magazine that makes me look like I'm disturbed or a loser or something. Great. That's what I want. To be summed up and classified.*"

I feel sick reading this. I reconsider everything. Why am I insisting that Fox tangle with his demons again, suffer for his art, expose his painful private life to the world? For my own personal revelation? Question, click, answer? I recall O'Malley's explanation of why Fox hated performing: "He felt like a monkey being trotted out on a stage to do a calliope show."

But I didn't want the monkey, I wanted the bird.

O'Malley says Fox is an avid reader, fluent in *The Iliad* and Aztec archeology. It's what he talks about over all those beers. "He thinks about things real hard," he says. When Fox told me he wasn't interested in talking, he wasn't being coy or stubborn or strange. He had thought about it. He made a decision. If I'd been honest with myself, it was right there in the songs all along, well before I showed up. It's what he told my wife on a dirt road in Vermont one day in 1998. It was the only sound that she could hear. A field recording of the last singer who ever felt what he sang.

> *Bring out the shroud*
> *The rebel prophet just got stoned by the crowd*
> *That walked away and laughed out loud*
> *At my baby crying* ✲

CONTRIBUTORS

EULA BISS is the author of *The Balloonists* and *Notes from No Man's Land: American Essays*, winner of the 2008 Graywolf Press Nonfiction Prize. She teaches nonfiction writing at Northwestern University, and is co-editor of Essay Press. Her essays have appeared in *The Best Creative Nonfiction*, the *Touchstone Anthology of Contemporary Nonfiction*, the *Denver Quarterly*, *Ninth Letter*, the *Iowa Review*, and *Harper's*.

TOM BISSELL is the author of *Chasing the Sea*, *God Lives in St. Petersburg*, and *The Father of All Things*. His new book, *Extra Lives: Why Video Games Matter—and Why They Don't Matter More*, will be published in 2010. He lives in Portland and teaches in Portland State University's MFA program.

FRANKLIN BRUNO is the author of *Armed Forces* (in Continuum's 33 1/3 series) and the poetry chapbooks *MF/MA* and *Policy Instrument*. He has recorded and toured with Nothing Painted Blue, The Mountain Goats, and Jenny Toomey; his current band is The Human Hearts. He lives in Queens.

RICH COHEN is the author of *Tough Jews* and *Sweet and Low: A Family Story*, and, most recently, *Israel Is Real: An Obsessive Quest to Understand the Jewish Nation and Its History*. He lives in the foothills of large mountains with his wife, his many children, and another man's dog.

SCOTT EDEN is the author of *Touchdown Jesus* (Simon & Schuster). A reporter living in New York, he received a master's degree from Washington University in St. Louis.

BEN EHRENREICH is the author of the novel *The Suitors*. He lives in Los Angeles.

STEPHEN ELLIOTT is the author of seven books, including the novel *Happy Baby* and the memoir *The Adderall Diaries*. He edits the on-line culture magazine *The Rumpus.net*.

JOE HAGAN is a contributing editor at *New York* and *Vanity Fair* magazines. He's written for the *New York Times*, the *Wall Street Journal*, *Rolling Stone*, and *GQ*. He lives in New York.

HOWARD HAMPTON published his first review—of the B-52's now-ancient EP *Mesopotamia*—in the Boston *Phoenix* in 1982. Since then he has written about music, movies, books, and other trails of the illuminati for such publications as the *Village Voice*, the *LA Weekly*, *Film Comment*, and *Artforum*. Some of this writing can be found in his 2007 collection *Born in Flames: Termite Dreams, Dialectical Fairy Tales, and Pop Apocalypses*, including more of his work for *The Believer*.

TAYARI JONES is the author of the novels *Leaving Atlanta* and *The Untelling*.

PAUL LA FARGE is the author of the novels *The Artist of the Missing* and *Haussmann, or the Distinction*, and also of *The Facts of Winter*, a collection of imaginary dreams.

JONATHAN LETHEM is the author of eight novels and three collections of stories and essays. He lives in Brooklyn and Maine.

SAM LIPSYTE is the author of *Venus Drive*, *The Subject Steve* and

Home Land, a *New York Times* Notable Book of 2005 and winner of the *Believer* Book Award. His writing has appeared in *Bookforum,* *McSweeney's, Open City, Tin House, NOON, The Quarterly, Esquire, GQ,* and *Playboy,* among other places. A 2008 Guggenheim fellow, he teaches at Columbia University's School of the Arts.

RICK MOODY is the author of four novels, three collections of stories, and a memoir. He plays music in The Wingdale Community Singers. He lives in Brooklyn with his wife and daughter.

PETER LUNENFELD lives in West Hollywood, around the corner from the Schindler House. He surfs a 10'4" Bruce Jones long board. His books include *USER: InfoTechnoDemo, Snap to Grid,* and *The Digital Dialectic,* all from the MIT Press. He is a professor in the Design/Media Arts department at UCLA.

DAVID ORR writes the column "On Poetry" for the *New York Times* Book Review. He received the National Book Critics Circle's award for excellence in book reviewing in 2004.

RICHARD POWERS's tenth novel, *Generosity,* is published by Farrar, Straus, and Giroux.

ED PARK edits *The Believer.* His novel, *Personal Days,* was a finalist for the PEN Hemingway Award.

GINGER STRAND is the author of *Inventing Niagara: Beauty, Power & Lies,* and a novel, *Flight.* She writes for a variety of magazines, including *Orion,* where she is a contributing editor.

MICHELLE TEA is the author of four memoirs, and of the novel *Rose of No Man's Land.*

WILLIAM T. VOLLMANN's latest book is *Imperial.* He lives in Sacramento.

ACKNOWLEDGMENTS

Jordan Bass, Charles Burns, Meehan Crist, Caitlin Van Dusen, Dave Eggers, Max Fenton, David Glantz, Jean Marie Hays, Scott David Herman, Laura Howard, Eli Horowitz, Andrew Leland, Gideon Lewis-Kraus, Juliet Litman, Dominic Luxford, Suzanne Kleid, Michele Knapp, Sarah Manguso, Brian McMullen, Heidi Meredith, Tony Millionaire, Michelle Quint, Angela Petrella, Ross Simonini, Eric Spitznagel, Brandon Stosuy, Vendela Vida, Alvaro Villanueva, Karolina Waclawiak, and Chris Ying.